Georgia Witness:
A Contemporary Oral History of the State

By Stephen Doster

GEORGIA WITNESS is published by:
Deer Hawk Publishing, an imprint of Deer Hawk Enterprises
www.deerhawkpublications.com

Copyright © 2012 by Stephen Doster
www.sdoster.com

Cover design by:
Ray Polizzi

Layout by:
Aurelia Sands

Library of Congress Control Number:
2012940188

Printed in the United States of America

Dedication

To all Georgians. Past, present, and future.

Table of Contents

Introduction

"A man is the living sum of his past. At the very moment at which he is doing something, he did that particular thing exactly in that way because of the hundred years before him that made him. This man is complete only because he is the sum of his ancestors and his condition – his times."[1] William Faulkner

If Faulkner is right–that man is the living sum of his past–then each man and woman is a reflection of the past and a contributor to history going forward. This book is an attempt to peer into Georgia's past through living windows: The eyes and ears of those who witnessed and helped shape the events that made Georgia what it is today, and who continue to influence its destiny. Most of the people interviewed are ordinary people, neighbors and coworkers, while others are more high-profile figures.

Many history books are projected through the lens of the historian who writes them. Those histories may or may not be accurate portrayals because historians are handcuffed by missing information about a person or event and always face the difficult task of deciding what to include and what to leave out. General histories often tell the reader what happened in a locale–the events and the people who shaped those events or of the people who were affected by them, with occasional anecdotal evidence. Histories often rely on secondary sources (books, articles, archived documents) and tend to be broad in scope, omitting much history due to the limited nature of the print

---

[1] *Faulkner at Virginia,* © 2010 Rector and Visitors of the University of Virginia; Author Stephen Railton, http://faulkner.lib.virginia.edu/display/wfaudio04, accessed November 12, 2010.

i

medium, editorial deadlines, or the historian's finite resources.

By contrast, oral histories tend to be narrower in scope. They are first person accounts of a place and its people, biographical sketches of the person telling his or her story, and by their very nature, offer anecdotal evidence as the primary means of telling the history of a place. Another advantage of oral histories is that they provide personal insights considered too insignificant to be included in general histories. The disadvantage of an oral history is that the narrator's memory may be flawed. Oral histories are not perfectly accurate historical accounts, but the same can be said of all histories no matter what form they take. Wherever possible, I attempt to fact check the narrators' details and include the researched information in brackets [ ] or in chapter notes. Also appearing in brackets, for clarification purposes, are words implied, but not spoken by the narrator.

There are two intended audiences for this book. One, is today's reader who may be interested in aspects of Georgia's history. The second audience are readers a hundred years from now who may want to know what the average Georgian's life was like in the 1900s-2000s, what they thought about issues of the day, and how those issues shaped their lives, which in turn will shape the lives of future generations of Georgians.

It should be noted that this oral history is by no means a scientific endeavor. While it is not a statistically representative sample–demographically or geographically– of Georgia's populace, an attempt was made to include people of varying backgrounds and ethnicities (e.g., those with African-American, Cherokee, or Mexican heritage), which I hope readers will agree, was achieved to some extent. An attempt to include all major areas and cities of the state was made, though a number of people from different locations declined to participate in this project.

Several of the people interviewed aren't originally from Georgia, and one or two others no longer reside in the state. But *that is* the history of Georgia in a nutshell and has been since its beginning; therefore, being a born-and-bred Georgian is not a prerequisite for inclusion in this book. Consider that Georgia's founder, James Oglethorpe, was neither from Georgia nor ended his days there. Georgia began as a polyglot of peoples, a crossroads of ideas, and an amalgam of religions from its inception and remains a true melting pot to this day.

Early travelers to Georgia met American Indians, Moravians, Salzburgers, Scots, Irish, English, Africans, Christians, Jews, and Muslims. Today, there is almost every other nationality on the planet as well. Not only does the state still attract visitors, the people of Georgia have also been relatively mobile and have had an impact on America and the rest of the world. To that end, I have included the narrators' descriptions of travel outside of the state and across the globe.

Several threads run throughout these narratives. Transitions that have impacted Georgia, like the movement from agrarian to urban-based workforces and the transition from train travel to automobile transportation, are two such threads. Other threads include discussions on education, politics, race, religion, and the empowerment of women in society. The narratives appear in approximately the order that each person was interviewed. There is a "music row" of sorts, in which three musicians who left home to seek their fortunes in the 1960s, '70s, and '80s, are presented one after the other. Vic Waters toured with a "galaxy of stars," including James Brown, in the '60s. Chuck Leavell came to Georgia and found success with the Allman Brothers Band in the '70s. He now manages over 2,000 acres of mid-state forestland when he's not touring with the Rolling Stones. Patrick McDonald's musical quest began in the '80s when a gym teacher encouraged him to join the high school marching band. He is now the drummer for country legend, Charlie Daniels.

If there is one word that describes a golden thread woven into these narratives, it would be "opportunity". Georgia was once known as the Empire State–an economic power and a place where people could come to build new lives. Georgia is still the land of opportunity, as the people in this book reveal. For Oscar Cruz, a second-generation migrant worker, Georgia has provided opportunities for his family to move up the socio-economic ladder one rung at a time. Senator Mattingly's narrative, the final chapter, encapsulates the opportunities Georgia offers. The "Opportunity State" continues to attract new residents and industry almost 280 years after its founding.

These narratives are the result of in-person and over the phone interviews using standard questions about how the person or his/her family came to Georgia, about education, about growing up, career, and so on. From there, the conversation moved in any direction the interviewee wanted to take it. The "ums," "ahs," and repetitions were removed; therefore, the narratives are not verbatim.

Like most projects, this book began as one thing and evolved into something else. In this instance, it started out as a continuation of a previous book of narratives, *Voices from St. Simons: Personal Narratives of an Island's Past*, in which Brunswick-area residents were contacted. Somewhere along the way, the idea occurred to broaden the scope to include people from across the state, to record their thoughts, aspects of their lives, and their impacts on the world around them. The result is *Georgia Witness: A Contemporary History of the State*. The people who appear in this book were either already known to me, picked at random, or suggested by others. I am indebted to Juliann Ashley, Sally Clark, Griffin Bell, Jr., Bruce Faircloth, Jerry Lynn Cato, Hobson Cato, Tyler Cannon, Terry Doster, Charlotte Doster, John Tyler Edenfield, Bob Dart, Judy and

David Wood, June McCash, Jeanie Pantelakis, Fred Fussell, and Nickie Reynolds for recommending people to interview. I thank my wife, Anne, for her encouragement in seeing this project through to completion. Finally, I thank all of the people who agreed to be a part of this project and who took the time to share their stories.

Griffin Boyette Bell, Sr.

Griffin Bell served as Attorney General under President Jimmy Carter. Prior to that, he was appointed to the Fifth Circuit U. S. Court of Appeals by President John F. Kennedy. Among his achievements, he oversaw the demise of Georgia's Unit System and restored public confidence in the Department of Justice and morale among DOJ workers after Watergate. Bell placed numerous women and minorities in government positions during his tenures on the court and at the Department of Justice. He was well thought of by members of both major political parties, serving as counsel to President George H. W. Bush during the Iran Contra Affair investigation. As an attorney with the Atlanta law firm of King & Spalding, he specialized in high-profile corporate investigations. His philosophy about law can be summed up in a commencement speech he made to Mercer students, "Always err on the side of doing right." Judge Bell granted this interview while in the latter stages of pancreatic cancer.

Photograph courtesy of the Jimmy Carter Library.

I was born in Concord, Georgia, nine miles northwest of Americus on Highway 30, October 31–Halloween–in 1918. Dr. Boyette delivered me in the house on my father's and grandfather's farm. We had to leave the farm on account of the boll weevil and moved into Americus. The boll weevil wiped out the farmers, state-by-state, starting in Texas. You couldn't eradicate it. It was a bug nobody knew how to get rid of. They tried all kinds of things, like tar, but none of them worked. It wiped out the cotton farmers.[1]

My grandfather had a country store on the farm. He was also the Justice of the Peace. When he came into Americus, he opened a grocery store. My father started out working for someone else as a day worker, and he finally got into the appliance business. He sold Frigidaire products. Then he got into the service station business selling Firestone tires and Shell gas. He had a good business–sometime in the late '20s. Back then, about half the roads in Georgia were paved and half weren't. Some of the roads were concrete. One road in this [Sumter] county, from Americus to Leslie, was concrete. They used concrete so it would last longer, and it did. Most of the roads were built by local convicts.[2]

Family

I have one sister. I had two. One died as a child. Elizabeth married and opened a ladies' clothing store–La Belle.

Politics

The first governors I remember were Gene Talmadge and Ed Rivers. Rivers and Talmadge would alternate as governor. People would say, "Why can't we get someone else besides those two?" My father took me to a Talmadge stump speech in Americus. I was ten or twelve years old. It was a pretty good-sized crowd. Every time they had a political gathering, there was a barbeque. He [Talmadge] had on an overcoat, and people were putting money in his pockets. It was the middle of the Depression, people weren't in good shape, and I couldn't get over the fact that people were putting money in his pockets and in his hands. It was small money, but nevertheless, money, and people didn't have much money at that time. I don't remember a thing he said.

Education

I went to a country school through the third grade. I skipped second grade. In those days, in county systems, most people got together and built their own schools. My grandfather had nine children, and he had a teacher living in the house. That's the way they educated in my father's time. The neighbors would send their children over to his house. By the time I came along, they had built a regular school building for several grades at Shiloh. Shiloh and Concord are not too far apart. Then I came to Americus and started in the fourth grade. Some of my childhood friends in Americus are still around; William E. Smith, a retired lawyer, and Walter Rylander. Jimmy Carter's cousin, Don Carter, now a retired vice president of Knight-Ridder, and I were friends and classmates. So the Bells and the Carters just knew each other.

High school, which went up to eleven grades, was almost like a prep school. We had three foreign languages: Latin, Spanish, and French. We had a great school. People would come from the adjoining areas and live with their relatives so that they could go to that high school. Professor Hale was the principal. Miss Waldrup was the English teacher. Miss Ross was a math teacher. Miss Shiloh was a history teacher. A man named Levitt was a science and biology teacher. Mr. Todd was the football coach. I got out of high school when I was fifteen. I was on the football team my senior year, the first time I got large enough to play. I played right guard, offense and defense. We had to

3

play both ways then. We didn't have but fifty people in my class. Over half were girls.

I went to Georgia Southwestern College. It was not unusual for people to get out of high school at fifteen when you have eleven grades. And when you skip a grade, it's easy to get out when you're fifteen. There was a girl in my class who got out at fifteen. She and I were the two "fifteens." I took general courses the first two years of college. At that time you could go to law school if you had two years of college. Now, you have to have a degree. Times were hard, so I decided I'd work for a while and then go to law school. I sold tires for Firestone out of a store where they sold them on a budget plan. I was a budget manager. In fact, I had to go to school. They sent me to a training school in Atlanta. From there, they sent me to a tire store in Bristol, Virginia, then to one in Augusta, Georgia. Then I came back to Americus and worked for my father. He was a Firestone dealer. Seems like all the companies trained their employees then. I don't know what they do now.

Every county had terms of court. Sometimes they were in session twice a year, sometimes quarterly, and sometimes every two months. They called a new jury pool—grand jury and petty jury—each time. I served on a jury one time, in Americus. I don't remember anything about it, except that it was for a crime. I'd just turned twenty-one.

I went into the military right after that. I was in the Quartermaster Corps, really in the Transportation Corps—a truck company commander. I went to OCS [Officer Candidates School], Fort Lee, Virginia, and became a second lieutenant. At that time, we had a big shortage of officers, so you got promoted fast. About two months after I was a second lieutenant, I was a first lieutenant. And then they created this truck regiment—twelve companies of trucks. Each one had fifty trucks—Ford Jeeps—and four officers. I was made a company commander, although I was still a first lieutenant. Later on, I got promoted to a captain, and I stayed with the company almost until the end of the war. We were in the CBI (China-Burma-India), and they took me and two others [companies] out of the ship while we were in San Francisco. They kept us running vehicles up and down the West Coast. I used to run these convoys from Long Beach, California up to Seattle, Washington on Highway 1. The traffic was light because people had to buy stamps to get gas, so civilians didn't have much gas. We'd camp on the way at different military bases. Sometimes, you'd be gone several days on one of those trips. We transported radar trucks and other vehicles that had to be shipped through the ports on the West Coast. They'd send them by rail to Stockton, California, where they had to take them off; they'd been shaken up on the rail badly, particularly the radar trucks and other sensitive trucks. We'd move them on the highway and load them on the ships.

After the war, I went to Mercer Law School. Macon was a nice, slow moving town. The state economy was still based on farming. They had a number of airfields around Macon, two airports in use. Every town of any size had an airbase. I wanted to get into law ever since I was a little boy. My father encouraged me to be a lawyer. My grandfather had a brother who was Chief Justice of the Georgia Supreme Court. He was a Bell, too.[3] So my father got the idea that I would be a lawyer. I worked for a law firm in Macon while I was still in school.

Segregation

I never really thought about segregation until I got home from the war [World War II], and I passed a country school one day while I was in law school. It was just a poor building, and all the children were outside at recess, I guess. I was riding with another law student, and I said, "You know, this won't go on. Look at that building, and

5

think about the building the whites have in this county." It was over near Thomaston, Georgia. That's the first time I started thinking about the segregated schools. You can't keep people down forever, and I think the war probably gave me that inspiration. When Truman integrated the military. That was a big step forward. And when *Brown vs. the Board of Education* was decided, the Supreme Court made a terrible mistake in trying to have a total race-balanced integration, when all the plaintiffs asked for in the case is that they be allowed to go to the school nearest their house. If they had just given them that, we'd have had neighborhood schools, and the schools would have gotten integrated because neighborhoods mix. Instead of doing it right, they tried to do it in a revolutionary way, and we've denied two generations of children a good education. I never voted for bussing. I was one hundred percent against it. I think you ought to integrate, but I don't think you ought to have race-balance.

Law

I passed the bar in '47 and started practicing law in Savannah in 1948. Savannah was great. I lived down on the Vernon River–Vernonburg.[4] I had several mentors, all of them great lawyers. I owe my success to them. I had two in Savannah–Mr. Thomas Mayhew Cunningham and Mr. Alexander Lawton, [District Attorney] Spencer Lawton's grandfather. At that time, Lawton and Cunningham was the oldest law firm in Georgia. I left there after four years and went to Rome, Georgia, to represent a client. The chairman of the board of the Georgia Central Railroad lived there. His lawyer killed himself, and he asked me to come up there and represent him. I'd been doing work for him in Savannah. So I stayed up there two years. I was recruited by King and Spalding [law firm] after six years of law practice. Judge King was a noted lawyer, then a Solicitor General of the United States under President Wilson, and later on a judge on the Fifth Circuit Court of Appeals. Mr. Spalding was an astute business lawyer who put Georgia Power together out of a bunch of small companies. Judge King rode a horse from South Carolina to Atlanta after the Civil War. Mr. Spalding rode a horse from Ashland, Kentucky to Atlanta, which was being noted as a place that was going to grow. When they got to Atlanta and started King-Spalding [1885], there were about twelve thousand people.

After that I became a judge on the Fifth Circuit Court of Appeals, the same court Judge King was on. I was assigned by Governor [Ernest] Vandiver, Senator [Herman] Talmadge, and Senator Russell to be John Kennedy's campaign manager in Georgia. There was a big battle over the appointment. Who was going to get it? Which state? The circuit has six states in it, the largest court in the country. And there was somebody from Florida trying to get it and somebody from Texas. So I didn't know until the last minute that I was going to get it. I was happy, but my wife didn't think much of it–just went along with it. I had an office in the Atlanta courthouse and another office in New Orleans, which is the headquarters of the Court.

The [Georgia] Unit System was rigged to begin with, because every county got two units, minimum, and the most any county could get was eight.[5] The little counties ran everything. The sheriff and county commissioners, usually, were in charge of politics, so they didn't need to commit fraud on top of that. Of course, they might have had fraud in some places, but it wasn't widespread. When I had the case, I ruled that they could put in an electoral system. But then they took it to the Supreme Court of the United States, and they ruled that the state had a one-man-one-vote decision, they had already rendered in some other case–that you couldn't have an electoral college.

I wrote the opinion to get rid of the unit system. It was a three-judge district court. At that time you had to have three judges pass on it. Two district judges and one circuit judge. I was circuit judge. In that case we had two circuit judges. Judge [Elbert] Tuttle was on it, too, and Judge [Frank] Hooper was a district judge. I wrote the opinion knocking it out. The Supreme Court dictated it when they said this court had jurisdiction. Before that they said it was a political question, and not to be decided by a federal court. Then they changed that in 1962. After that, if you had jurisdiction, you couldn't help but knock it out; it was so unfair. If you measured it against the equal protection clause, it failed.

I was later appointed Attorney General by President Carter. I didn't know it was coming. I was asked by President Carter, who was at the time just a [presidential] nominee, to be thinking about somebody to be Attorney General. And I worked on that until December the 6th. He called me at ten o'clock at night wanting to see me. I put it off until the next morning. I went up to the Governor's mansion the next morning at seven o'clock to meet him, and he told me that he decided I had to be the Attorney General. He had interviewed all of these people from out of town, and he said, "I asked every one of them the question, 'Who would be a good Attorney General if not you?' Without exception they said you would be. Based on that, I decided to make you the Attorney General."

My first inclination was not to do it. I just didn't want to go back to working for the government. I just got out of the government. My wife didn't think too much about it [the appointment]. She just went along. I rented an apartment in Washington at Watergate.

Morale at the Department of Justice was down. They had a lot of temporary people in there. They always change about seventy-five people when you change parties. We were succeeding Republicans, so we had about seventy-five open jobs. And then some other positions had to be changed, like the head of the FBI. It took a year or more to get staffed up. I went all over the country, addressing prosecutors, U. S. marshals, and anybody that worked in the Department, trying to get the morale up. And we did. It worked out well. I made my schedule available to anyone who wanted to see it. It has not been done since. I thought it was a good idea to let the public have confidence in the Department. That was what I was trying to do. All the Justice Department doors were locked except one, when I got there. It was like being behind a barricade. That was part of the aftermath of demonstrators who were against the Viet Nam War. The first thing I did was to get all the doors open. But I knew all about the Justice Department. I was a federal judge for fourteen years, working with Justice Department lawyers. The prisons are run by the Justice Department. That was a big advantage that I had. Once you've been in the Department of Justice, you always carry recollections of it, and Department Attorney Generals help each other. I've had good relations with all of them.

Rooster Pepper Sausage

My rooster pepper sausage recipe came from Bainbridge, Georgia. My former law partner, Charlie Kirbo, and I were down there quail hunting. This farmer gave us some sausage and said it had rooster pepper in it. We didn't know what rooster pepper was, but we didn't tell him. It's a hot pepper about the size of your little finger. The sausage was really good and hot. We later on got some rooster pepper at the farmer's market and had some sausage made up. I started talking about it in Washington and had a press conference and said "rooster pepper." It became quite a news story. You can buy this rooster pepper in Haralson, Georgia, at Williams Grocery Company. They make a lot of sausage with or without rooster pepper.

Verdict

I was on the Military Court of Review for the Guantanamo Bay prisoners, but I had to give that up because I got sick. I'm in my last days with [pancreatic] cancer. It's not treatable. I'm doing the best I can, living out my time. I'll be 90. I figured the Lord has given me a very good life. I had a good career, and I haven't done anything to complain about. I think there is a higher power. Some people call it fate. I call it God's plan. I don't know which one it is. I never have understood it. Whatever it is, I think there is a higher power. In looking back over my life, I think I've been touched very much by some higher power; otherwise, you couldn't have all the good luck I had. When the doctors told me I have untreatable cancer, two-to-five months to live, the most peaceful feeling came over me. I said, "Well, I suspected as much. I accept the verdict, and I want you–there were five doctors in the room–and my family to know I'm at peace, and we're not going to worry about it. We're just going to run time out."

Scandals

I'm reading a book that's just out about the Teapot Dome Oil Scandal. If you think things are bad now, you should read that book and see what went on in the Harding Administration. The Attorney General was taking bribes, the Secretary of the Interior was taking bribes, and they were making them give them a percentage of the oil rights and all kinds of things. Some people had to go to prison. There was so much money that they ran the risk. A lot of times in the corporate world, they try to cover up something–some bad news, and the stock market is affected by it. They don't want to put any bad news out. It comes out sooner or later. Things like that happen because their lawyers didn't stop it. The lawyers know when something is wrong, and if they have anything do to with it, they should stop it. That's where the trouble comes.

NOTES

[1] The boll weevil entered the United States from Mexico in 1892, and spread to all cotton-producing states by the mid-1920s. One positive impact is that it brought about more economic diversification in Georgia and other Southern states.

[2] "The chain gang system relied upon the idea that prisoners were repaying their debts to society through labor on public projects, which the state government supported because it could be done 'on the cheap.' By 1911, the Georgia Prison Commission reported that 135 of the State's 146 counties utilized convict labor on road projects." *New Georgia Encyclopedia*, www.georgiaencyclopedia.org/nge/Article.jsp?id=h-2635, accessed March 12, 2011.

[3] Robert Charles Bell, Chief Justice for the State of Georgia from 1943-1946.

[4] Located on White Bluff Road, Savannah. Settled by German craftsmen in the mid-1700s.

[5] "In effect, the system of allotting votes by county, with little regard for population differences, allowed rural counties to control Georgia elections by minimizing the impact of the growing urban centers, particularly Atlanta. All 159 counties were classified according to population into one of three categories: urban, town, and rural... Based upon this classification, each county received unit votes in statewide primaries. The urban counties received six unit votes each, the town counties received four unit votes each, and the rural counties received two unit votes each." *New Georgia Encyclopedia*, www.georgiaencyclopedia.org/nge/Article.jsp?id=h-1381, accessed March 12, 2011.

Ruby Marie Crawford

Ruby Crawford and her twin sister, Ruth, rose from humble beginnings to earn law and accounting degrees and enter the banking and real estate professions. They campaigned for Georgia politicians from Eugene Talmadge to Jimmy Carter and have appeared on "What's My Line?" and "Oprah"! Their success was due to a combination of hard work and the fortitude to overcome discrimination against women who aspired to professional careers. Among their many other achievements, Ruby and her sister helped bring about laws that allowed women the right to serve on juries in Georgia.

Photograph courtesy of Sarah Hassinger.

I was born on February 5th, 1919 at seven o'clock in the morning in Temple, Carroll County, forty miles west of Atlanta. My neighbor up the street, Dr. T. M. Sprewell, delivered me. My father was William Hampton Crawford, and my mother was Elizabeth Lois Grey Crawford. Both were born in Temple, Georgia. Daddy was born in 1879, and Mother was born in 1885. He lived on a 60-acre farm growing up, and mother lived on a 40-acre farm. Corn and cotton were the main crops. Daddy's farm raised cattle and also made liquor. It was legal in those days. They had all kinds of fruit trees, an apple cider mill, and they raised and butchered their own hogs and beef. He used to drive cattle to Atlanta to sell–walking all that distance and spending the night along the way.

They named me Ruby Marie and my twin sister Ruth Marian. We owned two farms until my sister and I were several years old. We used to go there and help pick beans, but we never actually lived on the farm. We lived in the town of Temple. I had an older brother, Dayton Hampton Crawford, who was twelve years old when we were born, and an older sister, Mary Joan, who was five when we were born. Our brother absolutely adored us and was like a father to us, but our five-year-old sister resented us very much. She didn't like us at all and stood out in front of the house and tried to give us away to everybody who passed by asking them if they didn't want some little old twin babies. Ruth and I used to say we came into the world unwanted, and it warped our personality [laughs].

My brother went to Florida in the late '20s to try to find employment. Jobs were scarce at that time. We were going into the Depression. He lived in Florida until he retired and moved back to Douglasville, Georgia. He died about fifteen years ago. My sister [Joan] is 94 years old now.

Transportation
Our transportation to Atlanta back then was by train. We had a little train on the Southern Railroad. Temple is between Atlanta and Birmingham, and there was a little train they called *Accommodation*, and it truly was an

accommodating train, because people who worked in Atlanta or went to school there rode the train. It came through Temple about seven o'clock in the morning and took an hour or so to get to Atlanta. It left Atlanta about 5:15 or 5:30 in the afternoon and returned. There was a lot of commuting from Temple, Villa Rica, Douglasville, and other towns between Temple and Atlanta. The train ticket was about seventy-five cents one-way, but I'm not sure. Seems like it was less than a dollar.

We used to ride the *Nancy Hanks* [train] to Savannah for the Georgia Bar meetings. We had so much fun I don't remember how much time it took to get there. Seems like we left around 4:30 in the afternoon. We got on the train, and they started serving cocktails, and we ate on our way to Savannah. It was just the greatest thing. We traveled on Pullman trains to Washington, DC and New York. Ruth and I usually had a bedroom. I think maybe one time we had just an ordinary berth or bunk. The first time we went up there, it was for sightseeing. Later, we went to things like the U. S. Chamber of Commerce meetings or to help host Congressional dinners.

Growing up

I enrolled in school in Temple, Georgia when I was five years old and graduated in 1935 at sixteen. I spent my sophomore and junior high school years in Villa Rica. We moved to Villa Rica for a while. My father had a business over there, but we moved back to Temple for my senior year. My father had a restaurant and a grocery store. Ruth and I used to cook all the pastries for the restaurant, and we worked in the grocery store. My first job, at age fourteen, was working as a telephone operator on weekends–on Sundays alone–and made dollar a day. You said, "Number please," and then rang the number. People would call and say, "Do you know where Dr. Baskin is?" "Do you know where Dr. Sprewell is?" "Where is Mrs. Smith?" They acted like you were supposed to know where everybody was. Ruth and I relieved the operators in Tallapoosa, Bremen, Temple, and Villa Rica when they would go on vacation, so we knew a lot of telephone numbers. But we loved it.

The best teacher I ever had in my life–my star teacher of all time–was Carlos Hamil. He was my seventh grade teacher, and when we got into high school, he taught us algebra and geometry. His brother Craxton Hamil was the superintendent of the school, and his wife, Louise Knutson Hamil, was the principal. They were great teachers. I've never known better teachers in all my life. In all the schools and colleges Ruth and I have attended, no one was ever a better teacher. They were from Bowdon, Georgia, west of Carrollton.

Eugene Talmadge began my interest in politics. When I was thirteen years old, we had a snow in Temple. He came there on a flatbed truck campaigning for governor on his three-dollar tags and his red suspenders.[1] Ruth and I handed out literature for him. That was our first exposure to political campaigning. Our high school competed in the Ready Writers contest, and my essay on Gene Talmadge won, so I went to the district meeting. I knew Miss Mitt and Herman [Talmadge]. Herman, Ruth, and I were great friends. He kept a picture of his mother, Ruth, and me in his office in Washington until he came home. I still have that essay, but wouldn't know where in the world to find it. Herman asked me for it. Seems like I sent it to him, but I'm not sure.

I started working the day I graduated from high school. An editor of three newspapers liked some articles I had written in school and the essay contest he sponsored that I won, so he offered me a job writing for his newspapers. I started working on Monday morning before I graduated that night. I wrote about everything from social to obituary to sports–everything that was news, I wrote.

Gone With the Wind

We stood in line several hours at Five Points for the *Gone With the Wind* parade to see Clark Gable and all those stars. The First National Bank of Atlanta [now Wachovia], where we later came to work, was on one corner of Five Points. We stood in line on that cold, cold day waiting for all those movie stars to come by. It was such a thrill. We didn't go to the premiere ball that night. Clarke Gable was in an open car. My heart still flutters.

I knew Margaret Mitchell. We used to have breakfast together a lot. Ruth and I came to Atlanta to get an education and work in the bank at Five Points. In the bank building was Jacobs Drugstore. They had a soda fountain and served breakfast, lunch, ice cream, banana splits, and things like that. She used to come and breakfast at the same fountain where Ruth and I did. She was delightful. Her brother, Stephens Mitchell, was a lawyer, and I knew him later through the bank and being a lawyer myself. She was struck by an automobile on the corner of 10th Street, crossing to go to the theatre. It was very tragic.

Twins

Ruth and I were truly identical twins. We could tell what each other was thinking. We knew immediately when we met someone if the other one liked the person or not. We talked in unison. People said, "You all finish each other's sentences," or "You say exactly the same thing at exactly the same time." We dressed identically all the time.

Ruth and Ruby Crawford, Christmas 2000.

Small Town Life

Chain gangs used to come by the house doing work on the highway, doing work on the sidewalks, cutting weeds. They wore those black and white striped uniforms. Some of them had chains on them. They were black and white prisoners working side-by-side.

Our town was very segregated. We knew the black tenants on our farm. We loved them, but we couldn't socialize with them. They went to separate churches. Having a grocery store, too, we had blacks as customers. In my father's restaurant in those days, we had a counter in the back of the store for the blacks and a counter in the front for the whites. That's the way things were in those days. The grocery store and Crawford's Family Restaurant were adjoining in the same building. The building is still there. I'm not sure what's there now. We served primarily fried chicken and country-fried steak. Daddy made the best hamburgers in the world, but Daddy was famous for his wonderful chili and beef stew. People would come from other towns just to eat his chili. Mother was known for her chicken stew. Traveling salesmen would say, "I'll be here on the twenty-third of this month. Now, be sure you have chicken-and-dumplings on that day." Ruth and I cooked the pies. I got a letter from this boy who was serving in Okinawa saying that when he was in the foxholes at night he dreamed of having a piece of our coconut pie.

Ruth and I wanted to be doctors, but we came along during the Depression years, and nobody had any money. There was no student aide or HOPE [Helping Outstanding Pupils Educationally] Scholarships, so we couldn't go to medical school. We thought we'd work a few years and then be able to go to medical school. Elbert Reeves, an insurance man from Atlanta with Jefferson Standard Life, who came out to Temple, used to eat lunch at my father's restaurant. He thought Ruth and I were whiz kids. He said, "You two are wasting your time in this small town. You need to be in Atlanta." He was a friend of bankers in Atlanta. He had Freeman Strickland, who was a Senior Vice President, mail Ruth and me an application to come to work at the First National Bank of Atlanta. Mr. Reeves did the same thing with the C&S [Citizens and Southern National] Bank, Mills B. Lane's bank. We were thinking about going into the civil service and weren't too interested in the banks. We filled out the forms, but didn't come over for interviews.

On January 2nd, 1943, the phone rang in my father's store. We answered it, and it was the First National Bank of Atlanta saying that they were very impressed with the information that we had furnished. I guess they thought that anybody who could work at four or five jobs–we were working at the restaurant, grocery, telephone exchanges, newspaper–would make good bankers. They asked us to come in for an interview. They said, "We have a policy of not hiring relatives, but in your case we're willing to make an exception and will hire both of you." So we came over, and they made us a good offer. The telephone company offered us a job in the Accounting Department in Atlanta, but the bank offered a little bit more money, so we went with the bank and started in 1943 in the Bookkeeping

Department running the Burroughs bookkeeping machine. We had the best boss in all my years of working–William V. Austin. I heard that to get into the Trust Department was the ultimate in banking, but it took years to be able to get that. Before the end of the first year, I got a call from our Vice President of Personnel, William Adamson, also from Carroll County. He was a man so many people sort of feared because he was the hirer and the firer. They looked on him as a bear. I thought, "Oh my goodness. What in the world is he calling me up to his office for." I thought I was going to get fired and tried to think, *What have I done? What have I done?* I went up there, and he said, "We've been observing your work, and we've been very impressed–etcetera–and we'd like to give you a job in the Trust Department. I about fell out of my chair. So then I was transferred to the Trust Department as manager of the real estate division. By that time, Ruth and I had been taking American Institute of Banking courses, and we took two courses in law. We became so interested in law that we enrolled in the Atlanta School of Law's night courses.

Ruth and I enrolled the second week we were in Atlanta. We started at Draughon's School of Commerce studying secretarial science and accounting.[2] At the same time we started at the American Institute of Banking [AIB]. We had two courses in law, Commercial Law and Negotiable Instruments, and that's how we became interested in studying law. When we got a few years into our AIB courses, we started in the law school and just loved it–couldn't wait to go every night. We got our Bachelors' of Law in 1947 and our Masters' of Law in 1948 and were admitted to the bar in 1948. I've been a member of the bar since then.

I did legal work in the bank, became in-house counsel in the Trust Department, and taught law. I taught the same law courses I had taken through the AIB for sixteen years. They hired me as an instructor. Immediately after law school, we went down to Georgia State College to major in accounting and taxation, working on our BBAs. I taught law-for-the-layman at the YWCA and also lectured in New York at the Kennedy-Sinclair Trust Institute. I used to guest lecture at Emory on estate planning, and I taught some of the evening law classes at Emory. As I said earlier, Emory is where I wanted to go to be a doctor when I was a girl. But when I graduated from high school, women couldn't go to Emory.

Ruth and I used to feed those hungry dentists at Emory University. We lived in Druid Hills near Emory. Some of the dental school students had a hard time making ends meet and ate at our house. We met Norman Doster; he wasn't that bad off. He was dating another girl at that time. In fact, he had given her a ring. They broke up, and so he was on the loose. He came up to the bank one day to have lunch with me in our dining room. My little secretary was there, and I introduced them. Barbara is from Atlanta. I chose her out of a selection of people who interviewed. We went on to lunch, and nothing else was said. Then we were going to have a house party at Jekyll, and I invited several dentists to stay at our house. Norman said, "I really don't have a date. How about that cute little girl you introduced me to the other day." I said, "Oh, Barbara? Yes. I'd be happy for you to bring her." So, he brought her down there, and I can still see them headed out to the beach in her little bikini and him in his swim trunks headed out to the ocean to go swimming. So, romance blossomed, and the rest of it is history.

Making History

At the time I became a lawyer, women could not serve on juries. Ultimately, I was admitted to practice before the United States Supreme Court. That was one of the big projects I worked on. After years and years of struggling, in 1954, we finally got a bill passed in the state of Georgia to get women first-class citizenship. We felt like we were treated like second-class people since we couldn't serve on juries. I just got through doing a documentary for the 80th anniversary for the Georgia Association of Women Lawyers. At the same time we were working on the jury bill, we were working at Georgia Tech and Emory. Back then, even women who were lawyers couldn't be members of the Atlanta Lawyers Club–only men. We had all the discrimination you could imagine.

Ruth and I are bankers, accountants, lawyers, realtors, and lecturers. I love banking, but I like law the best. I've just been made a Fellow of the American Bar Association. One third of one percent of lawyers become Fellows. I thought I was reading someone else's mail when I got the notice.

Neil Wilkerson, a lawyer who teaches business law and writing at Kennesaw State University, is writing a book about me and Ruth. It's called *Running on Full*, because he thought Ruth and I run at full speed all the time. Mayor [William B.] Hartsfield used to call us 'the 24-hour Crawford twins." He said, "The only reason Rome wasn't built in a day was because Ruth and Ruby Crawford were not there." Mayor Hartsfield and Tollie were some of our dearest friends. We were neighbors in Atlanta. They came out to my mother and daddy's 50th and 55th wedding anniversaries, and they came to the funerals.

Friends

They used to call the Atlanta airport Candler Field. Mayor Hartsfield had so much to do with getting the big bond deals to enlarge the airfield to make it a first-class airport. So they named it Hartsfield after him.

I knew Asa W. Candler. He was one of the sons of the original Coca-Cola Candlers–just a delightful man. When he had transactions at the bank, he didn't send his secretary or somebody else; he'd come down himself, sit at the desk and talk to me.

Lewis Grizzard was a friend.[3] I'm still friends with his wife. I haven't read a funny article since he died. He could make something funny out of anything in the world. He was from Moreland, Georgia, south of Newnan. Ted Turner is about the only person in Atlanta that I don't know well.

Ruth and I once appeared on *What's My Line?* in New York in 1954 with John Daly, Dorothy Kilgallen, Arlene Francis, Robert Q. Lewis, and Bennett Cerf. At that time we were the only twin members of the American Bar Association. Dorothy Kilgallen thought we demonstrated twin eggbeaters, Arlene Francis guessed we played twin pianos, and Bennett Cerf thought one was "Coca" and the other was "Cola." Merle Oberon was the guest artist, and we got to meet her.

Touring

The American Banking Institute decided they wanted to hire some bankers to travel across the United States on a public relations tour. They chose Ruth and me to be their representatives going from city-to-city to convince people to come into banking as a career. We were on radio and television in Washington, DC, New York, New Orleans, and Mexico. I wonder how in the world we were chosen for that. We were both president of the Georgia Association of Women Lawyers. We were chosen by Kennesaw State University as Phenomenal Women of the Year. We were the first women in Atlanta to be inducted into the Atlanta Hall of Fame.

Ruth and I were "Peanut Brigaders." We started out with Jimmy Carter when he announced he was going to run for the Presidency. We had just retired from the bank and thought, "Before we start in on our new career in real estate, if he's going to run, we're going to help him." I first knew him when he was in the legislature. Ruth and I campaigned in all the southern states. I campaigned in all the New England states, and she stayed home and kept the doggies. I slushed through the rain, sleet, snow and ice. I spent 17 days in New Hampshire and Vermont alone on one trip. He had us up to the White House five times the first year he was in office.

Hank Aaron and I go with the [Jimmy] Carters on their winter vacation trips. Last year, we went to Cancun, Mexico; the year before, to Crested Butte. Hank Aaron, Ruth, and I have the same birthday–February the fifth.

Ruth and I were featured in a book that Maryln Schwartz, a syndicated writer on the *Dallas Morning News* wrote–*A Southern Primer: Why Princess Margaret Will Never Be A Kappa Kappa Gamma.* We were written up as the "Moonlight and Magnolia Crawford Twins." It's really a book about Southern manners, charms, and customs. Oprah Winfrey read the book and told her producers, "I have to have those twins on my program." So Ruth and I had been up to Amicalola Falls on a Friday night for dinner and didn't get home until midnight to check our messages. One was the *Oprah Winfrey Show.* It said, "We want you in Chicago on Sunday afternoon to appear on the show on Monday morning." Ruth and I were flabbergasted, but we had such a busy weekend planned, so we changed our schedule around and flew up on Sunday afternoon and were met by someone holding placards with our names, and we rode in a stretch limousine. Everything was first-class, and she was really warm and charming. It was really more of a program on the difference between Northern and Southern women and the charm of Southern women.

Mary Mac's

For six years, I was a hostess at Mary Mac's Restaurant, a tearoom to begin with, on Ponce DeLeon and Myrtle Street.[4] Ruth and I critiqued the food and helped John Ferrell run it. He had worked with us in the real estate office, Northside Realty. He came to me one day and said, "Ruby, I understand Mary Mac's is up for sale, and I've always wanted to run a restaurant. If I buy it, will you help me run it?" I made the rash promise of saying yes. We loved it until I couldn't work there.

Real Estate

On the [2008] real estate crash, people just got too careless wanting to make more money, which seemed to be in real estate. The loans they were making wouldn't have been made under our old regime–we had younger bankers coming in with the mergers–it was not the same First National that we used to have, which was a very conservative bank. When I first started in banking, we wouldn't have thought about making some of these loans. But the competition got so keen, and as the banking personnel changed, the [real estate] field looked so lucrative, I guess they became careless and made loans they wouldn't have ordinarily made in order to have all the income coming in. Until we decided to go shopping, we were doing fine. We went out and bought that thrift company in California. That's what did us in. It was so heavy in sub-prime and all the real estate loans that they made, and so we suffered for it.

Going to Church

I go to three churches: Peachtree Road United Methodist Church, the Temple United Methodist Church, and the Jekyll Island Methodist Church. We tell everybody that we pass our sin around among the three churches, because no one church can take it all. Charles Stanley [First Baptist, Atlanta] used to eat at Mary Mac's. He's one of the most popular ministers in Atlanta. In all the years Ruth and I worked at the Atlanta Convention and Business Bureau, I do believe that other than visitors asking "Where is Stone Mountain?" and "Where is the Cyclorama?" the next question was "Where is Dr. Charles Stanley's church?"

They knew him from television and radio. His son, Andy, is also a minister.

Georgia Then and Now

Georgia is more progressive and more aggressive in getting business to move here than when I was growing up. It seemed we were sort of at a standstill, so to speak, in that we didn't seem to go out to bring companies to Georgia and particularly to Atlanta. When I came to Atlanta, we had three-hundred-and-something-thousand people. Now, it's over five million.

Coming from Temple, Georgia and doing everything we've done, I can't believe it–God's hand.

NOTES

[1] The burdensome cost of automobile tags was a cornerstone of Talmadge's 1932 campaign. "In an economic situation of staggering complexity, everyman could understand the three-dollar tag, and it would benefit the poorest of voters. It was common-denominator stuff." William Anderson, *The Wild Man from Sugar Creek: The Political Career of Eugene Talmadge* (Baton Rouge: Louisiana State University Press, 1975), 68.

[2] Both Ruth and Ruby served as presidents of the American Society of Women Accountants.

[3] Syndicated humor columnist, author, and speaker.

[4] Established in 1945 by Mary McKinsey.

Willie Mae Robinson

Willie Mae Robinson was born on Sapelo Island, Georgia, during the Great Depression. She recalls how the people of her community, Raccoon Bluff, were forced to give up their land and relocate to another part of the island, a small-scale trail-of-tears that still pains her to talk about. In this narrative, she recounts the Geechee way of life, once endemic to Georgia's barrier islands. Mrs. Robinson descends from Bilali Mohammed (a.k.a., Mohammet), an African Muslim slave well known to historians, who managed the plantation on Sapelo in Thomas Spalding's absence. Eventually, her family moved to Savannah where she became active in the Civil Rights Movement. Like her forebears, Mrs. Robinson's tale is one of making opportunity out of adversity.

Willie Mae Robinson

My name is Willie Mae Hall Robinson. My maiden name was Hall. I was born in Raccoon Bluff on the northern end of Sapelo Island on July 7, 1937. My dad's name was Charlie Sams Hall. Sams was his mom's maiden name. My mother was Sarah Jane Gardner. Both were from Sapelo. My dad's daddy was from the Hog Hammock.[1,2,3] Mom's folk were from Raccoon Bluff.[4] Aunt Kate–Katie Underwood–my Daddy's auntie, birthed me. She was the midwife for just about everyone who lived on Sapelo. She used to walk from Hog Hammock to the Bluff to deliver babies. The new ferryboat [from Sapelo to the mainland] is named for her. There were seven children in our family. Four of us were born on Sapelo Island, and the other three were born in Savannah's Charity Hospital. That hospital is now closed. It was during the days of deep segregation. There were two black hospitals, Charity and Georgia Infirmary. My son, Reginald, was born there. The Charity hospital is now Mercy Housing, nice little apartments for low and moderate-income people. They renovated Georgia Infirmary and do a lot of cardiovascular work there. Reginald is now a doctor [MD, obstetrics & gynecology].

The Mainland

To get to the mainland, you took a passenger boat–the *Janet*. It was a little, low-flung boat that could hold about fifty people. It ran at least twice a day, in the morning: coming to the mainland and then going back, and in the evening: coming to the mainland and going back. There have been several ferries since then. We learned how to swim in the rivers and creeks. We used to have irrigation ditches that were kept up and were clean. I would catch crabs in those ditches. I got stuck in the marsh one time going to get clams. I panicked and was sinking down. My cousin, Earle, said, "Willie Mae, be still. The more you struggle, the worse it gets." He made me be still. Then he said, "All right, now lift one foot." I lifted it and walked on out.

Sunday Service

I went to First African Baptist Church at Raccoon Bluff. A Sunday service would take a couple of hours. You come in and a couple of deacons would line hymns. They would say the words–speak the lines–ahead of the people singing. You did it *a cappella*. Sometimes, it was almost ethereal. I still get goose bumps just thinking about it. You'd sing, and then a couple of people would pray. You'd have a prayer service first, then you'd close that part of the worship down, and the preacher takes over, and you start the regular Baptist service. You'd have communion once a month. There were two churches on the island, and everybody would go to one church. The first Sunday in May was First African Baptist. The next month it was St. Luke's. It was a small island, so everybody participated. Each church had its own preacher. The church leaders sat on special benches for the deacons on one side and deaconesses on the other. Everybody else pretty much sat together.

Barefoot

I loved going barefoot. We'd go barefoot most of the time except when Mom said, "Get your shoes on," because she didn't want any colds going around. But I didn't like to wear shoes. We used to use kerosene lamps before electricity came to the island. My Uncle Charles Hall, Daddy's uncle, had the only store on the island. It was in the [Hog] Hammock. It's still there.

Seeing Spirits

Some people talked about conjuring, but we weren't big into that sort of thing. My dad used to see ghosts when he'd be walking at night. When you see one, you were supposed to cuss it, and it would go away. Haints [haunts] used to ride people, and people used to talk about that. People had horseshoes nailed over their front door to keep out evil spirits. But we weren't big into that kind of stuff.

Property Theft

Raccoon Bluff is a high bluff overlooking what used to be a narrow river that's very wide. As a matter of fact, a lot of the bluff is being eroded as the river widens due to natural forces, but some of it is man-made. That's a long story that has to do with the State stealing property, and I say that literally. We've been fighting it for years. There were some of our family who lived in Hog Hammock because they were working for folk at the "big house" as we used to call it. There are some folk now who wouldn't dare think about calling it the big house. They call it a mansion. But that's the way it was. When my dad was a very young man, he worked for R. J. Reynolds, Jr. [tobacco heir] at the sawmill located on west sided of the island near the river.

Willie Mae Robinson in her youth.

To get around the island, you either walked or rode on a wagon, a buckboard. Some guys rode horses, but most folk hitched the horse up to the wagon. Everybody had a garden–sweet potatoes, corn, beans, okra, peas–you name it. Everybody had hogs and chickens. When we moved to Savannah we had a big chicken yard. Country folk used to always do things like that.

Dancing Girl

Since I was a very active girl, I learned dances and songs, and when the adults would get together to have reunions, they'd say, "Willie Mae, come and sing this," or, "Come and do this little dance." I was always glad to oblige. That was a lot of fun. I used to think I could sing, and I wanted to perform.

African Influences

If you were going to say "hip," like your hipbone, we would say "kimbo." That's a West African name for "hip." My mom used to tell me, "Take your hand off your kimbo. You're too grown." Some of the research by Rena Green, who worked for the state of Georgia in Atlanta, has us coming from West Africa. She came here to my house when Daddy was alive. We have some of the family tree that she researched. They [researchers] had found a book that they thought was African language, and it turned out to be Arabic. The little book is in Athens in a library.[5] It was writing from memory of our ancestor, Bilali,[6] who was the overseer for [Thomas] Spalding's plantation on Sapelo. I descend from Bilali through my mother. Some of my cousins' and aunties' names come down from him. Mom and Big Momma used to talk all night long. It was fascinating listening to the things they used to do. They were great storytellers. That's what made life interesting–stories.

A page from the Bilali Muhammad Document. Image courtesy of the Hargrett Rare
Book & Manuscript Library, University of Georgia Libraries.

Sapelo

People on Sapelo still make baskets. Some folk teach their children. Allen Green [basket-maker] was my cousin.[7] We used to be big buddies. He was a no-nonsense man who used to talk about what used to be. I never used to go to Sapelo without going to Cousin Allen's house and talking with him and Annie Mae, his wife. He used to live in the Bluff, but when they moved us, he had to move down to Hog Hammock.

I went to Cultural Day back in October and bought a basket from Jerome Dixon. We have a preservation organization, the Sapelo Island Cultural and Revitalization Society, SICARS.[8] Almost everybody on Sapelo is related in some way. As a matter-of-fact, Mom and Dad were cousins. Since they didn't have a means to go back and forth to court off the island, they just made sure they didn't court second or third cousins. You wouldn't even think about courting a first cousin.

A Big Shock

My moving to Savannah was the result of them making us move from Raccoon Bluff. Some people died as a result because their heart was broken, and they never rallied from it. I don't remember the beginning of it because I was a little girl. The last move was around 1952-'54. They wanted to move us because they wanted the highest land. They didn't want any blacks down there. First, they made it a hunting preserve. One man, a judge, built a big, fancy house there. He lived in it for a couple of years. The next man who lived there was land developer, but the state put so many legal hurdles in his way, he was never able to actually live there. The house is still there.

The state has gone through years of legal wrangling with us. Big Momma, my mom's mom, owned thirty-three acres there, and they kept fighting us, saying money was loaned. Some of the documents they produced were hand-written IOUs for small amounts of money, which they said were never paid, and so the land reverted to the state. They did all kinds of wrangling. It all just ended last year in court [2008]. The state of Georgia has it now.

We moved to Savannah when I was about five years old. No one liked having to move. It was a very sad and frightening time for us. A lot of Daddy's folk had already moved to Brunswick and Savannah. Momma's folk had moved to Jacksonville and New York. Momma and Daddy found this little house at 537 Hartridge Street, and we moved in there. The house is still there. Moving to Savannah was a big shock. I went to East Broad Street Elementary, right across the street from where we lived.

The Spoken Word

We were Geechee on Sapelo. That's all I heard all my life until about fifteen years ago, when they started calling us Gullah. I think the difference is that Gullah has more to do with language, and Geechee has more to do with foods. People in Savannah used to tease me about the fact that we were rice eaters. When we first moved from Sapelo, our accents were extremely thick and heavy, and folk used to laugh at us. When I was at East Broad Street School, they use to laugh at me so much, many days I'd run home crying because they teased me about the way I talked. We had a sort of drag, and I tried my best to get rid of that. Even today, I wouldn't try to say certain words the way we did on Sapelo, because it brings up too much hurt. It's more the way we pronounced words than the actual words. By the time I was a young woman, we got rid of most of the words we used to use. We were speaking the same words that everyone else was speaking.

Walking Along

In Savannah, we'd buy clothes at Yachum & Yachum, and Lang's Department Store on West Broad Street, which is now MLK [Martin Luther King Boulevard], and there were one or two Penney's downtown. After I became a teenager, I used to buy clothes at Lerner's.

When it was time to go to Cuyler Junior High School, a mile-and-a-half from Hartridge Street, we had to pass all these white schools in the area. Cuyler is now the EOA, Economic Opportunity Authority, on Anderson and Ogeechee Road. We walked there in little groups because we couldn't afford bus tickets. I was coming home one day, and a little white boy ran down off his porch on the corner of Gwinnett and Drayton. I don't know why he picked me– there were four or five of us, but he picked me. He ran up and said, "Nigger!" and spit on me. I was so angry. I was already angry for having to go from Hartridge to Cuyler. I boxed that little boy right in his mouth, and the blood seemed like it just popped out, and we had to run like crazy. I stayed away from there for a while. I didn't go back in that direction because I was afraid. I went a couple of blocks up before crossing over Forsyth Park. We used to call it Extension Park. Every time I pass that house, I still think of it. That little boy would be in his sixties now.

A Party

We'd occasionally go back to the island, but mostly people from Sapelo would visit us in Savannah. Other people called my grandmother Mother Betsy, but she was Big Momma to me. She was "living on premises," as they say, at Sea Island because she was the cook for the Alfred Joneses. Their house was on the beach. Alfred Jones was the cousin of Howard Coffin[9] who owned the big house[10] on Sapelo. When they went out of town, she would either stay on Sapelo Island or spend time with us. As a matter of fact, the Joneses would drop her off sometimes to spend a few days or a week with us. When I was ten or eleven, they would let Big Momma bring me to Sea Island with her and stay in her room. It was a five-car garage with rooms above, and Big Momma had a nice room. I would stay with her for a week. Once, they threw a big party for a few hundred people. Big Momma was the cook. My uncle, Philip Dixon, was their butler. His wife, my Aunt Celia, was called the nurse because she took care of the Joneses' children. Uncle Philip would sometimes come and pick me up in Savannah. He and Aunt Celia lived on St. Simons near the firehouse.

Big Momma

Big Momma used to smoke a wooden pipe. I used love to light Big Momma's pipe for her. It's a wonder I didn't start smoking. Big Momma's husband was William Gardner. He was the [Sapelo] island's doctor. He was not trained, but he had a lot of Indian in him. If you saw one of his photographs, you could see that he was more Native American Indian than anything else. You'd think that he was full Indian–Cherokee. Whenever anybody became ill

35

on the island, they want to Pa Bill. He knew the various roots, seeds, leaves, and everything to make medicine. He healed people, not from witchcraft [root], but from his knowledge of using natural medicine.

Big Momma learned some of it. She saved me from influenza when I was seven or eight years old. I almost died. I was on St. Simons, staying a couple of weeks with Aunt Celia and Uncle Philip. I was out in the yard eating figs that evening and playing with the children. All of the sudden, I felt real sleepy, and I went to the back steps, sat on one step and put my head down on the step above and went to sleep. When I woke up, Big Momma was holding me in her arms trying to get some tomato soup down me. They said ten days had passed, and don't remember anything that took place. Uncle Philip had brought Big Momma over to his house to take care of me. She had made up something. When they brought me home, they sent a jar of it that I still had to take. It was syrup fired with lightwood–kindlin'. It had rock candy in it, corn liquor, and something else. It got rid of that flu. They called it influenza. It was Big Momma who saved my life.

Civil Rights

I was very active as a young woman in the Civil Rights Movement and did lots of Civil Rights marches. Marching and running, because I didn't want to go to jail. When policemen would come on the scene with dogs, I knew every alleyway or little cut, as we called them, and I'd run like crazy. I knew so many people, I could slip into a house. I was not going to jail if I could help it. We had meetings every week at various churches for the most part. When we did the marches, it would be in one of the squares downtown or out in front of one of the churches. The big marches would be in the middle of the streets going in town. I never took part in the sit-ins where they arrested the folk. Once they would get a sit-in started, I would make sure to go to those places and sit. But I wasn't going to go when they knew they were going to be arrested. It was a pretty intense period.

Three or four years ago, we worked with an interracial-interfaith group, and we did a remembrance of civil rights in the city of Savannah and produced a journal from it. We made a timeline for Savannah. Our theme was "50 Years+, Civil Rights in the City of Savannah." SCAD [Savannah School of Art & Design] printed up about 5,000 copies. We gave them away. We wanted the children to know. The children today have no idea of what went on. Every once in a while, or in February, they see little snippets of information. So, we ended up with a big march, and it's all documented with a timeline. If you don't know about history, you're subject to repeat it.

Going to University

I went to Savannah State University and then got a scholarship to get a master's degree in social work at the University of Chicago. I was the Assistant Professor of Social Work Administration, which meant I administered government programs, wrote proposals and got funding. I did most of my research and was politically active, so I would go up to Washington [DC] all the time and advocate for it. I was young and full of energy. I took students on trips. It was a rewarding career working with the students and seeing them make progress. It grew me as well as it grew them. One time, I was walking down the street in Accra, Ghana, and I heard someone yelling, "Mrs. Robinson!" I thought, *Who in the world knows me here?* I turned around, and it was one of my former students. When I went in 1969 to Ghana, there were some people who said I looked like I was from there. They took me to a village, and you could see the same facial features. We looked alike. We rode into a rural area that was a fishing village, which seemed normal because our people [on Sapelo] were fisher people and hunters. And we did look alike–a lot alike.

Religion

Little Bryan Baptist on Gwinnett and Price was the church I went to for a number of years. For the past thirty-eight years, I've been a member of Saint Matthews Episcopal Church on Anderson and MLK. Once I learned something about the true history of the Baptist church, there were certain things I couldn't live with, and that's why I changed. It's human nature for people to think that they know God's mind. But people don't know God's mind. While I believe the Bible, it has been interpreted and reinterpreted by people who put what they want in it. It's still factual, but it's also taken on some beliefs of people who did the interpretation. I wouldn't begin to tell people what God meant for this or that. It's up to God through the Holy Spirit to let us know. All I know is that God says we should love each other, and all that hate stuff is sheer stupidity. God made humankind, and we can see it in nature all the time that some are different from the majority, but so what?

At one time I was in line to become a priest in the Episcopal Church and spent four summers at Sewanee, Tennessee at the [University of the South] School of Ministry but got waylaid. I did complete the four summers, but so many things happened in my family. The Bishop was waiting for me to take exams, but I didn't take them.

The Women

Women who have had to take on big households–not just their own nuclear family but others in the community–get around a lot. You love to travel. That's pretty much my life. I used to be so busy that I took two vacations. I'd take one, and then about six months later, I had to take another just to get myself together. I'm somewhat of a loner. When I was a little girl, we never had any privacy because we had that little house, and I always had to sleep with a sister. It seemed like I could never have any time to myself. When I became an adult, especially after the separation and divorce, I just thoroughly enjoyed my solitude. I still love being by myself, at least sometimes. I've gone on three-week vacations by myself. In about 1980, I went to Europe by myself. I bought a twenty-one day Eurail Pass for Germany, France, Spain, and Italy. I like to plan things, so I talked with the lady at AAA in Savannah who was the expert about Europe. She sat with me for days on-end giving information. She found fairly inexpensive places to stay. For example, in Paris I had a nice, safe little hotel room. She told me what I should do and shouldn't do and who to talk to in order to see different things. I had a cousin, Robert Cutts, who lived in Berlin. His house was my base. I spent four days with him, and he gave me some orientation. I wanted to go to Oberammergau to see the Passion Play.[11] I'm a very serious Christian. They had just taken down the wall separating East and West Germany when I went, so I had the opportunity to see East Germany before it changed too much. It was extremely dreary. It was awful. Very depressing. Once we had to run because this huge crowd of skinheads with a huge flag–I've never seen such a big flag–were running behind Middle Easterners. My cousin said they were Iranians. He said, "Willie Mae, we better get out of here because they don't like black people either."

Barcelona was beautiful, absolutely gorgeous. I want to go back there. I loved Italy and the Vatican. I just had a marvelous time. When I was on the overnight trains, I'd get myself a little couchette [couch that unfolds into a bed] with a little bottle of wine, have dinner, and read. The folk come and turn it down at night so that you have your little bed. I don't think I would want to live anywhere on a permanent basis except right here in the U. S., and if I couldn't live in Savannah, I'd probably like to live in

Charleston or somewhere like that. I'm an old-fashioned person. I love going places, but the best thing in the world is to come back home.

Then, when I came back to Savannah, I bought an Amtrak three zone pass. I couldn't do the whole three months, but I did about a month. I got on the train here and went up to Philadelphia, cross the top of the U. S., then came all the way down through California, then the Grand Canyon. I just like doing things like that by myself.

Change

With Barack Obama coming into office–I can't even express it. I have to pinch myself periodically, because it's something that I didn't think could happen so soon. When God decides something is going to be, then things happen to bring it about. It's overwhelming. I started to go to the inauguration, because I could stay with my cousin in Washington who wanted me to come. But I thought about those huge crowds, and you can't get out of huge crowds if you wanted to, so I decided I better stay here and look at it on the TV.

Sapelo River

Nothing in this particular life is forever. It's the spirit that's more important than all these physical trappings. My parents are buried in Behavior Cemetery on Sapelo. I'm going to be cremated and have the ashes thrown in the Sapelo River.

NOTES

[1] A settlement named after Sampson Hogg, a slave. William S. McFeely, *Sapelo's People: A Long Walk Into Freedom* (New York: W. W. Norton & Company, 1994), 101.

[2] Owner Thomas Spalding "encouraged family formation in family-oriented villages–hammocks." Ibid., 57.

[3] "…the family changed its name [from Hogg] to Hall long after the [Civil] war." Ibid., 83.

[4] "Raccoon Bluff is located on the eastern side of Sapelo Island about five miles north of Hog Hammock." Ibid., 29.

[5] The Bilali Muhammad Document is a handwritten, Arabic manuscript on West African Islamic Law. It was written by Bilali Mohammet in the nineteenth century. The document is currently housed in the Hargrett Rare Book & Manuscript Library at the University of Georgia.

[6] "…Bilali, originally from Guinea…was a [slave] plantation manager supervising 500 to 1,000 slaves–without white overseership. He was also a religious father, an *imam* (Arabic) or *almaamy* (Fulfulde) who in the 1840s began to write a thirteen-page manual in Arabic for his Sapelo Island, Georgia, *umma*–the only known antebellum African Muslim community in the United States. Allan D. Austin, *African Muslims in Antebellum America: Transatlantic Stories and Spiritual Struggles* (New York: Routledge, 1997), 6.

[7] "Just to the west of Matty Carter's place…is a faded red-on-white sign: The Basket-Maker, Allen Green, Sapelo Island, Ga. Green's baskets are works of art–an art derived in method and pattern from Africa–and visitors interested in coastal culture seek him out." McFeely, *Sapelo's People, 27.*

[8] A nonprofit corporation whose mission is to preserve and revitalize the Hogg Hummock Community.

[9] Hudson Motor Company executive, Howard Earle Coffin, purchased Sapelo Island in 1912. In 1926, he purchased Sea Island

(called Long Island and renamed Glynn Isle) and, with his cousin, Alfred W. Jones, founded the Sea Island Company.

[10] The "big house," built on the ruins of Thomas Spalding's home, is located about 2 miles south of Hog Hammock.

[11] "Passion play: A dramatic presentation depicting the passion of Jesus Christ: his trial, suffering and death. Performed since 1634 as a tradition by the inhabitants of the village of Oberammergau, Bavaria, Germany... The town's residents vowed that if God spared them from the effects of the bubonic plague ravaging the region, they would produce a play every ten years thereafter for all time depicting the life and death of Jesus." Source: Wikipedia, http://en.wikipedia.org/wiki/Oberammergau_Passion_Play, accessed March 4, 2011.

William Hadley Brown

Bill Brown grew up in an era when trolley cars were common sites in small towns, telegraphs were the main form of instant communication, and young men barnstormed the country in bi-planes, performing feats of aerial acrobatics. In some ways, his childhood was the Georgia equivalent of Tom Sawyer's, where children created their own entertainment and the great outdoors was at their beck-and-call. His family's roots in Georgia extend back to a time when Florida still belonged to Spain. In this narrative, he recounts his family's post-Civil War involvement in the lumber business, life during the Great Depression, and his work in the shipyards during World War II. Bill also offers an interesting account of how Georgia's poet laureate, Sidney Lanier, came to pen his immortal "Marshes of Glynn."

Bill Brown

My full name is William Hadley Brown. My father, Simon Hadley Brown, was born in Camden County. I was born in Brunswick on December 3rd, 1918 at 4 Glynn

43

Avenue, which is now the Chamber of Commerce office. My mother, Ethel Grey Dart, was also born there in 1892. The house was built around 1890. There were five children in our family–two boys and three girls. Fortunately, they are all still living. I have a brother, Bob Dart Brown. He lives on St. Simons. My oldest sister, Sarah, lives in Eastview, a subdivision. My second sister, Jane, has a condo on the Island at Deer Run Villas and also one on Singer Island in Florida. The youngest sister, Delia, lives on the corner of Lanier Boulevard and Walnut, right across the street from me.

We grew up in the neighborhood called Urbana, named after Urbanus Dart, my great-grandfather, who owned a considerable part of Brunswick at one time. He had a number of children. My grandfather was his youngest son, William Robert Dart. Urbanus was the son of Cyrus Dart, who came down with the Continental Army when Florida was still a Spanish territory. He was assigned to the outpost at Colerain on the St. Mary's River down there in Camden County.[1] He was a doctor, and later he moved to St. Simons, where he was the port doctor. One day, he and my great-grandfather, Urbanus, and a Negro oarsman were rowing out from St. Simons to inspect a ship somewhere in the sound. They encountered rough water, and the boat capsized. Cyrus and the oarsman were drowned. Urbanus swam back to shore. Had he not been a good swimmer, I would not be here today. Their bodies–Cyrus and the oarsman–were never found. Urbanus was born in 1800, so he must have been a teenager at the time.

Back in the 1870s when the lumber mills were flourishing on the island, there were around a thousand people living there. About two-hundred-and-fifty were white and seven-hundred-and-fifty were black. I imagine they lived primarily around the village area. I'm not positive. The mills were on the Frederica River where Epworth is now [Gascoigne Bluff]. Getting to Brunswick

44

was by boat until the causeway [F. J. Torras Causeway] was built in 1924. The causeway engineer was Fernando J. Torras. He later became the city manager. Some people said he couldn't build the causeway, but he did it. The city and county jointly issued a bond to pay for the causeway, but the city had a better bond rating, so it owned fifty-one percent of it. The toll went to pay off the bond. They pumped the sand out of the bottom of the rivers to build the causeway. They built the road right on top of the marsh, so it had a tendency to sink and leave dips in the road, which they corrected later on when it was rebuilt. The day of the dedication, we sat on the porch at 4 Glynn Avenue and watched the parade go by. They had a big celebration in the park on St. Simons Island at Gascoigne Bluff facing Frederica River.

Acquiring Land

My great-grandfather lived in Brunswick. His sons built a sawmill on St. Simons somewhere around where the Sea Island Yacht Club is now [south of the Frederica River bridge]. That was during the days when the Dodge-Hilton mill was in operation. Four or five of his sons wanted to start the sawmill business. They asked him to divide up the land he owned in Brunswick and let them invest it in the mill, and he said he would not do it. So he borrowed $42,000 and pledged the land, 2,000 acres, and loaned them the money. In 1872 or somewhere about then there was a worldwide panic, a depression. They lost the mill, and he lost all of his land. I've been a little scared of a mortgage ever since.

He acquired the land [he owned in Brunswick] in 1830, I think. They had a yellow fever epidemic. People abandoned their land here. He and another party came in and claimed a good part of the land. He wound up owning a substantial amount of the property in Brunswick. He gave the land to most of the churches that were in Brunswick at that time–the Methodist church, the synagogue, St. Mark's, the Presbyterian Church, the Baptist church, and the First African Baptist church and several more. Before the Civil War, the blacks used to be with the Baptist church. After the war, they pulled out and started the First African Baptist church. He gave them the land for that church on Amherst Street. They still invite me over there for their anniversary celebrations once a year. The African Baptist church members used to come down there and have baptisms in the creek at the foot of Gloucester Street. They'd march from Amherst Street down Gloucester Street singing hymns.

Brunswick, early 1900s. Group of African-Americans on their way to a baptism at Back Landing which was located at the foot of Gloucester Street. Courtesy of Vanishing Georgia, Georgia Archives, Office of Secretary of State.

I went to Glynn Grammar School, Prep High, and Glynn Academy. I graduated in 1937. I wasn't particularly interested in sports. I spent all of my free time playing in the creek in front 4 Glynn Avenue, sailing, rowing, and swimming. I didn't have time for sports.

The Swimming Hole

Urbanus gave all of his children 100 x 250 lots along Glynn Avenue. On the east side of Glynn Avenue is a piece of land that was jointly owned by all the children right near where the Sidney Lanier Oak and monument is. On the edge of the marsh [just south of the current monument location] they had an open-air pavilion where they periodically had dances on summer evenings with a local band playing music. This was back in the early 1900s and up through the 1920s. People would come out and swim there at high tide. The bathhouse, where people could change clothes, was built there on the bank of the creek. They built what we used to call a wooden pen with a roof over it and sides, 1 x 4 inch vertical slats, around the perimeter and a wooden floor. Children could swim in there at high tide. That's where I learned to swim. Alongside of it, they had a dock on the west side. After I learned to swim, I would try to get courage up to dive off the dock into the deep water out there, and I was afraid if I went down, I'd never come up. As I was standing there trying to make a decision whether to jump or not, my cousin, Hal Myers, poked me in the ribs, and I jumped off the dock. Fortunately, I came up. When the [F. J. Torras] causeway was opened in '24, everybody went to the island, so there wasn't any need for a swimming facility in Brunswick.

My grandfather and his sons built a 100-foot tugboat called the *U-Dart* right on the bank of the creek. Back in the 1800s, Brunswick was a right lively port. They needed tugboats to tow the ships in and out of the harbor.

Lanier's Bath House. Brunswick, Ga., Historic Postcard Collection,
RG 48-2-5, Georgia Archives.

Brunswick, ca. 1900. Construction of the *U. Dart* in front of the
home of Urbanus Dart at
Gloucester and Richmond Streets. Note the people sitting portside
and on the stern.
Courtesy of Vanishing Georgia, Georgia Archives, Office of Secretary
of State.

There used to be a right angle turn at Glynn Avenue and Gloucester Street. Later on when traffic began to pick up, people unfamiliar with the area would fly down Gloucester and make that sharp turn. One Sunday during the lunch hour, a car from Savannah turned over into the creek. Fortunately, nobody was drowned. Another time, a circus truck heading back to Sarasota, Florida, missed the turn at night and dropped the elephants out in the marsh. They got the elephants back on land and turned the truck upright. Some of the local fellas that had been on the Island drinking, came along and saw several elephants in the road. Several of them stopped drinking for a whole month.

Building A Road

Back in the 1930s, they dredged out a basin there and pumped up the original land for the Howard Coffin [recreation] Park. Dart Creek came in and touched the land at the foot of Gloucester Street–Back Landing [the corner of Gloucester and Glynn Avenue]–and made a horseshoe bend out in the marsh and came back and touched the land there in front of Lanier's Oak where the veterinarian's office is, on 9 Glynn Avenue. The reason that [water] basin is out there in front of 4 Glynn Avenue is because when they extended the road to the foot of the Sidney Lanier Bridge, the Highway Department made a survey and concluded there was sand under the marsh, and they were going to create a canal and use the sand to build a road. They had a contract with a dredging company that had an 8-inch [diameter] dredge. They pumped out the marsh and the muck and couldn't find any sand down there and went broke. So they had to hire a larger dredging outfit that came in with a 24-inch pipeline and dredged that basin down to fifty feet and pumped the sand from that spot [near the F. J. Torras Causeway] all the way to the Sidney Lanier Bridge. That's why that big basin is out there, and when they finished dredging, it was fifty feet deep. Now, it's filled up from a lot of tides and a lot of silt. Eventually, the marsh will fill back. It's hard to believe that it was fifty feet deep at one time. When you look out there at low tide, you can see all the mud out there. It was all marsh one time except where the creek came up in there.

Brunswick, ca. 1918-1920. Aerial view of the first golf course in Brunswick, now the Windsor Park neighborhood. The road seen running north/south [Lanier Boulevard] was paved with oyster shells. The marsh area on the left of Lanier Boulevard in this photograph was filled in with sand dredged from the marsh and is now Howard Coffin Park. Gloucester Street, bottom of photo, runs east/west. Courtesy of Vanishing Georgia, Georgia Archives, Office of Secretary of State.

Fun With Guns

My grandfather had built a dam on a lot that lay east of Glynn Avenue. I was riding my bicycle one day up under a palm tree there and hit a palm frond, which dislodged a wasp nest. They lit onto me. I left my bicycle and ran home. We used to play in a grass field there. Someone had loaned us a .28-gauge shotgun, which was an unusual size for a shotgun. One afternoon when I was about ten or twelve, my brother Bob and I went out to shoot pigeons. About that time, a policeman on a motorcycle came around

50

the bend at Glynn Avenue and Gloucester, so we dropped the gun and ran off. We spent the rest of the afternoon looking for the gun in that tall grass. We had a lot of old guns stored in the trunk room on the second floor at 4 Glynn Avenue. One of them was a .45-70 caliber long-barrel buffalo gun. We found a jar of cartridges for it. One of us slipped out the front door with the shells, and the other took the gun out the back door. We went around to the river lot. We put a log against the dam, and I persuaded my brother to load the gun and fire the thing. He fired it, and split the log. The recoil nearly knocked him down, and the black gunpowder made so much smoke you couldn't see Saint Simons. We had an old double-barrel shotgun that was so old and worn, you had to push up on the barrel and down on the stock to fire it accurately. We had some old shells. Sometimes they'd fire, and sometimes they wouldn't. Sometimes they'd hesitate. You'd fire the thing, and nothing would happen. You'd lower the gun, and about that time it would go off. When it wouldn't fire, you'd have to hold the gun down for the shot to run out the barrel.

Elephant In The Room

Circuses that came to Brunswick would set up the tent down at the south end off of Union Street about where Second Avenue is. There was an open area there in those days. One day, one of the elephant's got loose and walked over across Union Street to Mrs. Lillianthal's home. She told the police, somewhat excitedly, "There's an elephant standing on my front porch!" Can you imagine a little Jewish lady calmly saying that?

Flooding

My father had a Buick back in the '20s. Around 1926, a hurricane came through here. I had an aunt who had a convalescent home on St. Simons near where the King & Prince Hotel now is. My father went over there to get her and one elderly lady guest from Atlanta, and bring them

51

back to town. My aunt had a cat and a crow in a cage, and he brought them all back, too. By the time he got to the end of the causeway, the tide had come up, and water was in the road. The car stalled out, but the wind was blowing from the northeast. The Buick had a high back, so he put the car in neutral, and the wind blew him all the way up to 4 Glynn Avenue. That night, the old lady would get up and walk to the window and say, "I wonder how far we are from the water." The water was about two feet deep under the house. The city police finally came out and carried us to the courthouse. We spent the night there.

Brunswick, Oct. 2-3, 1898. Home of W. R. Dart on Glynn Avenue after flooding caused by the hurricane of 1898. The water rose to six inches above the window sills. Note the items that have been put out to dry. Courtesy of Vanishing Georgia, Georgia Archives, Office of Secretary of State.

Bill Brown (April 2011) standing in front of his childhood home
on Glynn Avenue,
now occupied by the Brunswick Chamber of Commerce.

I used to ride the *Emmeline* and the *Hessie* to St. Simons before the causeway was built. It was about an hour ride one-way. One trip I recall, in 1923, they carried a Buick on the foredeck of the *Emmeline*. There weren't many cars on the island then. There was an old wooden pier on St. Simons that swayed with the wave action and had cracks in the decking. As a little boy, I was afraid I'd lose a foot in one of those big cracks. They put a gangway from the deck of the boat to the foot of the ramp. They drove the car up the gangway, up the ramp, and down the length of the pier.

Brunswick. Steamboat, the Hessie. Courtesy of Vanishing Georgia, Georgia Archives, Office of Secretary of State.

Occasionally, they had a special deal where a train came in from as far away as, say Fitzgerald, Georgia. The people rode the train to Brunswick, boarded the ferry to the island, spent the day over there, came back at night, got on the train and went back to Fitzgerald. The railroad and the ferry worked together on that. A pretty good crowd would come down from inland towns.

After the Civil War, when there was a hotel on the [St. Simons] Massengale tract, my grandfather and his brother-in-law from New York built a dock out in front of the hotel. People would disembark at the St. Simons pier and get on a trolley pulled by mules to the hotel at Massengale. They were going to run a ferryboat to carry hotel guests directly from Brunswick to Massengale. Just before they started, the person who owned the ferry line also claimed riparian rights on the beach, so that operation fell through.

School Days

One of my grandfather's brothers, Jacob, was a friend of Sidney Lanier.[2] I read a little memorandum he had written saying that one night he was walking down Newcastle Street and passed Friedlander's Emporium, a beer hall, where he heard the melodious notes of a flute coming from within. Jake went in and Lanier was in there playing his flute. They chatted and then walked from Newcastle down Gloucester Street and sat on the edge of the creek on a moonlit night with a spring tide, and Lanier got his inspiration to pen his poem, "The Marshes of Glynn." My mother said he got his inspiration out of Friedlander's beer barrel.

Brunswick, ca. 1900-1910. The Marshes of Glynn with Lanier's Oak at the right.
Courtesy of Vanishing Georgia, Georgia Archives, Office of Secretary of State.

In school, we had the choice of memorizing "The Marshes of Glynn" and either writing or reciting it. I didn't like to write, so I met after class with the English teacher and recited it. I can't quote any of it at the moment, but I have a copy in my office. Miss Jane Macon was one of my English teachers. She taught me and my brothers and sisters. She also taught my father. She came here as an elementary school teacher. One day, my father skipped school. That afternoon, on the way home, Miss Macon passed by their residence, and his sister, Aunt Susie, was playing in the front yard. Miss Macon said, "Susie, I'm sorry that Hadley was sick today." Aunt Susie said, "He's not sick. He's around there playing in the back yard." When he got to school the next day, Miss Macon gave him a switching. And when he got home, his mother gave him another one. I married in 1946, and Miss Macon was still teaching. My wife was a home economics teacher. Miss Macon told them at the first faculty meeting that Mrs. Brown's father-in-law said that she (Miss Macon) had made a Christian out of him when she gave him that whipping [laughs]. He never skipped school again. Miss Macon retired and lived in a house on the corner of Monck and Egmont Streets. She was walking across the street to the post office and was struck by a car. Later on, she died as a result of her injuries.

R. E. Hood, Ralph Hood, was the principal of Prep High when we moved from the grammar school. He was the principal there for three years. Then, when we moved over to Glynn Academy, he also moved. So we had him for seven years. He was a very interesting fellow. He also taught a class in civics or something like that. One day, he was telling us how important it was to eat a good breakfast every morning. He said, "How can you be sure to eat a good breakfast?" Carl Fowler held up his hand and said, "Don't eat supper!" The first day of school, we had an assembly. Miss Elder, who was later Mrs. Jeter, was standing on the side. Walter Gregory kept talking while Mr. Hood was at the podium. Miss Elder told him to be quiet, but Walter kept on chatting. She grabbed him by the shoulders and shook him until his head was about to pop off, put him back down in the seat, and he never said another word. Walter went on to become a Marine Corps pilot in World War II. We heard that he was patrolling off the California coast one day and spotted bubbles coming up in the ocean. He called for permission to bomb the Japanese submarine. He bombed the thing and put the outflow of the Los Angeles sewer plant out of commission.

Love Letters

When we sold the family residence to the Chamber of Commerce, we were cleaning out the house. On the second floor, there was a trunk room. In one of the trunks, we found a shoebox of letters my grandfather, William Robert Dart, had written to his first wife when he was a steam engineer and machinist, working at a sawmill on Union Island up in McIntosh County. She was here in Brunswick, and they were writing back and forth. He got sunburned one day, and she was chastising him. When he was feeling kindly toward her, he signed his letter, "Love, Billy." When he was irritated with her, he'd sign it, "Yours Truly, William Robert."

Trolley Cars

The trolley cars used to run down Gloucester Street to Lee Street, turn, and run out to Hercules [industrial plant]. We walked from 4 Glynn Avenue to Lee Street to catch the trolley for a ride into town. I was in the barbershop on Newcastle Street and saw the trolleys going down Newcastle to the barn on the last day they ran. They closed them down when the automobiles came in. This was in the early 1920s. The trolley barn was on Newcastle Street about where the Harold Pate building is located. This office building was the former county jail.

Life of Eli

There was a fellow, Eli, whose parents had been slaves. He lived in a little cabin behind the Shady Rest Tourist Home where McDonald's is now located at 1803 Glynn Avenue. He did yard work for all the neighbors in Urbanaville. *Amos and Andy* was on the radio in those days, and we'd invite him in and let him sit in the parlor to listen to it. He thought that was great. He'd slap his knee and laugh with it. Someone asked him if he had any burial insurance. He said, "No. I know the city can't keep me but three days." When he died, the only black people at the funeral were the undertaker and the preacher. The rest of the people were all white people from the neighborhood. He was a great fellow.

We had a battery-powered radio, and you had to string an antenna outside in the air. One of my aunts, a nurse, was a fan of Rudy Vallée. She used to listen to him, and you had to use earphones to hear. The radio station was up in Pittsburgh, I think. The batteries would last several months.

At The Beach

I worked as a deckhand on the Army Corps of Engineers survey boat for a few months. When the Corps had to run harbor surveys, we carried the survey parties from Savannah out. They'd survey the rivers, the harbor, and the channel from St. Simons on out to sea before they'd let a contractor dredge. After they dredged, we'd have to come back and run another survey and make sure they dredged the proper amount. The dredging may have caused some erosion by the St. Simons pier. There was more beach there at low tide than there is now. They had a platform across the cockpit where a lead man could stand and cast a sounding line with a lead on the bottom of it. When the line was vertical he'd read off the depth to the top of the water. They had a recorder who wrote down the number he'd call out. One day, the waves in the channel were four or five feet high, and the lead man was calling out, "Twenty-six-four, twenty-seven-four, twenty-six-four." I don't know how he estimated down to the tenth-of-a-foot with the waves running that high. They dumped the dredged sand further out off to the south of the channel in the ocean. We went down to Fernandina to do survey work for several days. This was back in 1936. My brother worked on that survey boat before I did. They had to go up to Burnt Fort on the Satilla River. The drawbridge attendant in Woodbine was a little reluctant to go out and open the bridge for them. They told him they had dynamite on the boat and were coming up the river and that he'd better have the bridge open by the time they got there. He hurried up and opened the bridge for them. The boat had a right substantial wake, and it washed out all through the swamp out there. This old farmer came down at Burnt Fort and said, "It sure do make a ripple, don't it."

One night, we got a telegram for one of the crewmembers on the dredge that a family member had died, and they needed him to come home. So we had to deliver the telegram to the dredge. Our boat was moored near the foot of Gloucester Street and we ran out to the dredge, which was on the far end of the channel. We ran alongside and asked them to throw a heaving line. I put the telegram in a twist in the line and sent it back to the dredge for delivery to the crewman. We brought the crewmember back to town. That's how communication was in those days before two-way radio.

Port of Brunswick

Hunter Hopkins was the mayor I remember most. Malcolm McKinnon was a county commissioner who was very active when the causeway was opened [1924]. They named the airfield on St. Simons for McKinnon. Back in the '20s, where Redfern Village is on St. Simons, there was a small grass airfield. Around '26 or '27 they brought in a squadron of Navy bi-planes. They had a crank you put in the side to start the things up. The U. S. Navy owned the south end of Blythe Island at one time.[3]

They used to have air shows and barnstormers who'd give people a ride. I remember when Paul Redfern landed. My father was active in the Chamber of Commerce at that time and helped promote his flight to Rio. There was a lot of interest in aviation then. Lindbergh had just flown 3,000 miles to Paris. Redfern's flight was a 4,000-mile solo flight. I was there on Sea Island when he flew his plane in and landed on the beach, and I was there when he took off on a hot August morning. They built a hanger for him on the edge of the beach. It was a green plane with white letters on the side–"Port of Brunswick." He didn't get off the beach the first time. The second time he finally got off and flew out of sight. His plane was so heavy with fuel, it looked like he was about ten feet over the top of the waves. The last thing we heard was that he'd flown over a ship down there [in the Caribbean] and dropped a message asking for directions to land. They turned the ship toward land, and he flew off in that direction. Nobody ever heard from him again.

Paul R. Redfern with friends. Brunswick-Brazilian flight. Caption reads [...] "friend, Ed Lambright, Paul R. Redfern Brunswick - Brazil flight." Paul Redfern was the first aviator to attempt to fly nonstop from the United States to the Caribbean on a solo trip. In August 1927, at the age of 25, he took off from Brunswick, Georgia, but never reached Brazil. Neither he nor his plane have ever been located. An airfield on St. Simons Island, Georgia, was named for him, which later became Redfern Village. In 1938 Metro-Goldwyn-Mayer produced a movie about him entitled Too Hot to Handle, starring Clark Gable. Photo courtesy of Vanishing Georgia, Georgia Archives, Office of Secretary of State.

Jekyll Island was a private reserve back then. Occasionally, you'd slip over there at night and look for turtle eggs. Seems like the causeway to Jekyll and the Sidney Lanier Bridge were started in the late '40s when Thompson was governor. Then he lost the governorship, and Talmadge stopped construction on the bridge and the causeway. He called it "Thompson's folly." Talmadge was going to leave those piers out in the river as a monument. Then it became a good idea to complete it. Several years later, in the 1950s, the Highway Department completed the bridge and the causeway. Talmadge came down and dedicated the bridge and acted like it was his idea, but it was really M. E. Thompson's.

We used to go in a little fifteen-foot sailboat to camp on the beach of Little Cumberland Island. Larry Miller's family had a cottage on the north end of big Cumberland. My brother Bob, Larry Miller, David Gould, Clinton Knight, and I went over there one time in our sailboats and landed at the big dock. We walked across the island and got somebody to bring a car down there to haul our gear to the landing at Christmas Creek. We put our gear in a rowboat with an outboard on it and spent the night on Little Cumberland. It rained on us, and it wasn't a very pleasant evening. Somebody brought French bread and syrup for dessert. But the bread was so porous we ended up taking a bite of bread and drinking the syrup. Another night, we camped on Little Cumberland and were boiling some turtle eggs over a fire. Alfred Brockinton, the harbor pilot who lived on St. Simons, used to take turtle egg parties from Atlanta there. He came ashore near where we were camping. Alfred stayed with us while the party walked down the beach. We asked Alfred if he would like a cup of coffee, and he said he would. So we got our coffee pot and turned the flashlight so we could pour into the cup, and all the bugs flocked to the light and filled the cup up. He wasn't very happy to have a cup full of bugs along with his coffee. Later on, a little boy from the Atlanta party came back and asked if he could have one of our boiled eggs. He said he'd eaten one of those green ones up the beach, and it wouldn't stay down.

Several of our party climbed up the old abandoned light house on Little Cumberland to sleep on top of it and get a little breeze up there. Clinton and I stayed on the beach and tried to sleep on the beach, which was as hard as concrete and there were sand flies and mosquitoes. We woke up at daylight, and I was ready to come back to Brunswick. Rattlesnakes used to crawl up the stairs of that lighthouse, and they had pulled up the ladder to the last ten feet to where they were sleeping. They thought nobody would disturb them, but there was a balcony, and I went out on it and woke them up. I'd had enough and was ready to come to town.

The government built that lighthouse. The St. Andrews Sound had a lot of vessels coming in there and going up the Satilla River in the 1800s. They exported cotton from the upriver plantations. They had little steamboats running up and down the rivers. Sailing vessels came in from out in the ocean, and they'd tow them up the river to pick up timber and cotton or whatever the plantations had to sell.

Edwin Fendig and his brother Neal told me about sailing off of Jekyll one Sunday and they saw an alligator on the beach. They landed and caught it and put a piece of board under its stomach and tied his tail down where he couldn't flap it. They put it on the sailboat and sailed back to St. Simons and dragged the alligator on the beach. They went up to get a Coca-Cola. When they came back the alligator had got up and was walking down the beach, and the Sunday crowd on the beach was scattering.

Plane Ride

My first plane flight was during World War II. I went down to Florida and went over to St. Petersburg and then rode a train to Atlanta. I took a flight from Atlanta to Savannah on a twin-engine DC-3. I'd read in the brochure that they had enough power to fly on one engine. We landed in Augusta, and about five minutes after taking off again, the right engine started sputtering. The pilot flashed to tighten our seatbelts. I had mine so tight I could hardly breathe. Someone got sick and threw up in the aisle. We flew on to Savannah and came in rather steeply. The right wing dropped, the pilot pulled it up, and I wrenched my back trying to help him lift it. I didn't get nervous until I looked out the window and saw a fire engine and an ambulance riding along beside us. He reversed engine and slowed the thing down. I thought we were going to roll out of Chatham County, but he finally got the plane to stop. I rode the bus to Brunswick and couldn't eat anything but milk toast for two days. That was my first plane flight, and I got my money's worth.

Roadwork

There were several oaks there where the Lanier Oak is now. They preserved it when they were rebuilding the roads. Glynn Avenue originally had a 75-foot wide right-of-way. My father was in the legislature at one time and got a bill passed authorizing the Highway Department to four-lane Highway 17 the length of the coast of Georgia. The city of Brunswick widened it at Glynn Avenue and took ten feet off the family property at 4 Glynn Avenue, which was my mother's home. My grandfather, William Robert Dart, put the title in trust in the name of his wife and the children, including my mother, so that he did not lose it when the sawmill went under on St. Simons. So, my father wasn't too happy about losing ten feet off the front of the property. But Brunswick four-laned Glynn Avenue all the way to the city limits. In those days, the rural counties between Brunswick and Savannah weren't very interested in tourists. The Highway Department would only pave the road if a county provided the right-of-way, and those counties never would furnish the right-of-way. So they never got the highway four-laned in the '30s.[4] Traffic used to come down Glynn Avenue to Gloucester Street, from Gloucester to Newcastle past the Oglethorpe Hotel, Newcastle to G Street, and by the courthouse to Norwich Street and back to Gloucester. They ran the tourists all the way through town so all the merchants would get a shot at them.

Downing Company

The Downing Company was a big operation. They bought rosin from the turpentine and producers operating in South Georgia and shipped the rosin out of Brunswick in barrels. They would finance these turpentine operators who tapped the pine trees to draw out the sap. Then they'd make turpentine and rosin from the sap. The Downing Company would buy it and sell it, mostly overseas. It was the early 1930s when they finally went broke. There was a box factory on the 2600 block of Glynn Avenue, the Georgia Veneer & Package Company. They'd bring in gum logs from the Altamaha River and soak them in a pond. With the thin veneer, they made boxes and hampers for the Florida vegetable and fruit pickers to use. Glynn Avenue [Highway 17] ran right through the plant. You had part of the plant on one side and part on the other. Later on, they straightened out Glynn Avenue and eliminated that passing through the plant. Hercules is a big plant near there. The Atlantic Refining Company had a plant at ARCO [west side of Brunswick]. My understanding is that they imported crude oil from Venezuela, expecting the wells in Texas to go dry. Later on, they closed it and moved back to Port Arthur, Texas. Then the pulp mill came in to that location in '36 or '37.

The President

When Eugene Talmadge was running for Agricultural Commissioner [1926], he made a speech on the steps of the old city hall one night. There was a right good-sized crowd in the street. He told the crowd, "They say I stole from the state. And I say 'yes, I stole from the state, but I stole for you!'" Everybody applauded him and elected him.

When Calvin Coolidge came to Sea Island, there was a lot of publicity surrounding that visit. The Sea Island Company carried the President to their hunting lodge at Cabin Bluff in Camden County. The New York newspapers chartered an amphibious plane to fly reporters down to cover an upcoming turkey hunt. The plane landed in the Cumberland River at low tide. The people on the deck tried to wave them off the submerged sandbar. The pilot waved back, struck the sand, and stood the plane on its nose. That night, they had an oyster roast for the President. Arthur True, a Sea Island employee, was standing next to the President to open oysters. He opened one, and with the oyster knife in his hand, he offered it to the President. At that moment, he felt the barrel of a .45 caliber pistol in his back as a Secret Service agent told him to drop that knife. Early the next morning, the hunting guide was ready to carry the President out to the turkey stand. However, no one could find the President. Finally, one of the black employees informed the group that the President was "commoding around, but he would be there shortly."

World War II

During World War II, I worked at the shipyards. I graduated from Emory where I studied business administration. When I got out and came home and went to work in the J. A. Jones Shipyard in Brunswick, which built Liberty Ships. I started out marking the patterns on the sheets of steel. Liberty Ships were 441 feet long. You'd mark the outline and bring in the burners to cut them out. That wasn't very exciting, and I asked to be transferred as a ship fitter. I worked with a fellow named Echols from Patterson, Georgia. We assembled the parts of the ship by fabricating them in the yard and putting them up on the deck. Mr. Echols was raising tobacco. He'd get up and tend his tobacco crop in the morning, get on a bus, ride to the shipyard and work the second shift, go back home, and do it again the next day. Working down inside the ship and coming up all the time, I caught a chill and got strep-throat, so I went over to the Brunswick Marine Yard as a time-keeper for the remainder of the war. It was a smaller shipyard at the foot of Dartmouth Street and Bay Street that built Army freighters and Navy oilers and the bow sections for landing crafts. We had about 200 on the payroll. They hauled the bow sections up to Charleston for assembly with landing craft. The Brunswick Marine Yard was already a long-established business with a railway that hauled shrimp boats and other boats out of the water to work on. They originally got a contract to build three harbor tugs. Then later, they got contracts to build the freighters and oilers and the bow sections during the war. The Navy oilers were about 200 feet long.

Moxham originally got the contract to build the Liberty Ships. Daniels Construction Company built the shipyard near the present location of the Sidney Lanier Bridge. My brother helped build the ways for the Liberty Ships. When the war came along, Brunswick had 15,035 people. After the war started, something like 16,000 people were on the payroll at the big shipyard. People were renting some of the bedrooms by the shift. The movie theatre operated around the clock. Everything was blacked out around here. They got behind on the delivery of the ships, so the government took the contract away from them and gave it to J. A. Jones. One day, my brother and I were riding our bicycles through Windsor Park to work on the second shift. I went over the handlebars on my bike and skinned myself up. Dusted myself off, rode to the yard, and went to the clinic to get patched up. Right ahead of me was an old fella from Fargo, Georgia, on the edge of the Okefenokee. Apparently, he had malaria–a bit of a fever. He was talking to the nurse who was taking his history. She said, "What's your occupation." Well, he didn't know what "occupation" meant. She said, "How did you make a living?" He said, "I ain't never made 'ary 'un" [one]. There was a new tack welder who came on the second shift one day. He climbed the steps up to the platform level to the deck, and there was 441 feet of rusty deck metal in front of him. He looked from one end to the other and said, "Hit's a terrible pile of iron to float in the water, hain't it?"

Brunswick, 1943. The U.S.S. Samalness on the day it was christened and launched at a Brunswick shipyard. Courtesy of Vanishing Georgia, Georgia Archives, Office of Secretary of State.

Apparently, the previous timekeeper at the Brunswick Marine Yard was selling moonshine on the side. He had little trouble being sure workers paid him for it because he handled the checks. It took me several weeks to convince the employees that I wasn't also selling moonshine. They hired an elderly gentleman named W. G. Price as my assistant. We found that some of the men wouldn't show up for work, but would get a friend to punch their time cards. He stood in the gatehouse and made sure everybody punched his own card every morning. Mr. Price was about 75 years old and walked with a limp. We had a little office on the yard. One day, they were moving the bow section of an Army freighter from the yard down to the ways to put it in place. They had two steam cranes that would pick the thing up, one on either side, and walk it down there. When they got it ready to lower it into position, the brake slipped on one crane, and the bow fell off and pulled both crane boons down until they crossed. Well, steam sprayed all over the yard. The operator of one crane jumped out and broke his hip, and there was a lot of commotion. When it was all over, I looked for Mr. Price and found him walking back to the yard. He had sprinted two blocks up Bay Street.

I was in the Coast Guard Auxiliary. The Golden Isles Marina was our base, and we'd go out at night and anchor in the sound to listen for German submarines charging their batteries. When they were running on the surface, they'd use the diesel engines. At night, they came up to the surface and ran the generators to recharge the batteries. We never heard any. One Monday morning, we were coming in, but had difficulty cranking the engine, so I was late going to work and wore my Coast Guard uniform. I walked up to the timekeeper shack and saw the clerk, a young girl, sitting at the desk. When I went around and opened the door, she had disappeared. She had been to Hinesville on Saturday night and met a soldier, and they got right friendly. He said, "I'm coming down to marry you." She thought he had arrived and hid under the desk.

When my brother went in the Navy, they said they didn't allow nicknames. He had a hard time convincing them his name was not Robert, it was B-O-B. He was born on my aunt's birthday. Her name was Robbie Dart, and the family just named him Bob.

When the shipyard closed down, I went into real estate in 1945. My father was in real estate. In those days, you didn't have to have a license. In 1950, when Glynn County reached a population of 50,000, they came out with a Georgia license law, and they gave me a broker's license. My wife and father also got a broker's license. Along about '52 there was a bit of a recession. I gave up my real estate license and got an insurance license. Two years later, I decided that was not my field. Every time I saw a client, I had the feeling they were thinking, "Here comes that so-and-so selling life insurance." So I gave up my insurance license, went up to Atlanta, and got my real estate broker's license back in 1954 and have had it ever since. Down cycles aren't much fun, but they happen. I've seen them before. Just hang on. This one [2008] is worse because banks went overboard lending to people that shouldn't be getting loans. A lot of people bought houses who should not have. The government is partly responsible, and the banks are partly responsible.

It was pretty tough during the Great Depression. One day, my father wrote five letters to prospects. Postage was two cents, and he didn't have a dime to mail the letters. He borrowed money from the American National Bank. One day, Ike Aiken, the president of the bank, saw him on the Post Office steps and said, "Hadley, you need to make a payment on the principal." My father said, "Ike, make out another note for whatever you want, and I'll sign it." Ike didn't push him anymore on that. Fortunately, we didn't have a mortgage on 4 Glynn Avenue. Jeff Brown at Phoenix Brown's grocery store extended us credit, and we were able to eat. So things were right tough. Around 1937-'38, things began to pick up a little bit.

My father was in the legislature back in the early '30s. He ran on the reform ticket. There were some shenanigans going on at the courthouse he thought ought to be cleared up. They had a ballot where they could tell how everybody voted. There was a poll tax and things like that. This was around 1932. He went to Atlanta and had four or five bills passed to correct some of the problems down here. He came home feeling real proud of himself. Frank Scarlett, who later became a federal judge, was a local lawyer and a friend of Governor Eugene Talmadge. The courthouse crowd hired him and put him on a train to Atlanta. He got Talmadge to veto most of the bills [laughs]. But things got a little better after that. My father was in the legislature a couple of times. They ran a fella, Cogdell, who finally beat him. My father served a couple of terms as a representative, lost out and came back as a state senator. In those days, Glynn County, Camden, and Charlton rotated the senator seat.

The sheriff used to confiscate moonshine during the year. On Election Day, they'd pass it out by the drink. One election night, I saw a voter at the top of the stairs at the courthouse. He was rather drunk and missed the top step and rolled down the stairs. When he hit the floor, he shook his head and walked out.

My father and Frank Scarlett later became good friends. When Frank was appointed a federal judge, he was having to hold court in the Glynn County Courthouse. He wanted to get a federal building built so he could have a federal courtroom. He persuaded the city to buy some land, and the city got my father to negotiate the purchase. One time, he and Judge Scarlett went to Washington to see Senator Russell about some of the funding for the project. When they went into Senator Russell's office, Judge Scarlett introduced my father, and the senator said, "Oh, I know who you are. You worked for Charlie Crisp when he ran against me in 1932." My father said, "That's right. But I want you to know I wasn't mad at you; I was mad at him [Scarlett]." Crisp was from Cordele, I believe. My father had been traveling all over southern Georgia trying to sell timberland and handing out Charles Crisp cards all over south Georgia. Senator Russell remembered that.

Frank Scarlett was holding court down at the old courthouse one summer day. I met Ed Burford, an attorney cousin of mine, on the courthouse steps, and we started telling jokes. One told a bigger story than the other. Finally, he went one way, and I went the other. The next day somebody told us, "It's a good thing you left when you did, because the judge sent the bailiff to run you in." The jury

71

was sitting there listening to us through the open window rather than paying attention to proceedings in the courtroom.

Judge Scarlett was a rather unique federal judge. My father had been doing business with Rayonier, and he knew the Rayonier lawyer, Warren Jones, down in Jacksonville. Jones got appointed to the Appeals Court. My father was in Jacksonville one day and took Judge Jones out to lunch. He came back and told Judge Scarlett, "Frank, I saw Judge Warren Jones, and he sends his regards. He thinks a lot of you." Judge Scarlett replied, "If he thinks so much of me, why the hell does he reverse me all the time?" Judge Scarlett got appointed to a three-judge panel to hear a civil rights case in Atlanta. There was a liberal federal judge up there who always ruled in favor of the blacks. Scarlett appeared at the hearing, pulled some papers out of his pocket, and gave them to the Atlanta judge. "Here's my dissenting opinion," he said. The Atlanta judge said, "What do you mean 'dissenting opinion'? You haven't heard the case. You don't know how I'm going to vote." Scarlett said, "Well, if you don't know how you're going to vote, you're the only fella in this room who doesn't."

Unfortunately, these days, it seems like there's a lot of unnecessary violence in the community, which we didn't have in the old days. It's not just Brunswick. It's everywhere. On the other hand, we have a symphony orchestra now, which we didn't have before. I'm showing my age, but I think things were a lot more pleasant when I came along. You wonder if we're really making progress.

Bill Brown on a sailboat, 1930s.

NOTES

[1] "Near the navigable end of the St. Marys a small outpost known as Coleraine or Colerain became a popular trading site for Creek Indians and outlaw traders looking to skirt the laws of English Georgia and Spanish Florida. They could sail up the St. Marys to Coleraine and sell illegally obtained goods at quite a profit to the Indians, if they were willing to accept skins in exchange." Archives of Camden County, from the Editors of Roadside Georgia.
http://roadsidegeorgia.com/county/camden.html, accessed February 4, 2011.

[2] "Sidney Lanier was born in Macon on February 3, 1842. He graduated from Oglethorpe University, when it was located near Milledgeville, in 1860 with high honors. When the Civil War (1861-65) began, he volunteered to serve in the Confederate army. In 1864 he was captured and held as a prisoner of war for four months in Maryland, during which time he contracted the debilitating tuberculosis that plagued him for the rest of his life.... Lanier found his purest voice in the religious vision of "The Marshes of Glynn," which was inspired by the poet's visit to Brunswick. Set in southeastern Glynn County, the poem begins with a rhythmic description of the thick marsh as the narrator feels himself growing and connecting with the sinews of the marsh itself. Then as his vision expands seaward, he recognizes in an epiphanal moment that the marshes and sea, in their vastness, are the expression of "the greatness of God" and are filled with power and mystery." The New Georgia Encyclopedia,
www.georgiaencyclopedia.org/nge/Article.jsp?id=h-533, accessed February 4, 2011.

[3] Thomas Butler King, of Retreat Plantation on St. Simons, was once under consideration for Secretary of the Navy. He proposed constructing a naval base in Brunswick, and land was set aside on Blythe Island for that purpose.

[4] As of 2010, Highway 17 remains four-laned only in parts of Chatham (Savannah) and Glynn (Brunswick) Counties.

Irene Hurt Cordell

Irene Cordell is a descendent of Major William Horton, who served under General James Oglethorpe, Georgia's founder. Major William Horton was also in charge of military operations in the general's absence. The tabby ruins of Horton's home on the north end of Jekyll Island are still standing. Mrs. Cordell recounts a number of little-known aspects of Georgia's history, including her great-grandmother's aid to Union and Confederate soldiers–black or white–during the Civil War, her grandfather's presiding over the Leo Frank trial, and her father's work for the Coca-Cola Company. She grew up in Atlanta with Gone With the Wind *author, Margaret Mitchell, as a neighbor and family friend. She and her father were with the Mitchells when Margaret was fatally struck down by a car on Peachtree Street.*

Irene and Howard Cordell celebrating their 50th wedding anniversary at the Cloister Wine Cellar, 2009.

I was born in Atlanta, Piedmont Hospital, January 20th, 1940. Dr. Upshaw delivered me. My mom was Irene Horton Hart-Hurt, and my dad was Toulman Williams Hurt, Sr. My dad was born January 16th, 1899 in Atlanta, and my mom born May 3rd, 1899 in Union Point, Georgia. My mother's mother was Georgia Irene Horton from Augusta. Her father was James William Horton from Jackson County. Then the next one [ancestor] is James Horton and then William Horton. There may be one generation between James and William Horton. I'm not sure. When my grandfather was elected Attorney General, the family moved to Atlanta.

I used to listen to stories that my grandmother, Ma-Ma, told me. My mother's family were all teetotalers. If you didn't drink or smoke, you could live in one of my great-great-aunt's houses behind the big house in Union Point. So, they tormented my grandmother, Ma-Ma, incessantly. They would talk about a "black" Douglas in the Hart's lineage, some kind of knight. And Ma-Ma would tease about that, and they would say, "At least we didn't make whiskey like William Horton." He made beer for the regiment at Fort Frederica and sold it to the Indians, but anything like that they called whiskey. He was a tall man, about six-foot-two with red hair. Then, I heard about how he came over to America in a ship with the Wesley brothers, John and James, and tap-danced on deck above their berth.[1]

Ma-Ma would tell us all kinds of tales about how wild William Horton was. I wish I could resurrect her just one more time to ask a couple of questions. I'm the only one who listened to her stories. He's buried under the narthex in Christ Church, Savannah. The body was exhumed and interred there. I went by the church once, but nobody there seemed to know about it. But I think there some letters about it in the University of Georgia Library, which indicate that his body was exhumed, they found red hair, and he was tall.

My mother took me to the ruins of his house on Jekyll a long time ago when I was really small. We all picked up shells from the tabby walls, and I still have that shell. It was really strange when an archaeological dig was later begun at his home site on Jekyll Island. You get a funny feeling. I can't explain it. Uncle Hal Hart, "Big" Hal, worked with the museum on Jekyll because of the connection with William Horton.

William Horton House ruins, Jekyll Island. A covered porch once extended out in the front of the house.

My great-grandmother, Mariah Virginia Collier Hart, lived at Union Point near Greensboro. That's where the railroads met. That's how it got its name. Why Sherman never came there, I don't know. Mariah was the first and only female Civil War patriot, and I am in the UDC [United Daughters of the Confederacy] under her. She had a wayside home in Union Point. She would take soldiers– Yankee, black, Southern–off of the trains. There were fourteen other ladies who helped her. My great-grandfather, James Brook Hart, had a store, and she kept a 700-page ledger using his store paper. When the train of men stopped, she would get their information–name, company, where he was from, who his parents were, how he was injured, what he ate, what happened to him after that. Some of them she buried. Some, she sent to Augusta. She did this daily. She and the ladies cooked a phenomenal amount of food. People--Howell Cobb and Robert E. Lee–donated money, ham, chicken, eggs, flour. If someone gave lace off a petticoat to make a bandage, she wrote it down. The house she lived in, she called Hawthorne Heights, is still standing.[2] It was in the family until about 2005. It's right in the middle of town. The store was downtown, and it's gone. She'd take men off the train and put them in the store, too. People would come through looking for lost men, and if he came through there, she had a record of him. A lot of people were reunited. She sold the original ledger to somebody for money to put monuments on the graves of people who had died. Then it was donated by someone in Chicago to the University of North Carolina. Knox College, near Chicago, bought it from the University of North Carolina. I have a copy of the ledger.

Rattlesnake Bites

There was a governess at Union Point that was bitten by a rattlesnake. One of the slaves took a chicken, cut it right in two, and put it on that rattlesnake bite. The chicken turned as green as a gourd, and the woman lived. The hot blood drew the poison out of that woman's leg.

Memories

My grandfather, Judge Hart, presided over the Leo Frank trial.[3] Ma-Ma, his wife, said he felt like there wasn't enough evidence to hang Leo Frank. It ruined Governor Slaton politically.[4] They had Leo Frank moved, and the mob got him moved in Milledgeville, because at that time

Jews were despised more than anybody. Judge Hart was the first to take an environmental case to the Supreme Court and win. Tennessee mills were dumping dyes into the rivers, and it was coming in to Georgia killing the fish and poisoning cattle. He was killed while hunting on his Union Point farm in 1916.

I have a lot of unusual memories of growing up in Atlanta. My dad's cousins bought Cola-Cola from Asa Candler. My mother's best friend was Laura Candler, and they went to Washington Seminary together with Margaret Mitchell. My dad graduated from Tech High. He got a scholarship to Georgia Tech because my grandfather was the civil engineer for the city of Atlanta. My dad had helped his dad lay out Fort Gordon and several big bridges. He knew what to do. So he went to [Georgia] Tech and did his freshman year in one week and became a sophomore. He played baseball for Georgia Tech. Then, Bob Woodruff bought Coca-Cola, and they pulled Daddy out of Tech and got him to work for the Coca-Cola Company. He was the production manager, so he set up syrup operations in different places. The syrup was sent to the bottling plants. They always spoke of the syrup and bottling operations as two separate companies.

They had what was known as the "Hurt" process in the production of Coca-Cola. So he knew everything that went into a Coca-Cola, how much to order, and so on. He knew the secret formula but would never tell it. He would go to sleep, and my brother and I would start talking to him because he talked in his sleep. He could tell you how much fencing you'd need to enclose a fifty-acre farm or something like that. He could figure it out in his sleep. Then Brother would say, "What is the secret formula for Coca-Cola," which would wake him up fast. He never would tell! Before I was born, my dad, my mom, and my brother lived in New Orleans. My dad set up that Coca-Cola company in New Orleans; then he went to Cuba to help set up a company there. They had no air conditioning in New Orleans. Mother said they would play bridge and put their feet up on ice cubes under the bridge table. Daddy said they ruined a damned good frog pond when they built New Orleans. He had to go to work sometimes in a rowboat.

My memories of World War II were from the tail end of that war. I recall there was rationing in Atlanta. You could buy two pairs of shoes. Thompson-Bolen-Lee had radium X-ray machines you could stick your feet in. We used to love to play with it. But that's radium. I'm sure all of those employees are dead now. Everybody who was anybody bought shoes there. If you didn't get your shoes from Thompson-Bolen-Lee, you just didn't qualify. We rode the trolley, which my great-uncle, Joel Hurt, brought to Atlanta. We'd go to Thompson-Bolen-Lee, which was downtown on Peachtree [Street], maybe right across from where Macy's is now. Everybody stuck their feet up under those machines to take pictures of your feet. So it was good that you only got two pairs of shoes, because we would have been eaten up with cancer, I'm sure.

Aunt Mary and Uncle Hal had a house at what is now Epworth [Gascoigne Bluff] on St. Simons. I remember seeing crashed airplane parts near the toll bridge there.[5] The reason why we had to leave their house was because my first cousin's boyfriend, Perry Ballard, caught a bunch of crabs in an umbrella and turned every last one of them loose in Aunt Mary's house. We were just visiting that summer. Perry's son is now an oncologist in Atlanta. Most of the roads on St. Simons and Sea Island then were made of sand, shells, and sometimes black dirt.

We originally lived on Morningside in Atlanta, then we moved to 189 15th Street, which was right there in midtown. I went for one year to Washington Seminary, then in the third grade, I went to Spring Street. That Washington Seminary building was torn down. It was a colonial home on Peachtree near Brookwood Station. I've still got photographs of it with my mother on the steps. Washington Seminary is now a part of Westminster. When I moved to 15th Street, the Keenans lived up the street. They raised their grandchildren. One of them was my best friend, Louise Loomis. Louise's mother died having her. The Keenans had made a whole lot of money in Coca-Cola, and they were quite wealthy. They had a chauffeur named Claude who drove us around everywhere, and we rode to school in a Cadillac limousine [laughs]. They had a white nurse named Miss Mert who went along with us and sat in the back seat with a beige-plaid lap rug. I don't think the limo had heat. It was after the Lindbergh baby had been kidnapped, and the Keenans were so afraid that someone might kidnap Louise or Greg, her brother. Miss Mert went everywhere we went. Claude used to dress up like Santa Claus. He was a thin black man. They had a big playroom, and Claude would get up in the chimney and drop down. When Mama told me there was no Santa Claus, I wasn't shocked about that. The biggest shock was to discover that Santa Claus wasn't a thin black man. Louise was killed in the Orly airplane crash.[6]

Irene with her mother in front of the Fox Theatre, 1944.
Note the man in uniform at the ticket window.

We started going to Sea Island when I was about five. It seemed like it took forever to get there. We'd go from Atlanta down Highway 441. It was three good throw-ups before you got there. There was no air-conditioning, and I'd be in the back seat of my aunt's Cadillac or Daddy's. My aunt would stop and start when she was driving. Lumber City was a good place to throw up. It was a long trip.

My uncle married Mary King. The King brothers owned King Hardware. Before I was born, they moved to

Miami. Someone said the paint in the paint store dried up in Miami, so he briefly moved back to Atlanta, and then he moved to Sea Island and had the Number One cottage, which is still standing. It's way down on the end, maybe on 37th Street, because they thought they were going to build the Cloister Hotel on the north end. Instead, they built it on the south end. So the first cottages are down at the other end. There were palmetto palms that would scrape you on the way to the beach, and sandspurs. There was so much beach, it seemed you almost walked for miles--to a five year old--to get to the water. I don't know what has happened to it. Now, the water is almost in your backyard. There were little gullies in the beach where the crabs were. You could turn umbrellas upside-down in those gullies and catch crabs and bring them back to the house in your umbrella.

Once, my mother and I got thrown out of Atlanta's Piedmont Park. There was an African-American named Gene Wilburn that delivered pharmaceutical drugs to our house, and my dad liked him and befriended him. Dad talked to him about driving a truck for Coca-Cola Company. Then Big Gene, Eugene W. Wilburn, got sent to World War II. So his wife, Josephine, a caterer, and Little Jean, their daughter, came and lived in a guest wing behind our house on 15th Street. While Big Gene was gone, little Jean went everywhere with me. I took piano lessons, and she learned from me. She could play better than me. I took ballet lessons from Madame Alexander and taught little Jean, and before long, she could dance better than me. She could do everything better than me.

One day, Mama and I walked down to Piedmont Park, which was straight down the street. We were swinging, and a man came up to Mama and said, "Mrs. Hurt, you have to leave the park." Mama said, "Why?" And he said, "Because you have that little girl [Jean] with you." She said, "Well, I'm responsible for her." I remember Mama turning blood red like a beet. Her neck was...she was furious. She said, "Excuse me, you'll let that dog walk in this park, and you won't let this little girl..." I mean, we weren't doing anything. They made us leave. But later, I don't know who Mama talked to, but they apologized to her. And now Jean George, she married Langston George, Sr., is just one of the most outstanding individuals in Atlanta, Georgia. She's the principal of a grammar school.

Big Gene couldn't read or write, but he learned to read and write in the service. When he came back from the war, Big Gene went on to work for the Coca-Cola Company, and he ended up driving for Bob Woodruff, the chairman. He also drove President Eisenhower down to Ichauway Plantation.[7] He was the most outstanding individual I have ever known.

Athens

They thought my Daddy had cancer and they took his lung out, so they retired him from the Coca-Cola Company, and we moved to Athens, Georgia, to look after my grandmother who was sick. I missed my 15th Street friends. I went to Chase Street Grammar School and then to Athens High. We read the Bible every morning, said the Lord's Prayer, and pledged allegiance to the flag. I think when I got to Chase Street, we used to bless our school meals.

I worked at Jim Heery's Clothes Closet in downtown Athens. I was his first employee. And I worked for my cousin. She owned a florist shop, Van Cleve's. She was Van Cleve Wilkins. She married a Cochrane. I worked for her for fifty cents an hour. Made a fortune. My best thing was to take red pipe cleaners and shape them into letters, like SAE, and put them in the middle of a chrysanthemum. Everybody wore those. We dressed up for football games– high heels and everything. Everyone wore flowers to the football games, and you dressed up. Seems like they began the last of September. It was cool weather. Francis

Tarkenton played at Georgia. I went to high school with him at Athens High. Just about every Athens High player the year we won the state championship–Francis, Billy Slaughter, George Giesler–went to UGA. Francis was very dedicated to athletics. His dad was a minister. Actually, his brother, Dallas, was a very good athlete, too.

I graduated from the University of Georgia with a major in home economics, which isn't a major anymore. I lived at 100 Hart Avenue off of Broad Street. The Home Economics building was Soule Hall. I loved college. I pledged Phi Mu my freshman year, '58. Howard Cordell and I got married my sophomore year.

Margaret Mitchell

My mother knew Margaret Mitchell. They went to school together at Washington Seminary, an all-girls private school. Mother and Margaret were in the same grade. In the classroom, my mother didn't make fun of anybody, but she said there was a girl the others called the "Black Plague" and another girl they called the "Yellow Peril." Margaret was one and the other girl became a famous opera star. They were not the most popular girls in the class. My aunt, Ann Hart or Big Ann, was a year older and was editor of the school annual. This was 1916 or 1917. They all submitted stories to be printed in the annual. Of course, my aunt turned Margaret's story down and put her own story in there. She had the right to do it as editor of the annual. Margaret's story was called "The Little Sister," which was about a Mexican that was trying to rape this little girl. The big sister killed the Mexican. You think back to *Gone With The Wind* and the soldier on the staircase–so "The Little Sister" was once again created. My aunt's story was the dumbest thing I've ever read in my entire life, about a 14th Century German soldier trapped in a cave. Big Ann used some very big words. Then it was almost like she got to the pinnacle and couldn't figure out how to end her story, so she just wrote that the cave opened up, and they walked out. Made no sense!

Big Ann married Dr. Murdock Equen, an ears-nose-and-throat specialist in Atlanta. He bought the Poppinheimer house and turned it into a hospital called Ponce de Leon Eye, Ear, Nose and Throat Infirmary. The infirmary is still alive and well; it's just not in that house. He also invented a magnet that could, without surgery, remove metal objects, like safety pins, that had been swallowed. He got the Woodrow Wilson Award, I think it was called, for medicine. The X-ray machine was in his hospital. He'd put you to sleep first. The largest thing he ever removed was a baby bedspring. He never left the city limits of Atlanta, and he had a car phone back in the 1940s.

Mrs. Murdock (Ann) Equen with daughters Anne (standing) and Carol. From June 7, 1948 *Life* magazine article.

Big Ann became quite the socialite. In other words, kiss the hem of my skirt, and you shall debut, and if you didn't do it, you didn't make your debut, or you didn't get into the Junior League. She was quite influential. They were in *Life* magazine [June 7, 1948]. My mom was the direct opposite. In one of her books, Margaret referred to Big Ann as a canker sore that just cropped up on your face when you didn't want it. Big Ann supposedly kept Margaret out of the Junior League. So Margaret did not like my aunt at all. Well, I think Margaret was kind of wild. She'd dance with a ruby in her navel at the [Piedmont] Driving Club.[8] Then, when the Junior League was having the *Gone With The Wind* premiere party, Big Ann realized that Margaret was not a member and said they needed to ask her. Mama said, "You'd best not." They went ahead and asked her, and Margaret, of course, cursed them out.

Right before the movie premiere party, I believe it was December 11th, 1939, Big Ann wrote an article for the *Atlanta Constitution*, stating that she had turned down Margaret Mitchell's school annual story. I can't remember what else she printed. This was twenty years after high school, and Margaret had already won the Pulitzer Prize for her book. So Margaret wrote her back. Boy, she reamed my aunt out. She wrote those two letters with such vim and vigor that on the back of the paper it's almost like Braille. If you could read backwards, you could read it with your fingers. She was that mad. Those letters show a different side of Margaret. There was also a telegram Margaret sent to Big Ann stating she was going to sue her if Big Ann did not hush. We still have that telegram. My mom was the easy-going, unpretentious one, so Margaret maintained her friendship with my mother, but she certainly did not like Big Ann.

They had the premiere of *Gone With The Wind* at the Driving Club in December of '39. Mother didn't get to go because she was pregnant with me. Margaret was very attractive but kind of short. She didn't come all spiffed up to the premiere party. And after the book and the premiere were so successful, she wanted to rest from her public, so nobody would have suspected that she was in the maternity ward of Piedmont Hospital, which is not where it is now. It was on Piedmont at that time. Nobody seems to know what she had, but she talked about how she wasn't well. "Adhesions" is what I think they referred to, but Mama never said that. She just said that Margaret was hiding from her public.

The day I was born was the worst snowstorm in the history of Atlanta. My dad had to get Mama to the hospital. He went out to the car to get something and slipped and temporarily passed out underneath it. Dr. Upshaw lived in Marietta, and he was having trouble getting to the hospital. Finally, we get there, and Mother was having a bad time; she was forty years old, but there was an intern on duty, and Margaret Mitchell came in and kept bringing my mother coffee, which is a horrible thing to give a pregnant woman, but she was trying to help. She wasn't doing it to be mean. Finally, Dr. Upshaw got there. I don't know what happened, but I had a pint of Dr. Upshaw's blood, and mother had a pint of the intern's. Mother told me later they did it direct, from arm-to-arm.

Margaret lived in the Piedmont Apartments. That was her last home. She had a huge, fluffy cat. We later moved one block from 15th Street to the Piedmont Apartments, and John and Margaret Mitchell were right there across from us. Well, one day, Daddy and myself walked up to 10th Street to a shop. I guess it was a doughnut or ice-cream shop. John and Margaret were there getting something to eat. They were going to a play afterward. So we were all together in that shop; then they started to cross the street to go to the play at a women's theatre. John kept going when he saw a car swerving, and Margaret turned to go back. I guess the driver tried to go behind them. But he was definitely drunk. If John had grabbed her to keep her from turning and going back, it wouldn't have happened. Daddy and I were sitting there, and we heard the screeching of tires and looked out. The cabdriver who hit Margaret Mitchell stopped. Daddy had a billfold in his coat pocket, more of a folder than a billfold, and he took it out. He had a picture of me in it and took it out and wrote the tag number of the taxi driver on the back of it. Daddy was always kind of like that. It was a frightening thing, and Daddy wouldn't let me see anything. I just remember him writing that tag number on the back of that picture. I may still have it somewhere. Then Daddy rode in the police car with that cabdriver who, Daddy told me later, was drunk. There are so many stories about where it occurred. It was on Peachtree down below 14th Street. John rode in the ambulance with Margaret, and that doughnut man had to take me back home.

I have always thought it was an interesting twist of fate that Margaret was there when I was born, and I was there when she was hit by that car, which led to her death.[9]

NOTES

[1] "…one of Horton's female servants was put ashore 'for Drinking and indecent behaviour'…. Horton was furious with the Wesleys and fed up with their pious ways. To show his contempt he awakened them late one night, according to John Wesley, 'by dancing [on the deck] over our heads.' However, Horton, a gentleman both in rank and heart, acknowledged his rude conduct and 'begged…pardon the next day.'" June Hall McCash, *Jekyll Island's Early Years: From Prehistory through Reconstruction* (Athens: The University of Georgia Press, 2005), 47.

[2] Images of Hawthorne Heights can be seen at: http://unionpointdda.org/9.html, accessed May 11, 2011.

[3] Leo Frank (1884-1915), superintendent of the National Pencil Company, Atlanta, was accused of raping and murdering of a pencil factory worker. He was sentenced to life in prison but was lynched by a mob on August 17, 1915.

[4] Georgia's 60th governor, 1911-1912 and 1913-1915. "Believing that Frank had not received a fair trial…Slaton commuted Frank's sentence from death to life imprisonment…A mob threatened to attack the governor at home, but a detachment of the Georgia National Guard under the command of Major Asa Warren Candler…dispersed the mob. Slaton fled the state…Slaton never held another publicly elected position." The New Georgia Encyclopedia,
http://www.georgiaencyclopedia.org/nge/Article.jsp?id=h-2137,
accessed April 11, 2011.

[5] A Naval airplane training center was stationed on SSI during WWII.

[6] "On June 3, 1962, many of Atlanta's civic and cultural leaders were returning from a museum tour of Europe sponsored by the Atlanta Art Association when their chartered Boeing 707 crashed upon takeoff at Orly Field near Paris, France. Of the 122 passengers that died, 106 were Atlantans (eight crew members also died; two stewardesses sitting in the tail section survived). In an instant the core of Atlanta's arts community was gone. Thirty-three children and young adults lost both parents in the crash. Mayor Ivan Allen Jr. traveled to Paris to assist

with the recovery efforts." New Georgia Encyclopedia, http://www.georgiaencyclopedia.org/nge/Article.jsp?id=h-1103, accessed March 29, 2011.

[7] A nature reserve established in the 1920s by Coca-Cola chairman Robert W. Woodruff. Located in Baker County, southwestern Georgia.

[8] A private social club founded in 1887.

[9] "Mitchell was struck by a speeding automobile as she crossed Peachtree Street at 13th Street with her husband, John Marsh, on her way to see the British film *A Canterbury Tale* at The Peachtree Art Theatre in August 1949. She died at Grady Hospital five days later without regaining consciousness. The driver, Hugh Gravitt, was an off-duty taxi driver. He was driving his personal vehicle at the time, but his occupation led to many erroneous references over the years to Mitchell's having been struck by a taxi. After the accident, Gravitt was arrested for drunken driving and released on a $5,450 bond until Mitchell's death several days later. It was discovered that he had been cited 23 times previously for traffic violations. Georgia Gov. Herman Talmadge announced that the state would tighten regulations for licensing taxi drivers. Gravitt was later convicted of involuntary manslaughter and served 11 months in prison. His conviction was controversial because witnesses said Mitchell stepped into the street without looking, and her friends claimed she often did this. She was buried in Oakland Cemetery in Atlanta."
Wikipedia, http://en.wikipedia.org/wiki/Margaret_Mitchell, accessed April 11, 2011.

Samuel Alan Massell, Jr.

Sam Massell, Jr. served as Mayor of Atlanta from 1970 to 1974. He is the youngest person to serve in that capacity. As mayor, he brought mass transit (MARTA) to Atlanta and brokered the building of the Omni Coliseum. Massell has enjoyed successful careers in association management, real estate brokerage, and tourism. He is currently president of the Buckhead Coalition, a nonprofit civic organization founded to nurture the quality of life and guide the orderly growth of Buckhead. In 2004, Georgia Trend Magazine *added Massell to its "Most Influential Georgians Hall of Fame."*

Photograph courtesy of Sam Massell.

My full name is Samuel Alan Massell, Jr. I was born August 26, 1927 at Piedmont Hospital when it was in downtown Atlanta. Later, the Atlanta Fulton County Stadium was built there. My father was Samuel Alan, Sr., and my mother was Florence Rubin Massell. I understand Massell is a French name, but we don't know how the family received that, which was probably a change from the original. My father was born in Atlanta. My mother was born in St. Louis.

My father's family came from Lithuania. My paternal grandfather came here and went in the wholesale grocery business. He had three sons and three daughters. My father's older brothers were born in Lithuania before the turn-of-the-century [1900].

As a child, I didn't know a depression was on the way. We'd see a peddler come to the neighborhood pushing a cart or buying rags or scrap metal. But I just thought that was a normal business operation and didn't know it was a sign of a depression or poverty. I worked all the time, from childhood up, but it wasn't because I was ever told that I needed to earn money in order to provide for shelter or clothing. I was taught the work ethic–that it was the proper thing to do for males. Females weren't expected to do so; males were. And I worked, whether it was operating and owning a little soft drink stand or selling flower seeds or selling newspapers or magazine subscriptions. I always worked at something.

Coca-Cola used to have a little yellow box that they would make available for kids on corners to sell pop, as it was called. When I was nine or ten, I actually had two of those [boxes] nailed together, because my business got so big, and I sold all kinds of soft drinks. Occasionally, we would put in other things, like candy bars. For a while, my dad got me a little pushcart that I could put ice cream in and go up and down the streets and have my buddies push it for free ice cream. My dad printed cards for me with

"Bud's Place" on them. I was called "Buddy" up until I went to college. My drink stand was on the corner of North Decatur and Oakdale roads in front of a vacant lot, which I thought was a forest. There is now a single home there–a small lot, in fact. North Decatur was a major artery. That's where the traffic was, and there was some building around the area. So I gave young friends of mine free Cokes when they put circulars in mailboxes up and down the street.

We lived at 1280 Oakdale. We were in the last block of Oakdale, which had an interesting number of residents, including Bert Parks of Miss America fame. His real name was Bert Jacobs. And there was Herman Talmadge who became governor and U. S. senator. It also included Larry Gellerstedt, who became president of the Metro Chamber of Commerce and the CEO of Beers Construction Company. It also included the brother of Justice Duckworth, state Supreme Court justice. Druid Hills was a high-income area of yesteryear and still is a very stable community with larger homes and single-family residences. It's in DeKalb County. It's not in the city limits of Atlanta.

I went to Druid Hills School, which was elementary and high school at that time. I went there for 11 years in the same building. It's still there-high school only. Then, I went to the University of Georgia. I went to all the colleges– University of Georgia, Georgia State, Georgia Tech, Emory, Atlanta Law School, and Woodrow Wilson College of Law. I didn't get kicked out of them [laughs]. I started at the University of Georgia. I was the president of my college fraternity chapter as a first-quarter freshman– unheard-of. But the reason was that it was 1944, when most of the able-bodied men were off at war. Most of the fraternities had closed up entirely. The fraternity I pledged was in a little apartment over an office in downtown Athens. There were two other pledges and one active member, and he flunked out of school. So the alumni had to rush up there and initiate all three of us, and then they had to hold an election. I didn't need but one vote. I had mine sewed up, so one more vote gave me a landslide. Later, I came back after I went into the Air Force during World War II and got legitimately elected president of a real chapter with a real fraternity house.

The reason I left Georgia was because if you were a male, you could be everything on campus–head of every chapter or organization. I was very involved with extracurricular activities, so much so, that it was interfering with my academics. I was literally running from one meeting to the next. I decided the best thing to do was to cut it off cold turkey–just leave. So I transferred to Emory, where I went for a year. I didn't do anything but go to school, come home, study, go to bed, go to school. Didn't join a single organization. Then I was drafted and went in the Air Force. I was teaching administrative management in the Air Force. The war was about over. I was bored to death and needed and wanted the excitement the University of Georgia offered and returned there for a year.

Then I decided to transfer to the Atlanta Law School where my dad had graduated and which was easier than the law school at the University of Georgia. I was not a good student, but smart enough to know that if you just keep going, you can absorb something by osmosis. While I was going to the Atlanta Law School two nights a week, I also enrolled at Georgia State University, also at night. I was working in my dad's office and going to two night schools at the same time. I got my degree in business. After that, I also got my law degree at the Atlanta Law School. I started Woodrow Wilson for a Master's in Law, but I got married and I gave up my academic work. Georgia Tech was just some night courses I took–public relations, primarily. That's the reason I went to all those schools.

When I went into real estate, I was in downtown Atlanta. My office was located about two blocks from the Georgia State University campus, and they had parking for students at $10 a month. I had already graduated. So I enrolled in another course at Georgia State, because I could get that $10-a-month parking. I even took the course, which cost about $35.

World War II brought Atlanta to a standstill. There was no construction. At one time, my father and his two brothers were in real estate development and built some of the apartment buildings still standing on Boulevard and Park Place. They built a lot of warehouses, some of which are still standing. That Jones warehouse downtown on Marietta Street was the largest warehouse in Atlanta. They built a number of small retail centers that are still standing in the Little Five Points area and Emory and other suburban areas. When the Depression came, they split up, and my dad went into law. After the war, my Uncle Ben Massell went back into real estate development and became the largest developer in Georgia. He built most of the office buildings in midtown Atlanta, and he was the largest taxpayer in Georgia. The *Atlanta Journal-Constitution* called him "Mr. Real Estate." He was a tycoon and built a fortune and had a really good reputation for philanthropy. After World War II, he started building Midtown–all the office buildings, seven and eight story buildings, up and down Peachtree, West Peachtree, and Spring Street. He built the Government Services Administration (GSA) building at Peachtree and 7th, which is a half-million square feet, the largest building in Atlanta at that time. It has now been converted into loft apartments. Many of his older buildings have been converted, so they were strong enough to withstand time, but not good enough to continue in their initial design.

There were plenty of shortages during the war. Gasoline was rationed. Meat and other foods were difficult to find. My maternal grandfather, Sol Rubin, had a department store–Rubin's–downtown at Peachtree and Ellis, I think. It was right across from Davison's department store, which later became Macy's. But his store did not make it during the Depression.

My parents used to drive the family to Daytona every summer. It was an all-day trip. That was during the '30s. In later years, we started going to Tybee Island near Savannah. My parents had a Reo, which was a luxury car. They had two of them. We had a two-car garage in tandem, one in back of the other, rather than side-by-side. And we had servants' quarters there–a yardman, a cook, and a part-time maid. The first car I had was a Packard convertible, a hand-me-down from my sister who had received it new when she turned sixteen. When I turned sixteen, it was given to me.

Prejudice

Being Jewish, I encountered prejudice, from time to time. I was not aware of much of it as a child. Druid Hills School was a county school, and, as such, it had school buses that went out to rural areas and picked up barefoot kids in blue jeans. But being in the more affluent community of Atlanta, it also had chauffeur-driven kids in limousines. We all played together and studied together. It was, for me, a great teacher of humanity. At the time, I didn't realize I was being taught this. The fact I felt comfortable, and my parents didn't suggest anything different, I didn't have any bias or prejudice about people from different socioeconomic backgrounds. Now, they were all white, because schools were still segregated then. But I think that sensitivity toward people from different walks of life helped me later with the broader community and in my political career. In later years, when I was in politics, I did confront prejudices at times. I had a cross burned in my front yard, 2750 Wyngate, during a campaign. There were other instances I could recite. The cross burning didn't scare me, but it shocked me to know that such a thing could take place in my neighborhood. No one was ever arrested for the incident.

Our synagogue was bombed when I was a young adult. It tore off part of the side of the building. It was sad and scary for something like that to happen. They caught and tried the person they thought did it, but he was not convicted. It also brought about a warm feeling from the reaction it generated in the community at large, which came forth with hands of friendship from all walks of life, to express regret and anger and to help. It really helped build a better city as a result.[1]

Influences

Buddy (Marshall) Mantler, the guy I worked for on my first job, taught me one thing I never used. He taught me how to delegate authority. Damn it, I still don't do it! I was chief of publication for his trade journals. He was head of a national organization of women's and children's apparel salesmen, like a union. Every six months or so, I'd go in and get a raise. One time, I went in and asked for a raise, and he said, "No, I'm going to fire you." It scared me to death when he said that. I said, "Why? I've done a good job. I've done everything you wanted." He said, "Oh well, okay I'll give you another $50 a month raise. And I'll do that every six months or so for the rest of your life if that's what you want. But it's time you made a real living. You should be in real estate. I will call Sam Goldberg over at Alan Grayson Realty Company and set up an interview for you." He pushed me out the door. I went over there and interviewed and took the job. I paid more in income taxes the first year than Mantler had paid me in salary. So it was like a bird pushing his baby out to fly. It was a pretty wonderful lesson.

Many people have influenced my life. Margaret McDougal was chairman of what was then called the White Democratic Executive Committee and was later changed to the City Executive Committee. She was a sterling example of integrity, which was very enriching in my life. Helen Bullard was the political guru during the times I ran for public office. Both of these women are since deceased. They guided me dramatically. One time, I was seeking the presidency of the Board of Aldermen, and I was being called to meet with a group of the black leadership in what is called a screening session where they would sit and ask you questions and decide if they would endorse you on the ticket. They were very important sessions, and I asked Helen to prepare me for it. She said, "What do you mean prepare you?" I said, "Well, they're going to ask the tough questions." She said, "Like what?" I said, "What if they asked me what I think about mixing white blood and black blood in the hospital?" Now remember, this was back during the '60s, and it might not sound like much today. She paused and looked at me and said, "Well Sam, what *do* you think?" It was like lifting an anvil off my shoulders, because in that way, she was teaching me to be honest, and to be myself, and don't try to second-guess people politically.

One night, I was with Margaret, Helen, Ralph McGill,[2] and Henry Toombs, a prominent architect who designed the Little White House in Warm Springs for President Roosevelt. We were at Toombs' home with Eleanor Roosevelt. I was Vice Mayor and president of the Board of Aldermen at that time. Ivan Allen, who was mayor, was out of town. When Mrs. Roosevelt was getting ready to go back to the airport, I said, "Where is your security?" She said, "I don't have any security." I said, "You're not going to go to the airport without a policeman. I'm going to get one for you!" She says, "Oh no, you're not!" We argued, and I finally had to compromise and said, "Well, I'm going to get a policeman to follow you," which he did, all the way to the airport. But she was quite independent.

Politics

When Sol Rubin would come over on Sundays for family dinners, there would be a lot of good-natured arguing about business and politics or current events. I was a child listening some, maybe playing on the floor. One time, I heard my father talking about a politician, and he said, "At least he's honest." And my grandfather, Rubin, said, "Well, that's nothing. Everybody is supposed to be honest." And that meant a lot to me. I'll never forget him saying that and what that translated to.

My father loved politics. He used to take me around to rallies. When he was a lawyer, as a hobby, he used to publish a monthly newspaper called the *Atlanta Democrat*. He got me involved either selling ads or handling circulation, or even occasionally writing something for him. That was one of the motivations for me to get into politics—having a father who thought well of it, and I thought well of my father. But I give most of the credit or blame to a friend named Charlie Goldstein who lives in Miami, Florida now. He was a school friend at Druid Hills and was running for president of the student body, and he asked me to paint his signs, which I did. I was an introvert up to the age 15. I had two or three friends and wouldn't have dared ask the popular girls for a date or to a dance. Anyway, he got elected and turned around and said, "Buddy, I'm making you student body treasurer." I said, "You're crazy. I don't want to be treasurer or anything else." But he made me do it. There was no turning back. From then on, I became active in everything else at Druid Hills and later at college. Then, I got very involved after college in the Atlanta community—services like the Atlanta Humane Society, the Atlanta-Fulton-DeKalb Muscular Dystrophy Association, Anti-Defamation League, and other civic and service organizations. And that's very similar to politics. The main difference between civic service and political service is that in civic service, they ask you to do it, and they don't pay anything. In political service, you ask the public to let you do it, and they pay you a little stipend. Otherwise it's very similar. I spent 22 years in different elected offices.

The reason I ran for mayor of Atlanta was "opportunity." Almost every step of the way was an opportunity, from being on the City Council at Mountain Park, Georgia, to being secretary of the Atlanta City Executive Committee, to being president of the Board of Aldermen, to being mayor. Each was an opportunity that presented itself. One time, I was running for president of the City Council, and I went to a rally at the Druid Hills Country Club, one of my opponents was standing next to me in the men's room, and he said, "Sam, are you an opportunist?" And he meant it sarcastically. I thought for half a second and said, "Yes, I am an opportunist. If one comes by, I'm going to grab it." That's what I've been doing all my life.

The [1969] mayor's race was an open race with Ivan Allen, incumbent. I had been president of the City Council, I felt I could make a contribution, and I felt I could get elected. I was the more liberal candidate and had several opponents. One of them happened to be black, articulate, knowledgeable, attractive, and a former member of the Board of Education elected by the city. He had a following as head of a teachers' guild. He later became a state senator. One of the highways near my home is named for him–Horace Tate. He couldn't get elected because the population was predominantly white then, as was the registered voters. The black leadership told him he couldn't get elected, so they supported me. I had a major white opponent, Rodney Cook, who was more conservative. He had the support of the business community. I ended up getting 90% of the black vote and 10% of the white vote. Four years later, after a really good term of working well with blacks and whites across all lines, the African-

American community then had a majority in the registration. They had their own candidate who they could get elected. I got 90% of the white vote and 10% of the black vote, and I lost that election to Maynard Jackson.

I thought it was a very normal thing that once blacks had a majority they would want to have involvement. When whites had a majority, they wanted to run the show. It was fair and square, and they had the numbers, and they won. Over the years, I remember when blacks weren't even allowed to vote. Then I saw where blacks were not only voting but were able to be the swing vote to elect whites. And then I saw where blacks had enough votes that they elect their own. Today, we are in a phenomenon where blacks run against each other. All of this shows growth and is healthy for the community. The majority of the population in Atlanta is African-American, so it's highly appropriate that they also run the government.

I appointed the first woman to the City Council, Panke Bradley, in its hundred-and-twenty-five year history. Back then, the charter allowed mayors to fill vacancies, which I did. She's a planner, and she did a fine job. In the early '70s, it was shocking to people that I would do something like that. Incidentally, I gave them an inch and they took over. Now, there is a majority of women on the council–the president of the council is a woman, the mayor is a woman [laughs].

This is also [during] a transformation from white to black. That was a major difference that took place. I was in between the two, trying to keep them together, understanding each other, and being sensitive to each other's needs. I gave a speech toward the end of my administration before the Hungry Club, which is a club of African-Americans that meets monthly. The title of my speech, which was printed in its entirety in *US News and World Report*, was "It's Time for Blacks to be Able to Think White." I was saying that for years, whites of goodwill had been urging other whites to try to think like blacks, to understand their needs and the suppression that they've suffered and to try to understand their thought process in order to share the qualities of life. I was saying to the blacks, "Now you're going to be in control. You're coming-of-age where you're going to be electing mayors and council members and Board of Education people, and it's time you understand how we think so we can work better together." It didn't go over very well, but I stick by the idea that anybody is better off if you can understand how the other guy thinks.

MARTA

I restructured the method of financing the proposed MARTA (Metropolitan Atlanta Rapid Transit Authority) to provide both bus and rail mass transit for Atlanta. And I got through the legislature the right to put on a sales tax, which had been retained by the state up until then. No city or county or authority had the right to put on a sales tax–only the state. So this was a real breakthrough and took a great deal of effort. We campaigned very hard for it. Two or three times, I went up in a helicopter with a bullhorn over the expressway during bumper-to-bumper traffic saying, "If you want to get out of this mess, vote 'Yes'!" This being the Bible Belt, people thought God was talking to them [laughs]. I believe in free transit. I almost had our mass transit program, free. We did run it [fares] for $.15 for seven years. If I had been back in office, that would have been my top priority. That's one of the main things I regret is not being able to bring the fare back down lower than that. But every major city in the world has traffic, and we're a major city. My wife is from Hogansville, Georgia, population of a couple thousand. They don't have any traffic. They don't have the amenities–museums, art galleries, large churches, mega stores, parks–that we

[Atlanta] provide by having traffic. I just see it in a different way. Traffic is how you pay for amenities.

Being Mayor

The appointing of the first black department heads in the city's history was something for which I was proud and providing the first enclosed coliseum–the Omni–which later allowed us to hold the National Democratic Convention and other major events here. I worked out the real estate deal on the coliseum where, if they never sold a single ticket, the taxpayer still didn't have to pay for any of it. The mass transit system later allowed us to hold the Olympics here. I developed the Woodruff Central City Park in downtown Atlanta. All of these things with no call on *ad valorem* taxes, incidentally.

Some of the ideas for doing these things, you steal from other people. Some, you dream up during the night. I had a good chief administrative officer, George Berry, who I give credit to for making me look better than I was. During a period when a group of major mayors in the country were lobbying for different issues, we decided the issue in Atlanta was going to be transportation, and to make the point that we needed money to help with traffic problems. One day, I had some of the most prominent mayors in the country–Lindsay from New York, Daley from Chicago, Alioto from San Francisco–out on the 10th Street Bridge early in the morning for a news conference, looking down over the expressway to see the bumper-to-bumper traffic. What I didn't know until later, is that George Berry had arranged to have a police car with the blue light blinking parked about three blocks south of there so the cars had to back up [laughs]. He wasn't taking a chance that I wouldn't have bumper-to-bumper traffic. He made sure I would.

Sometimes, you get frustrated as mayor. We had what was called a weak mayor system, so you have to use persuasive powers to get the council to support you. It was a partnership. Today, the charter is different. It's a strong mayor system, where the mayor makes all the appointments and budgets and decisions. When I came out of office, I felt tremendous relief from pressures I'd had all the time but had never really been bothered by them because it was part of the job. But when I came out, it was like having anvils lifted off my shoulders. I could go to the restroom without a policeman watching me. I didn't have to read every single locally printed publication to keep up with the pulse.

I had run-ins with Lester Maddox who was governor and lieutenant governor when I was mayor. I had J. B. Stoner attack me in his newspaper. I never had any run-ins with Herman Talmadge. In fact, we were friendly. He had named me on his honorary governor's staff back when he was governor, before I was in office. Eugene Talmadge was a demagogue, a racist and crude. Herman was more sophisticated. He chewed tobacco, but he had to be taught how to do it just to keep up an image.

Probably my biggest public run-in with Maddox was when I had come up with a two-city plan, which was an annexation program that would take all of unincorporated north Fulton and put it in the city of Atlanta and all of unincorporated south Fulton and put it in College Park. This would have created two very large cities, geographically. It would have added a lot of population to Atlanta and a larger tax base. We had the vote in the House, and we passed the House. We had the vote in the Senate, and Lester Maddox blocked it. I used to have a Monday morning news conference every week, and all the reporters were trying to get me to say something ugly about him. And I said, "That's his prerogative. That's behind us. I'm not going to discuss it."

When the news conference was over, I said, "Now, do y'all want something for the Gorilla Ball?" The Gorilla Ball was an annual event for radio and TV guys only, not the print media. It's where they took their outtakes–things they messed up, said the wrong things, things they couldn't use on the air. Some of it was racy stuff. They would have a big party once a year and have a contest to see which radio or TV station had the funniest bloopers. They had food, and a lot of whiskey, and a trophy. I used to be invited, although I was an interloper. They got along with me. We used to have a lot of fun, and I'd usually pull some prank on them. One time, we arranged where I would come out in judge's robes and try one of the reporters, find him guilty, exile him to Dothan, Alabama, put him in a car and haul him to the airport and put him on a plane with a one-way ticket. He thought he was going to get off–that the mayor's limousine would be waiting for him at the end of the runway. But the plane took off to Dothan, and he didn't have any money to get back. That made national news. He was on NBC news that night. Anyway, for the Gorilla Ball outtakes, reporters asked me, "Mr. Mayor, what do you think about Lieutenant Governor Maddox killing your two city plan?" And I said some very ugly things, which I'm not going to repeat. The TV and radio guys had what they needed for the Gorilla Ball. The funniest part of this is that there was a newspaper reporter who tape-recorded this. He knows that it's in fun and off the record. He takes it over to Maddox without telling him anything about the background. He said, "Do you want to hear what Mayor Massell just said about you?" And he plays it to him. Of course, Maddox goes ballistic, and it hit the news. The newspapers back then wouldn't print the words I used. He threatened me–"You apologize or else." I waited a day, and then I'd send an emissary over to the capitol to ask him what "or else" is. And he'd say, "I give him 24 hours." Then I'd wait 23 and half hours and send the press back saying, "Can I have more time?" It stayed on the front page of the newspapers for about four days before he finally realized I was pulling his chain.

So yes, we had some run-ins. But don't forget, politicians are members of a fraternity, like other groups that are very competitive publicly. But privately, you sit together, you drink together, you joke together. We were friendly, privately, up to his death, but he was much more conservative in his philosophies than I. I don't know whether he liked me or didn't like me. That never surfaced.

We did receive threats on my life while I was mayor. I had a security aide who was with me during the daytime. He would start up the car before I would get in it, and we would drive a different route to work every day. I used to read the hate mail, and we kept a file of it. One day, I got a letter that was signed–not a hate letter–saying what a good person I was because the person who wrote it had seen me the night before at the wrestling matches with my son. He thought it was very commendable that I would take time from my busy schedule as mayor to take my son to the wrestling matches. The typing was from an old typewriter on which the ink would fill in between the "Es" and the "Os." I looked at it and said, "This is so familiar. Bring me the hate mail file." We pulled it, and, sure enough, the same guy who was praising me had written two or three times threatening to kill me, which were unsigned. The GBI [Georgia Bureau of Investigation] went out to his home. We decided he was an elderly white man who was not going to kill me. The first time someone threatened to kill me, I called Police Chief Herbert Jenkins to tell him about it and to see if there was anything I should do. He said, "Sam, don't worry about it. The guy who's going to kill you is not going to tell you." And that's the truth, usually. It made me feel a lot better.

NOTES

[1] "The infamous dynamiting of the Temple on October 12, 1958, is believed to have been perpetrated by people upset with the work of the Temple's rabbi, Jacob Rothschild, in particular his participation as a guest speaker at a 'brotherhood' program at Atlanta's First Baptist Church the preceding May. Contrary to the public reaction during the Frank case, however, the general Atlanta population was generous in its outpouring of support for the Jewish community after the bombing. Indeed, the bombing of the Temple sent moral shockwaves through the city of Atlanta and beyond. Just after the bombing, U.S. president Dwight D. Eisenhower remarked, 'I think we would all share in the feeling of horror that any person would want to desecrate the holy place of any religion, be it a chapel, a cathedral, a mosque, a church, or a synagogue.' Support, including telegraphs, cards, and financial gifts, came from numerous Atlanta churches. Writer Melissa Fay Greene notes that such sympathy and fellowship from Christians in Atlanta led Rabbi Rothschild's wife, Janice, to label the crime as "the Bomb that Healed." The New Georgia Encyclopedia, http://www.georgiaencyclopedia.org/nge/Article.jsp?id=h-3169&hl=y, accessed February 24, 2011.

[2] Pulitzer Prize-winning editor of the *Atlanta Journal & Constitution*.

Patrick McLean Demere

Patrick Demere was neither born, nor resides in Georgia. However, he descends from Captain Raymond Demere who served under General Oglethorpe, who were both at the Battle of Bloody Marsh, a pivotal moment in Georgia and American history, and who resided on St. Simons after Oglethorpe's regiment disbanded. By focusing on one family's past, Patrick's research affords interesting perspectives on the state's early settlers and succeeding generations. He also provides details–involving his family– about the story behind Mary the Wanderer, perhaps Georgia's best-known ghost.

Patrick Demere and children.

I was born on June 20th, 1966 in Memphis, Tennessee at Baptist Memorial Hospital. My father was McCarthy

109

Demere, and my mother was Ruth Mary. Her maiden name was Pidgeon. They were both from Memphis. When my father went to Southwestern College here in Memphis, which is now Rhodes College, he changed our last name pronunciation from "Dem-er-ee" to "Deh-mere." His father, Clifton, never changed the pronunciation. In my opinion, my father changed the pronunciation because it was a little sissified for a rough-and-ready river town like Memphis in the 1920s and '30s.

My grandfather, Clifton Demere, was born in Palatka, Florida. His mother died when he was a child. His father's name was James Barnard Demere who was born either on St. Simons or in Camden County, Georgia. James was a train engineer in Savannah at one time and also a steamboat captain. I found references to him being on the Suwannee River, the Mississippi, the Cumberland River in Nashville, Tennessee, even up as far as West Virginia. He ran an excursion boat, taking people from one point to another, and a packet boat, which carried goods. In the late 1800s, he put my grandfather [Clifton] into an orphanage in Nashville. Eventually, my grandfather moved to Memphis to work for a company called E. L. Bruce Company. It was a hardwood flooring company then. He was chief engineer. My great-grandfather, James Barnard Demere, is buried in Belleville, Illinois. Clifton was always bitter about being put in an orphanage. That's how we ended up in Memphis.

My father was a plastic surgeon and an attorney. He went to the University of Tennessee Medical School and was a doctor in World War II. He served in the European Theatre from 1943. He said, "D plus eight," so he got to Normandy eight days after D-Day and was in the Battle of the Bulge.

I've been able to trace the Demere family back to 1580. I found a reference to them being from a region called Chatellerault just north of Poitiers, France. There is a little village near Chatellerault called Mairé. It was originally spelled Méré. From what I've been able to ascertain, a commoner there would have been referred to as Deméré– "of Méré"–which basically means he's from that village. Méré is either a Gallic or Roman word. It may have belonged to a person named Marius and meant "property of Marius." Marius is a Roman name. Gaius Marius was related by marriage to Julius Caesar, and Marcus Aurelius Marius was Emperor of the Gallic Empire in 268 AD.

I have not been able to identify anybody in France with that surname, and there are only about one hundred of us in America. The earliest ancestor I can trace is Louis Deméré may have pronounced it "D'mayr-ay." Over time, the Demeres of Savannah, Florida, and Texas pronounce it "Dem-ree." My inference is that if you take Deméré with the accent on the last two "e's" or the last "e" with a British accent, it would sound like "Dem-er-ee."[1]

The first Louis Demeré was from Poitiers, France, one of the first protestant strongholds. He was a silk merchant. His son, also named Louis, had a son named Isaac who was born in Nérac, south of Bordeaux, France. Most Protestants moved to the southwest of France as the persecution against them became more acute.

Raymond Demeré, my direct ancestor, was born in July of 1702 in Nérac. The way I learned all of this is because right before Raymond, died he filed a lawsuit contesting his grandparent's estate, and he had to document his genealogy. He had two sisters, Margaret and Catherine, and a brother, Paul. Their half-uncle, Francois Cayran, who changed his name to Francis, purchased a commission in the British Army in 1719. In 1725, when Raymond was twenty-three years old, Francis helped Raymond get a position as an aide to William Stanhope who became the first Lord Harrington [for whom the Harrington section on St. Simons is named]. Stanhope was a Brigadier General and Envoy Extraordinary and Plenipotentiary to Spain in Madrid. So, Raymond was back and forth between England

and Spain for about ten years. He evidently learned to speak Spanish, which, along with his native languages, French and English, would aid him greatly in the future.

If you looked at his writings over the years, English had to be the primary language for him. Whereas Paul lapsed into French, Raymond always wrote in English. In 1733, James Edward Oglethorpe was in the process of founding Georgia. My contention is that either Stanhope introduced Raymond to Oglethorpe or helped him get a Captain-Lieutenant's commission in the 42nd Regiment of Foot under Oglethorpe. King George II gave Oglethorpe permission to raise the regiment, and in 1737, all the commissions for the new regiment were granted. Raymond purchased his commission as a Lieutenant and was placed in Major William Cook's Company of Oglethorpe's 42nd Regiment of Foot. Cook was an experienced British officer who held a commission as early as 1707. Oglethorpe was commissioned Colonel, Cook was commissioned Major, and Raymond Demeré was commissioned Lieutenant on the same day, August 25th, 1737. So Raymond Demeré was involved in the raising and the formation of the 42nd Regiment from its very beginning, and he left England to arrive in Georgia on 8 May 1738. At one point, he served as Oglethorpe's emissary to the Spanish governor, Montiano, in St. Augustine.

My inference on the Battle of Bloody Marsh, based on the accounts I've seen, was that there was the first skirmish at Gully Hole Creek [near Fort Frederica]. Then Oglethorpe assembled Raymond's company of the Regiment and the Highlanders and positioned them somewhere near where the Battle of Bloody Marsh monument now stands [on the Demere Road curve]. I'm guessing that the actual battle was on either side of present-day Demere Road. Demeré was on one side with fifty or sixty regulars, and the Highlanders were on the other side. The Highlanders loved to fight, but the British Redcoats were the dregs of the earth. Most of them had been emptied out of prisons or cast-off of other regiments. Whenever a new regiment was formed, they used the opportunity to get rid of their troublemakers. The only way to train them was to beat them. Rain started to fall during the battle, and some of the Redcoat platoons "retired"–retreated in disorder. They panicked and ran. You got sixty guys standing there with the Spanish in front of you. Because of the rain, their weapons were useless. Two or three start to run; then fifty start to run. Oglethorpe rode up on them and made them regroup, which Demeré did. Another officer, who was never named and never court-martialed, refused. There's no record of who that officer was. Officers in the British Army were rarely reprimanded. They were gentlemen. There was a different set of rules for the enlisted men and the officers. So, Demeré and the others turned around went back. Oglethorpe was a wild and reckless kind of guy. He pressed a full attack and beat the Spanish back to the south end of the island.

After Fort Frederica closed, Demeré accumulated land. If you look at colonial records, he was a pretty litigious guy and applied for land. He got islands granted to him. He eventually got William Horton's land on Jekyll. He started acquiring thousands of acres of land from Charleston and on down the coast to Cumberland Island. He became a farmer. The regiment disbanded in 1748. He became a Captain of one of the Independent Companies of Foot that reported to the Governor of South Carolina. All they did was change destinations. The Company wore the same uniforms–the red scarlet coats with the popinjay green facings and lining. If you go to Fort Loudoun today and see a reenactment, the uniforms they use for the South Carolina Independent Company of Foot are exactly what the 42nd Regiment of Foot had.

Paul Demeré, Raymond's brother, came to America after Raymond. On Christmas Day, 1740, Paul purchased his commission as a Lieutenant in a Grenadier's regiment under William Horton. I have no idea of the age difference between Paul and Raymond. Paul died at Fort Loudoun.[2]

Raymond built a house, Harrington Hall, just northwest of the roundabout where Frederica Road and Lawrence Road meet, about where the [new] Sea Island stables are today. It was probably constructed of tabby or wood. Harrington Plantation was located where the North and South Harrington Roads are now. Those roads literally mark the boundary of Harrington Plantation. He was granted a lot of land over the years–500 acres on the Ogeechee River, Lot #65 at Hardwicke, two lots at Frederica, 1,000 acres at Newport, a 538 acre island called Great Turkey Buzzard Island, Demeré Island which is now known as Champney Island, one mile southwest of Darien, 150 acres of land adjoining Harrington Hall, 500 acres near Darien, 425 acres in St. John's Parish [modern Bryan County], 50 acres and a lot at Frederica [St. James Parish; now Glynn County], 600 acres on Jekyll Island vacated by the death of Major Horton and 500 acres adjoining. In all, Raymond and Paul Demeré accumulated over 3700 acres by Crown Grant. He had 26 slaves. When Fort Frederica was being rebuilt in 1762, he furnished cedar posts, timber, roof, hinges, lead, Spanish Brown [a paint], carts and horses, Negro slaves, and the use of a great boat.

Raymond Demeré is seated next to the fireplace in this painting: "Peter Manigault and His Friends," Goose Creek, South Carolina, ca. 1760 drawing by George Roupell, courtesy of the Winterthur Museum, Winterthur, Delaware.

There is no record of Captain Raymond's wife. His son, Raymond, Jr., was born in 1752 on St. Simons. He also had a son name Raymond, born in 1733, who had a son named Raymond, born in 1804. To make it even more confusing, Paul Demeré had a son named Raymond, born in 1750, who had two sons named Raymond. One died as a young child in 1785, the other was born in 1791. He is the progenitor of the Savannah Demerés. I descend from Captain Raymond Demeré's son, Raymond, Jr.

Captain Raymond Demeré died on about April 21st 1766, probably at Harrington Hall. He was 64. He was most likely buried at Frederica. Mulberry Hall was the home of Raymond Demeré, Jr. It was located where the Malcolm McKinnon Airport on St. Simons is now. They called the house "The Grove" and the land "Mulberry Grove Plantation," not to be confused with Mulberry Grove north of Savannah, General Nathaniel and Katy Greene's home where Eli Whitney invented the cotton gin. The land probably shared the imprint of the airport. William Bartram, the naturalist, visited St. Simons and had dinner at Mulberry Grove with Raymond, Jr. He wrote about having venison and honey with water and brandy for dinner.

Paul Demeré's son, Raymond II, was a Patriot who joined the American Revolution when he was twenty-six. He was a delegate to the Georgia Provincial Congress, was in a couple of battles, and was Aide-de-Camp to General William Alexander, one of the founders of present-day Columbia University. Ironically, years earlier Paul Demeré got a commission in the British Army that George Washington wanted.

My ancestor, the St. Simons Demeré, was a Loyalist. I think that he probably went to north Florida during the Revolution. The two Demeré families diverged greatly after that conflict. The St. Simons Demerés got burned out every time there was a war. During the American Revolution, Raymond, Jr.'s house and plantation were burned, and during the War of 1812, the plantation was burned again. Eugenia Price wrote about that time period.

The two Raymonds were first cousins, born about two years apart. They were well acquainted with one another. After the American Revolution, Raymond II helped my ancestor, Raymond, Jr., get his citizenship restored. Raymond II died after the war in a horse riding accident.

All of the Demeré gravestones at Christ Church on St. Simons belong to my ancestors. The bodies are not there. The gravestones are big slabs made in Baltimore. They used big slabs because when there was a hurricane, the coffins would float to the surface when the ground became saturated. Those big stones effectively kept them where they belong. Robert Houstoun Demeré, Sr. of Savannah told me that when he was a college student during World War II, somebody called him to say an airport was being built on St. Simons on the old Demeré (Mulberry Grove) property and that the old gravestones were going to be plowed under. So he drove down from Savannah, loaded up the gravestones, and took them to Christ Church. But he didn't dig up any bones or bodies. I never did get the slabs' exact original location.

When one St. Simons Raymond Demeré died, the son would rename himself "Senior." So you have to go by birthdates. In 1824, as a hurricane was approaching the island, Raymond Demeré (born 1804), had a fight with his father, Raymond Demeré (born 1773), over a girl named Mary his father brought back from Charleston as his ward. Apparently, the father was a wastrel. Maybe the son fell in love with her. Who knows? Something happened. The son left for Darien in the morning and tried to come back that night to the north end of St. Simons. The hurricane covered the whole island in six feet of water, and the son and five black oarsmen were killed. The story is that Mary was so distressed that she walked from Mulberry Grove Plantation to the St. Simons Sound and drowned herself. That's how the story of Mary the Wanderer came about. No one knows her last name. Someone wrote a story once and gave her the last name of McCabe, but there is no historical reason for that. I don't know where she is buried. Those Raymond Demeré's gravestones are at Christ Church. Who knows where Mary is buried? If she wasn't a Demeré, she wouldn't have a marble headstone. She probably had a wood headstone.[3]

The father, Raymond, died in 1832. The remaining oldest son, Joseph, was also a wastrel. He mortgaged everything in the 1830s. There was a huge cotton depression then. The last Demeré born on St. Simons was in the early 1840s. The Demerés left the island when the matriarch, Anne Demeré, died in 1847.

Patrick Demere (l) and 1760 detail of his ancestor, Raymond Demeré (r), from Roupell drawing (courtesy of the Winterthur Museum, Winterthur, Delaware).

My direct ancestor, born on St. Simons in 1813, was Lewis Demeré. The Demeré fortunes had declined, but he married well to Virginia Barnard whose ancestors had been in Georgia since Oglethorpe. Lewis and his brother, Paul, moved to Camden County, where the Barnards had a plantation on the west side of the Satilla River near Burnt Fort. There's nothing there now. In 1853, Lewis' father-in-law sold that plantation, and they moved to Marion County, Florida, near Ocala. They'd all pick up and move together–brothers, wives, cousins. Then Lewis and Virginia, my great-great-grandparents, moved to Cedar Key and then finally to Demere Key, which has a natural harbor.[4]

Demere Key, Pine Island, Florida. Image courtesy of Google Earth©.

Lewis may be buried there. I talked to someone who did an archaeological dig, and there are Indian bones there. Virginia moved back to Ocala, then the [Civil] War broke out. The last I heard, Demeré Key was owned by a group of dentists. Paul was a lighthouse keeper on Sanibel Island, and there is a Demere Road on Sanibel.

There were Demerés all over the place during the Civil War. Lewis and Virginia's son, Raymond Barnard Demeré, enlisted in 1861. I have a photo of James Barnard Demeré, and he looks exactly like my younger brother.

The only Demeré artifact that survived in my family is a tea-caddy spoon that was made for the wedding of Anne Demeré and John Fraser, which Eugenia Price wrote about.[5]

Demeré-Fraser wedding spoon. Photograph courtesy of Patrick Demere.

I have visited St. Simons quite a few times, and the first time was really the only time that it seemed familiar. That was about 20 years ago, and the island was not nearly as developed as it is now. I have the same feeling now when I visit other once remote areas, the feeling that you cannot return. I get a little *deja vu*, however, when I pick up Mrs. Cate's *Early Days or Our Todays.* It is a neat feeling to have someone say, "Demere? We have a street here named Demere." More often, friends from Memphis returning from Sea Island or St. Simons will say: "They pronounce your name wrong down there. We set them straight!" I will then have to explain the pronunciation change occurred here, not there.

NOTES

[1] "Much can also be inferred from the many misspellings in letters to and about Raymond and Paul Demeré, who themselves signed many letters in the mid-1700's both *Demere* and *Demeré*. These obviously phonetic misspellings include: *Demaré, Demarie, Dimory,* and *Demeree.* This leads one to believe that Raymond Demeré pronounced his surname *dim-er-ay*, obviously with a French accent. Almost five centuries later, differences in the spelling of the family name are mainly regional. There are families of the same line in America now that use the acute accent mark on the last two *e*'s (*Deméré*) as did the earliest progenitors quite often; on the last *e* (*Demeré*); or not at all (*Demere*). Also, the pronunciation varies geographically from *dim-er-ee* to *dim-a-ray* to *d'mayr*. In addition, some former slaves took the last name, and their descendants can be found today with the names Demere and Demery." Notation by Patrick Demere.

[2] "During the French and Indian War (1754-1763) the British Colony of South Carolina felt threatened by French activities in the Mississippi Valley. To counter this threat, the Colony sent the Independent Company of South Carolina to construct and garrison what became Fort Loudoun [in present-day Vonore, Tennessee]. This move helped to ally the Overhill Cherokee Nation in the fight against the French and guaranteed the trade would continue between the Cherokee and South Carolina. In the course of the fort's four-year existence, relations between South Carolina and the Cherokee Nation broke down. In August, 1760, the Cherokee captured Fort Loudoun and its garrison." Source: http://fortloudoun.com/?page_id=10, accessed February 12, 2011

[3] Does the specter of a lovely young girl with long flowing hair and sorrowful eyes still roam the beaches at the south end of the island? Many say they have seen her with her lantern held high, waiting and watching for the lover who went off to the mainland and never came back. One who encountered Mary years ago was Carolyn Butler, a former third-grade teacher at St. Simons Elementary School. The thing Carolyn saw wasn't human in form–it was more like a big white blob– but it put a tremendous fear into both her and her dog, Boots, who ran away from home as a result. "You just know when you've seen a ghost," she said, "You've never been colder in your life and then you break out in heavy perspiration." Don W. Farrant, *The Lure and Lore of*

the Golden Isles: The Magical Heritage of Georgia's Outerbanks (Nashville: Rutledge Hill Press, 1993), 73-74.

[4] Demere Key is an archaeological site west of Pine Island, Florida. On June 13, 1972, it was added to the U.S. National Register of Historic Places. The island is named for its early owner, Lewis Deméré (1813-about 1880), who was born at St. Simons Island, Georgia. He and his wife, Virginia Clancy Barnard Deméré (1821-1900) and son, Raymond Barnard Deméré (1843-1905) lived on the island until about 1880.
Wikipedia, http://en.wikipedia.org/wiki/Demere_Key, accessed February 13, 2011.

[5] The spoon is about 3.5 inches from top to bottom, engraved with the Fraser of Lovat crest: an elk or stag whose rack appears to have five points each side. Above the figure is a curved scroll of about 180 degrees on which the upper case French words Je Suis Prêt, meaning "I Am Prepared." The silversmith's marks show that the famous London silversmith Francis Higgins made them in London in 1821-1822. The marks are: "FH" (Francis Higgins, maker), "Leopard's Head," "Lion Passant" (made in London), "Date Letter" (small case f, meaning 1821-1822), and "King's Head."

William Francis Ladson, Sr.

William Ladson remembers when cotton, timber, cattle and hogs were big industry in Moultrie, located in southwest Georgia. It was a large enough town to attract politicians like Governor Eugene Talmadge and President Franklin D. Roosevelt, both of whom Mr. Ladson remembers addressing crowds from Moultrie's courthouse steps. Colonel Ladson describes traveling to the Citadel by train, the main mode of long distance transportation by land at the time. He was stationed at a coast artillery post, one of many that once, but no longer, guarded America's seaports, and he served in Korea where he found himself working alongside Kim Il- sung, the future leader of North Korea.

William Ladson

My full name is William Francis Ladson, Senior. I was born in Moultrie, Georgia on October the 9th, 1915. I was born at home–822 2nd Street, SE. Dr. Everett Daniels was the doctor who delivered me. He was the main obstetrician for the people in the city. There was another doctor, Doctor Hitchcock, who was the main obstetrician for the people in the county. The original house burned down, and Father rebuilt on the same property. Our new, modern home was designed and built in 1922 by G.W. Milligan, an architect and building contractor. It is considered a landmark in Moultrie today. My father's name was John Elzie Ladson, Senior. He was from Montgomery County [Soperton]. According to the genealogy, two brothers, James and John Ladson, came over from Ireland and settled James Island and Johns Island just outside of Charleston, South Carolina.[1] Then they migrated to Georgia.

My father was the only member of his family who was able to get an advanced education. He attended the Macon Secretarial School. Upon graduation, he got a job as a secretary for a lumber company in Sigsbee, Georgia, a very small community about halfway between Macon and Moultrie. There was a hardware salesman he became familiar with, who told him a similar job was open in Moultrie at Southern Lumber Company. Dad, one weekend, went down and interviewed for it and was hired at a higher salary. That's how he ended up in Moultrie. He died in 1980. One family bible recorded him as 96 years old, and the other one recorded him as 97. So he was born in either in 1884 or 1885. Mother was from a little town east of Tifton called Brookfield. Her full name was Anna Laurie Rhodes. When her father died, her mother moved to Moultrie and opened a boarding house a block from the railroad depot. When Daddy arrived there to accept his job in 1908, he asked the conductor where would be a good place to stay. The conductor said, "You couldn't find any better place to stay, and especially to eat, than with Miss Rhodes." And he directed Daddy how to find it. Grandmother Rhodes had five or six daughters, and she had plenty of help. That's where Daddy met my mother.

Moultrie had between 8,000 and 12,000 people then. The whole area around there was agricultural. Cotton was king, and that prompted the opening of the Moultrie Cotton Mill to process the cotton into cloth. Swift & Company came to Moultrie in about 1914 and opened a tremendous hog and cattle processing plant. They operated salesmen out of Moultrie and shipped to the various markets. They also ran what they called a commission company that bought hogs and cattle from the surrounding area. They slaughtered them and processed the meat there. They used to say the only thing that they couldn't use of a hog was his grunt.

When my father took that job in 1908, the local lumber operation, Southern Lumber Company, was owned and operated by Mr. Anton Huber[2] and Mr. John N. Norman. The Normans and the Hubers are original pioneers of Moultrie. Mr. Norman lived up at Norman Park between Moultrie and Tifton. There was little junior college there named Norman Junior College. To run a lumber company, you need a lot of money, and he was doing business with the Moultrie Banking Company. Mr. Norman, being of a strong bible-based Baptist faith, objected vigorously to Mr. Huber's growing neglect of their business operations and his extended absences from time to time. This resulted in Mr. Huber buying Mr. Norman's interest in the Southern Lumber Company in a put-up or shut-up confrontation.

Well, Mr. Huber would disappear at times, and sometimes, he was owing money to the bank, and it was due. Mr. W. C. Vereen had the Moultrie Banking Company and the Moultrie Cotton Mill. He called my father down to the bank and said, "It seems like every time I call out there, you're the only one that answers the phone. I'm foreclosing on Mr. Huber, and I can't locate him." Mr. Vereen says, "Now, you go over there to the courthouse steps, and I want you to bid it in." My father said, "I don't have any money to bid." Mr. Vereen said, "Don't worry about that.

You go over and buy this company, and I'll take care of it."
I imagine Mr. Huber was pretty upset when he got back,
but there was nothing he could do about it. He owed the
bank money and was apparently indifferent towards
honoring his obligations. Mr. Vereen was not known for his
patience. So my father bid on it, and Mr. Vereen put him in
the lumber business, which marked the beginning of a
personal and business relationship between the Vereen and
Ladson families over the years. My father was later able to
pay the loan off and changed the name to Ladson Lumber
Company.

I went through the Moultrie public school system. Back
then, the elementary school was called the grammar school.
We had about 16-18 students in my first grade class. My
second grade teacher, Mrs. Outler, and my third grade
teacher, Miss Martha Kelley, were two outstanding
teachers. We had eleven grades. The junior high was a two-
year set up, 7th and 8th grades, before you went into senior
high. The high school is now the Colquitt County Arts
Center. We'd walk to school–about three-quarters of a
mile–walk home for lunch, then walk back to school. I
didn't make varsity due to my size. We had a very active
YMCA, and they were sponsoring teams. Most of my
athletic work was done there. The American Legion
sponsored junior baseball. I played more baseball with the
American Legion than anything else. I was a catcher.

One day, a friend, George, and I decided to make some
wine to liven up parties. They were called "proms" in those
days. You had punch served at the various houses back
then. We did make it and bottled it, but failed to use tannic
acid, which aids the process of fermentation. We stored the
bottles, about fifteen of them, at the top of our garage in a
closet my father had to store his hunting clothes and guns.
No sooner had we stacked them in there and closed the
door and started down the steps than they started going off.
They exploded. We went running back up there, afraid to

open the door. Finally, we decided the last bottle had busted. It took us about two days cleaning up before we were finally satisfied and hoped Daddy would never go up there. My father never did find out, thank goodness.

When times got hard, the price of cotton went down to ten cents a pound, and the price of a number one hog went down to two or three cents a pound. There was no way a farmer could raise a hog or grow cotton at those prices. They had to diversify, and my father was one of the leaders, and that's when they brought in tobacco and later what they called the "Spanish peanut" used in candy and peanut butter. Before that, the only peanuts grown were what they called "runners." As soon as they developed, you turned your hogs on them to fatten them. This was during the '20s and the first couple of years of the '30s. My father had a wholesale lumber business, Ladson Lumber Company. Mr. [Grady L] Doster was secretary-treasurer. But instead of buying timber on what we called "the stump"–in other words, you don't own the land, you cut the timber and haul it off–my father would buy the land before he harvested the timber; then he would stump the land and convert it to farmland. So, that's how he got to be such a big farmer.[3] What put my father out of the lumber business was Roosevelt's program of Social Security and income tax deduction. To do this, it would have been a hardship on my father. You had a bunch of little independent sawmill operators–men that had nothing but small sawmills and no money to finance themselves.

Well, we would agree to get a saw miller to move into an area where we had bought the land and owned the timber and cut it. He would hire people, and we would pay them off every week. I would go up on Thursday evening and pick up the saw miller's time book and come back. On Friday, we'd go in the bank and get the cash and put it in a little brown envelope, and I'd take it back to the saw miller on Saturday at noon before shutting down operations for the weekend. Most of the laborers were transient. They would make two or three pay periods and move on. There was nothing permanent about it. My father saw that it would be a nightmare trying to keep up with Social Security and tax deductions for this type personnel, exclusive of the increase in his office force required to maintain record accounting and control. By this time, the tenant farming and sharecrop operation had become so vast, my father closed out his wholesale lumber business and concentrated on his farming operations.

When my father decided to close out, his brother, W. B. [Bazzell] Ladson, was in full blossom in lumber. Uncle Baz had just obtained about forty thousand acres of virgin timber up in either North or South Carolina. He was an operator. He wasn't much of an administrative man. World War II had started and the government was buying most of it. Well, Mr. Doster just went right in and took over the office and administrative work. It was enough to keep them busy for several years. They moved up there with their sawmill and set up operation.

Integration

We didn't have any problems that could be referred to as race relations. Times were difficult, and there was a feeling of interdependence. Of course, there was always that separation of facilities–separate schools, separate public toilets and water fountains. Martin Luther King was successful in getting the federal laws passed that integrated. It's the best thing that's happened. I used to haul cotton pickers for my daddy. This was long before mechanical cotton pickers came in. You were dependent upon these people to pick your cotton. That was the only way. I'd pick them up early every the morning. We'd pick cotton, then I'd weigh them up and pay them in the afternoon, load them up, and carry them back home. I never had the first minute of trouble. I had a very good relationship.

Church

I'm still a member of St. John's Episcopal Church in Moultrie. The first mayor I remember was a Huber, then Evans Reynolds. For vacations, most people in Moultrie would go to the mountains or Pablo Beach, which is now called Atlantic Beach outside of Jacksonville.[4] Mother always took us for five days to Pablo Beach. When I go to the Mayo Clinic in Jacksonville, it's located just off San Pablo Road.

Holidays

Christmas was much like it is today. Mother would put up a tree. We would have presents under it and a big Christmas dinner. But there were no lights on the outside of your house or downtown. Friedlander's was the big department store growing up. It was right across from the courthouse on the east side. They went out of business about ten or twelve years ago. It couldn't compete with Wal-Mart and K-Mart. One of the brothers running it told me, "Wal-Mart and K-Mart are selling goods for the price I have pay to buy them. I can't compete with that." Mr. Friedlander was one of the original Jewish families that had migrated to Moultrie. He was very successful because he had diversified commodities. He had to carry clothes suitable for farmers as well as clothes suitable for the in-town clientele. He bought up a lot of real estate around there. I don't think Moultrie will have a mall. The outcroppings are places like Lowes, Home Depot, and Wal-Mart. Where Wal-Mart sets up, there are always a group of stores that set up around it.

Most July Fourths there was always a big celebration with families and politicians. They were held mostly at the fairgrounds, south of the courthouse, out on the edge of town about a half or three-quarters of a mile south of the courthouse. Eugene Talmadge used to come and make a speech. He'd take off his coat, open his collar, and flash those red suspenders. Everybody was buying red suspenders back then. He was a perennial governor until he died.

Citadel

We had a local Baptist preacher named Dick Gresham whose family was originally from Charleston. There was an old Gresham Hotel there in Charleston. He knew about the Citadel and tried to get young high school graduates interested in it. This was during the Great Depression, and the Citadel was certainly the school I could most economically attend. I believe it cost my Daddy between $800 and $900 a year. The first year there, you're treated pretty roughly. They claim that when you went through the Citadel, they developed the whole man. Every attempt during your first year, was to see if you could take it and stay. Generally, a lot of people left, but I managed to hold on.

THE CITADEL
CLASS OF 38
50TH REUNION

Bill Ladson

I used to catch a train in Thomasville to Savannah and then have about a four-hour layover there, then catch the train on up to Charleston. There was a train called the ABC–Atlanta, Birmingham, and Coast–that ran through Moultrie. That particular line ran from Atlanta and terminated in Thomasville. It had Pullman service for sleeping accommodations. You had to go to a common lavatory [men's room] at the end of the car to dress, undress, shave, and wash. It was a room there about ten by twelve feet with four or five lavatories [sinks] and a couple of commodes. If you were using a Pullman accommodation, you had an upper berth [bed] and a lower berth. The upper berth pulled down, whereas the lower berth was one of the two seats that faced one another. There was a common curtain that closed to give you privacy. You could sit up in the lower berth, but in the upper one, about all you could do was lie down. Once you got up [in the morning], the lower Pullman beds were converted into seats that faced each other. On the Atlanta-Thomasville train, there was no dining car because it just ran over night. The train from Thomasville to Savannah was purely a local, coach cars only train. So was the one I'd catch up to Charleston.

I'm currently one of the oldest Citadel alumnus and apparently, the oldest still able to travel. After my second year, times had got so hard, that I wasn't able to go back. I stayed home and worked with him [John Ladson Sr.] on the farms for two years. During that time, Roosevelt was elected and began to turn the country around. My mother insisted that I go back, so the class I graduated with was 1938. Charleston gets in your blood real early. It's hard to explain. It's a wonderful city and will never change. I met my wife there. She was a nurse at Roper Hospital while I was a cadet. I had a classmate that was going with her roommate. I didn't know any of the young ladies in Charleston and wasn't particularly interested until Clyde

Morton and Geraldine decided I needed a little social life. They wanted me to meet Geraldine's roommate. So I agreed. Her name was Johnsie Elizabeth Sarratt. Her mother's maiden name was Johnson. After the Citadel, I went to work for a general contractor named W. F. Scott & Company out of Thomasville, Georgia. I started keeping payroll and working with the local superintendent. I had a B.S. in Engineering, so I was trying to pick up everything I could as well as do the administrative work.

Politics

The first president I remember much about was Coolidge. There was a fellow named Smith, a former governor of New York, running for the presidency. I forget who he was running against, but he was defeated because he was a Catholic. Way back in those days, there was a lot of suspicion of Catholics. Roosevelt was the only President I remember coming to Georgia. He came when he was canvassing for individuals he wanted elected. We had a senator named Walter F. George, in my estimation, one of the last statesmen.[5] All we have now are politicians. Apparently, Senator George would not rubber stamp everything President Roosevelt wanted to put through in his New Deal. So Roosevelt canvassed for a man named Walter Camp, who was running against Senator George, but George stayed in the senate until he retired. He was highly respected by both Republicans as well as Democrats. Roosevelt was asking people to support his choice and not Senator George. He spoke from the [Moultrie] courthouse square. He was standing, but he couldn't stand too long. They didn't have a public address system, but you could hear him pretty well. I was standing within fifty feet of him. He was very popular in Georgia because he had polio, and he would come to Warm Springs.

In February of 1940, I was called into service and sent to Fort Barrancas, Florida, opposite Pensacola, contiguous to the Naval flight-training center.[6] It was an old coast artillery post. When I went to the Citadel, they had only two ROTC in one infantry and the other coast artillery. All engineering students were required to be artillerymen. My commission was in the coast artillery, but the coast artillery went out with the development of the Air Force. Anywhere in the United States where there was a coast artillery, it closed.

The one time in my life I made a mistake I'll always regret is when I let the mayor, Lonnie Johnson, who was a good friend of mine, talk me into getting out of the service and coming back there [to Moultrie] as City Manager. It entails running the public works and the administrative as well. It's an excellent field to get in, but I think I can best sum this up with the passage that appears in the Gospels when Jesus said, "A prophet is not without honor except in his own home town." You can apply that to my situation there. They caused enough trouble that they even impaneled a grand jury and had me indicted. That was 1950. I demanded a trial. They didn't think I would do it. I had a jury trial and got a direct verdict of acquittal.

After that, I went to work for the military airlift command at Belleville, Illinois right across the river from St. Louis. I was an engineer working on construction. I wasn't there but a short time when Korea hostilities had broken out, and I got ordered back to active duty. Thirty days after I reported, I was on my way to Korea and started off as the Deputy Commander of an engineer combat group. I took an engineer combat battalion about the time they were having the first truce talks at Panmunjom. I had a searchlight company, and we illuminated the battlefield. But I used four of them to mark the corners of Panmunjom at night and balloons by day to keep some of our Air Force people from getting the idea of emptying their ordnance on the way back from a mission and maybe shooting up the place. They were old World War II carbon-type searchlights mounted on a steel wheel frame. We pointed them up in the air.

I became personally acquainted with Kim Il-sung, the father of the present Kim Jong-il, the Premiere of North Korea today. He was the North Korean representative, their chief negotiator. I had to be over there every time they went into session. He first shocked me by asking me about my wife by name and my two children by name. I couldn't help but wonder how he got that information. He was a chain-smoker. He had a little ivory cigarette holder that had a curve in it. It went upward after it left his mouth, and he had it in his mouth all the time. He smoked their cigarettes. I guess they made some kind of tobacco [product] from China. I never offered him one, and he never asked for one. That assignment was in addition to my work of commanding a combat battalion. When they separated the two Koreas, he became the Premiere of North Korea. When he died, his son took his place.

I had a great respect for the South Korean soldiers. Their officers are brave, and they are good fighting men. They are dedicated to their country. It's a shame that they are divided. It really is. I didn't have any respect for the North Koreans. They were good fighters, but the Chinese did most of their fighting.

Family

I had one brother, Jack [founder of the Ladson Genealogical Library, Vidalia, Georgia], and two sisters, Carolyn and Mary. My wife, Johnsie, died April 14, 2006 subsequent to an extended period of suffering from manifold medical problems. Had she lived until August 20, 2006, we would have been married 68 years. We had two children, a son, William F. Ladson, Jr., and a daughter, Tommie Jean Ladson. Bill Jr. completed the Navy's Aviation Flight Training at Pensacola, Florida. Upon completion of his five-year obligation with the Navy, he, his wife and two small children returned to his wife's hometown, Macon. Bill Jr. entered the Walter F. George School of Law, passed the State Board, and began a successful law practice. He had a very successful practice for several years until he developed a cancer of the esophagus. After it was diagnosed, he was gone in six weeks. It was that rapid. That was 1999. He was 54 years old. Right in his prime.

Manual Labor

The biggest surge in population in Colquitt County has been the immigration of Mexicans. A large percentage of farming requires manual labor. It takes harvesters. That's where the influx of Mexican laborers found their home. Mechanically, you can only do so much. To add to that, we had truck farming–the growing of tomatoes, peppers, and cabbage. They would make at least three crops of cabbage during a year, sometimes four. Moultrie is still mainly an agricultural town. Old-timers used to say every time there was newborn, someone left.

NOTES

[1] Fort Sumter, site of the first Civil War battle, is located near the eastern tip of James Island. The bombardment of Fort Sumter was initiated on James Island at Fort Johnson.

[2] "In 1891 the Anton Huber Co, a contracting firm, was established. Mr. Huber's firm was responsible for building the first brick buildings in the area. In 1898 Mr. Huber built Moultrie's first water works and light plant, which was later sold to the city. He also had a lumber company and owned extensive real estate." Colquitt County Heritage Book Committee, comp., *The Heritage of Colquitt County, Georgia, 1856-2003* (Marceline, Mo.: Walsworth, 2003), 9.

[3] "At the height of J. E.'s various enterprises, he maintained over 8,000 acres of land in timber, pasture, and cultivation." Ibid., 24.

[4] "In the late 19th century, developers began to see the potential in Duval County's oceanfront as a resort. In 1883 a group of investors formed the Jacksonville and Atlantic Railroad with the intention of developing a resort community that would be connected to Jacksonville by rail. In 1884 the first residents of what would become Jacksonville Beach moved in, and a railway station, post office, and small tent community was formed. The community was named Ruby, after the daughter of one of the first residents. The name was changed to Pablo Beach in 1886, and the first hotel was constructed. It was incorporated as a town in 1907. The name was changed to Jacksonville Beach in 1921, emphasizing the connection with Jacksonville." Wikipedia, http://en.wikipedia.org/wiki/Jacksonville_Beach,_Florida, accessed May 20, 2011.]

[5] "George resigned from the Supreme Court of Georgia to run for a seat in the United States Senate, which became available due to the death of Thomas E. Watson. George won the special election but rather than take his seat immediately when the Senate reconvened on November 21, 1922, George allowed the appointed Rebecca Latimer Felton to be official sworn in, making her the first woman seated in the Senate and serving until George took office on November 22, 1922, one day later." Wikipedia,

http://en.wikipedia.org/wiki/Walter_F._George, accessed May 21, 2011.

[6] "Fort Barrancas sits on a bluff overlooking the entrance to Pensacola Bay. The natural advantages of this location have inspired engineers of three nations to build forts. The British built the Royal Navy Redoubt here in 1763 of earth and logs. The Spanish built two forts here around 1797. Bateria de San Antonio was a masonry water battery at the foot of the bluff. Above it was earth and log Fort San Carlos de Barrancas. American engineers remodeled the Water Battery in 1840 and built a masonry fort on the bluff between 1839 and 1844, connected by a tunnel to the Water Battery. This is the current Fort Barrancas. A $1.2 million, eighteen-month restoration project led to its reopening in 1980." National Parks Service,
http://www.nps.gov/guis/planyourvisit/fort-barrancas.htm, accessed May 21, 2011.

Floyd Harvey Faust

There was a time in Georgia's not too distant past when many of its cities and towns had their own baseball teams. Beginning in the 1800s, thirty-seven communities boasted teams belonging to twelve organized leagues, while other semi-pro or "outlaw" leagues cropped up in other parts of the state. Floyd Faust came from Leesport, Pennsylvania, to Georgia in the early 1950s to play on the Pittsburgh Pirate's minor league team, and he never left. An injury prematurely ended his hopes of playing professional baseball, but his short-lived career stats speak for themselves. Faust was inducted into the Minor League Hall of Fame in 2006. His involvement in numerous civic activities is evidence that Pennsylvania's loss has been Georgia's gain.

Floyd Faust and friend.

My name is Floyd Harvey Faust. I was born on August 6, 1930, in West Leesport, Pennsylvania, about nine miles north of Reading. My father was Samuel Faust, and he was born in Hamburg, Pennsylvania, north of Reading. My mother was Florence Seaman Faust. She was raised in Dauberville, about five miles north of Leesport.

I had an older brother who was drafted into the Army during World War II. Another brother, one year older than me, and I just missed being drafted. If the war had gone another year or two, we would have all been in it.

We didn't have a Little League or anything like that back then. We played in the cow pastures, just getting groups together. My baseball really started when I hit high school–Ontelaunee High in Leesport. That school is no longer there. The principal would give a devotion every morning during assembly. My junior year, our baseball coach, Kenny Matz, lived fifteen miles from where I lived. He wanted me to play for the Mohnton American Legion baseball team. He'd pick me up, take me over there for all the practices, and take me to all the games. I thought that was the greatest thing anybody could have ever done for a young guy. I batted .404 and led the league in the American Legion. I stayed in touch with him for years. It wasn't too long ago that he died. He lived to be way on up there in age.

I hoped to play professional baseball right out of high school, but I broke my leg the second game of my senior year sliding into second base. We really didn't learn how to slide properly then. After I graduated, another fellow and I decided we'd enlist in the Marine Corps. I was in Parris Island for training and then Portsmouth, Virginia. They were playing baseball where they stationed me in Portsmouth. Man, I was on that team before you knew it, playing center field, and I learned then how to slide. The word got out among the coaches, and I played for different civilian teams along with the Marine teams. I spent three years, nine months, and a few days in the Marines and was signed to a professional baseball contract, a one-year renewable contract, with the Pittsburgh Pirates upon my discharge. The contract was for $200 a month. My second year, I got $250 a month. That's all they were paying back then. We enjoyed the game so much in those days, we would have played for nothing.

They sent me to Brunswick to play on the minor league team, the Brunswick Pirates, in the Georgia-Florida League.[1] I had never heard of Brunswick, Georgia. I never knew what a sand gnat was until I came here for spring training. We stayed at the Oglethorpe Hotel. When they assigned me to the team after spring training, I stayed at Maynard's Tourist Home in the 1600 block of Reynolds Street. The house is still there. The biggest thing that impressed me about Brunswick was the easy life that people were leading. It wasn't a bang-bang-bang thing like with the people up North where people were all the time rush-rush-rush. The people were so easy-going, so courteous, and so friendly. They were the old Southern people. Now, today, you have your mixture from all over the country down here. It's not quite the same, but I still love Brunswick.

The minor league stadium, Edo Miller Park, is still there. There were eight teams in the league–the Brunswick Pirates, Fitzgerald Red Legs, Albany Cardinals, Waycross Bears, Valdosta Tigers, Thomasville Dodgers, and the Tifton Indians. The American Cordele Royals were in the league at that time. In 1953, I played right field, and in '54, I played centerfield. My batting average the first year was .280. The second year it was .273. In '54 I was listed among the top five ball players in the league for most hits, most runs, total bases, most doubles, most triples, most home runs, most extra base hits, and set a new Georgia-Florida League record for 76 stolen bases that year.[2]

The highlight of my baseball career was the opening night of the '53 season. The local merchants gave away different things for the first hit and the first homerun. I was the lead-off batter and thought, *I've got the best chance for the first hit.* Well, I walked. But by the time I came up for the second time around at bat, nobody else had got a hit. Guess what I did? I hit a long home run. So, I won it all. The Brummetts who owned Roger's Jewelers gave me a 17-jewel wristwatch. I got shirts and a $25 war bond from one of the sponsors. The thing that really impressed me was they passed a hat around the stands, because here I am, a little fellow, and I guess they thought, *Wow! He did great!* They collected $116. That's something you never forget.

The longest homerun I hit was over in Waycross. I hit the scoreboard in left-center field. Long years after that, somebody from Waycross moved to Brunswick, and I was introduced to him. He said, "Floyd Faust. Yeah, I remember that name. They put your name on the scoreboard for hitting it with that homerun." Apparently nobody had ever hit that scoreboard. The stadium is still there, but the sign is long gone.

Faust in Marine Corps baseball uniform.

The best ballpark I liked was in Albany. They had a great park, but it's no longer there. On the whole, most of the ballparks were nice. Tifton was about half-and-half. Our '53 season coach was Jack Papke. In '54 it was Frank Ozeak. They were good coaches. Jack was still a playing coach. He was a catcher. There wasn't a lot of teaching going on. I had mastered base stealing and hitting from my time in the service. Stealing bases came naturally. I had no problem keeping them busy throwing to second. The Georgia-Florida League started, I believe, in 1935. Brunswick didn't get into the league until 1950. The old record was 69 stolen bases. I stole 76. Practically all those 76 bases I stole were second base.

My coach, Ozeak, didn't believe in stealing third. He said, "If you're on second, you'll score anyway if there's a hit." But I could have stole third so easy so many times there's no telling how many bases I might have stole. It's easier to steal third because you can get a better jump. You get a longer lead off of second than you do on first with the first baseman standing on the bag. More than once I ran half way to third and had to dart back to second quick. I wanted to go so badly, but he [Ozeak] wouldn't let me do it. If I got picked off, it was a rare occasion, because it's not something I can remember. It's easier to steal on a right-handed pitcher. As long as I could get my routine jump, I was in high gear on my second step. I even stole home a time or two. You've got to know how the pitcher delivers the ball and pick your pitch. You got to know what pitch you want to run on when you see what the count is. With a curve ball, you got a better chance of stealing home. The coach would let me go depending on what the score was, and he knew if I got the right pitch, I had a chance to steal home.

We traveled in an old school bus. The first year, I was just another ballplayer in the bus. The second year, I was the bus driver. We usually played a two or three game series, so we'd stay overnight in a hotel. After the last game of a trip, if we got through playing, showered, and left by 11:00 o'clock at night, they all slept coming back to Brunswick while I drove the bus. I have to think that driving affected my playing. Back then I had to stop many a time because cows were lying out on the highway. They liked the warmth. They didn't have a law then that cows had to be penned up and off the streets. Cows used to eat along the road. Many a time, I had to come to a screeching halt. You'd come around a curve, and see them lying there. We had to get up, get out, and chase cows off the road.

We carried fifteen guys on the team if I remember correctly. The payout for fifteen players was about $1600 a month.[3,4] Room and board were covered by the organization. You walked from the boarding house to the field. The season lasted from April to August. Since my older brother, Cliff, lived in California and had his own business, I spent time out there with him after the '53 season.

I played with Gene Freese, a shortstop who became a major leaguer.[5] "Whammy" Douglas, who was blind in one eye, set a new record for the Georgia-Florida League at 27 and 6. Mario Cuomo [52nd governor of New York, 1983-1994] played for the Brunswick Pirates the year before I got there. In 1952, he played in the outfield, played 81 games and batted .244. We led the league in 1954. We played 140 games. The biggest turnout at a game we had was 5,000 people. The total attendance was 54,475 for the summer. I was in the '54 all-star game.

I hurt my shoulder right at the end of the '54 season. Doctor Howard Coe, our team doctor, diagnosed it as bursitis. He said, "The fluid that lubricates your shoulder joint has dried up. It's like an old hinge that isn't oiled regularly and gets tight. You can get out of baseball because you aren't going to be able to throw with that arm."

144

I was offered a contract to go to Williamsport, Pennsylvania, for the April league up there. I told my dad I wasn't going to sign that contract. He couldn't believe it because I had so much going for me, so I signed the contract and went to spring training in Texas, but I had no arm–couldn't throw. That's when they gave me my release. When I got out of baseball, I started to work in insurance for Metropolitan Life in Brunswick. It was hard to go to minor league games to sitting there and watching and not being a part of it. The minor league team left Brunswick in '68.

I never did have surgery and learned to live with it. I got on a fast pitch softball team here in Brunswick and then managed my own team. I switched over to slow pitch softball. I could play third base and throw side-armed, and it didn't bother me. We played in Georgia and parts of Florida in different tournaments. In 2001, forty-seven years after I left baseball, my son, Kurt, and I were hunting on Sapelo Island. I tripped a cypress knee [stump] coming down a bank and busted my right shoulder–tore the rotator cuff. After Doctor Gurley got in there and sewed it up, he came in the hospital room that night and said, "Mr. Faust, I sewed up that bad tear in your rotator cuff. But you also had a nasty tear in your rotator cuff from way back in your life. When did you ever hurt that arm before?" I told him, "Only one time, playing professional baseball." He said, "Well, back then, they didn't have the knowledge they have today. Had they known it was a torn rotator cuff back then, you would have been playing the next year with no problem." Now, I can raise my arm over my shoulder as good as ever.

I used to go to the Exchange Club turkey shoots out on 4th Street, and one of the guys on the Exchange Club invited me to join. The year I joined, in 1963, the fellow that ran the turkey shoots, gave them up. I told the president, "This is the one reason I joined the Exchange

Club. I loved the turkey shoots. I can't believe you're not going to have them anymore." Sid Evans and some of the others sitting by me said, "Floyd, why don't you take it over?" So that's how I got started in it. This year [2010] will be the 46th straight year I've been running the turkey shoots. They run for nine nights before Thanksgiving, but not on Sundays. We hold them out at the fairgrounds starting at six o'clock. Twelve people shoot for each turkey. We put an "X" on a piece of paper. The person whose pellet is closest to the "X" from ninety feet wins. We give them a slip, and they go by the store to pick up the turkey. Last year, in nine nights of shooting, we gave away 298 turkeys to the winners. In 45 years, I've given away over 9,000 turkeys. From day one, I've listened to over 120,000 rounds of ammunition go off. I'm hard of hearing in my left ear because of that.

Floyd Faust at November 22, 2000 Exchange Club turkey shoot.

Kurt and I hunt on Ossabaw Island about every three years.[6] You have to apply for a lottery to the state Game and Fish [Department of Natural Resources, Wildlife Resources Division], and you have to be drawn. You usually get in about every three years. We take tents and camp at a place they have over there. It's a three-day hunt. We also put in for our grandchildren. It's called a parent-child hunt. Last year, I took three grandchildren and two great grandchildren. Each child has to have one parent there to supervise. We've been doing that for many years. Last year, we went on the archery hunt. I killed a real nice 118-pound six-point with a bow and arrow. Kurt killed two himself. We eat a lot of deer meat. I make a lot of deer jerky and take a lot to the Exchange Club and to church. We bury the deerskins in the ground.

Petting Farm

About twenty years ago, I started a petting farm for the Exchange Club, taking my own animals. There are five pens for the animals and one big pen where the kids can come in, walk among them. I took out sixty-two animals last year. I have a miniature horse, about three years old and three feet high, a dozen goats, ten geese, twenty-five chickens and roosters, rabbits, a peacock, turkeys, a little of everything. I keep them at our house, right on the marsh. It's a good expense, but my wife and I are not into partying and drinking and all that. I'm a non-drinker and non-smoker, so what money I spend is for the animals, and it's money well spent.

Still in the Game

I taught both of my sons to play baseball. Kerry was a good infielder. We'd to go the Ballard ballpark. I coached a lot of Little League teams. I still follow professional ball. I'm looking forward to the Phillies tearing up the [New York] Yankees this year. The Phillies were my team growing up. I lived only about seventy miles from Philadelphia.

Southern Charm

The biggest thing I was impressed with when I first moved here, was the Southern people. Each time you saw them, this week or the next week, they were shaking your hand. Everyone was so friendly. You didn't have that up where I lived.

NOTES

1 "In 1935 the Georgia-Florida League was organized, with Albany, Americus, Moultrie, and Thomasville representing Georgia. Tallahassee and Panama City made up the Florida part of the league and would be the only Florida cities ever to play in the league. Dothan, Alabama, was also admitted for the 1942 season. The league survived through the 1958 season, only breaking its stride from 1943 through 1945 for World War II (1941-45). During this twenty-one-year run, Brunswick, Cordele, Cordele-Americus, Dublin, Fitzgerald, Tifton, Valdosta, and Waycross, along with the original four Georgia teams, played at least one year in the Class D circuit. Albany was the only team to play every year during this stretch. In 1962 the Georgia-Florida League reorganized with four teams and played Class D ball. When Classes B, C, and D were eliminated in 1963, the league moved up to Class A baseball. This was the last year of operation for the Georgia-Florida League." The New Georgia Encyclopedia, www.georgiaencyclopedia.org/nge/Article.jsp?id=h-838&hl=y, accessed January 17, 2011.

2 Floyd Faust is listed in 7 out of 10 records based on top 5 offensive positions for the 1954 season: most hits (153, #5), most runs (143, #1; second place was 102), total bases (242, #3), triples (10, #2), homeruns (14, #4), extra base hits (51, #3), stolen bases (76, #1; second place was 34). Faust place #6 in doubles (27, 2 behind the #5 player). John Bell, *Georgia Class D and Minor League Baseball Encyclopedia: A Statistical History of the Georgia-Alabama League, Georgia-Florida League, and Georgia State League* (Carrollton, Georgia: Vabella Publishing, 2001).

3 Compare 1954 semi-pro baseball salaries with what ballplayers were making in 1920s: "In 1923, $500 a month was needed to support the Americus, Georgia semi-professional baseball team payroll for sixteen players and other expenses." John Bell, *Shoeless Summer: The summer of 1923 when Shoeless Joe Jackson played baseball in Americus, Georgia* (Carrollton, Georgia: Vabella Publishing, 2001), 7.

4 By mid-season, the Americus team had signed Shoeless Joe Jackson and other "ringers" whose salaries averaged $60 per week. Jackson earned $75 a week. Ibid., 43.

[5] Gene Freese played professional baseball for 12 years with various National and American League teams.

[6] To cull the deer population.

Lucian Lamar Sneed

Lucian Sneed is the Administrative Director of the Georgia Tribe of Eastern Cherokee (Georgia Cherokee Indians). His European roots in America extend to 1634, but his Cherokee Indian heritage goes back much further. In this profile, he discusses how the Cherokees came to be in Georgia and how they were forced out. He also provides an interesting account of how Ball Ground, Georgia got its name and shares a bittersweet incident involving an ancestor during the Civil War.

My name is Lucian Lamar Sneed. I was born in Atlanta, Georgia, on February 18, 1936 at Grady Hospital. We lived off of Grant Street close to Grant Park. My father was John Olin Sneed, and my mother was Emma Louise (Jackson) Sneed. I graduated from Henry Grady High School next to Piedmont Park, then attended Georgia State College and Emory University Law School. I graduated from Emory in 1965 and worked for the federal government as an attorney in the Department of Defense dealing with companies that had government contracts.

My father was a writer for the *Atlanta Journal and Constitution*. I'm named after Georgia's historian, back in the 1930s, named Lucian Lamar Knight.[1] My father also did book reviews for various authors, and Knight was a prolific historian and author. They became such friends that I was named after him. My father was well educated, but he wasn't that interested in history. It just seems like the name Lucian Lamar not only passed on a historian's name but a historian's interest in history. What's in a name? It's strange that I have a historian's name and a Ph.D. in history from the University of North Carolina, and I've loved history all my life.

My ancestors have been in Georgia since 1734. They were originally from England. The family estate still exists there. The Sneed family came into Virginia in 1634 and formed a farm adjacent to what is now George Washington's farm. As the family kept growing, they looked for more land. They migrated down to North Carolina, and many stayed there.

As soon as [James] Oglethorpe opened up Georgia, people were looking for new and free land. It was a hundred years after 1634 that my great-great-grandfather came into Georgia. His name was John Thomas Sneed. He settled in what is now Wilkes County, Georgia. Washington is the county seat. It was from there that Cherokee lands were opened up in the late 1820s by virtue of the Cherokee Land Lottery in which Georgia literally stole the Cherokee peoples' land in north Georgia. They sent surveyors up there and divided it into 160-acre tracts. Along the Gold Belt, it was only 40-acre tracts. The Gold Belt is about a twenty-to thirty-mile strip that runs out of North Carolina northeast to southwest, through Georgia past Carrollton, and into Alabama. The first gold that was discovered in Georgia was in White County. It runs lawyers nutty when they're doing title searches on land because all land lots are 160-acres with the exception of Georgia's gold-bearing district.

Georgia held a land lottery in Milledgeville, the state capitol, in 1820 and '30. They had three lottery drawings. John Thomas Sneed was a veteran of the American Revolutionary War. Veterans or their widows and children got first draws into the Cherokee country. That's how my white ancestors came from Washington, Georgia, into north Georgia.

The lottery land was in what is now Lumpkin County, but John Sneed didn't stay there. He moved further on up into Union [County], which was part of Fannin County at the time. That's where he married his Cherokee wife, Mary

Stacy, and that's where my great-grandfather, John Harrison Sneed, was born.

The first whites in the Cherokee country during the 1700s were traders. At the time of the Cherokees' removal in 1838, the Chief of the Cherokees, John Ross, was only one-eighth Cherokee. But his family had come in as traders and had big trading posts in north Georgia.[2] They traded in deerskins. The Cherokees and the Creeks almost wiped the deer population off the face of Georgia because the Europeans wanted deerskins so much that they were over hunted. Deerskin is supple and soft. The Europeans used it to make shoes, luggage, upholstery–anything in leather. We have more deer today than existed back then.

The first [modern European] contact with the Cherokee people was by Hernando DeSoto in 1540. He came up from Florida. His narratives in dealing with the Cherokees show they were totally different from other tribes. People try to paint all Native Americans with one brush. They were as different in many ways as Europeans are. All Europeans are not the same complexion and have different colors of hair. The Cherokee were lighter skinned people. The first whites who came down from New England and down the North Carolina coast were Vikings. The Celtics were also here around 1000 to 1200 A.D. So there were mixed races coming into the country way before Christopher Columbus. He never set foot on the American mainland. The closest he got was Cuba and the Bahamas Islands. DeSoto writes about seeing red-haired, blue-eyed Cherokees who were very tall and lighter skinned. The Lower-Florida Indians were shorter, stockier people. So you ran across different racial traits as you went around America because they had contact with people way before Columbus ever discovered America.

The Southeastern Indians per se were more advanced, and that would include what people refer to as the Creek. But "Creek" is not descriptive of that group of people. The main people that made up the Creek family of tribes were Muskogee. They came along after the mound-builders. The beautiful gigantic mounds down in Macon and over in Cartersville and Etowah were built by mound-builder people who later became Creeks, a confederation of Southern tribes. The whites gave them the name "Creek."[3]

No tribe in America named themselves. They were usually named by other tribes referring to them. It is believed that "Cherokee" is a Choctaw word meaning "mountain people." It's chopped–"Tsa-la-gi." In the Choctaw language, it refers to "people who live in the mountains" or "the cave people who live in the mountains." It refers to people who live in high places. It's very difficult to get an absolute translation from any Indian language into English.

The Cherokees are not native to the Southeast. They are part of the Iroquoian group of Indians we now find in upstate New York, all the way into Canada. Cherokee is not a unique language. It is Iroquoian. "Chattahoochee" and "Chattanooga" [north Georgia/southern Tennessee] are Muskogee [Creek] words. It has never been truly explained, but apparently there was a falling out among the group of people that comprised the Iroquois Nation, and they almost had a civil war. A large group of them migrated south around 900 to 1000 A.D. Migrations don't happen all at one time. Small groups at a time moved south. When they [the Cherokee] were a warrior society, their biggest enemies were their kinsmen to the north. They would raid back north into the Iroquois country, and the Iroquois would raid south into the Cherokee country.

The Cherokees drove the Creeks out of north Georgia. The Creek territory went all through north Georgia, Tennessee, and up into Kentucky. The Cherokee drove the Creek south of the Chattahoochee. The Chattahoochee River running north of Atlanta through Roswell was the boundary line between the Cherokees and the Creeks. Most of the arrowheads you find in north Georgia and Tennessee aren't necessarily Cherokee. Many would be pre-Cherokee, the Muskogee people.

Battle Ground

My great-grandmother is a descendent of Nancy Ward. If you look at a Georgia map, northwest of where I live now in Cumming, is a little town in Cherokee County called Ball Ground. Ball Ground got its name from a battle between the Cherokees and the Creeks in the late 1700s, right around 1800, over disputed land to the west, near Carrollton. They both claimed they owned the land and had a battle. Back then, many women went with their husbands to battle. They already had rifles at the time. Nancy went with her husband, and he was killed in the Battle of Taliwa. She picked up his rifle, and they said she fought like a "piga," a man. As a result, she was rewarded by being named the first "beloved woman" of the Cherokee nation. She's buried on the Georgia-Tennessee line just east of Chattanooga.[4]

But that battle was not conclusive, so they decided to play a ballgame–an Indian ballgame called stickball, a forerunner of lacrosse–between the Creeks and the Cherokees to decide once and for all, where that boundary line in west Georgia was. The Cherokees won the ballgame, and the Creeks agreed to a permanent line between the two nations. However, the Cherokee word for ballgame meant "little brother of war," because they didn't play ball like they do today in lacrosse or baseball. They actually used those sticks to break bones. It was not unusual for two or three people to get killed in a ballgame. They would get wounded, maimed, killed. There were about twenty participants on each side. There were other ancient societies that settled disputes this way.

The early traders had come in before and married Cherokees. There were many whites who came in from the

155

late 1700s up until the 1830s who had come into North Georgia for various reasons. Gold was "discovered" in 1828 in Georgia. The Cherokee people by that time were not warriors, they were farmers. So whites just invaded the Cherokee country looking for gold. Once they got here, they didn't leave. That's what brought a lot of them in. When white men came as explorers, very few brought women or existing families. They were usually young, white adventurers from Ireland, Scotland, England or wherever. They married Native Americans and had mixed-blood children. The South is full of people of mixed blood. Our insurance commissioner for the state of Georgia [John Oxendine] who is running for governor is a member of the Lumbee Tribe over in North Carolina.[5]

There was plenty of land there, so the Cherokees welcomed them as neighbors, but the whites didn't want to be there as neighbors, they wanted the land for themselves. At the time of The Removal, the Cherokees were known as one of the five "civilized" tribes. They didn't call themselves that. The white government saw the Southeastern Indians as being progressive as they were. They had their own newspaper, their own laws, their own constitution. One of the things the Federal government wanted the Cherokees to do was to become as white as their white neighbors. In other words, adopt the white man's way of living. Many succeeded very well. Some of the Cherokees owned slaves. They had large plantations. The Vann House in Chatsworth is a good example. It's a mansion even by today's standards. It's a red brick building with white columns built by an area chief name James Vann, a wealthy man who owned 500 slaves. What they did in order to be accepted as part of the culture was they very quickly adopted the ways of the whites. They might have been too successful because they built beautiful farms and plantations.

One of the Ten Commandments states that thou shalt not covet. Well, Georgia and the surrounding whites saw how beautiful the Cherokee country, farms, and plantations were, and they wanted the land. The Indians had no rights, so the whites could literally steal the land. The Cherokees, in *The Cherokee Nation vs. the State of Georgia*, won the case in the U. S. Supreme Court. Their case was that Georgia was trying to encroach on their lands. The Supreme Court said the Cherokee is a sovereign nation, and Georgia has no claim to Indian lands. That was about 1830. Andrew Jackson was the President at the time.

You can liken it to the 1960s when the Civil Rights laws were passed. Schools and hospitals became desegregated. Prior to the 1960s "separate but equal" as ruled constitutional. After *Brown vs. the Board of Education*, the Supreme Court ruled that separate cannot be equal. That's after John Kennedy was assassinated and Johnson from Texas was the President. The Arkansas governor refused to integrate the schools, and President Johnson had to send federal troops to Arkansas to enforce the policy of allowing blacks into white high schools. It also happened in Alabama. Johnson had no choice but to carry out the ruling of the Supreme Court. When you take your oath of office as President, you will carry out the law of the land. When the Supreme Court rules, that is the law of the land. Well, the Cherokee Nation won their case, but Andrew Jackson basically told the Supreme Court to take a flying leap. He sent an army to the South and carried out the removal of the Cherokees contrary to the Supreme Court decision. The removal was not only illegal, it was immoral, unethical and criminal. One third of the people who were rounded up to be removed to Oklahoma died either in the holding camps or on the trail from Georgia to Oklahoma. One third of an entire nation of people died as a result of the horrendous treatment of the white government and the federal soldiers.

My ancestor was exempt from The Removal. My great-great-grandfather was white, and all families that had a white head of household were exempt from being removed. If you count North Georgia, Northeast Alabama, a portion of Tennessee and North Carolina, there were probably a thousand families that were exempt. From the time the gold was discovered in 1828, Georgia wanted the Cherokee land and outfitted marauding gangs of thugs referred to as Pony Club gangs. Georgia gave them the guns and horses. They had camps along the Cherokee's boundary line, the Chattahoochee River, and whatever. They would raid Cherokee country, rape women, shoot Indians at their pleasure, steal their cattle, burn their houses down. And that went on for a number of years. A lot of the Cherokees said it's not worth it and migrated west in 1815, 1816, 1817. They were referred to as the early settlers that went west. Then in 1838, when the rest of the tribe was removed, they went west as well. The early settlers had already set up a Cherokee government in the West. So, when the larger part of the Cherokees were removed and sent west, the early settlers said, "Y'all will have to come under our laws because we already have an established government." They didn't recognize the elected officials or John Ross as their chief anymore. There was almost a Cherokee Civil War. But John Ross's faction won and they built what we now know as Tahlequah, Oklahoma in Cherokee County.

Nathaniel Gist was a fur trader who came through the Cherokee country. Some traders didn't marry. They just met Cherokee, had children, and went on their way. Nobody knows what happened to him. He had son named George Gist. His Cherokee name was Sequoyah. He was half Cherokee, but was raised totally as a Cherokee. He saw how the whites could communicate with each other by sending messages on a piece of paper. He is the only man in known history who was totally illiterate, who developed a system of reading and writing which is referred to as the

Sequoyan [a.k.a., Cherokee] syllabary. The English alphabet uses one letter at a time. There were only 86 syllables in the Cherokee language, so he developed a letter representing a particular syllable of the Cherokee language. He worked on it for about five years. One of the reasons he developed it was so that Cherokees in the East could communicate with kinsmen in the West. They printed a bilingual newspaper in 1830, part English, part Cherokee. Sequoyah moved west to teach the system of reading and writing that he had developed to his kinsmen. The average Cherokee could learn to read and write in seven days. He spent the rest of his life traveling around the West, teaching. Many of the Cherokees didn't stop in Oklahoma. They went to Texas, and some went into Mexico. He died on the way from Texas to Oklahoma and is buried in an unmarked grave. Nobody knows where it is. The Sequoyah syllabary is still taught in the schools of the Eastern Band of Cherokee Indians in North Carolina and in Cherokee Nation in Oklahoma. They're starting it in pre-school, about two to three years old, so they can keep the language alive. I can converse in Cherokee and read some words, but you have to grow up being taught it.

Many came back East right after the forced removal to the north Georgia mountains. Georgia was so bad, they finally took refuge in North Carolina around Murphy and over toward Andersonville. There was a great Cherokee leader named Junaluska. There's a whole mountain range right across the Georgia line in North Carolina named for him.[6] The Eastern Band of Cherokee Indians in North Carolina are Georgia refugees.

William McIntosh was chief of the Creeks at the time of their forced removal. He had a plantation over in Carroll County on the Chattahoochee River. His first cousin was the governor of Georgia. So you had a mixture among the cultures going way back. By signing over all the Creek lands and allowing his people to be removed to Oklahoma, he was killed by his people. It was not murder. The Creek and Cherokee nations passed laws stating that any leader under any pretense who signed a document transferring Creek or Cherokee land was under penalty of death.[7] Many of the Cherokees who signed the 1835 removal treaty were killed when they got to Oklahoma in 1838.

The American Civil War almost split apart the Cherokee Nation in Oklahoma. A Cherokee general in Oklahoma was one of the last to surrender. Half of them sided with the North, and half sided with the South. Here, in the East, a white mountain lawyer named Will [William Holland] Thomas, who served as the Cherokee's legal counsel buying up lands, recruited a whole band of Cherokees known as Thomas' Legion to fight for the Confederacy. They stayed in the Southern mountains guarding the passes and valleys to keep the North from coming through. They were among the last group in the East to surrender during the Civil War. I had two great-grandfathers on the white side of my family who fought for the South at Gettysburg.

My great-great-grandfather, named Presley Jones and who was in his 70s, was killed in Covington by Sherman's troops when they left Atlanta and were going towards the sea. As the Federal troops were coming down the road, they ordered him, this old man, to pull his horse and wagon off the road to let them by. The Southerners were so proud that they weren't going to let a Yankee tell them to get off the road, and they just shot him dead.[8]

All of his sons were off to war, but he had a grandson who was on the wagon with him as well as a little black boy. They carried him back home to Oxford, right next to Covington. Back then, you didn't have funeral homes. General stores sold caskets, but when the Federal army came through, they confiscated all the lumberyards and things like caskets for their own troops. The boy, who was about ten years old, wasn't going to put his granddaddy in the ground without having a coffin. He tried to get wood at the lumberyard, but it had already been confiscated, so he tried to sneak in that night after dark to get enough boards to carry home. He was caught by Federal troops, and the next morning they were going to hang him right there in the lumberyard because this was done under Martial Law. There was no trial, and he was considered a thief even though they stole the lumberyard from the owner. A Yankee captain drove by and saw that they were going to hang this ten-year-old boy, and he asked the troops why. They said, "He was stealing government property." The captain went up to the boy and said, "Son, why did you need this lumber?" And he told the story about how the day before the troops killed his granddaddy and that he was the only male at home, and it was up to him to bury his grandfather. Well, it touched the captain so much that he ordered them to release the boy and have the Yankee carpenters build a coffin for my great-great grandfather, dig the grave, and assist in the burial of the old man. The captain also had a sign painted and nailed to an oak tree in front of the house stating, "This home and family is under the person protection of Captain so-and-so." I once saw the sign myself, but I don't know whatever happened to it. The grave is in the Oxford cemetery.

When my father was coming up, you didn't even declare yourself as being Cherokee. Georgia, and all the Southeastern states treated Indians the same way they did Negroes. The same laws that applied to Negroes applied to Indians. Georgia passed many laws against Cherokees–no Indians could own land, they could not vote, they were considered colored people and therefore, could not go to white schools or white hospitals. It wasn't until 1947 that Georgia recognized its Cherokee descendants and removed many of the laws, though they weren't enforced for at least 40 or 50 years. So, it was not "cool" to be recognized as Indian. Urban legends came about because if you were a little darker complexion, you'd say "Our people were Black Dutch or Black Irish." There were no Negroes in Holland or Ireland. But when you're dealing with ignorant whites who didn't know that much about the various peoples of Europe, you could pass with a dark complexion as long as you weren't Negro or Indian. It was only during the 1960s, during the Hippy Movement, when they rebelled against everything that many claimed to be Native American, but they weren't. If they were late for work, they'd say, "I'm Native American. I don't live on white man's time, I live on Indian time." Well, that's insulting to people of Native American descent. But it was cool to play Indian, and a lot of thieves came along. People actually started up fake Indian groups and would print up cards. One claimed to represent the Southeastern Cherokee Confederacy. Some of them got seats at various colleges and universities that were reserved for truly minority people. Any time there is a buck to be made, a con man will come out from under a rock. They apply for grants, and many have been very successful. We work with the Cherokee Nation and the Eastern Band to expose these fake groups. We have a website, www.cherokeefraud.com, and we name some of these people.

When I was in my late teens, you could go squirrel hunting in Dekalb County and drink out of any creek. You didn't need bottled water. Now, almost every stream is polluted from one source or another. It's not necessarily my Native American heritage that makes me want to scream out. Seeing what has been spoiled over the years by urban sprawl makes most people of my age unhappy.

NOTES

[1]Lucian Lamar Knight was an editor for the *Atlanta Constitution* and was the Georgia Archives' founder and first director.

[2] "Short, slight and reserved, he wore a suit and tie instead of deerskin leggings and a beaver-skin hat.... his mother and grandmother raised him in a traditional household, teaching him the tribe's customs and legends.... After his mother died in 1808, Ross worked at his grandfather's trading post near present-day Chattanooga, an important way station on the road to the West." Brian Hicks, "The Cherokees vs. Andrew Jackson," *Smithsonian* magazine, March 2011, 51.

[3] "These were the Indians known to the Charles Town traders as the Ochese Creek who had migrated eastward to take advantage of the superior trading opportunities afforded by the South Carolinians. Crane has argued and John R. Swanton agreed that Ochese Creek was the early name for the Ocmulgee River. The tribal name 'Creek,' the same authorities agree, developed from the habitual shortening of the term 'Ochese Creek Indians.'" Harvey H. Jackson and Phinizy Spalding, eds., *Oglethorpe in Perspective: Georgia's Founder After Two Hundred Years* (Tuscaloosa: The University of Alabama Press, 1989), 198.

[4] "Also present at the Treaty of Hopewell was the war woman of Chota, Nancy Ward. Her bravery in battle against the Creek Indians years earlier had earned her the title of Ghighau, or Beloved Woman. Respected women were often allowed into the predominately male Cherokee council house. These women played important roles in the tribe and could at times override the authority of the mail council." Vicki Rozema, *Cherokee Voices: Early Accounts of Cherokee Life in the East* (Winston-Salem: John F. Blair, Publisher, 2002), 74.

[5] "The Lumbee are the present-day descendants of the Cheraw Tribe and have continuously existed in and around Robeson County since the early part of the eighteenth century." http://www.lumbeetribe.com/History_Culture/History_Culture%20Index.html, accessed March 4, 2011.

[6] During the 1814 Battle of Horseshoe Bend, in which forces under Andrew Jackson and Cherokees attacked a Red Stick faction of

163

the Creek Indians, Junaluska "saved Andrew Jackson from an attacker, prompting the Tennessean to declare, 'As long as the sun shines and the grass grows, there shall be friendship between us.' But in the peace treaty he negotiated with the Creeks, Jackson confiscated 23 million acres of land...some of which belonged to the Cherokees." Hicks, *Smithsonian*, March 2011, 52-53.

[7] "Just before dawn on April 30, 1825, Upper Creek chief Menawa, accompanied by 200 Creek warriors, attacked McIntosh at Lockchau Talofau to carry out the sentence. They set fire to his home, and shot and stabbed to death McIntosh and the elderly Coweta chief Etomme Tustunnuggee." New Georgia Encyclopedia, http://www.georgiaencyclopedia.org/nge/Article.jsp?id=h-3541&hl=y, accessed March 4, 2011.

[8] This incident was recorded in a diary by Dolly Burge, a northern widower who inherited a Southern plantation near Covington, Georgia. On July 24, 1864 she details a Union Army raid: "They cruelly shot a George Daniels and a Mr. Jones of Covington, destroyed a great deal of private property, and took many citizens prisoners." Dolly Sumner Lunt Burge, *A Woman's Wartime Journal: An Account of the Passage Over a Georgia Plantation of Sherman's Army on the March to the Sea, as Recorded in the Diary of Dolly Sumner Lunt (Mrs. Thomas Burge)* (Atlanta: Cherokee Publishing Company, 1994), 20.

Claryce Sutton Strother

Claryce Strother grew up in a time when meeting a real "Yankee" was a rare event for some Southerners. She describes what it was like growing up on the coast during the 1930s and '40s. Her husband's store, J. C. Strother Co., is located in the heart of the village on St. Simons. More than an icon, it is one of the oldest family owned and operated businesses in the state. She also discusses an incident from her days as a teacher that still weighs on her conscience.

Claryce Strother. Photograph by Chris Johnson.

My name is Claryce Sutton Strother. I was born November 27, 1927 at home, 1615 Macon Avenue in the Urbana[1] section of Brunswick, right behind the Hadley Brown home, which is now the Chamber of Commerce. My maiden name was Claryce Sutton. I didn't have a middle name, so I just used Sutton. My sister, Rosalie,

165

made up her middle name–Catherine. My father was Leslie Gordon Sutton. He had the Royal Crown Cola bottling company in Brunswick. There was a cola war going on at that time. Coca-Cola and Dr. Pepper were the two other bottling companies. The bottling plant was at the end of Gloucester on the block where the Brunswick library is now. When my daddy sold it, the man who bought it wasn't really able to look after it, so it sort of went to the dogs.

We used to play with the Brown children and would all go down to the creek to the swimming hole. They had a nice dock down there. It was located beyond where the Lanier's Oak is, directly into the marsh. I don't believe that's the original Sidney Lanier Oak. They just move the sign from one oak to the next [laughs]. Highway 17 was just a two-lane road. We used to swim in that little hole that is now covered up by Highway 17.

Helen Keller stands beside Lanier's Oak which inspired some of the poems written by Sidney Lanier in the 1870s. The Marshes of Glynn are in the background. Vanishing Georgia, Georgia Archives, Office of Secretary of State.

166

I lived in Urbana until I was ten, and then we moved over to Windsor Park, 1414 Palmetto Avenue. It's the third lot off of Glynn Avenue. The house was built in 1938. Windsor Park had been a golf course and was *the* new neighborhood. I went to the old Prep High building on the Glynn Academy High School campus for the first two grades. Then they built Sidney Lanier Elementary, and I went there through the sixth grade. Seventh and eighth grades were at the old Prep High building, then I went to high school there at Glynn Academy. There was the old Glynn Academy building, the Annex, and the gym. The principal was Sidney Boswell. Miss Beulah Lott taught geometry and trig. Miss Tracy taught algebra. She liked the boys, but she didn't like the girls, and I was dumb in algebra. Miss Jane Macon taught English. She was sort of the boss of the school. She was very straight-laced and wanted us to behave ourselves, and we did. Everybody was in awe of her, and I guess that's why they named Jane Macon Elementary School after her.

The local high school girls used to go over to St. Simons when we were growing up in the '40s. A lot of boys were there, and we danced with the sailors. Somehow or the other, Billy Strother would find me every time I'd come over. Billy and I knew each other in the sixth grade. He had a brother named JC, Jr. who was killed during World War II on Normandy Beach in 1944. Billy was too young to join the military. They didn't take the only surviving son from a family, so when JC, Jr. was killed, Billy didn't have to go.

In the summertime, we hung around the Howard Coffin [recreation] Park. I lifeguarded at that pool a couple of summers. Every time they came to teach the lifeguard class, I'd take it again. Also, during the summer we'd go to the Casino and dance there at night. They had a jukebox, too. The thing that impressed me so much, was that there were all ages of people–granddaddies dancing with grandchildren. That was such a wonderful neighborly thing going on. They had a big skating rink down around the pier. People used to skate to music, and you sort of danced on skates. In that same area, the Cofer family had a bar with a jukebox and dance floor that extended out over the water. At that time, the Navy boys hung out over there, and one of my friends married one. I remember being anxious to see a Yankee. I had never seen a one before, and the one I zeroed in on was Peggy Wilson. The Wilsons had a yacht yard on Mackay River. She had a brother named John.

Claryce Strother, 1945 high school graduation photograph.

During World War II, we'd also go to dances at the Oglethorpe Hotel. There used to be a train station right behind the hotel. Our wedding reception was there in the ballroom. Back in those days, you just spoke to everybody, drank a little punch, and ate petits fours.

The Oglethorpe Hotel, Brunswick, Georgia. Designed by Stanford White and built in 1886. Formerly ranked with the best hotels on the Continent. One block long. Historic Postcard Collection, RG 48-2-5, Georgia Archives.

I went to GSCW, Georgia State College for Women, in Milledgeville. That now is Georgia College. It was an all girls' school at that time. I had planned to transfer to the University of Georgia my junior year, but I was so involved and had all my friends there, and decided to stay and graduate from GSCW. I was studying Distributive Education, which was sort of like marketing, preparing for retail management. I worked one summer at Gordon's Department Store on the corner of Newcastle and Gloucester in Brunswick. I didn't really want to be in business, but couldn't think of anything else I wanted to do. I had my eye set on Billy Strother. I just wanted to marry him [laughs].

After college, I came back to Brunswick and taught third grade at Arco Elementary School at the end of Newcastle Street where they had the refinery[2], and waited on my husband to finish college, and then we married in the First Baptist Church in Brunswick. It was across the street from where the current one is. For our honeymoon, we drove to the north Georgia mountains.

Learning to Teach

I had prepared to go into retail and fashion. Mr. Boswell, then the superintendent of education, was desperate for a teacher and talked me into it. We lived on Seabreeze Drive, across from the St. Simons Elementary School. It was a dirt street. Teaching was not what I had prepared to do. During my first year, one of my little boys kicked me. Mrs. L---, the principal, found out about it, and she made me spank him with a big ol' wooden paddle that had holes bored in it. And this little kid was so meek and mild. He did not deserve a spanking. So, I gave him one hit, and she motioned for me to keep going. I bet you to this day, that child still bears the scars of that paddling. It is still on my heart to try to find that kid and apologize. I had never spanked anybody. I didn't know how to do that. His name was Tommy. I'm not sure now what his last name was. There was another little boy, Tommy Thomas, who was a hell-raiser, but I made a buddy out of him. My sister suggested that, because she had taught school, and she said, "Just have him be your special helper." So, when he arrived in the mornings, I'd say, "Oh, Thomas, I'm so glad you're here. You can help me do so-and-so," like no one else was capable. He was just an angel after that.

The Business of Doing Business

My husband was the son of JC [John Carl] Strother, who started the hardware store in St. Simons. JC came from Metter, Georgia. He opened the hardware store in 1928. He built it in the village across the street, catty-corner, from where it is now–closer to the pier. He originally came to build a seawall on St. Simons.

Strother Hardware store. St. Simons Island village.

The King & Prince hotel was a naval station during World War II. They needed housing during World War II for liberty shipyard workers and Navy personnel, so JC built Oglethorpe Park.[3] He bought a tract of Wesley Oaks over to Vassar Point for five thousand dollars and built the houses. He called it Oglethorpe Park because [James] Oglethorpe was so well known and, too, there is Oglethorpe's trail that runs north-to-south through the property.[4] My house is the last house on the right at Oglethorpe Park. During Hurricane Dora in 1964, we evacuated to Swainsboro because we had relatives there. The motel we stayed in was called the Tick-Tock. I just thought it was wonderful. We had a great time at the hurricane party. When we came home, we had about ten pine trees down. Our house was on the marsh, so we got a lot of wind. The water came up in our yard but not into the house. Oglethorpe is on high ground. When you first come into the entrance, you're on a rise.

Once other builders came to the island, JC stopped house construction because being in the lumber business, we didn't want to compete. That's really not kosher to compete with your customers. So we went into the building

171

supply business instead. He worked at the hardware store all of his life. It's been in business since 1928 because our prices are competitive and we provide good service. It's one of the oldest businesses in Georgia run by the same family.

Cassina Garden Club

I was a member of the Cassina Garden Club, but when my children got in school, I got out because the club met at three in the afternoon. The Cassina Club studied horticulture and the history of the area. The club maintained the slave cabins on Gascoigne Bluff. They're still doing that. It's their big project.[5]

Slave cabins at Gascoigne Bluff. Photograph courtesy of Jonathan Doster.

A group of us started Cotillion in 1954. Our purpose was to have two formal dances a year. Practically everybody on St. Simons belonged to it. The dances were held at the King & Prince Hotel out on the Oleander Patio. It had a bandstand. The purpose was to have big bands. There was no TV, and we didn't have the opportunity to see the big bands. We had Sammy Kaye and bands like that. Now, it's disintegrated into a cookout thing over at Rainbow Island, near the entrance to Sea Island in the spring. We're having a Night In Paris this coming Saturday [February]. Gloria Olsen and I are the two charter members who are still active.

NOTES

[1] Named for Urbanus Dart, who once owned large tracts of land in Brunswick.

[2] Arco is a neighborhood located north of downtown Brunswick established near the Atlantic Richfield Company (ARCO) refinery.

[3] "...professional archaeologists were digging Saturday at St. Simons' Oglethorpe Park, looking for traces of a Native American culture called the Swift Creek. They were an elusive community that lived on St. Simons between A.D. 500 and 800. Archaeologists recognize the culture by the elaborate paddle-stamped ceramics they made.... team archaeologist Fred Cook...thinks a large portion of Swift Creek remains lie in the yards of the homes nearby. The ancient village likely followed along a high ridgeline that runs through the neighborhood today."
Carole Hawkins, Times-Union, May 25, 2008. Jacksonville, Florida, http://www.jacksonville.com/tu-online/stories/052508/geo_282629455.shtml, accessed March 19, 2011.

[4] James Edward Oglethorpe, Georgia's founder, constructed a "Military Road" that ran from Fort Frederica, located on the west side of the island, to Fort St. Simons located on the south end. Part of the road runs through Oglethorpe Park.

[5] The slave cabins were part of James Hamilton's plantation and were later part of the Hilton-Dodge Lumber Company's operations. The cabins were listed on the National Register of Historic Places in 1988.

Victor Lewis Waters

Vic Waters was raised knee-deep in the rich cultural and musical influences of coastal Georgia. He set out to make his mark on the music world in the 1960s and has enjoyed a long and interesting ride. Vic and his bands shared the stage with top performers of the day and once toured with James Brown. In this narrative, he talks about race relations in the 1950s and '60s and what it's like traveling America with a 12-piece band. When "the road" finally got to him, Vic returned home, where he resumed a musical career on a smaller scale. In addition to his ability to weave stories in song, Vic is an author.

Photograph by Bobby Haven.

My name is Victor Lewis Waters. I was born April 27, 1944 in Reidsville, Georgia. We moved here to Crescent, actually Belleville Bluff, when I was ten weeks old. My parents were R. S. Waters and Rudine Waters. My dad was from Glennville, and my mom was from Surrency, over by Baxley. My dad was never in my life. The reason we came here is because my grandma, my mother's mother, was at Belleville Bluff. She was a cook at Roscoe's Place, a restaurant that also rented rooms and outboard motor boats. It was a fishing camp located where Pelican's Point restaurant is now at the end of Sapelo Drive. It was a great big ol' white, two-story building with a restaurant and a big dance hall downstairs. They had square dances sometimes on the weekends. A little country band came over from Brunswick.

My mom and my aunts were the waitresses, and we all lived in that place. I lived there until first grade when me moved up the road about two hundred yards. My grandma had bought a house in 1945 at the end of World War II. She paid $100 apiece for the two lots it sat on, and the house cost $800. It was an Army barracks at Camp Stewart [Fort Stewart Military Reservation]. She paid $90 to move it from Hinesville down to here. She still worked down the street at Roscoe's. In 1955 or '56, the Barnett family bought it from Roscoe Norman and changed the name to the Sandpiper Inn. In 1964, it burned to the ground.

Roscoe owned all the property from Roscoe's Place, which is the point of Belleville Bluff, all the way up past the Buccaneer [the Buccaneer Club, a restaurant] at the end of White Bluff, which is about a half mile along the river there. He sold the lots on the riverside for $250 apiece, and the ones across the road cost $100 per lot. I bought my house on the river for $50,000 in 1977. It would appraise for half-a-million dollars now, not because my house is so cool, but because of the land it's sitting on. I've got deep water at low tide. There are shrimp boats seventy-five feet long tied up behind my house. You can leave my house and go anywhere in the world at low tide. Anytime you can to do that, the rent's going to go up. My next-door neighbors are asking $800,000 for their houses. By the way, they are still $50,000 houses.

You can try to teach a kid how to play piano by giving him lessons, but if you don't have a piano in your house, that's just a waste of effort. There was always a piano in my house and always a guitar leaning up against the wall, so I just always had played music. You walk by and someone is showing you how to make a chord. My mom had me take piano lessons, but I wasn't learning anything. My best friend, Hunter Forsyth could play amazingly well. He'd say, "No, man, put your fingers here and go do-dee-do-dee-do-dee-do-dee-do." Boogie-woogie. And I thought, *This is fun if you do it this way. Don't teach me how to play, show me how.* Forsyth now lives right here in Valona, five miles from my house. He's in the shrimp fishing industry. He and his wife, Suzanne, are "aristo-crackers." They have direct lineage from the French who settled here years and years ago. He's got fingers just about as big around as a bratwurst. It's a wonder they can fit between the keys, but he can play angelic music–Chopin, Beethoven–believe it.

When I was growing up, we didn't have race problems at all. I lived in Belleville Bluff, right here in Crescent, where seventy-five percent of the people were black, and I was the minority. However, when I was a little kid, eight or nine years old, Mr. Jeff Baker [African-American], who was about seventy, called me, "Mr. Vic." He said, "Yes, sir," and "No, sir," to me and every white person. Looking back over that I think, "God, that was so wrong." I'm embarrassed by it and feel weird about it, but that was the way he was brought up. He owned the only dump truck around here. Every time somebody had trash to haul off, they'd call Jeff Baker. Nowadays, around here, every time we have an election, it's just a black/white issue. You have a black candidate and a white candidate. The black people vote for the black one, and the white people vote for the white one. It ain't the right way to be, but that's the way it's evolved.

I went to school here in Darien through the eighth grade, then went to Benedictine Military School [BC] in Savannah. I tell people I thought I was going to acting school because my mother jabbed me in the chest with her little bony finger and said, "It's about time for you to learn how to act." I lived with my aunt and uncle up there because BC didn't have a dormitory facility.

The first night I ever sang in my life was when I was in a band called The Emeralds in Savannah, during high school. We were playing at the Desoto Hotel. It wasn't called the Desoto Hilton then. It was for the Georgian Ball, a big ball for fraternities and sororities. Our singer got in a car wreck. It was an hour late getting started. Finally, we got a phone call saying he wasn't going to make it. So they said, "You sing." I didn't want to, but I did. The first song I sang was "Brown-Eyed Handsome Man," by Chuck Berry. We sounded like two cats fighting in a dipsy-dumpster, but we thought it was great. I never was into that Elvis thing. I was more into that rhythm and blues. I liked all the black singers.

We were taught by Benedictine monks who came out of Belmont Abbey [College]. We were never sexually assaulted, but we got our ass beat on a regular basis if you messed up. The head disciplinarian was Father Alquin. He walked around with a drumstick up the sleeve of his habit. If you got out of control, he'd slap you across the back of the head with it. Father Bede Lightner was the principal. I was the high school drum major since I was the tallest guy at six-three. So I carried the mace and led the band. We were coming back from Forsyth Park, where we went for close-order drill one day, and rolled off on a peppy song. I started dancing around in the street like one of the drum majors from Beach High. Father Bede was standing on the front porch of the rectory and saw me. He came flying across the campus with his robes and habit flying. He ran up and said, "Waters, you blankety-blank S-O-B!" He drew back and just popped me right in the mouth. But we didn't have any problem with discipline there. You got in trouble, you got your butt whipped.

They used to give us a smoke break at ten o'clock in the morning and one o'clock in the afternoon. We'd go stand outside the classroom and smoke cigarettes like they wouldn't hurt you. Here I was in the 9th grade, smoking Winstons. And the teachers would be standing there smoking right alongside of you. Nobody told us that later on in life our lungs were going to be parched. To tell the truth, I liked all of my teachers. You just had to do what you had to do. We had two civilian teachers. The Spanish teacher was Orlando Diaz, from Cuba. Charlie Moore was my algebra teacher. He graduated from Benedictine and was one heck of an athlete and is in the Savannah sports hall-of-fame. He was only about five or six years older than me. We all wanted to call him Charlie. He said, "You can call me 'Coach,' or 'Mr. Moore,' but none of this 'Charlie' stuff." We'd go, "Okay, Charlie." Father Bede later on got married and dropped out of the priesthood. Then his wife died of cancer, and he went back into the priesthood.

When I first became a young adult coming home from high school to see my mom every Sunday afternoon, my buddies and I would go riding around with a cooler full of beer. If you got stopped by the law, they would just take you home and tell you, "Boy, don't you get back in that car until you sober up. Now, behave yourself." Nowadays, they'll take you straight to the cage, which is good. We don't need people out there drinking and driving. We thought we were cool, but in reality, we were just blithering idiots.

179

The Benedictine Class of '62, what's left of us, meets every St. Patrick's Day at eight o'clock in the morning in front of Pinkie Masters Tavern in Savannah, which is right around the corner from the Cathedral of St. John the Baptist. We have this thing called "Benedictine Survivors." There was a camaraderie that came with going through that Benedictine system that is like no other I've ever experienced. The survivors meet the first Tuesday of every month at Johnny Harris' Restaurant to have lunch. It's just like we were back in the eleventh grade. That's for anyone who went to the old school, not just the class of '62. The Benedictine I went to was on Bull and 34th Street. It was connected to Sacred Heart Church in downtown Savannah. In 1965, they built a new school off of Eisenhower Boulevard. All the new boys from that school aren't part of the "Survivors." They wear khakis and golf shirts for uniforms now. Back then, we wore those grey wool West Point uniforms every day.

When I got out of there, I went down to St. Petersburg, Florida to be in a band. Bobby Barnes graduated from Benedictine in 1960 and went back to St. Pete where his family was. He called me up and said they needed a piano player. The day after I graduated, I was off and stayed on the road until I was 30 years old. The band was The Impacs. That was 1962. When I first started out, I was the piano player. I started doing a song here and a song there. First thing you know, I was doing all the singing because the singer had quit. Then I stopped playing piano and became the front man. Just singing and dancing.

Bobby Barnes, who played drums, came up with the band name. We'd gone through every single name for a band that you can think of to try to sound cool. One day we were practicing over at Bobby's house in his daddy's garage. Bobby was changing the oil in his car, and he had a can of Impact motor oil in his hand. He said, "How 'bout the Impact Motor Oils?" Just being a wise guy. This other guy said, "You drop that 'Motor Oil,' and 'The Impacts' don't sound too bad." And a little bell kind of went *ding*! Everybody said, "That's it!" But it was spelled I-M-P-A-C-T. Someone said, "We ought to call it The Impacks, with a 'k.'" But we just made it The Impacs.

We were on King Records first. That was James Brown record label, which Syd Nathan owned. We cut two albums that were out on the national market. One was called *Impact! by the Impacs*, and the other was called *A Week-End With The Impacs*. We were out on the road then with Dick Clark and the Caravan of Stars. It was us and the Dovells, Lou Christie, Gene Pitney, and Brian Hyland who sang, "Itsy Bitsy Teenie Weenie Yellow Polka Dot Bikini." We traveled with Dick Clark for a whole summer. It was another one of those bus deals, man. Everybody on the bus, except, of course, Dick Clark. He would fly in and introduce the bands. That was in 1965. East coast and out to Texas.

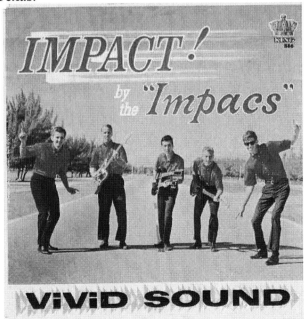

Image courtesy of Vic Waters.

I had only been in the Impacs for a couple of months when we were booked to do a show with Roy Orbison. I was stoked because he was one of my favorites and a big, big star. We rehearsed for a week, just learning his material. I was always so impressed with his powerful voice. The thing that amazed me most about him, was the control he had over his voice. It sounded as if he was pushing his pipes to the max, when in reality he was singing so easy we had to turn the PA system up to the point of almost feeding back. He was a master of vocal control. I've never seen anybody since then that could do that. When he hit the high notes at the end of "Leah" or "Crying" it sounded like the windows were going to break.

We wore suits, man, and spent most of our money on them. We had a manager named Jay Angelo whose son played guitar in our band. Jay was in the car business in St. Petersburg. He ran a Ford Motor dealership down there, and everybody in the band drove brand new Fords. We bought a lot of clothes at Arnold's Menswear, a downtown store where you could buy a purple tuxedo. That's where we bought most of our clothes. Then, when we were in Chicago, we came across a clothing store up there called QueTiki that specialized in show biz clothes and bought these tuxedos. They had them in every color. We'd wear a purple suit the first show and maybe a really bright blue suit the second show. It was way after the Beatles came along that bands started dressing however they wanted to with jeans and T-shirts. When you got to a town you were going to be in for a day or so, you'd take your suits to a laundry and get them all done at one time. The manager we had took money out of our checks for the uniforms. He got 10% right off the top for being our manager, then another 15% came off for uniforms and equipment, because you were always breaking a PA system or blowing a speaker. You had to have a little slush fund. But he always treated us good and never ripped us off that I know of. He was so into making his son a star that he did everything he could. He's the one who got us on King Records. At the time, we were the only white act on King Records. They had James Brown, B. B. King, Hank Ballard and the Midnighters, and Little Eva.

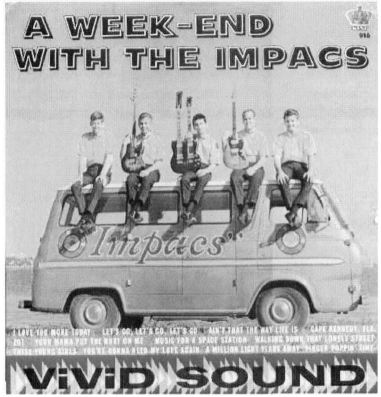

Image courtesy of Vic Waters.

I left the Impacs when they decided to turn more toward the "British explosion." I joined a group from Athens, Tennessee, called the Big Brothers. I was still into the R&B thing and just couldn't see changing my whole style of doing things. Soon after I joined the Big Brothers, we left for Manhattan.

It was the time of my life. I turned 21 years old playing with the Big Brothers at the Peppermint Lounge in New

York City on 45th and Broadway. I had my first legal cocktail, a Vodka Collins. You know–"Give me something tough." [Laughs] That was during "The Twist" days. The Peppermint Lounge was the home of the twist. We also played next door at the Wagon Wheel Lounge. We played at the Roundtable. All of this was in Manhattan. We stayed up there one time for an eight-week stretch. I put my brand new Ford Excel 500 in a garage because you can't find a parking place in New York, so I had it in storage. I went back over there. Somebody had broken into it and stole my radio, battery, my cool spinner hubcaps, stole all my stuff. When we played the Peppermint Lounge, we had to do five shows a night. We started at nine o'clock at night and didn't get off until six o'clock in the morning. There were three bands on the show. We'd come out and play our set. Then band number 2 would play, then band number 3 would play, then we'd come back on and play another set. By the time you do your five thirty-five to forty minute sets, it's daylight. The crowd would change over all the time. It was two doors down from the Ed Sullivan Theatre where David Letterman is today.

I got my draft notice two weeks before I was to be married. I took my case to the draft board and got a 90-day deferment. During that time, I enlisted in the Army Reserves where I spent the next six years. Our musical career went to hell during those years. I did basic training at Fort Benning, Georgia and my AIT, Advanced Infantry Training, at Fort Gordon, Georgia. I was in the MPs–the 317 MPs [317th Military Police Battalion]. They activated the 503rd MPs out of Fort Bragg, North Carolina, so they sent my whole battalion up to Fort Bragg. I spent the rest of my time in Fayetteville, North Carolina directing traffic. Everybody else was going to Viet Nam. I was the luckiest SOB in the world. Every day, our CO [Commanding Officer] or First Sergeant would say, "Any day, boys, we're going to be mustering up and going to Saigon." Every day,

I'd wake up and think, *Oh, Jesus, today is going to be the day.* First thing you know, eighteen months had gone by, and I was a short-timer still in Fort Bragg.

When I got out of the Army, we put together a band called The Entertainers, a big twelve-piece show band with seven horns and a five-piece rhythm section. It was actually two bands—the Impacs and a band from Roanoke, Virginia called the Spinners, not the R&B guys but a rock-and-roll band. Those guys were cool, man. They'd switch instruments after each song. The guitar player would go to bass, the bass player would go to organ, the organ player would start playing saxophone, then at the end of that song, they'd switch instruments again. But the guys weren't making any money. So our drummer, Bobby Barnes, and I went to them and said, "Why don't we merge these two bands and make one big powerhouse band?" And they could all sing, too. We put that band together and started getting a lot of attention in the Florida area. We couldn't think of a good band name. Some guy at a club said, "Boy, you guys are really good entertainers." I was against the name—Vic Waters and the Entertainers. It sounded like we had a really big ego—like, we were THE entertainers. But it stuck. Then, we broke out and started doing the Dallas, Vegas, and New York thing. By the time we got to Vegas, I left the band and headed home.

Vic Waters and The Entertainers. Images courtesy of Vic Waters.

Muscle Shoals was the spot where Aretha Franklin, Wilson Pickett, Sam and Dave came from or came to. Well, all the musicians behind those black artists were white guys. Rick Hall, David Hood, Jim Keltner, Duane Allman. It was black people singing it, but the soundtrack was made by white boys. They'd bring in black artists to do the singing. Most all the black musicians out there were either doing blues or jazz. Dan Penn was from Sheffield, Alabama, near Muscle Shoals. He and Rick Hall, David Briggs, and Mike Leach put that Muscle Shoals sound together. A lot of them moved over to Memphis because it was a bigger city. There weren't many black venues then. The races were separated. We did play a few black clubs.

They'd be like, "Look at these white boys playing this music." Because a lot of the people in the audience weren't aware that Aretha Franklin's band on the records were white boys.

When we recorded in Memphis, it was with American Studios. When we recorded with King Records, it was in Cincinnati. Some people wrote that the Impacs were going to be the next Beach Boys. We thought we were cool. We were just kids. We thought any day now, they were going to start bringing the money to the house in wheelbarrows. Like I said, Syd Nathan owned King Records. A lot of people considered him the father of the R&B movement because he had James Brown and Freddie King on his label. About the time we were there, there was a big payola scandal. They put all these DJs in jail for accepting money. Alan Freed got busted. Dick Clark even got investigated. Come to find out that Syd Nathan blew the whistle on them to a federal grand jury. It got to where no DJ in the country would play a King record. They'd just throw it in the trash. And you couldn't blame them. So, we finally got out of that contract and went with Capitol Records.

We recorded original songs and wrote most of the Impacs songs. With the Entertainers, we did a cut called "Taking Inventory" by Eddie Floyd who wrote "Knock on Wood," and "The Greatest Love," by Joe South who wrote all of those Billy Joe Royal tunes. I played piano with Billy Joe Royal in Savannah in a club called the Bamboo Ranch back when I was in high school. Buddy Livingston was a bass player who owned the club.

We worked with James Brown and all kinds of different people. The Entertainers had a manager and a booking agent named Hugh Rogers who booked us in Atlanta at a place called James Brown's Soul City Ballroom out on Cheshire Bridge Road. It was big joint that seated about a thousand people. Billy Watson, James's partner who later owned a chain of clubs in Atlanta called "Billy's," owned most of that business. He paid James Brown a royalty to use his name on the marquee. James would do so many gigs a year at Soul City. My band had been hired to come up there and do our show, but we were also backing up this chick named Marva Whitney, one of James's protégés. She had three ladies who played violins. She was doing Barbara Streisand music.

The first time I met James Brown was backstage at Soul City. It was me and all of my band, part of his band, and Marva. I said, "Hey James, if Marva wants to do any of the songs I'm doing in my show, I'll just drop them out and let her do them." Because I was doing a lot of cover tunes–R&B, Wilson Pickett stuff. He was only about five-foot-five, a little short guy. He pointed up at me and said, "Hey! You don't call me 'James.' You call me '*Mister* Brown.'" He started snapping his fingers. "And I'll call you…What's your name?" I said, "Vic Waters." He said, "I'll call you 'Mister Waters.'" I mean, he called me down in front of my band. Embarrassed me to death. He's got all these bodyguards, and I'm thinking to myself, *Man, if we were in Crescent, Georgia, you wouldn't talk to me this way.* So, we went out and did our show.

We had a smoking band. Matter of fact, Maceo Parker left his band and came and played with my band for a while. He was a lead alto-sax man who's won a bunch of Grammys in the jazz field. When I first met James, he was so into this blackness, and I was just like an employee. "Hey, boy. Time to go on stage." One night, I was coming off the stage and James Brown says, [imitating Brown] "Vic, we got off on a bad foot. We need to get on the good foot. Just call me James. I'll call you Vic."

Vic Waters backstage with James Brown. Image courtesy of Vic Waters.

We toured with him that summer. He flew everywhere. He had his own Learjet even back in those days. But his band and my band were on that stinking bus full of sardine cans and Vienna sausages. It smelled like a cross between sardines and pomade [laughs]. We did Atlanta three or four different times and Fort Lauderdale, Florida. James cut this song called, "Say It Loud, I'm Black And I'm Proud." This was when they used to have answers to songs. Usually a guy would put out a song like "Save The Last Dance For Me," and a girl would put out an answer like, "I'll Save The Last Dance For You." We were going to American Studios in Memphis to record. We were with Capitol and Crazy Horse Records. Dan Penn suggested that I write an answer to "Say it Loud." I wrote a song in the car on the way to Memphis called, "I'm White, And I'm All Right." At that particular time, they were having race riots all over the country. They were burning down Watts, burning

Detroit, burning Fort Lauderdale, and burning Chicago. It was a horrible time.

So we started doing these gigs called the Mayor's Youth Opportunity Council, where we would go in with his band and my band, and we'd play these songs to try and get the black kids and the white kids to stop hitting each other in the heads with sticks and stones. We went down to Fort Lauderdale where they had just about burnt half the city, and we did this thing for the Mayor's Youth Opportunity Council, a big concert at the War Memorial Auditorium. James came out and did, "Say It Loud, I'm Black And I'm Proud," then we came out and sang, "I'm White And I'm All Right." Lavern Baker was on the show. She and I did this thing–when I look back, it was really corny–but she'd put on a white glove, and I'd put on a black glove. Lavern would step up, hold that white glove up, and say, "A great American, John F. Kennedy said, 'Ask not what your country can do for you. Ask what you can do for your country.'" Then I'd step out on the stage and hold that black glove up and, "And look what George Washington Carver did with one little peanut." Then she would quote another white American, and I'd quote Martin Luther King. Then the spotlight would hit the middle of the stage, and we'd walk toward each other and put those two hands together in a soul brother handshake. The crowd would go crazy, and everyone would say, "It's going to be so wonderful." We'd close the show, and they'd go burn another building.

Vic Waters onstage with James Brown. Photograph courtesy of Vic Waters.

"I'm White and I'm All Right" charted at the lower 100, but that song title scared everybody off. When the DJs read the title, it reeked of racism. But it wasn't. It just said that you don't have to be black to have soul. You can go on YouTube and play it. We had a record Joe South wrote called "The Greatest Love." We put it out, and it was doing really well, then Billy Joe Royal put his version out, and his record charted higher. Back before that, around 1963, the Impacs had a record on Cameo-Parkway Records out of Philadelphia called, "I'm Going To Make You Cry." It got up to sixty-something on the charts. The records charted high enough to keep us working.

James could have been a baseball player. He played a little semi-pro ball for the East Augusta Rockets, and he was semi-pro prizefighter in the lightweight division. He was only 5' 5" and weighed about 125 pounds back when he was a skinny little dude. If it hadn't been for James Brown, I wouldn't have had a career, because our band was

191

doing just about every song he ever wrote at that time. I was in the studio with James when he recorded "I Don't Want Nobody To Give Me Nothing (Open Up The Door, I'll Take It Myself)." I wasn't playing on the record. I was just in there watching. Maceo Parker, James Brown's alto sax player, and Melvin Parker, James's drummer, were the backbone of that band. They were brothers. Maceo would put these great tracks together, and James would just come in the studio and sing over the tracks. He'd make suggestions, and Maceo would tell everybody what to play. They'd just get that funk thing going. He'd tell Maceo what he wanted, and Maceo would get some sort of lick. They'd go into the chorus or the bridge, and James would sing. He was doing rap before rappers were around. But Maceo Parker never got as much credit as he should have. He should have been co-writer on just about every one of those songs. I never felt like I was in the presence of creative genius with James. I just felt like he was another dude with a band, because my band was just as good as his band. We had twelve pieces that were strong. He was more famous, but I didn't think he was going to be legendary until he died.

You don't hear songs anymore that has any kind of funk in them because everything is so perfectly done now, it's almost like they're mechanical. A lot of today's country and rock singers won't go onstage without a pitch modulator. If one has a tendency to sing sharp when he gets a little nervous. He sings out of pitch. That modulator puts him right in tune. When it comes shooting out of the speakers, it's dead on the money. That's a common practice. Just about everybody out there is now doing it. The future's here.

We worked with Billy Joe Royal, Joe South, the Classics Four, Wilson Pickett, Dee Dee Sharp, Ray Stevens, and lot of different people. Unfortunately, we were always the opening act. Back in those days, all the stars didn't have their own bands. They'd travel light. They would come into town and pass out the charts, and my band would back them up. Hugh Rogers booked the gigs, and they'd want to use us because we had a twelve-piece band that could play and musicians who could read music. They'd come in with a briefcase and pass out the charts–tenor sax, alto sax, trombone, trumpet, organ–and we could play those charts; where lot of those little four-piece rock-and-roll bands doing Beatle music played by ear, and every song was in the key of E. So a lot of times the big acts would just ask for us. We were a tight band. The guys are all over the place now. Jerry Michael is in Nashville. He had a song he wrote and produced that was on the Oak Ridge Boys *Elvira* album. He got about quasi-rich off of that one song. He had a couple of Aretha Franklin cuts. The guy that was producing our records was Dan Penn, who is in the songwriter Hall of Fame. He wrote "Give Me A Ticket For An Airplane" for the Box Tops, "Do Right Man, Do Right Woman" for Aretha Franklin, the "Dark End of the Street," and "I'm Your Puppet."

My band brought Ray Stevens from Nashville to Tampa for a show. We backed him up, and we gave him $600 to come all the way to Tampa and go back to Nashville. He could fly down there for $100. But people [musicians/singers] didn't make a whole lot of money like they do now. He was primarily known for his novelty tunes–"The Streak" and "Ahab, The Arab." But Ray is one of the true musical geniuses of our time. He wrote "Everything is Beautiful." He made it with those novelty songs, but he did those for money. He could chart out a hundred-piece orchestra.

We'd be in Dallas for two weeks, New York for two weeks, Atlanta for two weeks, then we were booked in Vegas to play with Redd Foxx and Frankie Laine. That's when I quit the band. I was tired of being on the road and living out of a suitcase. Shad, my oldest son, had just turned six years old and had to start school. My other son, Mason, was a year-and-a-half. So we had to have a landing zone. We couldn't be out on the road playing rock-and-roll music like a bunch of gypsies. I called Hugo Hornsby who ran the Ramada Inn in Eulonia. He had a little lounge there called The Whale's Tail. I said, "Do you use live entertainment there?" He said, "Yeah, I got some organ player from Ludowici who sounds like he plays funerals in the daytime. So I came from a twelve-piece band to a one-piece band sitting on stool with my flattop singing "Sapelo River." That's how the whole transition came about. I just couldn't stand being on the road anymore.

I told Sherry, "We can go back to St. Petersburg where your next door neighbor is ten feet out your bedroom window, or we can come up here and live in my grandma's house." There was nobody living in that old house that she paid $800 for, because all my family had moved to Savannah or wherever, just get out of these woods. I didn't think Sherry would ever go for it because she was born and raised in St. Pete. She was a beach girl–Tampa Bay big city girl. We came up here for about a week, and I didn't think I'd ever get Sherry to go back home. I really wanted to go back to the city because there wasn't much of a future in music around Crescent.

One day, Melissa Fay Greene called me and said, "I was wondering if I could interview you. I'm writing a book." She gave me the premise for *Praying For Sheetrock*.[1] She came out to the house and stayed here for about three days. That book's supposed to be non-fiction, but a lot of it is fiction. A theatrical company up in Chicago did a play on that book. A lot of the people here in town like our mayor, David Bluestein, and Mary Lou Forsyth, who owns the Darien Telephone Company, flew to Chicago to see it. I asked, "How did they portray me?" They said, Vic, oddly enough, you're the only one they got right." They [the theatrical company] had me sitting on a stool with my guitar, and between scenes, I [the actor] would sing a little bit of one of my songs–"Born and Raised on the Sapelo River." The one they really centered on was "The Saga of the Great Sapelo Bust," this song I wrote about the big pot [marijuana] bust. They portrayed [Sheriff] Tom Poppell as a big ol' fat, pot-bellied guy with suspenders and a shotgun and a pistol hanging on his hip, chomping on a cigar. Number one, he didn't smoke. Number two, he didn't weigh but 125 pounds soaking wet. Never carried a gun. Unless it was Sunday, he always had on a pair of khaki pants and a white dress shirt. That was his uniform. They had him blown out like Boss Hogg. I was glad I didn't go.[2]

I wrote that song after reading the whole story in the newspaper. I wasn't there, but it [the marijuana bust] took place right across the river from my house. There was this dude name John who was a snitch. He's dead now, died of cancer. He was a paid informant. He had told some people with our local enforcement that there was a boat coming in on that particular night. Then he told the GBI [Georgia Bureau of Investigation]. He played all these law enforcement agencies against the middle, and each one of them had paid him for his tips. So, they were all there, but nobody knew that the other guys were going to be there. The GBI guys were in the woods of Sutherland Bluff, which is now all big million-dollar homes, where we used to go camping. There wasn't a single house on that bluff back then. The GBI were hiding up there waiting for this boat. Tom Poppell and Wayne Renfro, who owned the S&S Truck Stop at the time, were going out there in Tom's boat. They were out there to intercept the thing. The Highway Patrol all had on their jungle fatigues, looking like they were going deer hunting. They were hiding in the woods. When the boat came up the river, everybody started moving in. But nobody knew who the other people were and just considered the other people were the smugglers. They all got up there and started shooting at each other, and it was all cops. Everybody out there were cops except for the four guys on the shrimp boat. Anyway, they arrested the people on the boat, and John walked away with some money.

Back in 1975, as a friend once told me, every shrimper in the county had a new Lincoln Town Car or a pickup truck. Not like shrimpers now, who can't even afford fuel for their boat. There were several [marijuana] drop-off points. They'd bring them right up to a dock. They were unloading it all over the place. But that night they were going to unload at Sutherland Bluff. It's a big, high bluff with a smooth little beach where you could just nuzzle the bow of a boat right up to the shore, and there were dirt roads big enough to get trucks in there. They were just unloading that one right there. The drugs came from South America. Some of the boats wouldn't go to South America. They'd just meet a cargo ship offshore. The banana boats out of Central and South America were the primary ones bring it up. There's always a banana boat unloading in the port of Jacksonville, Savannah, or Baltimore.

Tom Poppell didn't run the gambling joints. He just allowed them to be run. He had tons of land and tons of money, and you don't make that on $15,000 a year salary. Chico's Monkey Farm [on Highway 17] had an alligator that looked like he had the flu. That gator was skinny. He was about eight feet long. And they had a three-legged monkey. It was one of those places where you could stop and buy an alligator handbag. They also had punchboards, these little cards with numbers on them you'd punch through, and whatever prize was under there you'd win. The S&S Truck Stop was a notorious cat-house that used to run numbers [gambling]. They had a homemade lotto machine made out of a popcorn maker with an air hose hooked up to a vacuum cleaner that shot ping-pong balls into a tube. You could buy whatever priced number you wanted. They'd pay ten-to-one, so if you bought a $.10

number and won, you'd get a dollar. That was before lotto came along.

One of the stories in *Praying for Sheetrock* was about a tourist who lost his boat, motor, and trailer in one of those pecan shops at South Newport. When he went to protest to Sheriff Poppell and told his story, he says, "Gambling's against the law in this county. You telling me you were gambling? If you were, you're under arrest." So, the man just got back on the road. Poppell didn't look the other way. He got his share on Monday morning. The S&S was the only truck stop in the world that didn't sell fuel. They only sold coffee and women. Before it was called the S&S Truck Stop, it was called The Oaks. But the S&S burned down. It was located by a big oak tree on Highway 17 on the north end of the county. That tree is still there.

Tom Poppell put me on the Grand Ol' Opry. I was playing at the Whale's Tail Lounge out at the Ramada Inn at exit 58 on I-95 near Eulonia. I just did a flattop guitar solo. Just sat on a stool and did my little songs. So Tom came in one night, and he had this big ol' fat man with him wearing a pair of overalls and a pair of Uniroyal deck boots–the uniform around here. The guy was smoking a cigar. His name was Shot Jackson. Tom introduced me, and Shot said, "You're pretty good, ol' boy. You want to be on the Grand Ol' Opry?" I said, "Oh sure," thinking this guy didn't know the Grand Ol' Opry from nothing. I just kind of laughed it off. That was on a weekend, and about halfway through the next week, I got a telephone call from some lady who said, "Shot Jackson talked to you, I believe, about coming up to do the Opry?" I said, "Who is this, really?" She went through it all again and wanted to know if I wanted to do a fifteen-minute spot during the disc jockey convention week, which was in October.

Every major country act does the DJ convention week. They had it out at the new Opry house at the Opryland Hotel, not the Ryman [downtown Nashville]. I didn't know it at the time, but Harold "Shot" Jackson was the dobro player for Roy Clark's band, and he and Buddy Emmons invented the Sho-Bud electric pedal steel guitar.[3] There was a store in Nashville down on Broadway with a big sign out front–Sho Bud Steel Guitars. Shot was originally from Blackshear, Georgia, but he came down here all the time to go fishing. Tom had taken him fishing, and I just thought he was some ol' cracker from around here and came to find out he was "the man." He was in the Hee-Haw family band and all that.

Anyway, he booked me for a fifteen-minute show. I followed George Jones. Man, I was scared to death. Everybody backstage drew a number out of a hat, and that's when you go on, because they had such an ego problem–"Well, I don't want to go on behind the Oak Ridge Boys. I want to go in front of Tammy." That kind of thing. So you drew a number, and I drew 36, and George Jones drew 35. He went on before me. Everybody was supposed to do fifteen minutes, and he stayed out there for about forty-five minutes, and he was just killing them one song after another–[imitating Jones] "Here's another one I wrote: He stopped loving her today... And here's another one I wrote: Well, the race is on..." The crowd is going crazy, and I'm back there sweating bullets.

There was a stage director, a guy down in a hole with a shell on the stage that the audience can't see, but up on the stage you can see his head. He'd tell people, "Next. We got to cut to commercial." It wasn't on TV. It was on nationwide radio. He kept telling George, "Cut, cut." George would say, "Okay. But let me do this one more tune," or, "I had a request for this." He finally walked off, and the crowd was still standing and screaming when they introduced me. The crowd was still clapping for George when I went out on stage. The announcer mispronounced my name. He said, "From south Georgia, Rick Walters!" I went out there and said, "Hey, I'm Vic Waters, thank you, kindly." I did "Rolling In My Sweet Baby's Arms," a bluegrass tune and "Long Black Veil." They liked me, but they liked everybody. It was a free show. The staff band was tremendous. They'd come backstage with the rehearsal band, which was the guitar player and the piano player, and they'd chart everybody out. Then they'd go out there with the full band on stage and pass out the charts. They just blistered it. I mean, they were great. They paid me forty bucks. That was union scale for fifteen minutes. They lady who handed me the check said, "it's customary that we endorse the checks and give them to the Country Music Hall of Fame." So, I just signed the check and handed it back to her. But I didn't care. I just wanted to get my picture taken in front of that microphone stand that says "WSM Grand Ol' Opry." I got it hanging on my wall. This was 1978.

I moved to Nashville four times. The longest I ever stayed was sixteen weeks. Down here, I'm kind of like a big fish in a little pond. WYNR and the WAVE play all my records, but in Nashville, I couldn't get a record played. The music business doesn't have anything to do with Nashville. Nashville is in the publishing and the songwriter business. The joke up there is, "How do you get a songwriter off the front porch? You pay him for the pizza." It's cutthroat. It's hard to get a break. Garth Brooks had a manager from Tulsa that had all the money in the world—had tons of oil wells or something. He went up there with a million dollar check to the guy who produced Garths' first albums and said, "Listen, I'll back this boy's career with this check. If he doesn't make it, you can take it out of my cut." So they didn't have anything to lose, plus he came out there with Tony Arata, a Savannah boy who used to sit on a barstool on River Street singing Jimmy Buffett tunes. Tony wrote "The Dance." He went from being one of those Jimmy Buffett guys on River Street to being a jillionaire, because that song was not only number one on all charts, it was on three greatest hits albums. Country music isn't country music anymore. Brooks and Dunn would have been a rock-and-roll act if they had been around in 1955.

My son, Mason, went up to Nashville after graduating from Georgia [University of Georgia] to pursue a music career. He found out that there's a great guitar player or bass player bussing tables in every cafe. Under every rock in Nashville, there's a guy better than you are. He stayed up there for ten years. He's now a banker in Georgia who plays music on the side instead of being a musician that banks on the side.

One time, about 1974-'75, a couple of prominent ladies around the county, Hannah Tostensen and Mary Lou Jackson Forsyth, asked me to meet them at Archie's [Restaurant] for lunch. When I got there, they said, "We want you to run for county commissioner. We think that because you were raised out here in Crescent and all the black people know you and like you, you might have a chance to win that post from Thurnell Alston," the guy that was in *Praying for Sheetrock*.[4] "Some people are a little disenchanted with Thurnell." I came home, and my head was swelled up thinking, *Hey, they want me to be a politician. This is kind of cool.* I told my wife, and she said, "Are you out of your mind? Number one, you can't win–but if you could, which you can't, but if you could–you know how you hate talking on the telephone. It would never stop ringing, and it won't be people calling to say they love your new CD. They'll be calling to say, 'Where's that load of dirt you promised me for the road in front of my house that got washed out.' The phone would never quit ringing, and it would be someone complaining about something." I said, "Oh yeah. You got a point there." So, I decided to pass on that. And I couldn't have won.

I don't play bars anymore because I can't breathe. That cigarette smoke kills me.[5] But I still do shows. We worked a show a while back with the Neville Brothers and Delbert

McClinton, T. Graham Brown, and Sammy Kershaw. We opened up for those guys. So, I'm still having a little fun doing it. Delbert is the best white rhythm and blues singer I've ever heard. He played the harmonica solo at the beginning of "Hey, Baby," that beach music classic. Bruce Channel recorded it. John Lennon copied Delbert's harp playing on "Love Me Do."

Vic with Neville Brothers, Cyril (left) and Aaron (right).
Photograph courtesy of Vic Waters.

There's nothing like the coast. That's why 85% of the people in the world live within fifteen miles of a coast. We've got a port in Brunswick and a port in Savannah, but I live in the last little unspoiled place on the Georgia coast. That river, man. Being on the river is what attracts people here. Every time you look out at the river, it's different. When you live in the city and look across the street at your neighbor, it looks the same every time. When you look at the river, the tide's coming in, the next time you look at it the tide's high, the next time, it's low, next time, the marsh grass is brown, next time, it's green. It's always changing, and it's breathing.

*****

Vic Water's Band Timeline:
1956-1958 The Emeralds...Savannah, GA
1959-1962 The Versatones...Savannah, GA
1962-1965 The Impacs...St. Petersburg, FL
1965-1966 The Big Brothers...The Road and New York
1966-1967 The Impacs
1967-1970 The Entertainers...On the road
1970-1974 The Vic Waters Band...Florida
1974-Present Vic Waters Band

NOTES

[1] Winner of the Robert F. Kennedy Book Award.

[2] In her book, *Praying for Sheetrock*, Melissa Fay Greene writes that in McIntosh County in the early 1970s, "the epic of the civil rights movement was still a fabulous tale about distant places to the black people of McIntosh." Sheriff Thomas Poppell controlled the county through a "system of favoritism, nepotism, and paternalism" and manipulated the black vote to stay in office. New Georgia Encyclopedia, http://www.georgiaencyclopedia.org/nge/Article.jsp?id=h-2716, accessed March 7, 2011.

[3] The name, "Sho-Bud," was derived by combining the first three letters of "Shot" and "Buddy."

[4] Black civil rights activist elected to the McIntosh County Commission in 1978.

[5] Vic was diagnosed with throat cancer not long after this interview.

Charles Alfred (Chuck) Leavell

The road less traveled has some interesting twists and turns. Chuck Leavell, once a member of The Allman Brothers Band and now keyboardist for the Rolling Stones, made a conscious decision to take that road early in his life. How does the son of an insurance agent go from civil rights-torn Alabama to become a world-renowned musician/land conservationist who manages thousands of acres of Georgia pine? It begins with a Ray Charles concert...

Photograph courtesy of Chuck Leavell.

My proper name is Charles Alfred Leavell. Most folks know me as Chuck. I was born in Birmingham, Alabama, April 28, 1952. Leavell is a French name. Most of my own family pronounces the name "Level." Growing up as a child, oftentimes people would mispronounce it. Oddly enough, when I finally got a little bit of recognition as a musician, so many people pronounced it "La-vell" that I just gave up and said, "Okay. That's cool." We had family in Montgomery, Alabama–my Uncle Jay. We had family in Florida. We had family in the Atlanta area and others scattered out through south Alabama. We settled in the South as a whole. It was quite an unusual name. We were very curious whenever we would see anyone else with that name. There weren't a whole lot of us that we didn't already know about because most of us were related. There were a band of French folks that came over on one of the Mayflower expeditions that settled in Virginia and eventually moved down south through the Carolinas and from there, westward towards Georgia and Alabama.[1]

My father's name was William Alfred Leavell. Everyone knew him as Billy. He was an insurance salesman. Dad had two brothers, Emory and Jay, and three sisters. Emory was the firstborn. There was Louise, whom we called Aunt Lou, and there was Gussie-Mae, and another sister, Frankie. Lou lived in Atlanta, Gussie lived in a small town in Alabama called Lapine. Frankie lived in North Carolina, and Uncle Emory lived with his family down in Florida. Uncle Jay and his family lived in Montgomery. Dad worked for Guarantee Life and Protective Life. He eventually started his own company called Educational Trust, Incorporated. He sold primarily policies that dealt with setting aside money to put your kids through college. Ironically, he also sold cancer insurance, and cancer is what ultimately undid him.

My Mom, Frances Earl, was a Harrison from Greenville, Alabama. My mother and father were working in Montgomery at Kress, a department store that had a soda fountain. Dad was a manager, and they met and started dating. There was a little controversy because you weren't supposed to date anyone working with you. So, they kept it quiet as long as they could. Finally, they both left their positions and got married.

When I was very young, maybe four or five years old, we moved to Montgomery. We had a little eight-acre place. We had horses. Dad plowed a garden behind a horse with a manual plow. We had an old barn out there. My sister, Judy, and I used to play in a creek. That was my first experience with the outdoors, and I absolutely loved it as a child. I just loved living there. We eventually moved back to Birmingham for a time, and then settled in Tuscaloosa.

Young Chuck. Courtesy of Chuck Leavell.

I grew up in the days of segregation in the South. My memories of this are twofold. My mother was extremely non-prejudiced, and she made very sure that her children understood that all people are created equal. That was something preached a lot in our home. However, because of the influences around–your peers, most of the adult population at the time–it was not uncommon to have that prejudice, to separate white and black. My school was segregated until the time I started going to high school in Tuscaloosa, Tuscaloosa High.

I can remember very well when Governor George Wallace stood on the steps of the University of Alabama and refused admission to the first black person who tried to enter the school. There was a huge uproar throughout the community by both blacks and whites about this issue. After all that, the laws rightfully persisted to allow integration, and it began to filter into the schools.

When I was in high school, the first black student I recall was a black guy named Willie. I can't remember Willie's last name, but I remember liking him, and I was one of the only boys that would talk to him or spend time with him. My mother had taught me to accept these things. While a lot of my friends were just outraged that this could happen, I found Willie to be a really great guy. We had physical education, PE, together, and I remember being one of the few that would accept Willie, talk to him, and walk around with him and so forth. It was a time of a lot of tension. Later on, as I got into music, most of the great musicians were black people.

I was tremendously influenced by Ray Charles. To begin with, my family had some of his records. We had the wonderful record album, *Modern Sounds in Country and Western Music.* "I Can't Stop Loving You" was a hit, and you would hear it on the radio. There was another album called *Genius + Soul = Jazz.* I loved the texture of his voice. I loved his playing. I loved the fact that he was blending different kinds of music. At that time, I was probably ten or eleven years old. Then, when I was twelve years old, there was an occasion when my sister, Judy, had a date to go see Ray Charles who was playing the Coliseum at the University of Alabama. My parents also had an engagement that night and didn't want to leave me alone there in the house, so they told Judy, "You got to take Chuck with you," and she was okay with that. So I went to the Coliseum with Judy and her date. Ray Charles had such a great band. Every song, every change, every beat was just phenomenal. Billy Preston was playing organ with Ray. Ray gave Billy a one-song segment where Billy came out front and sang and danced. Fathead Newman was playing saxophone, and there were the Raelettes [female singers who provided backing vocals]. It just was a life-altering moment for me. I walked out of there thinking, *I don't want to be a lawyer, a doctor, or anything else. I want to–hopefully–play in a band that's anywhere near that good.*

I learned piano by listening to my mother. She was not a professional or a teacher or anything like that, but she played the piano. We had one in the house, so it was sort of for family enjoyment. I was the baby of the family. My older brother, Billy, was fourteen years older than me, and Judy was five years older. Oftentimes, when I was very young, it was just my mother and myself in the house. Dad was out working, and the two other siblings were in school. I would tug on her skirt and say, "Momma, play me something on the piano." I was really fascinated with it. I loved watching her hands move up and down the keyboard. I loved listening to the melodies and the harmonies. She played mostly standard tunes… "The Black Hawk Waltz," "The Spinning Songs"…fairly easy stuff that was out of a standard piano book. She read music quite well. She would encourage me to engage and play. As time went on, I began to sort the puzzle out a little bit just by working with her. My parents said, "Chuck's showing some promise in music. Maybe he would like to have lessons."

Eventually, I did take lessons for about six months. By then, my ears were so far ahead of my eyes that when the teacher wanted me to read music, I didn't really want to do that. I just wanted to sit at the piano and play. I didn't want to have to deal with that sheet of paper on the front of the piano, so I gave up lessons, but I always stayed with the piano. I learned through the good graces of folks showing me things I needed and through some painstaking times listening to records and trying to figure out exactly what was going on.

My cousin, Winston, who we called Windy, played guitar. He was Uncle Jay's son and a few years older than me. Windy and I would hang out, and he showed me things on the guitar. At that time, folk music was a big deal. We were listening to Chad and Jeremy, the Kingston Trio, New Christy Minstrels, Peter, Paul, and Mary, and Bob Dylan. Music began to blend between piano, guitar, and singing. I just hung with it. But again, when I heard Ray Charles, it changed my life.

I eventually found myself working with a group called The Jades. I was in high school at the time, and they were going to Stillman College in Tuscaloosa. The Jades were very much a Temptations-type band. They had the harmonies and the dance steps and did cover songs by the Temptations, the Four Tops, and so forth. They were excellent, really great musicians. They had a keyboard player named Freddy, and Freddy found himself confined to being behind the keyboards. The other four guys were up front dancing and singing, and Freddy wanted to be up there. I was hanging around a show somewhere, and we met. Somehow, Freddy heard me play, and he said, "Look man, I think I can show you some stuff that will help you out as a musician. Then, I can go up here and dance with my pals." I said, "Okay," and found myself in the rather unique position of playing with an all-black group and being a very young keyboard player on stage with them.

As you might imagine, in those times, I took a lot of heat from some of my peers because of that. It didn't make any difference to me, man. It was all about the music, and I was trying to learn, and I did learn a lot from Freddy and from The Jades. We played mixed audiences. There were some shows I recall that were for the black audiences, mostly around the college and maybe a theatre or two. Tuscaloosa is a college town, the University of Alabama, so there were a lot of fraternity parties, and The Jades played fraternity parties, as did a lot of other black artists of the day. It was a short-lived situation, probably six months or so, but it was certainly a great education for me.

My second career as an environmentalist, a tree farmer, pretty much came about by accident. I had made the decision that I wanted to pursue music as a career when I was around fifteen or sixteen years old. By the time I turned seventeen, I was really anxious to get out of school, and I actually did drop out of high school when I was a senior. The way it came about is there was a studio in Birmingham that hired me to play as a staff musician. There was a term back then called DE–Diversified Education. Basically, what that meant was you had a job. You got out of school in the middle of the day to go to your job. Most of the DE guys were mechanics or something like that. I was a musician. It was a very unusual thing, but they allowed me to do it.

So, I was playing in a band and working in this studio. Oftentimes, we would work on the weekend, which made for a long weekend. Or we would have to leave on a Thursday to go play in Oxford, Mississippi, and I would miss school. Friday and Saturday, we would play and come back on Sunday or on Monday sometimes. It got to a point where I was not attending school as I should have been. My grades were okay. I was no stellar student, but I was a C+ and B student. However, I'd get called into the principal's office at midterm, and they'd say, "Chuck, you've missed a lot of school here." And I'd say, "Well, yeah. I've got this job, and I'm playing." They said, "The state of Alabama has a law that says you have to attend so many days of school to graduate. You're a senior, and you really can't miss any more school. You have to attend the entire next semester if you want to graduate." So I was faced with this decision of playing music or staying in school. I was enjoying the music very much and went that route. My parents were not happy about that, of course, and there was a lot of discussion. "I'll go back to school and finish it up at some point. But right now, I'm making money and enjoying what I'm doing." Well, I never went back. I convinced my parents to allow me to go to Birmingham.

Universal Sound Studios was the one I was working for at the time. There were three or four studios scattered around Birmingham. This one got a decent amount of work. We would do jingles and commercials for local companies…just little things, nothing on a national or even state level, but it was good experience. When the clock wasn't running for a client, we would play for our own enjoyment, record things, and experiment. It was a wonderful thing for a young musician, and a great opportunity. This was when the Beatles and the British Invasion was huge. Music was beginning to be very experimental, and we were in a pretty good position to be engaged in that. We were influenced by the British music, by soul music, by country music, by gospel. You heard both black and white gospel on the radio on Sunday mornings. I remember very well spinning that dial on the radio and hearing the black preacher preach, hearing the songs the choir would sing, then tuning into the white church sermon as well. There were a lot of influences going on at the time. For me, the most interesting was the British Invasion. For one, it was all over the radio. Number two, it was so new and fresh and different. We had never heard anything like that. Groups like The Beatles, the Stones, The

Zombies, Dave Clark Five, Herman's Hermits, were all groups of interest to us musicians of the time.

Early Influences

I was also influenced by a guy named Paul Hornsby. Paul lived in Tuscaloosa and had been in a band called The Hour Glass, a precursor to The Allman Brothers Band. It included Gregg and Duane Allman, Johnny Sandlin, and a couple of different bass players. Paul had gone to California and had this experience with The Hour Glass and had done a couple of records out there. He played keyboard and electric piano, and Greg Allman played organ. Paul played guitar as well–a multitalented guy. Eventually, The Hour Glass broke up, and Paul came back to Alabama. He saw something in me, whatever it was, I'm not sure, and took me under his wing. He showed me a lot of things on the keyboard and encouraged me to sing. As time went on, Capricorn Records, owned by Phil Waldon, was born in Macon, Georgia. Capricorn was home of The Allman Brothers Band when Gregg and Duane eventually formed The Allman Brothers. Because Paul had known those guys and kept up with what was happening, he got the call one day that he should come to Macon and work at the studio. Well, I lost my mentor. Paul was leaving, and I was very upset about this. With a bass player friend, Charlie Haywood, I said, "Let's go over there and see what Macon, Georgia is all about."

We got in my burgundy Oldsmobile Cutlass station wagon and drove over to Macon. Paul escorted us around the studio, and I met Phil Waldon. I actually met my wife-to-be, Rose Lane White. She was working in the office at the time. There were only about five or six people in the office then. After seeing all of this, Charlie and I thought, *We've got to come over here!* And we were encouraged to come over. Paul and Phil Waldon, and a guy named Frank Fenter, encouraged us and said, "Come on back, and we'll see if we can find you something to do." Well, we did. We want back to Tuscaloosa…I was going back and forth from Birmingham to T-Town even though I was going to school in B'ham….and got most of the belongings we had and made the second trip over to Macon and flopped on somebody's floor for a couple of months. We started a band called Sundown, which was a combination of three or four of us from Tuscaloosa and some guys who were locals in Macon. We did a record that was on the Ampex label, a very short-lived label and a very short-lived band. But that gave us a start in Macon.

I didn't give a whole lot of thought that I was leaving Alabama and going to Georgia. It was still the South to me. The culture was pretty much the same. There was a different look. It was new in terms that I had never seen a whole lot of other cities, but the South was the South. I had traveled a little bit. We used to go to Atlanta to see our Aunt Lou. She was the secretary to the Secretary of State for Georgia, and she was engaged in the legislature and was the one that spoke, or read, all the bills that were introduced in the state of Georgia. Because of her connections, my sister, Judy, and I were at the capitol when we were very young. I had some connection in that regard.

As time went on, I started to get work as a studio musician and wound up playing with a guy named Alex Taylor, James Taylor's older brother. He was more of a blues singer than his brothers James and Livingston were. We did a couple of records for Capricorn. That was my first experience traveling all over America in the back seat of a Ford LTD station wagon with six people in the thing having wonderful experiences playing in clubs and a few theatres and opening up concerts for more known artists like The Allman Brothers and Jefferson Airplane. I began my real professional career in Macon. It took me a couple of years to get up courage to ask Rose Lane out because I had little or nothing to offer. By the time I worked my way up and was eventually asked to play in The Allman Brothers Band, I got the courage to ask her out. She accepted, and we've been together thirty-seven years now.

My parents had been concerned about my leaving Alabama when I was seventeen. I found out later my father had called the offices of Capricorn not knowing who he would get and introduced himself and spoke to a guy working there at the time named Bunky Odom. Bunky took the call, and my dad said, "Hey, you got my boy over there. I want to know what's going on. I'm just checking up. Please don't let him know I called." If I had known about it at the time, I would probably have been upset. But, by the time I did hear about it, three or four years later, it was a very endearing thing. My dad wanted me to be safe. He and my mother were very concerned.

Eventually, they accepted it, and my career began to blossom. Unfortunately, my father contracted cancer about the time I was playing with Alex Taylor. I was up in Martha's Vineyard rehearsing with Alex and got a phone call from my mother saying, "You may not want to hear this, but your father is very ill, and you may want to consider coming home."

"Why? What do you mean he's ill?"

"Well, he's going to be going in the hospital, and there's a pretty good chance he's not going to be around very long."

It was a very strange call to get. I was at a rebellious age. It was a very confusing thing to deal with, and of course, I did go home. Indeed, my father was in the hospital. I don't think he had more than a week from the time I got home until he passed away. It was a very, very strange thing. One of the things that was regrettable, was that my father and I were sort of coming to terms with each other. He was not happy that I was hanging out with hippies and playing rock-and-roll music. He wanted me to follow in his footsteps. But he had begun to accept that I had a life to live, and I had begun to accept that he was my dad, and that whatever he thought didn't matter in terms of our relationship. For instance, we had just had our first couple of drinks together. I remember very well coming home at one point and Dad saying, "Son, sit down here. Would you like a little whiskey?" I was not a big drinker and never really had been, but what a thing to have offered. It was almost a ritual in a way–father and son learning to be adults together. From my perspective, that was part of what it was about. It wasn't long after that, he went in the hospital. It just happened so quickly, and he was gone.

Stewardship

My wife, Rose Lane, comes from a family that has been connected to the land for generations. Her family acquired land from various purchases through the years, but very early on, the Faulk family–her grandmother's side–got tracts of land deeded to them in the land grant days of King George III. When we began to date seriously, she finally said, "You need to meet my family." Well, she brings me out to the backwoods of Twiggs County, Georgia where her family is from. She had not really divulged a whole lot about her family at the time, or I had not paid enough attention, so it was a bit of a surprise to come out and see that this family owned a lot of land. They were farmers and engaged in tending the land in one form or another. It kind of reawakened what had lain dormant in me for so long– that little short time of living in the country when I was a child. Once we finally tied the knot, we really began to come out here for holidays and weekends and so forth. The more I spent time with the family, the more I appreciated their dedication to the land. Then, in 1981, Rose Lane's grandmother passed away, and because Rose Lane's father preceded her grandmother in death, the land went to Rose Lane and her brother, Alton. The Allman Brothers had broken up, and I had just finished working with my band,

Sea Level. All of the sudden we woke up one day, and Rose Lane has inherited this land. It became a responsibility to carry on the heritage of stewardship that her family for generations had done, and I took it very seriously.

For a little time, I gave up music and started studying land use. It was a diversified farm at the time. They had cattle, row crops, and some timber. I realized that if I was going to pursue my career as a musician, row cropping and cattle was so much a day-to-day requirement that it wasn't going to fit me. I began to study forestry, and the more I studied, the more fascinated I became. I eventually enrolled in a correspondence course when I toured with The Fabulous Thunderbirds in the early '80s. It took about a year-and-a-half to complete that course. It was very useful, and I learned a lot from it. It seemed the more I learned, the more fascinated I became. Finally, we began to actively manage the land she inherited primarily for forestry use. But it's not fair to say forestry, because there are so many things that go along with it. It's not just trees, it's what lives within the trees, the wildlife, the biodiversity, the big picture of it all. That led me on a journey I had no idea I would take, but I'm very grateful to take it, because it gave me a second career.

What's in a Name

The way we came up with the name Charlane Plantation was taking my first proper name, Charles, and my wife's double-name Rose Lane. So we combined C-H-A-R and L-A-N-E to come up with Charlane.

Forestry Management

I'm happy to say that America as a whole is a shining example of good forestry management. Certainly in the Southeast–Georgia, Alabama, Mississippi, the Carolinas, Kentucky, Tennessee–there is a tremendous amount of well-managed forests. Other places in America that are

216

engaged in this would include, Washington State, Oregon, northern California and other states as well. Those are big states in terms of growing and managing forestland. It's interesting to note that in the year 2010, we have about as much forestland as we did a hundred years ago. And that's saying something when you have a population of almost 310 million people, when you've seen the growth that America has experienced since European settlement. Certainly, there are challenges.

Sometimes I talk about the "invisible forest health crisis," and what I mean by that, is we're losing a lot of natural land to growth and development. The metro area of Atlanta loses something on the order of one hundred acres a day to development. About 50% of that is lost to impervious surfacing. The Southeast as a whole from Virginia down to east Texas loses on the order of million acres a year to growth and development. Maybe it's slowed down a little bit now because of the economy we're experiencing, and housing is not what it was in years past. Nonetheless, we still lose land to growth and development every day.

That's the subject of a new book I've just written called *Smart, Strong and Sustainable: Growing a Better America.* My attempt with this book is to find ways that we can experience growth, because the growth is going to be there, like it or not. But can we tide it? Can we be smarter and be more careful? Can we address our energy uses and transportation issues? Can we address the big picture and try to slow down the loss of these natural lands? Can we find good community growth models?

That's a big concern of mine. In the introduction, I talk about when I was very young and we used to get in the car and leave Tuscaloosa and drive up to Atlanta to see Aunt Lou. There was a sign on Peachtree Street that depicted the population of the Atlanta area. When I was probably seven or eight years old, it had topped a million people. I remember thinking *Wow, a Southern city with a million people?* You thought about New York and expected to have a lot of people up there, but a city in the South with a million people was just phenomenal at the time. Now, at this juncture, Atlanta has over five-and-a-half million. So, it's grown five-fold since the time I was young and drove up to see Aunt Lou. That's phenomenal growth that we're experiencing. We just need to be careful what we do from here on out.

There are a very few small tracts of forest in the South and in other areas of America that we might term virgin forest, although that's a nebulous term because what's a virgin forest? Trees are like people. They do have a mortality, some a bit longer than others. What we might term an old growth forest in the South is where pine trees might live to be four hundred years old.

There's a plantation, Greenwood, in South Georgia, owned by a very wealthy family.[2] They are fortunate to have a little bit of land that has four hundred-year-old pine trees on it. They don't intend to use it commercially. It's wonderful to have that. The fact is there's very little of that in our country. But look, if a tree is going to live to be four hundred years old and dies, you're going to have a fresh forest come along. In the Southeast, we're on our fifth forest since European settlement, and that's not necessarily a bad thing. It's a wonderful thing to see a preserved forest, but it's also important to note that we can use this natural, organic, and renewable resource. It gives us so many things–materials to build our homes, schools, and churches. It gives us materials for books, magazines, and newspapers. My instrument comes from the resource of wood. Trees clean our air and our water. They provide home and shelter to wildlife. There are over 5,000 products we use in our everyday lives that contain some element of trees. Cellulose goes into things like salad dressings. It's a remarkable resource, and it's a renewable resource.

So, yes, we want to use it, but we also want to have areas that we hold back for aesthetic use just to see the beauty of the forest. What we try to do here at Charlane Plantation is a little bit of both. We have some trees that are over a hundred years old, and I just love to see them. I enjoy riding my horse in the forest and seeing these things. But we also have areas that we do use for production, and it's a good feeling to know that these trees growing on our land are going to make somebody's first home or to renovate someone's home, make books, or whatever the product might be.

If I had to guess, I suppose we've planted in the hundreds of thousands of trees. In the long view, when you're talking about forests, if I plant a seedling in the ground today, that seedling will eventually grow to be sixty or seventy years old before it's taken and given use. So, the trees I'm planting now are much more for our grandsons and heirs, than they are for us. We have harvested some trees that we put in the ground in the early '80s. It's a great feeling to walk by what used to be an open field we planted pines on that have grown to fruition and are being managed. Our view of forest management is select removal. We go in somewhere around age 18-22 or so for the first thinning. I like to say it's weeding the garden. You go in and take out the lesser trees and allow the other trees to live and grow and be healthy. Maybe another eight to ten years go by, and you weed the garden again. Some of the areas we planted in the early '80s that may have been thinned once or twice are now beautiful forest. It's pretty cool to walk by that and know you put them in the ground, that you've harvested some that are going to good purpose, and that they now give a lot of pleasure to walk within.[3]

One of the things we do at Charlane Plantation, is constantly riding around the place and looking up to see if you have any trees that might be struck by lightning or have diseased by insects. When I see that, I get the chain saw, take the tree down, and cut it up. I have a homemade grapple that goes onto the tractor so I can drag the log to a location where we load it up onto a trailer. I know a fellow about eighteen miles from me who has a sawmill. We have built innumerable buildings using that wood–our horse barn, the lodge, which is a 4, 500 square foot building guests stay in. My fencing for the horse pasture came from that resource. We renovated our own home that we live in, an 1850s farmhouse, using that resource. We have two grandsons, Miles and Rocco, and it's a nice feeling to think that when they grow up they'll say, "Granddad went out there, took those trees that were already dying on the stump, and put them to good use." Hopefully, these buildings will stand for a couple of hundred years or more.

Chuck with grandson, Miles. Courtesy of Chuck Leavell.

Separation of Music and Land

I try to keep my two careers separate. When the show is over and we go back stage, I'm happy to talk to people within the band that I work with, or people I meet, about environmental issues. But I'm not going to sit on the stage on one of my personal shows and talk about conservational issues. I think that's wrong. With all due respect to someone like Bono, who is a great humanitarian, I wish he would keep that message off the stage. I feel the same about any cause. I think entertainers are there to entertain, not to try to sway somebody to a certain way of thinking.

photos: courtesy Chuck Leavell
Chuck Leavell (second from right) with Keith Richards, Mick Jagger, Ronnie Wood, and Charlie Watts of The Rolling Stones.

While on tour, I sometimes put my mind to what is happening on our plantation…and of course, Rose Lane, and I miss our home greatly when we're gone. But I find it's best if I can just focus on my duties to the Stones or whoever I might be touring with.[4] Of course, we check often with our family that lives in Twiggs County, and with those that work for us on Charlane.

Land management and music are things I'm very passionate about. The interesting thing, perhaps, is that they both offer the opportunity to leave a legacy. Recorded music has been around for a pretty long time. We all enjoy listening to records that were made during the early days of recording. I'm in the middle of a project now that is a tribute to pioneering blues piano players from the 1930s, '40s, and '50s eras. To go back and listen to those early records, it's just astounding that they are there.

As a musician, I feel like you have an opportunity to leave a legacy through the recording and through the time that you have as a career on stage. The same opportunity exists as a land manager. You are leaving your footprint on this land. The mantra that we go by, and that most land managers go by, is that you want to leave the land in better shape than you found it. That's our mission, and hopefully, we're accomplishing that. I hope that someday, after I'm gone and my wife is gone, people that walk this land will say, "These folks did a pretty good job, and we now can take it from here." I want to see our grandsons appreciate this land and make it better than we made it.

NOTES

[1] "In 1630, a colony of French Protestants actually sailed from England for Carolina...in the ship Mayflower. Could it have been the same vessel that carried the Puritans to Plymouth Rock?.... For some unexplained cause they were landed in Virginia." The Charleston (S. C.) News, July 20, 1895, reported in the New York Times. http://query.nytimes.com/gst/abstract.html?res=F30D14FB3B5D15738 DDDA90A94DF405B8585F0D3, accessed November 3, 2010.

[2] Located near Thomasville, Georgia. Owned by the Whitney family.

[3] Leavell and his wife, Rose Lane, were named National Outstanding Tree Farmers of the Year in 1999 for the "outstanding management of their own forestland, Charlane Plantation." Leavell is a board member of the American Forest Foundation, the US Endowment for Forests and Communities, and the Georgia Land Conservation Council. He advocates on behalf of the environment on Capitol Hill and helped form "the forest component of the past two US Farm Bills." http://www.chuckleavell.com/bio.html, accessed June 17, 2011.

[4] "Chuck Leavell, from Dry Branch, Georgia...was a Stu [Ian Stewart] protégé and appointee. He first played keyboards on tour with us in 1982 and became a permanent fixture on all subsequent tours. By the time Stu died, Chuck had been working with the Stones for several years. 'If I croak, God forbid,' said Stu, 'Leavell's the man.'" Keith Richards, with James Fox, *Life* (New York: Little, Brown And Company, 2010), 464.

Patrick Lennon McDonald

Patrick McDonald has come a long way from banging on pillows with drumsticks as a child, to earning a living as the drummer for the Charlie Daniels Band. It's been a circuitous journey filled with ups and downs (including two bouts with cancer) that most people would have abandoned for more reliable careers. I pushed Pat into providing details of how he got from point A to point B and so on. His story is that of dedication to a vision, perseverance in the face of daunting odds, and saying "Yes" to little openings that lead to greater opportunities.

Photo by Wolf Hoffmann.

My name is Patrick Lennon McDonald. I was born December 8, 1965 at Glynn-Brunswick Memorial Hospital. My mother's name is Lillian Carnell "Conni" Youmans McDonald Purciarele. My father was Julius Lennon "Lennie" McDonald, Jr. He was a DJ at WYNR in Brunswick for years before they divorced, and he moved to Wilmington, NC. He died in 1995. They were both born in Brunswick. My maternal grandfather, Tracy Youmans, was born in 1910 in Blackshear, and my maternal grandmother, Carnell Benton, was born one year and one day later in Alma. They got married when they were 16 and 17 in 1928. Not long after that, they moved to Brunswick. They had one child, my mother. When my grandfather was young, he got a job as Howard Coffin's chauffeur. When Howard Coffin wanted to go somewhere, he was the guy who drove him around.[1]

My grandfather eventually ended up going into business for himself. His brother, Ed Youmans, owned an electric motor winding shop, Youmans Electric, on Albany Street in Brunswick. My grandfather opened Tracy's Auto Parts next door to his brother's shop. He eventually had a store on Norwich Street across from C. B. Greer Elementary and one on St. Simons in the village. The shop on Albany Street was a long building. On the right side was the auto parts store. On the left side of the building was my great-uncle's shop. Adjacent to their building was a little shack with a dirt floor. An old, colored man named Doc had a little business in there. Doc didn't see really well. He was almost blind. He sold peanuts, crackers, Nehi and NuGrape sodas out of that shack. I used to spend time in the auto parts store riding around on a creeper, the flat board with wheels that mechanics lie on to get under cars. I'd go over and get grape sodas from Doc. He buried most of his earnings in a metal box in that shack. When he died, he left a note for his family to go in and dig it up. For a guy selling sodas and nickel peanuts, he had saved a lot of money.

My grandfather eventually sold out to Brooks Auto Parts. I think his initial plan was to keep the stores and let my younger brother, Tracy, and myself eventually take them over. But his health failed due to stress, and he sold the stores when I was a child. He and my grandmother lived at 2006 Demere Road. His house, a little brick house, was the first one past the Island Art Center right across from McKinnon Airport. It had an old camshaft for a mailbox post. He and his brother-in-law built that house from the ground up in 1949. He lived there until he died in 1992. My grandmother lived there until she died in 1999. My brother bought it from the family estate and later sold it.

Now, there's a strip mall/office complex there. Before the sale, a housing inspector measured the house and told my brother he had hardly ever seen a house built that perfectly square. From corner-to-corner, forty-to-fifty feet, it might have been a quarter inch off plumb. They built it with their own hands and obviously took their time. It makes you look back and realize people used to do things right and took pride in their work. That's so rare to see these days. They had bricks left over, so he built a little workshop and a barbeque pit in the back yard. After he sold the auto parts stores, he got into charter fishing. He ran fishing charters out of the Sea Island dock. The people who were on vacation could take their catch to the Cloister Hotel dining room and have it cooked for them for dinner. But most people would catch the fish, take pictures, and then give the fish to my grandfather. He would bring home coolers full of fish all the time. We'd clean and wrap them and throw them in the freezer and later cook them on his pit or fry them up fresh. He used to take all the guts and scraps and bury them for fertilizer in his rose garden in the front corner of the yard. He grew some beautiful roses. To this day, I'm a bit of a seafood snob and don't want it unless it's fresh, because we always had fresh fish to eat growing up.

My father's father, Julius Lennon McDonald, Sr., was instrumental in setting up the infrastructure–the water mains and electrical lines–on Sea Island. He was in the engineering department. If they needed to tap into an unmarked water main, they'd say, "Call Mac." and he'd come over, point to the ground and say, "It's right there." He had glaucoma, and it eventually took his sight. His wife, Myrtle Lee McDonald, had a beauty shop in Longview Shopping Center for years and had a large clientele of ladies from Sea Island.

Growing Up

When I was born, we lived in a duplex on Ocean Boulevard right next to where The Crab Trap restaurant is located. We had to live there for a few months while we were waiting for our house to be finished. It was off Ledbetter Avenue, right off of Frederica across from the St. Williams Parish Hall. I remember getting excited every Christmas because they used to hang a big lighted star on the wall of the Parish Hall, and it was always my reminder that Santa Claus would soon be there. There was a little dirt road down Ledbetter Avenue called Bracewell Court. We lived at 110. The Bracewell family's house and business was on the corner. There was our house, then Pete and Joanna Buglino's house. Next to the Buglinos, lived an elderly couple, Lionel and Mary Tester. And on the end lived the Sanders (later Pridemore) family. The Buglinos owned all the property between our house and the Youngwood neighborhood. All of that was pasture for the Buglino's horses. My mom is a horse fanatic and used to tell people she couldn't get anything done because every time she was cleaning the house or cooking, she'd hear those horses running and run to the back window to watch them fly by. The Buglinos sold that property to the Stroud family and moved to Waynesville. The Strouds built Heritage Inn, a retirement home, there. It's now called Magnolia Manor. Philip Sheffield lived just across the property in Youngwood and was a childhood friend. He and I used to skateboard all around the place as kids. We're still friends today. More on him later.

I went to Busy Bee Kindergarten on Redfern Drive, one street over from Ledbetter. Philip's mother, Pegge "Pokey" Sheffield, ran it. The biggest moment in my life up to then was when my mom let me ride my little purple Schwinn bicycle to kindergarten when I was four years old. I'd ride down our road, go fifty yards through the woods along a drainage ditch, then turn left and go two houses down to school. She trusted me enough to do that. It wasn't more than a hundred-fifty yards from our house, but it seemed like miles to me back then.

When I was little, probably five or six, I got a little toy drum set for Christmas. It was one of those Sears Catalog, paper and plastic sets that fell apart in a week and ended up in the attic. I forgot about it. My big thing back then was the water and fishing. I shark fished on the pier all summer long. I used to get fishing tackle at Higdon's Bait shop, which is now Brogen's. I *lived* on the pier in the summer. I wanted to be a marine biologist. It was all about sharks and fish for me.

Rocky Career Beginnings

One year, I went to a St. Patrick's Day parade in Brunswick. They had these guys dressed as leprechauns on the fire truck, throwing candy. Candy was just raining down all over, and kids were scrambling to grab it all. The marching band came by, and I could feel the bass drum– BOOM, BOOM, BOOM–in my chest. I hated it. I literally couldn't stand the sound. It drove me nuts. I didn't like that feeling. I sat in the back seat of the car looking at this candy everywhere and kids running all over the place collecting piles of it and couldn't get out of the car because the drums bothered me so much. And now I play drums for a living. That's really ironic, because I hated my first experience with real drums.

When I was eight or nine I was in exploring mode one day and went up the in the attic and dragged those Sears drums back down, and the bug just bit me. I have no idea why I suddenly felt the need to try drums again, but I'm glad I did. They were covered in dust and all torn up. I pieced them together and tried to make something playable. I'd throw on a record or turn on the radio and just tap along. The only stereo in the house was in the living room. My mom had a pile of '70s vinyl records–John Denver, Eagles, Engelbert Humperdinck, Barry Manilow–what they now call "soft rock." I had a pair of drumsticks and would set cushions on the couch like they were drums and play along when it was too late in the day to play my little toy drum kit.

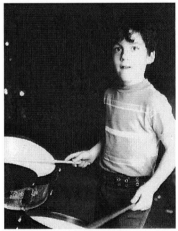

Patrick, age 9.

My mom wanted to put me in public school when I was five years old, but the Glynn County school system changed the rules that year and said you now had to be six years old to be a first-grader. Frederica Academy [a private school] would let me in at five, so my first two years of school, I went to Frederica Academy, located in the old hospital on the south end of Brunswick. The Sea Island bus picked up the kids on St. Simons and took us over there. After two years at Frederica, my parents decided to send me to public school, so I transferred to St. Simons Elementary. Being from a family of modest means, the cost was a bit high for our budget, and my mother said that she started noticing patterns in my behavior that gave her pause. Most of the kids there came from more affluent families and naturally, were accustomed to a bit more of a "privileged" life than we had. Kids are kids, and I apparently began showing signs of a more elitist personality than she thought I should have had. I guess I was hearing and experiencing things in school that were making me feel and act above my means, so she took me out and sent me to public school.

Mrs. Barone was the principal. I was there from third through fifth grade. Then I went to Glynn Middle School, right next to Glynn Academy in Brunswick. Glynn Middle was sixth, seventh, and eighth grades. By then, Mrs. Barone was the principal at Glynn Middle as well. My grandmother, Myrtle Lee, used to do Mrs. Barone's hair on weekends, so I'd see her in the shop often. I didn't get in much trouble in school, but when I did, I always got a "get out of jail free" card from Mrs. Barone. She'd pull me aside and give me a stern look and a lecture and send me back to class. Anyone else involved rarely got so lucky. I could hear the "whack" of the other kids getting the paddle in her office as I walked away. That was the first time I realized the truth in the old adage, "It pays to know people."

The Middle School music teacher was Margaret DeFino. Every day at the end of class, one student got to pick out a song from a box of 45 records and play it at the end of class–funk, R&B, rock, top 40. You could always tell what everybody was into by what they picked. I liked most everything. Mrs. DeFino asked Greg Parker, Joe

LeCates and myself, if we wanted to be in the chorus because she needed some male voices. We all joined up. We went over to Glynn Academy to see a chorus show one day. They had a drummer who played along with them. When it was over, I went to Miss DeFino and said, "I play drums, too. If we do a show, I could play." We did a Christmas show, and I played along with the chorus on "Jingle Bell Rock" in the cafeteria at Glynn Middle. The chorus sang along with a record player, and I played drums. She said, "I'm going to let you do an eight bar drum solo." And at that point I didn't even know what a "bar" was, but I somehow got through it. And that was the moment I realized it was really cool to play drums. It was my first taste of fame.

At Glynn Middle, the band program started in the sixth grade. I signed up for it. The band director was Mr. Frazier. I remember him as kind of a quirky guy. He went around asking, "What do you want to play?" The kid next to me said, "I want to play drums." Then Mr. Frazier pointed to me and said, "What do you want to play?" And I said, "Drums." He said, "We can't have a whole band full of drummers." At the end of the class he said, "I need three trumpet players, four trombone players, four drummers," and so on. Only two us in the whole class had said "drums." For some reason, I thought, "This guy's a bit too weird for me," and I transferred out of middle school band. In retrospect, I wish I hadn't because I had to do a lot of catching up in later years on skills I would have learned then.

I kept bugging my mom for real drums and eventually, she relented and found a little better drum set. I think my mom got that set from Betty Griner whose son, Emreid, had played briefly and lost interest. Betty and my Mom were friends and went to First Baptist Church together. That drum set was a little better than what I had but still a toy. I set it up in my room and played it every chance I got. I had to learn what drummers do by listening and figuring out what people on the records were doing. I spent a lot of time doing that. As I got better and my idols became more advanced, it was a continual challenge to see if I could pull off what they were doing. All the while, I continued to hassle my mom for better drums. At that point, I was in middle school, and my mom realized that I was serious about drumming and that it wasn't just a passing fad.

Patrick, age 13.

She and my grandparents took me to Dixie Music Center on Newcastle Street in Brunswick. I went in, and they had a used drum set in the window. Somebody had wrapped it in brown contact paper like you'd put on shelves, but I didn't care. They were real drums. I went in and sat down at it, and Mom said, "Is this what you want?" It was my first time sitting down at a real drum set. There was a guy in the back of the store testing out a guitar. He played some rock riff, "Smoke on the Water," or something, and I started playing along with it from across the store thinking, *Is this right?* He looked over at me. Then all the guys in the store turned and looked as well.

One of them said something to my mom. I guess I sounded okay because we took those drums home that day. That was one of the first times I got to sit down at a drum set and play with real people. Seems like that set cost around $250. The salesman kind of misrepresented it as a real, quality, pro drum set. As I learned more about drums, I realized it was pretty much a Taiwanese piece of junk, but it was better than everything I'd had up to that point.

Just before the start of my seventh grade year, Hurricane David threatened the coast, and we evacuated inland to stay with family in Alma. I remember packing up those drums and piling them inside my bedroom closet to protect them if the storm hit. I moved my dresser in front of the door as an added level of protection, thinking they'd be safer. I had no concept of the damage that floodwaters would have caused if it had hit us directly, but the drums were all I was worried about. Luckily, the storm skirted us, and the only thing that happened was that my first day of seventh grade was postponed one day.

I had that old drum set up through high school when I really got serious about it and needed real equipment. My grandfather took me to the Jekyll Island Aquarama to see Buddy Rich play.[2] He got us seats on the second or third row. The Valdosta State Jazz Band opened the show, and they had a really good jazz program. The drummer's name was John Hammond. Ironically, John is now a friend of mine and a working drummer in Nashville. There was a point during the show when he did some solo stuff, and I thought, *This guy is going to give Buddy a run for his money.* I was just a kid and didn't have clue as to what I was about to witness from Buddy. Buddy came out and played and did things that only Buddy Rich could do. I was sitting on the edge of my chair, totally sucked into it. It was the most amazing thing I'd ever seen. To this day, Buddy is revered as one of the greatest drummers to have ever lived. I was lucky enough to see him play three different times before his death in 1997. My grandfather knew then that I had been completely bitten by the bug. From that point, if I wanted something that had to do with drums, my family supported me a lot. They knew that, *This kid's going to be a drummer*. I don't know if they were happy about it, but they knew it.

In high school, my family thought *He's really serious about it. Let's take a little money and buy him something good.* They drove me to Jacksonville to Rhythm City, a big music shop. I was like a kid in a candy store. They had drums everywhere. I found this big ol' fancy chrome Ludwig drum set. I had to have it, and they bought it. It was around $1500. It was my first real, professional drum set. I used to polish it with a cloth every time I finished playing it.

When I got to Glynn Academy, one of the courses you had to take was Health and Safety. The class was taught by Theresa Adams, the girls' basketball coach. In the beginning of class she made us fill out a form—What's your name? Where are you from? What are you from? What are your hobbies? She went through each person's survey. When she got to me and read that my hobby was drums she asked, "Are you in band?" I said, "No." She said, "Why not?" I didn't realize that I could have even been in the band. I didn't do the Middle School band thing and thought that's what you had to do to be in high school band. She said, "I'll go talk to the band director. I'll get you in band."

Patrick, age 15

Tom Fouche was the band director. A couple of days later in class she said, "I talked to Mr. Fouche, and he wants to talk to you after class. Go over to his office and talk to him." I went in, and he said, "So you're a drummer? Why didn't you sign up for band?" I told him the story, and he said, "Do you want to join?" I said, "Absolutely." He got all the paperwork done, and they switched me out, and he got me into jazz band. At this point it was the second quarter of ninth grade, and marching band season is the first quarter, so I missed getting to march in the band my first year of high school. But I marched the remaining three years. Jazz band was actual drum set playing. Allen Amason was a senior who played drum set in the jazz band, and we swapped off on the drums during concerts and shows, alternating songs. He showed me a lot of stuff. At that point, I was just immersed in drumming, just soaking up everything I could soak up. I would have probably never joined the band if Ms. Adams hadn't taken the initiative to get me involved. I've always wanted to get a chance to tell her how huge of a fork in my life's road her interest in me turned out to be.

There's a popular drumming magazine called *Modern Drummer*. The magazine is full of trade ads, equipment reviews, and articles. I remember finding that magazine one day on the counter at Dixie Music Center. The reason I bought it was because the first real band that I was into–not my mother's records but something I discovered on my own–was KISS. Face paint, blood spitting, fire breathing, blowing up stuff…it was the coolest thing in the world for a young kid. Peter Criss, their drummer, was on the cover of the first issue I ever bought, and he didn't have his makeup on. KISS was always very secretive about their true identities, and I got to see for the first time on that magazine cover what he looked like without his cat whiskers. I talked my mom into getting me a subscription in high school, and I still subscribe to it to this day.

Spare Parts

For years, my mom worked for Kaufmann Associates, an advertising agency on St. Simons. The office was on Frederica Road at the foot of the McKinnon runway. All the doors had big numbers painted on them, and Kaufmann Associates was in number five. Sig Kaufmann was her boss. His son, Chuck, played guitar, and Chuck was good. He could really play. There was another guitarist on the island named Ewell Sasser. Ewell, Chuck, and a bass player named Cliff Gassett heard about me, this kid who could play drums, and called me to come play. I'd pile my drums in the car, my mom would take me over to the Ewell's house in Devonwood, and we'd just jam on tunes. We never really played anywhere, but that was one of my first experiences playing with a band and not just copying records.

Toward the end of high school, I got hooked up with a guitar player named Jim Mason. His brother, Dana, was a bass player, and they lived in Brunswick. They were trying to put a band together and called me. We worked up a bunch of songs, but we never did any gigs. Then it just petered out. Right about the time I was ending high school, Jim had joined a local band and started to play around clubs on the island. I got a call one day because the drummer had quit, they needed someone, and Jim had recommended me. That band was called Caruso. Stephen Harrison was a British guy whose parents had moved here from London. He was a couple of years older than me, but I knew him and his younger brothers because we were all in Boy Scouts together in Troop 248. His parents, Maynard and Valerie, opened the Horse's Head Pub in Longview Shopping Center. Stephen sang, Jim Mason played guitar, Scott Pendarvis played bass, and Johnny Murphy was on keyboards. We started playing at the Pub in the summer of 1983.

I was also working at the time at Ace Hardware in Longview Shopping Center for Hal Hart. That was an invaluable experience. My grandfather was always a tinkerer, a fix-it guy. I learned a lot from him and from working at the hardware store. Someone would come in with a piece of copper tubing and say, "This broke. I need to fix it." We'd go back to plumbing and play tinker toys. "Well, you can get this fitting and put this here, and do that..." They'd come in the next day or the next week and go, "Man, I got my refrigerator working. My icemaker works. Thanks for your help!" It was really gratifying. Hal taught me a lot about customer service and how important it is to go the extra mile to make your customers come back next time they need something. He was also a music fan, and he turned me on to a lot of music that I had never heard, like Pink Floyd, Frank Zappa, Traffic...bands I still love today. I learned all about PVC pipe and fittings, electrical fittings, plumbing, lumber, tools, paint....you name it. Now that I own a home and do a lot of that stuff myself, I can walk into Home Depot, pick out what I need and be done with it, instead of having to pay someone to do it for me. Hal was real cool about letting me gig a lot, playing The Pub until two or three in the morning and coming in late the next morning so I could sleep in a little longer.

Caruso got hooked up with an agency that booked bands for college frat parties in the Southeast. We'd drive to the University of Georgia and play a frat party, or go to the University of Alabama and play a dance. We'd all pile in one car, throw our gear in the back and go do it. If I ever die and come back as a musician, I'm going to be a flute player because a flute is small, you can carry it one little box, show up ten minutes before the show, and get out of there five minutes after. Setting up drums is a pain. I'm always the first one there and the last one out because I have to haul so much gear. Nowadays, playing with Charlie [The Charlie Daniels Band], there's a crew guy who does it all for me. He gets there in the morning and sets it up. I just kind of go there and look at the setup, do some minor tweaks to adjust things where they need to be and do the show. When the show's done, I throw the sticks out in the crowd and go to the bus. It's MUCH nicer than having to do it myself.

I have had a lot of equipment failures–broken drumheads, pedals, stands–and injuries over the years. I've hit myself in the face with a drum stick, torn out clumps of hair, smashed knuckles on drum rims…drumming is a very physical thing, and you will eventually lose focus and smack yourself across the nose! I especially remember one nightmare gig that made me realize I had to have some spare parts and tools with me at all times. It was right after high school when I was still working at Ace Hardware. I had found a strange lump in my neck. Ace Hardware had one of those old Coke machines where you pull the door open and pull out a Coke bottle. I was getting a Coke and pulled the door, and the reflection off the front store window hit just right where I could see this lump. The doctor did a biopsy, which turned out to be Hodgkin's disease, a form of lymphoma. I had to go through radiation treatment. One of the first things they did back then when you were diagnosed is they took your spleen out. They told me on Friday, "It's cancer. We've got to treat you." Monday morning, I was in the hospital in Brunswick having my spleen removed.

I had radiation therapy for five or six weeks–get up in the morning, drive over to Brunswick, lie underneath this big machine that zapped you with radiation, then go home and rest. This was 1983. The radiation knocked it out for a couple of years. So there I was, seventeen years old with a big bandage on my stomach from the spleen surgery. I was very sore and very weak. I could barely stand up and couldn't lift anything. We had to go to the University of Georgia to play a frat party. Halfway through the gig, I broke a snare drum head. The snare is the center of a drum set. You don't need a bunch of drums to do a gig but you HAVE to have a snare drum. I didn't have a spare, but I had a tom head [a thin circle of Mylar material attached to the top of a drum shell] that was the same size, but I didn't have a key [a tuning key used to speed up drum head changes]. So, I'm changing drumheads with a pair of pliers I found. It took ten minutes to do it. During a show, ten minutes is a lifetime. Stephen was out front trying to keep things going, and the crowd was getting antsy. There I was with a huge zipper scar down my stomach trying to get this drumhead changed to get through the gig. By the end of the night, I was totally wiped out. I barely got though the gig. That was the moment when I thought, *If I'm going do this for a living, I'm going to take a spare parts kit wherever I go.* I've got a box now that I built that's got drawers full of spare parts and tools. You could build four extra drum sets and a helicopter and have parts left over with what I haul around with me now.

Living the Dream

After high school, Caruso began doing roadwork down in Florida playing rock clubs. Scott and Jim left, so we brought in a guitar player named Rusty Fortner from Alabama and Billy Faure from Tampa to play bass. We played together for a couple of years and did well. The booking agency, ETA–Earl Tennant and Associates–was based in Orlando. Earl represented probably 15 or 20 bands. This was when nightclubs hired bands to play live music. We played Daytona, Miami, Tampa, Valdosta, Columbus, and Atlanta. Earl had clubs all over the southeast. You kind of just bopped around. He had clients who'd say, "We just had those guys a month ago. Who else you got?" And he'd just shuffle us around. We'd usually get there on a Monday and play six nights a week.

It was great for an eighteen-year-old kid, living the rock-and-roll dream. We'd stay in hotels. If you got two double rooms, you could fit four people in each one. There were five guys in the band and a sound guy and a lighting guy who drove the equipment truck. The band piled in my car. So, we had a little operation going. The booking agent would book the clubs, but we had to get our own rooms most times. We'd either call ahead or drive around a town until we found a place that was cheap. We usually tried to get one that had an efficiency [kitchenette]. Instead of everybody going to eat fast food all the time, we'd go to a local grocery store and load up for the week. Everyone took shifts and cooked. We were all just skinny kids. That's because we didn't eat. Not much anyway. A club might have a happy hour buffet with carrots and celery sticks and the occasional peel-and-eat shrimp, so we'd always show up early and raid the food before we played.

Caruso. Image courtesy of Patrick McDonald.

We pretty much played rock–cover stuff. We had a couple of original tunes, but nothing of any real substance. In that circuit, they had bigger bands do concert-type shows. One week in West Palm Beach, we opened for The Pat Travers Band and later the same week, the Steve Morse Band. It was great for me to get to do that because I got to get up close and really watch what the real, pro drummers were doing. One of the bands we played with at a club in Daytona Beach was called Dorian Gray. They were more of a hard rock band, and we were more like a pop band. We did Loverboy, Rolling Stones, INXS–pop hits. They did Mötley Crüe, Scorpions and Judas Priest—more heavy metal stuff. We spent weeks playing there during spring break. Out on the main pier in Daytona, there was a big building with a nightclub that had two stages facing each other and a huge dance floor between them. We would play for an hour, and they would play for an hour–three sets a-night, one-hour sets, seven nights a week.

The drummer in Dorian Gray was a guy named John Osborne. He was a good drummer and a great singer who sang lead on a bunch of songs. I got to know him fairly well. All the bands were real buddies because they shared the same dressing room. At some point, John's father passed away, and he had to go home for the funeral in upstate New York. Well, we were playing seven nights a week for six weeks at a pop with no days off. They needed a drummer, and I volunteered. I knew the majority of the material they did already, and I'd heard them so much, I knew their show. I played for six hours straight. I sat at my kit, did our set, jumped off my drum set, ran over and got behind John's drum set, played their material, then ran back over to mine. There was a point where I told their guitar player, "You've got to do a solo, man. I've got to go to the bathroom." At the end of it, I was totally exhausted, but they paid me thirty-five bucks. I thought that was a goldmine, because we didn't get any money. The band got paid, but we kept piling our money back into our PA equipment, because we got loans that we had to pay off before the band could take a paycheck.

The guitar player for Dorian Gray was Dave Chamberlin. Dave's younger brother, Steven, was a drummer, and he and John Osborne decided they were going to move to Los Angeles and become rock stars. Everybody rolled their eyes and thought, *Yeah. Right. Whatever.* They went out there, started playing, and eventually became Warrant, a big '80s "hair band." They had a lot of hits. John changed his name to Jani Lane. He went from playing drums for this bar band in Florida, to living in LA, dating Playboy centerfolds and being a rock star. Steven Chamberlain changed his name to Steven Sweet. He's still out doing it. I ran into him with Warrant on the road last year–hadn't seen him in 25 years. We're a lot alike in that we both still love to play drums and are still making a living doing it all these years later. A lot of folks give up on it when they find the lifestyle comes with more sacrifices than rewards most times. It looks glamorous from the outside, but it is hardly ever how it's made to appear. You have to have the undying fire in your belly to stick it out through the down times. And there can be a whole bunch of those in a lifetime of playing music.

The Caruso thing was still going when I had a recurrence of cancer in 1985. I had to quit the band and do chemotherapy. I went to Shands Hospital at the University of Florida, Gainesville, and did six months of chemo from August of '85 to January of '86. At that point, I was doing freelance work around St. Simons, playing jobs at the King & Prince Hotel and The Cloister. I found a teacher there, Bill Kotick, who played in the Sea Island orchestra. He was the house drummer at The Cloister. I was in my rock mode, and he was more of a jazz guy, so he started to teach me reading and turning me on to other things that I hadn't been exposed to. He had an idea that I had the raw materials, but hadn't polished everything and needed a chance. I was waiting tables as a wine steward at The Cloister. I'd get funny looks from a lot of the guests, because I'd wait on them as the wine steward one night, and the next night, they'd come back in for dinner, and I was in a tux behind Bill's drums subbing for him playing jazz standards–"Satin Doll," "Take the 'A' Train"–dinner music.

At that time, I decided I wanted to go to college and get serious about it. I applied to Berklee College of Music in Boston, but didn't get accepted. I filled out the application totally truthfully, and my lack of harmony and ear training knowledge made them deny me admission. My buddies who were on the drum line in high school had all gone to Georgia Southern College in Statesboro. They were telling me, "You should come up to Georgia Southern, man, and march in the band with us." Georgia Southern had an amazingly good drum line with some real monster players. I applied there and got in thinking I'd take a bunch of music classes and reapply to Berklee. I got a spot on snare drum and marched in the band at Georgia Southern with all my buddies from high school. We had a great time. That's really where my music reading chops got dialed in quickly. It was trial by fire. There was a ton of music to learn, and you had to be able to read music notation well to keep up. I used my ears a lot and was able to begin to see how the dots on paper corresponded to the sound I was hearing. It really all started to fall together and make sense to me while I was there. I did that for a year and reapplied to Berklee, and with a transcript that said I'd taken harmony and ear-training classes and got all A's, Berklee let me in.

I started Berklee in the summer of '87. That was when I got laser-focused and just immersed myself in practicing. I lived, breathed, ate and slept music and drumming non-stop. I was in Boston for two years and never saw much of the town. I spent 99% of my time in the practice room downstairs in the basement of the school. Coming from a little town like St. Simons, all I could glean for knowledge was what I could see off the television or what I could somehow decipher off of a record. I didn't really know exactly what everybody I idolized was doing, but I could hear it. I learned how to listen closely and figure it out. But I really hadn't had a teacher until I met Bill [Kotick] a couple of years prior. At Berklee, I found out there were names for a lot of the things I already knew how to do.

I ranked better than I thought I would with the other drummers. Berklee had a reputation of being this place with a huge pool of monster players just ready to take the world by storm. That's really not the case. They probably had five or six hundred drummers, especially in the fall. In the summer it was a lot quieter. There were guys who were way better than me, but there were a lot of guys who are just beginners, who had just recently decided that's what they wanted to do. If you had the money and didn't mind fudging your application, they would accept you. One of the reasons I didn't finish is because it's very expensive. My maternal grandparents had set aside money to help me pay for it, but it just cost too much. I started to see the ridiculousness of paying that much–$20,000 to $25,000 a year in 1987-'88. It was not cheap. It's twice that now. I never applied for a scholarship because I didn't think I could get one. I was under the assumption that, "I'm just this dumb kid from Georgia. There's no way they're going to give me any money. These guys are all great. I'm just happy to get in." Then I got there and realized there were kids there getting half of their tuition paid, and they had only been playing for two years. They had just applied for aid and gotten it. I went to the admin office and said, "I've already got experience. I've done gigs. I can already play." They said, "Well, now you're competing for money with the upper classmen. You're going to have to hang around for a couple of years before you can get a taste of that," because they only have so much money to give out. It just got cost-prohibitive. At the same time, I kind of grew up a little and realized that, in the real world, a degree that says you know how to play drums is worthless. If you get one that says you're qualified to be a music teacher, then you can go to a school system and apply and say, "I've got a music education degree." If you want to work in a recording studio, you've got to know how that works. Those degrees are valuable. A performance degree that says, "I know how to play a drum set"… nobody hiring cares about a degree. They just want to hear you play and know you can do the job.

I learned a whole bunch of stuff in school, but I learned more just hanging around with a bunch of other guys just like myself who were totally about drumming. We shared information and traded licks: "Here's what I just figured out…Look what I learned in this lesson." Drummers were really open with that at Berklee. Guitar players were guys who put their headphones on and practiced with their back to the door. They didn't want anyone to see what they were doing, like it was a secret. You could walk by a practice room and see some drummer doing something cool and ask, "What is that you're doing?" He'd say, "I'm playing a seven over three with my feet and a Samba in five on the top of it." I'd go to my room and try to work it out. Drummers are a different breed. The old joke is bands have four musicians and a drummer. It's somewhat true, although not in the condescending way the joke is usually told. Personality wise and thought process wise, we are a little different. Several guys I went to school with there are doing great in music. We talk to each other now and go, "Hey, it worked. We actually did something."

While in Boston, I studied privately about eight months with an instructor name Gary Chaffee. Gary was Chairman of the Percussion Department at Berklee back in the '70s [1972-1976]. He was a world-renowned teacher who taught some of the greatest drummers of our generation. I was lucky to get a spot with him. I wish I could go back and do it all again because I know I could get a lot more out of it now. I've always caught on late. There were other kids who had much more perspective and focus and knew what they were trying to do. Gary's thing was to give you a basic framework and then have you take it home and work on it and come back the next week and show him what you could do with it. I never really grasped that when I was there. I just thought you went to some guy who showed you what to do and when you came out, you were good at it. One day Gary said, "You've had enough school. Go play now. Take what you've learned and go apply it. More school is not going to help. Just go gig."

So I went home. There was another circuit of bands in Georgia and Florida that were part of a more Top 40 club scene. Pier Seventeen was a club at the Ramada Inn on Glynn Avenue in Brunswick. They used to have bands. I got to know guys in those bands, and they turned me on to their booking agent, Ted Skorman. My buddies in those bands told him, "This guy in Brunswick is looking for a gig. You need to find him something." One day I got a call. The agency put a band together to play on a cruise ship. It was all guys I'd never met. I ended up going to Reading, Pennsylvania and rehearsing in the basement of the bandleader's house over Christmas. It was cold, wet, miserable, and I was rehearsing these cheesy Top 40 tunes to play on a cruise ship out of Cape Canaveral. As we say in the business: when things get to be depressing…"Livin' the dream, Baby!"

We played in the big nightclub on the ship. We played there every night from 9:00 pm to 1:30 or 2:00 am. We'd leave on a Monday and do a four-day run to the Bahamas. We'd go to Nassau, spend a couple of days down there, have a day at sea on Thursday, and be back at Cape Canaveral on Friday. There were different levels of staff on the ship. If you were a waiter, plumber, or technician–most of those guys were Indonesian, Filipino, European–you stayed down below. You never saw them unless they were working. But cruise staff, which was what we were considered, were up a level. We interacted directly with the passengers. We were encouraged to "socialize–do not fraternize." Those rules got bent now and again. We didn't get to eat in the dining room with the passengers, but there was a captain's mess off to the side of the dining room with the same menu where the officers ate. We ate there every day. There were times when I thought I would puke if I had to eat lobster or prime rib again, because on a cruise ship it's all this fancy fare. That's all they had, and it's all you ate. We couldn't wait to get to Nassau and go to Taco Bell and just get a big, greasy, nasty burrito–something that wasn't lobster. Tough life, I know. But the best food in the world gets old fast when you eat it every day.

We had four-month contracts as a band. We'd play four months and take a couple of months off. The bandleader asked us if we were going to come back each time. I said, "Yes," three or four times. They paid good money, I didn't have to pay rent, had no bills, and ate for free. So I had this big pile of cash. The only hobby I had was scuba diving. I'd go diving when I had days off in the Bahamas. The guy I worked with on the cruise ship was a heavy drinker, very unpredictable and as a result, a bit of a nutcase. I finally told the agent I was tired of dealing with him and wanted something else.

Skorman hooked me up with a different band, and I did that for a year or so playing Holiday Inn lounges and nightclubs all over the southeast. We worked a lot. That led me to Sarasota, Florida, doing a house jazz gig at the Down Under Jazz Bar. I did the house gig in Sarasota playing jazz for a couple of years. Then I got offered a job with a local smooth jazz guitar player named Richy Kicklighter and decided to leave. It was time to do something else. About a week after I left, the Down Under went bankrupt. The IRS came in and chained the doors shut. I just barely got out of there. The rest of the guys in the band went to work one night and found the club closed and their gear locked up. They could see their equipment on stage through the windows, but it was confiscated. They had to go through a lot of rigmarole to get it back. I jumped ship just before it went under not knowing it would.

I played with Richy for a few months, but he wasn't working much. There was another guy in town, John Prestia, doing original rock-and-roll club work. I joined up with John and played with him for a few years in Sarasota from 1993-'97. John and myself and a bass player named Mike Rector played John's original songs and cover tunes and hopped from club-to-club every weekend. Mike left, and we got Bruce Waibel who had played with Gregg Allman's band on the "I'm No Angel" album and tour. We made a fairly decent living. I was also doing a lot of teaching and recording work. There were a couple of local recording studios, and I was kind of the first-call guy in Sarasota if you needed someone to play drums on a project.

I met two brothers, Brent and Scot Ware, on a session call in Sarasota. They had a fiber optic company called Amherst Communications and were very well off. They were heavily into Christian music and put together a big production with a giant band of people, and they financed it all. I played on their project and did occasional gigs with them at mega-churches and Christian music festivals. Brent called me one day and said, "We're moving the company to Nashville. You should come up there." Their only direct competition was in Nashville, and they thought, *We're going to be right in their back yard.* They still wanted to do the band thing because Nashville was, and still is, the seat of the Christian music world. I had already been thinking, *I've reached as high as I can get in Sarasota. I could stay here, make a living in clubs, and be here forever.*

I finally decided it was going to be Nashville, LA, or New York. From what I had heard, the recording scene and the work scene in LA was drying up. The climate had changed. Guys were bailing out of LA to go to Nashville. New York was more of a jazz thing, which I like, but it wasn't where I wanted to go. Plus it was cold, and I don't like snow. So I went to the gig one night and told John, "Man, I'm giving you my notice. I'm moving to Nashville." Coincidentally, John had always been into songwriting and had been in touch with a friend in Nashville about moving up there, too. He had come to the gig that night to tell the guys, "I'm folding the band and moving to Nashville." John has now been working with Tim McGraw for ten years, and he's well connected. He still plays restaurant and club gigs in Nashville just for fun, and I still play with him now and again.

I moved to Brentwood, a Nashville suburb, and lived in Brent Ware's basement. The first thing I did was get in my truck and drive downtown to a local jam night. I had to get out in the scene and get to know people. I got lucky and met the right folks. Within a couple of weeks, I was working club gigs and within three or four months, I got recommended for the gig with Tanya Tucker's band–my first real, road, traveling-on-a-bus, "artist" gig. That lasted about ten months. We traveled all over America. As is typical for Tanya's operation, she decides mid-stream to change things. She routinely fires musicians, and I was one of the guys who got let go. Sort of a rite of passage, I later found out. The local joke is you have to be fired by Tanya to have really arrived in Nashville. Don't worry about it. Don't let it get you down. Just keep on slugging it out. And that's what I did.

Next, I got a house gig at a club on Dickerson Road called the Starlight Club. I did that for a couple of years. The bass player, Dennis Gulley, was an engineer at Johnny Neel's studio. Johnny had played keyboards for The Allman Brothers in the '90s. I was starting to do session work doing demos and playing on actual records. Dennis called one morning and said, "Can you come over and bail us out? I've got Charlie Daniels' keyboard player, Taz Degregorio, here. He hired one of his buddies to play drums. The guy's not cutting it, and we're getting behind." I loaded up the kit and went to Johnny's, set up and played and got them back on schedule. I knew who Taz was because Philip Sheffield and I used to sit around and bang on the piano on St. Simons. Philip had learned "The Devil Went Down To Georgia." He had a drum set and I played along with him in his living room.

Two weeks later, Charlie's drummer, Jack Gavin, quit after thirteen or fourteen years. When Charlie auditions new people, he doesn't like to have a big cattle call and invite everybody in town. He goes to the guys in the band and says, "You know the players. I want you to give me the name of the one guy you think would be right for this." Taz told him about me, and everybody else had some other names. Four or five other guys auditioned. It wasn't what I really thought I wanted to do at the time. I was trying to get a Keith Urban, Tim McGraw, Alan Jackson, Reba McEntire kind of gig–one of the big time, CMT gigs. As it turned out, it's been the best thing in the world, because those gigs are not always what they're cracked up to be. Charlie Daniels is considered to be a legend act. He had his heyday twenty-five years ago. He's still out doing it. Everybody respects him. But he's not selling out hockey rinks like Rascal Flatts, Kenny Chesney, or Tim McGraw. Charlie *was* them in back when I was a kid on St. Simons playing along with his records in my bedroom, worrying about the folks in the nursing home next door, thinking they were going to complain about all this loud drumming.

I auditioned on a Saturday. Taz gave me a bunch of tunes and said, "Here's the material you need to learn for the audition." So I learned it all and played a couple of songs at the audition. Most of it was Charlie going, "I got this new idea... kind of a riff thing like this. Let's just pick this up." And we would just jam. He wanted to see if I had ears and could keep up. All those years of listening to records and figuring out parts by ear really helped me. My ears were pretty sharp. I had been doing it for years. So we just jammed a bunch of stuff and had fun. It's funny that I wasn't intimidated. I had been listening to him my whole life. Most artists know you can play, or you wouldn't be there. They want to hear how confident and solid you are. If you go in intimidated and scared, they can sense it. You going in thinking, *You called me because you think I might have what it takes. Well, I'm here to show you I have what it takes. So, let's do it!* If you relate to any celebrity on that level–*You're just a person like me and everybody else*– most of them appreciate because they're so tired of having their asses kissed.

The audition lasted forty-five minutes to an hour. He pulled me aside and said, "We've got a couple of more guys to hear. At this point, you're the frontrunner. But I told these guys I'm going to give them a shot. Tomorrow at six o'clock we'll be done. I'll make a decision and let you know."

The next day, the phone rang at six o'clock sharp. Charlie said, "It's your gig if you want it. It pays 'X' amount." I said, "Okay." At that point, I wasn't picky. He told me years later, "You know why you got this gig, right?" I said, "No...tell me." He said, "Because the night I told you it paid this much, you didn't argue with me. You just took it. You didn't nickel and dime me over this or that."

There are lot of musicians who look at it like they're here to make money, and if there's money to be made, they're going to get what they can get. Some people are very much about that. They say, "This is what I charge if you want me." I've never been comfortable with that. I figure I'm lucky to be playing for a living. The money always takes care of itself. When Charlie hired me, he low-balled just to see if I'd take it. I did, and he gave me a raise the next day before I'd even played a show with the band. Not being a stickler for money can be a double-edged sword in this business though. I have many friends who hire me to play on recording projects or side gigs, and I can't count how many times they've told me they wanted to hire me but didn't think I'd do the gig because they didn't have much money to pay. I always have to remind people that I'm not a money hound. If the gig or session is fun, and I know there will be great musicians on it, I don't care if they can't pay a dime. I'll do it for nothing just to have fun and be creative with great musicians. So many people are hung up on how much they can make that the leaders sometimes just assume that I'm lumped in that pile. They figure I have a "name" gig now with a big artist, so I won't take something that pays beneath my price. It can be trying at times to know I missed out on a really cool thing just because someone assumed I wouldn't do it because it didn't pay enough. Such is the life of a musician.

I started with the Charlie Daniels Band in March 1999. Charlie comes from the old school. He's a big Allman Brothers and Marshall Tucker fan. His philosophy is, "Let's get up and play some music and see what happens." That's the way it used to be done. [Led] Zeppelin and those guys took these twenty-minute tangents where they'd just explore, and that's what made it fun. Then the industry became more about the three-minute pop song–people coming to the show to hear *that* song, and they want to hear it *that* way. A lot of the Nashville machine is now about, *Here are the songs. The session guys play them. We put artist X on the album cover. She or he sings these songs. We hire a band. The band gets paid to go out and copy what was on that record. Stay out of the way. Be transparent. She or he is the star. Play it the same way every night, and don't vary.* Some of them are really extreme about that. Do not vary at all. "I don't want to hear da-da-DAT-da when it's supposed to be da-da-da-da." The record is law. The way you played it last night or three months ago is how you'd better play it tonight.

Charlie is totally different. The first rehearsal I came in as a new guy. I didn't know the abilities or the comfort levels of the rest of the guys in the band. I had just met them. I didn't know if the guitar player really doesn't know how to count well and all he knows is, *I come in when I hear "do-do-dat-dum", That's when my guitar part starts.* I didn't know this yet. I had been given the tapes of their live performances, and I played the stuff that Jack played. Just to clarify, I said during the rehearsal, "On the tape, Jack did this. Is that what you guys are used to hearing? If that's what you want to hear, I'll do that." Charlie said, "No, no. Just do you whatever you want." A couple of tunes later, I said, "On the tape Jack did bat-ta-da-do-dum. Do you want me to do that to lead it in?" After a couple or three times of doing that, Charlie stopped the rehearsal and said, "Son, I hired you to play drums because I need a drummer, you know how to do it, and I don't. You just do whatever you want to do and we'll follow you." That's an extreme rarity in the Nashville music world. I have friends on major gigs out of Nashville who still are stunned to hear that. It just doesn't happen often around town.

Charlie doesn't use session guys to make records. He doesn't hire outside musicians to play his material. He wants it to be a band thing. If The Allman Brothers had made *Eat A Peach* and didn't use Dickey [Betts] and Jaimoe [Johansen] and those guys, it wouldn't have been the same record. There's something about the collective sound of the guys you have as a unit. There aren't many bands in Nashville. It's all singers and songwriters. There may be a few Lonestar or Diamond Rio type bands, but generally it's solo "artists." It's very much a machine. You don't get bands that have character and sound like U2 or The Dave Matthews Band. They have their own sound, and you know it's them when you hear it. But it comes about because they play together, and all the personalities make them what they are. Nashville has always been a "song" town and not a "band" town.

When we tour, Charlie and his wife ride on their own bus. The band and crew ride on another bus, and then we have an equipment truck. We have three vehicles, which is way scaled down from what somebody like Rascal Flatts or Tim McGraw has. They've got fifteen trucks and eight buses. If we have to play, say St. Louis, tomorrow night, we'll get on the bus at midnight, socialize, get in our bunks, watch a movie, fall asleep and wake up the next morning in the parking lot of a hotel. About 10:00 or 11:00 in the morning, the crew will go to the venue with the equipment truck. They'll set up all the gear. Charlie stays in the hotel or on his bus. He does interviews, radio and phone-ins during the day. They take his exercise gear inside the hotel, move the beds out of the way, and set up a little gym for him so he can work out. He spends the majority of the time on the bus, because it's nicer than any hotel room, and it's home for him.

Patrick onstage with Charlie Daniels. Courtesy of Patrick McDonald.

We don't have to do sound checks. I have a drum tech that sets up my gear, but I like to tune the drumheads and do my own maintenance, so sometimes I'll go to the venue with the crew and tinker with my drums. Say the show is at 7:00. The van will come and pick us up at the hotel at 5:00 or 6:00 o'clock and lead Charlie's bus to the venue. Charlie does the meet-and-greet thing with fans before the show. When the show's done, he gets in his bus. He and his wife and their driver are off to the next town. After the equipment is torn down, put into the cases and loaded back into the truck, we'll go back by the hotel. The crew guys go in and get Charlie's exercise gear and throw that on the truck. Everybody has time to go in, grab a shower, and get cleaned up, get their stuff, get back on the bus and then go to the next show. That's pretty much our life for nine months of the year. I've traveled all over the U.S. and really haven't seen a lot of it. Everybody sleeps while we're driving. I had been over Hoover Dam a dozen times before I ever saw it because I was asleep every time.

We add new material to the set each year. Charlie lets everybody in the band that writes songs perform one song in the set. Taz, Bruce [Brown], and Chris [Wormer] do songs. Charlie Hayward and I don't sing or write. Every year when we do rehearsals for the new set, we have to do the hits–"Drinkin' My Baby Goodbye," "Legend Of Wooley Swamp," "In America," "Long Haired Country Boy," "Uneasy Rider," "The Devil Went Down To Georgia," "The South's Gonna Do It." Those are standards. What happens in between are the other songs. Charlie may write an instrumental he wants everybody to stretch out and blow on. Those songs, I have to think about. The standards, I don't. But it's still a rush to play songs like "Devil." Even though I didn't play on the original record, I always remember playing along to it as a kid in my bedroom on Bracewell Court. That's the last song in the set. You've got to make the audience wait. When you get to that one, you know that 60% of the audience is there to hear that song. As soon as we start that song, they go nuts–every night. When we play big festivals with 75,000 to 100,000 people, that's when you can really feel the energy.

We'll usually come up with the show at the beginning of the year, and Charlie will arrange what he wants. Over the course of the first few shows, he may move things around. The crew still puts set lists down; they'll tack them on the stage so you can see them. A month into the year, I don't even have to look at them. Charlie has a little talking schtick he does before each song, and from that, I always know where it's going. I use in-ear monitors, so I can hear everything he's saying. There are times when I'll be doing something—adjusting a stand or tuning, expecting to play the next song on the list, and Charlie will say, "I'm going to do one we did back in 1977." "Trudy" is one of those on-hold songs. It may not be in the set list, but you never know when he might pull it out and spring it on you. Sometimes, Charlie will tell us before the show that he had a request for "Trudy" and to be ready. But most times, he'll just play it. But that's what he pays us for. You've got to be alert. You can relax, but you have to keep your ears open. He likes to know he's got guys behind him who can turn on a dime and stay with him.

We've been to Iraq four times now to play for the troops there. The first time, they flew us on a 737 to Frankfurt, Germany. The plane was all white–no markings, all big first-class seats–what they use to fly congressmen when they go overseas. As the war went on and it got more expensive and budgets got cut, they started paying for us to fly commercial to Frankfurt because Frankfurt was the hub of military operations, and we would have to get on military flights–C-17s, C-130s. The last time, we flew commercial direct to Kuwait City, then transferred to military flights out of Camp Arifjan. Most of the time now, it's commercial flights going over and military flights when you're there. They issue us flak jackets and helmets on the military flights.

The first time we went was 2002. You could hear roadside bombs going off and explosions in the distance. One night, we were flying back into Baghdad in a Chinook helicopter. We were all exhausted. We had been playing all day, hopping around to all these little bases doing impromptu acoustic shows, and then finished the day with a big show on a major base. Just as we were flying into Camp Victory in Baghdad, the helicopter did this little jog in mid-air. I heard "Pop! Pop! Pop! Pop!" and looked out the back. The seats run down the side, so you're facing the center. They had the back door of the Chinook open, and I saw flashes from chaff grenades. One of the generals who was with us said, "Something's going on out there. They don't use those things unless there's a reason." When we hit the ground, they said, "Someone just shot at us. We took fire just as we were coming in." Our soundman, Bob, was sitting up front. They reinforce the undersides with Kevlar. Bob said he could feel the rounds hitting underneath his feet. The Kevlar kept the rounds from coming through.

A couple of years later, we played in Iraq again. When we finish a show, we sign autographs for every soldier who wants one. We may play an hour show and sit in the autograph line for three hours. One of the guys came through the autograph line and said, "Remember when you guys were shot at a few years ago?" We said, "Oh, yes." He said, "I was part of the recon team that went out and took care of those guys. There were about seven of them hunkered down. Let me assure you, they won't be a problem anymore."

In 2005, we were asked to play during the pre-game show at Super Bowl XXXIX in Jacksonville. We were part of a "current stars and their influences" theme show, and Gretchen Wilson was on the top of the charts at that time. Gretchen and The Black Eyed Peas were asked to perform and pick who they felt were their biggest influences. She asked Charlie to perform with her, and The Black Eyed Peas chose Earth, Wind, and Fire. It was an incredible experience to be a part of such a huge spectacle. It was by far the biggest audience I have ever performed for with an estimated viewing audience of 94 million people. The backstage area was like a Hollywood movie premiere, and I got to meet and rub elbows with a lot of stars that night. I've been a huge Earth, Wind, And Fire fan for years, and getting to meet them as a peer was one of the highlights of my career. Even though we played on the field as part of the show, we weren't given actual tickets to sit in the stadium and watch the game. Charlie was kind enough to purchase tickets for everyone, and we got to stay for the game and see the incredible Paul McCartney halftime show live in person as well as watch a great game.

I was a Rush fanatic in high school and went to see them play at the Jacksonville Coliseum. Neil Peart was my idol, and I dissected and learned everything he played when I was growing up. I saw .38 Special, Eddie Money, Van Halen, AC/DC, The Police...all of them there. Years later, I played there on the same stage where Neal Peart was sitting thinking, *So THIS is what it looks like from up here.* Twenty years ago, I was out there hoping I could get up there someday. It's surreal but gratifying to know I finally made it up there.   I still like playing "Legend of Wooley Swamp" every night. It's a cool, story song with a nice riff. And it carries a lot of childhood memories of St. Simons. Someone gave me a tape of it when I was little. I'd walk over across the nursing home lot to Philip Sheffield's house and say, "Man, you've got to hear this," and we'd sit there with our ears to the boom-box speaker. I'd be in my room playing and learning that song, and now I play it every night with Charlie.

Where it All Started

There are people that live on St. Simons today who have no idea what it was like back then. I remember when one area was woods where I used to play, now it's a multi-million dollar housing development. Or that fancy ground-lit tree in that guy's yard still has a knot on the branch from the rope where we hung our tire swing. There was a quaintness to it–a little encapsulated way of life that's gone. The hominess of it is kind of gone, but there are still places that remind me of it. If I go into a little auto parts store somewhere, there's a smell that reminds me of when I was a little kid playing on the floor of my grandfather's store. Or riding down in the village where Al's Garage used to be and is now a restaurant. If you pull up the tile you'd find the hole where the hydraulic lift was. The Union 76 gas station on the corner where I used to help pump gas is now a restaurant. Curtis Stephens' little homemade amusement park by the old casino is gone. The new casino itself is gone. It's strange to see all the people who live there now, who don't know the history of the place. But that's how life works. I only get back there once a year or so to visit my brother's family, but it always surprises me how many memories I relive each time.

When I was young, it felt like the island was hidden away from everything. I couldn't get away or do anything. I was just stuck on this little island. I dreamed of getting away and being a rock star. I wanted to be world-wise. Well, now I am a lot more world-wise than I ever imagined I'd be. But years later, driving through the pine forests, through Baxley and Jesup or around Jekyll Island, I realize that this is me. This is what I came from, and it's really cool and unique. It's nice to drive around St. Simons and be really proud of it. It's a special little place and still has a lot of character even though it's been glossed over and polished, and a lot of people have been pushed out. People with money have come in and tried to make it something it never really was to me. But what can you do? It's progress, good or bad. You can't tell them to tear it down and put it back like it was. That part's gone. I've been all over the planet–Asia, Europe, The Middle East–and all over virtually every corner of North America, and I've done and seen a lot of amazing things. I go back home to St. Simons and think to myself, *this is where it all started.* If it wasn't for this and this happening, and if these people hadn't been cool about me playing drums, who knows what would have happened? I met my beautiful wife Jessica during my time in Sarasota, and she gave me a beautiful little girl who is the center of my world. If I hadn't ended up going there when I did, I wouldn't have either of them. But I do, and it's all because one path led to another, to another and another, and here I am.

A few years ago, I saw Ann and Henry Wheeler, our next-door neighbors on St. Simons after the Buglino's moved out. Ann and Henry are saints for putting up with that horrendous racket I made as a kid learning to play. My windows leaked like a sieve. If I had the TV on, they could hear it. Ann told me, "You don't know how many times I wanted to come over there and hit you on the head with a steel pipe to make you quit making that racket!" And I said, "I owe you forever for not doing it. That allowed me to play and learn, and now make a living from it."

Because of all of these things happening in the past, that's why we're here. I can look back now and see the points on the tree trunk where the major branches sprouted. This guy told me this, which led me here, and this person did that, which got me to there. If they hadn't done that, I might have ended up selling auto parts.

NOTES

[1] Howard Earle Coffin, automotive engineer and executive, purchased Sea Island (formerly called Long Island, then Glynn Isle) in 1926, and co-founded the Sea Island Company with his cousin, Alfred W. Jones.

[2] "Bernard 'Buddy' Rich (September 30, 1917–April 2, 1987) was an American jazz drummer and bandleader. Rich was billed as 'the world's greatest drummer' and was known for his virtuosic technique, power, groove, and speed."…. Rich was born in Brooklyn, New York, to vaudevillians Robert and Bess Rich. His talent for rhythm was first noted by his father, who saw that Buddy could keep a steady beat with spoons at the age of one. He began playing drums in vaudeville when he was 18 months old, billed as 'Traps the Drum Wonder.' At the peak of Rich's childhood career, he was reportedly the second-highest paid child entertainer in the world (after Jackie Coogan). At 11 he was performing as a bandleader. He received no formal drum instruction, and went so far as to claim that instruction would only degrade his musical talent. He also never admitted to practicing, claiming to play the drums only during performances and was not known to read music. Wikipedia, http://en.wikipedia.org/wiki/Buddy_Rich, accessed June 3, 2011.

Johnny Ronald Edenfield

Reidsville State Penitentiary was opened in the 1937, in part to replace the old system of prison farms that housed many of Georgia's convicts. Ron Edenfield's father worked at Reidsville as a correctional officer, and the family lived in employee housing near the prison gates. Ron discusses aspects of life growing up in rural Georgia during the 1950s and '60s and provides a unique perspective on Georgia's main prison facility. As this narrative reveals, it is a world unto itself.

My name is Johnny Ronald Edenfield. I was born in Macon, March 14, 1955 at Bibb County Hospital. My father's name is Johnny Edenfield, and my mother's name is Mildred Louise Edenfield. He was from Twin City, a small town about twelve to fourteen miles from Swainsboro headed back toward Statesboro. He's from a small town outside of Twin City called Garfield. My mother is from Garfield, too.

We stayed in Macon until I was about four years old. We lived in a small house on Log Cabin Drive, which is downtown, right off Cherry Street. My dad worked in the flooring business for a while, putting down hardwood floors. My momma used to carry me to a place called The Georgia Theatre to watch movies. My dad was also a city bus driver in Macon and had a pretty terrible accident. An old man, who was almost blind, used to ride his bus every day. One day, he walked out in front of the bus and was killed. My dad wanted to get out of that business after that and get away from Macon, so we moved to Swainsboro. I went back a couple of times, and the house we used to live in is no longer there.

Back then, Swainsboro was just a small town. When I went to first through fifth grade, we lived in a two-story wooden house on North Main Street. Me and my sisters used to walk to school. One sister is a year younger, and one was three years younger than me. I was kind of like a mother hen. We had to walk about a mile to school and cross a busy highway to get to Church Street, where Swainsboro Elementary was, and I had to keep them out of the street. Momma would escort us across the highway coming home.

My first grade teacher was Miss Fran Deakle, and my second grade teacher was Miss Neal. The teacher who influenced me more than any of them was my third grade teacher, Miss Fordham. She was kind of different from anyone else–ten degrees off from everybody else. She let the students run the classroom, but she kept order. She had you do special projects. Somebody led the class in the pledge of allegiance every morning. And every morning she'd pick two people–she always seemed to pick me–to grab these little plastic pails to go to the lunchroom to get everybody a half pint of milk. If you didn't have breakfast before school, you got something in your belly before you got started that day to kind of hold you. It was nothing to see a lot of kids come to school barefooted. A lot were farmers' kids. Everybody was in that same group. I'd say we were poor kids too, but we weren't in quite as bad a fix as some of the rest of them. We went to school with good clothing and shoes.

At one of the schools was a two-story building they turned into a store upstairs that sold cokes for a dime and jars of pinwheel cookies that cost two cents a cookie. You could go there before school started or at recess. At that time, you went to one classroom and stayed there all day. You took all your subjects from that one teacher. It was that way up until I got to the sixth grade. We changed from elementary to middle school where you went to different classrooms.

Middle school was Swainsboro Junior High, about a quarter of a mile down the street from the elementary school. I only went one year there, to sixth grade. When we went on summer break, we moved to Reidsville. My dad was working at the Reidsville prison [state penitentiary] and was driving back and forth between Reidsville and Swainsboro. They have a housing project for the guards who work there. After a guard put in a certain amount of time, he'd put in for a house if you wanted to live there. You didn't pay any rent. They only thing you paid for was a telephone. Everything else came free.

They had a swimming pool and a tennis court for the people that worked there. They even gave you a gallon of milk free every day. They had a dairy farm. Back then, when you moved in, they would give you a little wooden box that had two slots just big enough to hold two quart bottles. You would get in your car and go down to the dairy and pull up, just like a drive-thru. You'd stick it [the box] out the window to the convict who is standing there. He takes the two empty bottles out and puts two full ones in and hands it back to you. You could do that twice a day; once in the morning before eleven o'clock and once in the afternoon before four o'clock. So everybody that worked there got a gallon of milk–free.

They grew a lot of vegetables there; still do, and if you worked at the prison, whenever, say, English peas were in, you could call up there and say, "I'm going to the field and pick some English peas." They'd say, "Well, come up here and get you a permit." They called them the "Rat Patrol," two or three people who did nothing but maintain the guard line. They rode around in a state truck and would stop if they saw something suspicious. But if you had a permit, you were okay. And everyone knew most everybody and knew their vehicles. My parents had an old 1963 green Pontiac. If the patrol saw a 1963 green Pontiac parked in the field, they knew Mr. Johnny was out there getting some corn or peas or tomatoes or whatever.

When we first moved there in the summer of 1968, we pulled a trailer. They had a very small trailer park with about ten trailers in it. About a year later, they had a trailer spot open a mile-and-a-half down the road right on the fence line of what they called the Industrial Building. We moved that trailer in there, and it caught on fire and got smoked up pretty bad. So, we got rid of the trailer and moved into one of the houses. Our address was Star Route, Box 1328. They did a lot of things back then to help the people who worked there. You didn't pay rent. You didn't pay an electric bill. You didn't pay a water bill. The only expense we had was a phone bill. That was when they were needing help in the '60s and '70s, and they gave those incentives to get people to come there to work.

The Reidsville prison was started in 1936 by the WPA for the federal government. Before they put any inmates in it, they sold it to the state, and the prison opened in 1937.[1] There was an area down the road from the prison towards the river called "The Old Camp" [possibly a Prison Farm]. I'm not sure if that was back before they built the prison. My dad worked at the prison for almost thirty years. We were living there when a young man, a guard named Dan Harrison, was killed. He got trapped in a "sally port," an area about ten to fifteen feet long between two dormitories. They [the inmates] were upset with him over something. Two dormitory doors got opened somehow, and they stabbed him to death. The way things worked then, you worked six days straight, then had three days off. The reason they had guards living there was if there was trouble, a riot or something, they had manpower who could go there immediately. They had a big horn that sounded like a freight train, which you could hear for miles. If you ever heard that horn, it meant that everybody that lived at the prison needed to put their uniform on and rush up there.

There are two prisons in Reidsville. GSP [Georgia State Prison] is a mile down the road and then there's Rogers State Prison, a minimum-security prison. Reidsville is a maximum-security prison. And you have a prison over in Glennville, one in McRae, one in Eastman, and a detention center in Statesboro. Just about any town of any size around here has one. One of the guys I grew up with just got promoted to Warden at GSP. I lived next door to him. When he got out of high school, he went to work at Georgia State Prison and moved up through the ranks from Correctional Officer 1 to Captain of the Guard and Warden at Glennville and now Warden at GSP.

When my dad first hired on, he was a correctional officer working security. The next job he had was running the sawmill that cut wood to build houses and other facilities around the state. After that they had an opening in the canning plant, and he got promoted to Canning Plant Supervisor. He ran the canning plant for the last 10-12 years he worked there. These are all prison-run facilities. They raise cows and hogs, and they have a slaughterhouse. They used to have chicken houses, but they don't keep them anymore. Prisoners worked in all these places. They had shotgun details–back then guards could carry shotguns–because they were working maximum-security prisoners. They work minimum and medium-security prisoners these days. Maximum-security prisoners are in their cells twenty-three hours a day.

Anytime there was an escape, the horn would go off, and everybody put their uniforms on and set up roadblocks. My dad had a detail called Detail 27 in the "roughhouse" part of the prison. He had seven [escaping] prisoners load up on a truck. They [the guards] tried to shoot them off the truck. When my dad came back to the house and said, "There's seven of them out, but we can't find any of them," you get a little antsy living so close. The seven just drove out and stayed gone for two weeks 'til they finally captured all of them. But I actually felt more threatened working there than I did living there. There's a little store that sits right across the road from the prison, and we used to walk across prison property, within twenty feet of the fence, taking a short cut to that store. Now, you're not even allowed to drive in that area. We used to play baseball in the field right next to the prison. I actually played pitch with prisoners inside the fence. I'd throw my baseball to them over in the prison yard, and they'd throw it back.

On the weekends, if you had some work that needed to be done around your house, you could go up to the prison, if you worked there, and check a prisoner out. There was a water boy named Carlos who carried water to field workers during the week. On weekends, my dad would go up to the prison dormitory and get the officer running the dormitory to check Carlos out for four or five hours and bring him to the house to help do work around the house. When he was through, he took Carlos back to the dormitory. Carlos was a trustee. He had a sweet tooth. My mom would bake cakes, and he'd eat all the cake he could before he left because they wouldn't let him carry cake back into prison with him. He'd just about eat the whole thing. One day, he said to my daddy, "Me and your son are going to walk down to the pond. I want to show him something." We walked down to the pond where a little stream was coming out. He gave me an empty lard can with a handle on it. He was a big man and could straddle that stream. These little catfish, about six or eight inches long, would come swimming by, and Carlos would lean over and slap them out of the water. Whatever he slapped out of the water I'd pick up and put in the lard can. Pretty soon we had thirty or forty little catfish. Momma cooked them, and he ate them, then Daddy took him back to the dormitory. I'm not sure what he was in prison for. I think it was armed robbery.

When we moved to Reidsville, I started seventh grade in Collins Junior High School, in Collins, Georgia, about fourteen miles from Reidsville, going toward Swainsboro. I guess we had less than 500 students in the whole school. At that time, we weren't integrated. It was all white. We had to get up about 5:30-6:00 every morning to get on the bus by 6:30 and ride for almost two hours before we got to school. Our bus driver was Charles Driggers. He drove that bus for almost thirty-five years. He had to pick up everybody at the prison. We'd take the bus to the high school in Reidsville, get off that bus and onto another bus, and then make the fourteen-mile trip to Collins. We'd pick up people almost all the way to Lyons, back in the woods on dirt roads. We'd finally get to school about ten minutes to 8:00. Same deal coming home.

When I was in tenth grade, at Reidsville High, is when they integrated the school. It was kind of rough to start with. There were a few fights and a lot of talk around town about it, but then everything eased down and went smooth after that. I played baseball for three years and football to two. I was left field and first base on the baseball team and center in football. The black students made our teams much better than what they were. We had losing teams for a long time. We had quite a few good [black] athletes. One who sticks out in my mind was Johnny Byrd. He was six-two, real muscular and fast. We had a quarterback who could throw the ball, and it seemed like Johnny Byrd was the only one who could catch it. He always got the passes thrown to him. I lost contact with him after school. There was a young black guy in Reidsville, Kaiser Fleming, who made our basketball team a pretty good team.

There were two guys [prisoners] named John Brooks and Leo Cosalino who were confirmed escape artists. They were in there for life and didn't care how much time they tacked on to them for trying to escape. It was really kind of funny, because they made it their job to embarrass the guards by escaping any way they could. One time, they stole clothes out of the laundry, made themselves uniforms and walked out the front gate when the shift changed. They escaped at least seven times while we were there.

Prisoners usually didn't get far. This place is surrounded by rivers. You got to cross a river, so the first place anybody headed was towards a river whatever direction you go. They had guard shacks around the rivers. The dogs were centrally located to get them to a river. They always set up a perimeter around the two rivers. I don't know of anybody that has escaped from Reidsville that's never been caught. The dogs would pick up on a scent from a pair of gloves or whatever the prisoner was working with. They'd take the dogs and let them run. Either they'd lose the scent or run up on them, and usually they'd run up on them at the river. My nephew had a job doing what they call "laying tracks." They have someone go out in the woods, lay tracks, and hide. Then they bring the dogs out and see if they can pick up on the scent. That's how they train the dogs. They have a dog yard with twenty or thirty dogs.

Women [prisoners] used to be kept here [in Reidsville]. There were two buildings. Building Number 1, and Building Number 2. Building Number 1 was the prison that you see now. If you were standing right in front of it and turned around, you'd see the other building down the road. It had enough room to house 500 or 600. That building is office space now. It doesn't house prisoners anymore. The women's prison moved to Milledgeville before 1968, because when we moved down here, the male minimum-security prisoners were already in that building [Building 2]. The women were gone.

I don't know of any celebrity prisoners coming to Reidsville. Martin Luther King and Wayne Williams were sent there.[2] If you want to know what the prison looked like, go rent "The Longest Yard." Burt Reynolds filmed that movie here in the 1970s. Everything you see in that movie, even the office that has strips of paper on the wall that say "Loyalty, Pride," was exactly like that. That was the assistant warden's office. It was not done up for the movie. That office was exactly like that. All that stuff was there before Burt Reynolds arrived. When they show him going to the prison in a van, there's a guard working a detail beside the road. Well, that was my father wearing a blue jumpsuit with a shotgun over his shoulder. The big pressing machines they showed going up and down during the football game were in the inmate's laundry. The big water tower they showed right outside the fence was about two hundred yards from the trailer we used to live in.

There were a lot of people that worked in the prison that were extras. They had pictures made with Burt Reynolds and got autographs. The football field was in the yard. They used to not keep inmates locked up twenty-three hours a day like they do now. That yard is probably about a half-mile by a half-mile of grass. They had enough room for a baseball diamond and a football field. My father used to coach the prison baseball team. It's a massive yard. It's used now just in case they have a fire or a riot. Used to, on Saturdays or Sundays, there'd be anywhere from eighteen hundred to two thousand people out there.

The Alday murders happened in Seminole County. There was a book written about it and a movie called *Murder One*. Carl and Billy Issacs weren't celebrities, but they were well-known murderers in this area. Carl Issacs, his younger brother Billy Issacs, their half-brother Wayne Coleman, and a black guy named George Dungee murdered a whole family. They killed a couple of people in New Jersey and headed south on a crime spree. The wound up at the Alday farm and murdered everybody at the house. Billy Issacs was only sixteen years old, and he turned state's evidence against all three of them. Bill Issacs was housed in Reidsville in the GSP A&B building. They were all four at this facility at one time.[3]

Back in the '70s, I was playing softball at the field the prisoners use. When they were locked up, all of young'uns could go down and play there. But I was playing softball there one night and went to slide into second base. One of the guys I lived next to stuck his knee out, and my chin hit his knee. It put a pretty deep gash in my chin, which needed sewing up. My dad carried [took] me up to the prison to get stitched up. Back then, you could get medical attention at the prison. We went up to the hospital floor, and the guy that was duty was Gary Steven Krist. In the '60s or '70s he and an accomplice, a female, kidnapped a woman named Barbara-Jane Mackle and buried her in a coffin in north Georgia [near Duluth, Gwinnett County]. He buried her alive. He put water and food in the coffin and left her there. He was holding her for a $50,000 ransom.

When he got caught, at first, he wouldn't tell them where she was at. Finally, he told them, and they went and dug her up. She was barely alive, but she survived. They made two movies about it.[4] Well, Gary Steven Krist was on duty that night. He was a male nurse before he got in all that trouble. He's the one that put the stitches in my chin. I didn't like it when he took that cloth and laid it over my face [laughs]. I really didn't feel anything after that. There was a cloth with a hole in it, and he put the hole right where my chin was and covered up my eyes. I took my hand and pulled it back down. He said, "You don't want the eyes covered?" I said, "No, I don't."

The prison guards in the '60s were always understaffed, and the prison was overcrowded. Now, it's one convict to a cell and has open dormitories, A & B Blocks, with bunk beds. Back in the '60s, there were two or three convicts staying in one cell. At one time, this place had like 3,500 convicts and 1,000 staff. They were outnumbered like 3-to-1. Now, they don't have as much turnover as they did before. Back then, it was a pretty unsafe place to work. In the early 1970s, a convict named Guthrie filed a lawsuit about the conditions. They [inspectors] came down, and sure enough, the conditions were way out of whack. They put it under court order, and the court order, issued by Judge Anthony Alaimo, changed it from what it was to what it is today.[5]

I hired on at Rogers CI [Correctional Institute] when they first built that prison, putting beds in, ice machines, and furniture. Then, we went through an eight-week training program at GSP. I went to work at Troy Textiles in Swainsboro. It was a big factory that printed cloth. I worked in the chrome room. We'd hook up these big copper rollers that weighed 150 pounds to a chain-horse and lower them into a tank with acid in it where they'd turn for twenty-four hours. When it comes out, the acid has put a chrome finish on the copper roller. You etch a design into the chrome, load it down with dye, and roll it across the cloth where it prints a design. I went to a place called Byrd Furniture after that, then did construction for a while. In 1974, I hired on with Winn-Dixie in Swainsboro as a meat cutter. I've cut meat for them for thirteen years. I work for Food Lion in Hinesville right now.

The '60s and '70s were a whole different time than what it is now. It was like a big family. Everybody knew everybody. It was nothing for us to be out walking the streets or for ten or fifteen teenagers to be sitting out in the yard at eleven o'clock at night. You always saw somebody out and about. Now, you go over there, and it's like a ghost town. You may see a few children here and there but nothing like it was back then.

There is a prison graveyard on a little patch of ground a mile or two behind where the females used to be kept, on the left side of the highway as you're leaving the prison area. There is no fence. There are no names on the markers. These are unclaimed people. Either their family couldn't bury them, or nobody claimed them, or they couldn't get in touch with their families. It looks like a military cemetery.

There are probably a hundred-and-fifty out there. Just white crosses in the ground.

Usually, when convicts are processed, the state tries to make it easy on the family. They try to put you in a facility where the family doesn't have to drive four or five hours to see you. But there are convicts from other states here. It's all about where you commit your crime, where you get processed, and what diagnostics center you get sent to, that determines where you wind up. Family could visit any day of the week. Whenever they had a visit, they'd send a couple of officers to bring the prisoner to the visiting room. If, say, a high-maximum inmate had a visit from their lawyer, they had a room that had a barrier between them because fisticuffs might start. When prisoners were released, they were given one suit of clothes, forty dollars, and a bus ticket to Savannah. In Reidsville, there was a place that has been torn down and a convenience store put up in its place. It used to be called Frank McCall's service station, and he had a waiting room there that they used for a bus station. Some convicts can't make it on the outside, and they eventually come back. It's home for them.

NOTES

[1] The Reidsville location was determined to be too remote for a federal prison. One was later built closer to Atlanta.

[2] On October 25, 1960, Martin Luther King was sent to Reidsville on a trumped-up traffic violation. On October 26, U. S Attorney General Robert Kennedy contacted Georgia's governor, Ernest Vandiver, to secure Dr. King's release. Two days later, on October 28, Dr. King was released. Wayne Williams, was convicted and sentenced for the serial murders of children in the Atlanta area during the late 1970s.

[3] Carl Issacs, Wayne Coleman, and George Dungee were sentenced to death for the 1973 murders. Billy Issacs was released from prison in 1993. Our Georgia History, http://ourgeorgiahistory.com/ogh/Alday_family_murders, accessed February 13, 2011.

[4] *83 Hours 'Til Dawn* and *The Longest Night.*

[5] Appointed to the US District Court by President Richard Nixon, 1971. "Alaimo was guided by his experience a prisoner in a German camp during World War II in many of his decisions, but especially in a 25-year-long lawsuit that focused on conditions at the Georgia State Prison at Reidsville. After taking the 1972 suit, Alaimo found racial violence and almost routine stabbings, rats in the prison's hallways, standing waste water in the cell blocks and sewer lines hooked into the drinking water. More than 3,000 inmates were crammed into a prison that should have held only 1,000. 'It was pretty sordid. I confess, I was shocked,' he said. Twenty-five years later and after taxpayers had spent more than $100 million to renovate the south Georgia prison, he closed the case, saying the state was then ready to operate a safe prison. As a World War II prisoner of war held in Germany, Alaimo knew what it was like to be caged. 'I cannot really describe to you the terrible feeling of claustrophobia which engulfed me when the gates of the camp closed behind me. The loss of liberty is one of the most serious injuries that can be inflicted upon an individual,' Alaimo said in a 2005 interview." *The Atlanta Journal-Constitution,* Metro Atlanta / State News, December 31, 2(

Harriet Bussey Black Gilbert

Harriet Gilbert was born and raised in Macon. She offers interesting insights into Georgia life during the 1930s and '40s and recalls the days when Macon neighborhoods that are now well-established were first being constructed. In addition to being an artist, she is a historian who wrote a history of the First Baptist Church in Brunswick. Among other aspects of Georgia events, she talks about her grandfather, Sylvanus Landrum, a tireless clergyman who preached to both Confederate soldiers and Union troops occupying Savannah during the Civil War.

Harriett Gilbert

My name is Harriet Bussey Black Gilbert. I was born at home in Macon on February 11, 1921. My father was Ernest Black. His daddy had left the family when he was a boy. His grandpa, Bret Davis, a preacher, educated my daddy. Daddy started working and taking care of his family when he was fourteen. He got a head start and did really well in the cottonseed oil business. He owned a company with a Mr. McKenzie and got to be the national president of the Interstate Cottonseed Crushers Association, which sounds dumb when you look at a cottonseed, but they make oil and mayonnaise and lots of other things.[1] During the war (WWI), Daddy went to Washington, DC a lot because cottonseeds could be used to make explosives, mineral oil, and other things. After the war, the demand went down. Cotton can catch on fire from the heat if it's compressed in a storage place. So they learned to keep cool air on it. Anything live like that has a soul, I think. My mother, Harriett, was born in Chattahoochee County. My sister's name was Margaret. Mother taught school in Camilla. Macon was not a big town, about 50,000, when I was a little girl. It had a wonderful old Baptist church downtown where my great-grandfather was the preacher for a while. His name was Sylvanus Landrum. He went to Mercer. In his day, Mercer was in Penfield, Georgia, [located 7 miles north of Greensboro], but it moved to Macon.[2]

When the First Baptist Church in Macon was going to be built, they sent Sylvanus on a boat trip to see what other churches looked like. He visited the President on that trip. You could do that then, before the Civil War. He came back and told them what he recommended they build. He went on to preach in the First Baptist Church in Savannah on one of the squares. It's still there. When he got to Savannah, the Civil War had started. Two of his boys died of yellow fever in Memphis. Sherman gave Savannah to Lincoln as a Christmas gift. He invited Sherman's whole unit to come to church, and they came.[3] I don't know if that appealed to the members. Sylvanus later went to churches in Atlanta, New Orleans, and Kentucky.

My mother's grandfather had his Eagle and Phenix Mill on the Chattahoochee River. He got some of his land after the Indians were forced out during the Trail of Tears. He had a Northern partner and didn't want to act like he was against the rebel cause, so he sent his son, my mother's father, to war [Civil War] when he was 15 years old. I've got a list of the people who were at Appomattox, and he was one of them. They called him a parolee, and he had to walk home at the age of 17. My grandfather also went to Mercer, and later taught Latin and Greek. My grandmother died when my mother was five, and a half-Indian and half-black woman named Aunt Rilla raised her. She liked to sew on the farm where she grew up because she didn't like to clean up. She had an older brother and sister. They killed hogs and made soap out of the fat and things like that. Her father was a wonderful old man, and he taught her everything. She wanted to go to college, but they didn't have money enough to send her. But he said, "You've got an Uncle Will, my brother, in Birmingham [Alabama], and if you go over there and as smart as you are, you will graduate from Birmingham High School. Just love him and be sweet to him, because he has money to help you." She wanted to go to Georgia Normal and Industrial College in Milledgeville. She graduated and became a teacher there. She made all the uniforms there. People offered to keep her because she was such a darling little lady.

Harriet, 1924.

We'd take a streetcar to the Saturday matinee and stay all afternoon. Every Saturday they'd show a continuation of a wild-west show. The first movie I ever saw as a child was "Sonny Boy" at the Rialto Theatre. It was the first Vitaphone talking movie.[4] I just bawled because the little boy gets run over, and Al Jolson sings to him. I just boo-hood, and my sister was very embarrassed. She was twenty months older than me. My mother had an aunt named Harriett who was married to a man who wrote *The Leopard's Spots* and *The Clansmen* [Thomas F. Dixon, Jr.]. They made *Birth of a Nation* out of both of them. That is a sad thing for me to know, because I had seen *Birth of a Nation*. It was awful. It was about how a black man had raped a white woman. Horrible. In my grandpa's diary, it says Woodrow Wilson liked it. [Dixon and future President Wilson were classmates at Johns Hopkins University.] The

279

way we thought about black people and Jewish people is awful to me. We were mad about a lot of things like that in Georgia.

Macon was nothing like Atlanta. We didn't think anything negative about Jewish people. They were thought of as among the best people in town. In Atlanta, they wouldn't let them in the country club. When I was a little girl and lived on Buford Place, I could sit early in the morning out on my walk and watch the help [black maids and chauffeurs] getting on the streetcars and walking to fix breakfast for everybody. I knew the names of most of them and where they lived. I'd talk to them. They were well dressed. They'd stay all day to make three meals. Can you imagine? There was one man who was Baxter Jones's chauffer. Beryl Ingram was his name. He was handsome, a really good-looking fellow. There were about five doctors and several lawyers on that street, so I guess every one of them had help. They'd come by and pat me on the head. There was a Catholic school for men called Stanislaus in the good part of town. Murphy Taylor & Ellis [realtors] bought it when it burned down in 1920. The street on one side of it was called Pio Nono, which meant "Pious the Ninth."[5]

When Murphy Taylor & Ellis bought it, they built houses all around it in a circle, then the street in a circle and houses around that. We moved in one of the second or third houses. The Ellises built one, then the Taylors, then we built one. We built a pretty little house on Stanislaus Circle. I was a loner. I had a little Scotty dog, and I walked everywhere, especially when they were building houses. You could watch what they were doing and sell lemonade to the workers.

Harriet Gilbert, about 1940.

I went to school with Mr. Woolman's daughter at Randolph-Macon College in Virginia. Mr. Woolman [Collett Everman Woolman, founder of Delta Airlines] lived in Louisiana. She'd go on the train with us to school. During World War II, he moved Delta to Atlanta. So, Delta was a part of my life. I graduated in 1942. My degree was in psychology and sociology, and I minored in Old Testament.

I remember when the stock market fell. It was a horrible thing. Banks closed. I had just come down to Brunswick. Mr. Jones on Sea Island was issuing paper money to people. This was the beginning of the Great Depression. My sister ran away and got married when she was seventeen. There was a place near Macon where you could get married. I didn't stay home so much. Mother and Daddy sent me on a trip out west that year. I went up to Montana and down to California, staying three weeks in Santa Monica. It was a wonderful experience. The next year, I went to Europe with a professor. I really never lived in Macon too much. I'd come back after I married and go to a party, and people would say, "Ernest Black only had one daughter." And I'd say, "No, he had two."

My husband was the sixth of the Gilbert brothers–
Courtland, John, Andrew, OP, Ben, James–to go to Mercer.
Macon was rather small then. I went to church, and James
would sit in front of me with his brother, Ben, not paying
attention to anybody. I would ask them if I couldn't drive
them home, but we never made any contact except for that.
I started going with a boy named Robert Dillard. James
moved into a house owned by the Dillards. One day, on my
birthday, Robert gave me a little pin and said, "I'm going to
quit going with you. James asked me all about you, and you
asked me all about him. I think this is a time for me to back
out." So the next Sunday, James asked me for a date. I was
a senior in high school, and we knew right away that we
loved each other. We were always so good. Many young
people wouldn't believe how good we were. Even when I
was a senior in college, and he was in training with the FBI,
I'd drive over there to spend the weekend. We went to the
Washington Hotel desk, and he said, "I want two rooms.
One for Miss Black on the second floor, and one for me on
the fifth floor." I said, "James, why did you do that?" He
said, "Because I've got a reputation. I'm a Federal Bureau
of Investigation agent." I thought it was because of my
reputation [laughs]. No young people would understand
that. I don't know if it was that generation, or because we
didn't have any birth control. It's so much fun to anticipate
marriage.

We married the week I got out of college. My mother
didn't like it at all. But I got out of college on a Monday
and came home on the train and married the next Sunday
afternoon. We drove off to Cincinnati where we started our
lives together. He had to be there on Thursday because he
had to start duty there. We lived a lot of places, and I never
could tell people what he did. He was working against
mobs, Germans, and Russians. The Germans had a group of
submarines that came to Ponte Vedra, Florida that June and
one in New Jersey. They were trying to do like the

terrorists want to do, disrupt our water and electric systems. They caught all of the spies, and all but one was killed. He broke down and told them a lot of things. They put James, posing as an inmate, in the Winnetka jail near Chicago with the father of one of them. He did find out a lot about one of the boys. James was in jail about ten days, but it seemed like a long time to me. I didn't know where he was. Seems, too, that anyone could tell James wasn't an old jailbird, but he wore old clothes. He was in a lot of surveillances. We moved to New Jersey where there was a big mess with a mayor or maybe the governor. That was rough.

James had a growth on the bottom of his spine, which he didn't know about until he tried to join the Navy. It might have been a fetus that never developed. So, he was upset. He called me and said, "I'm going to try for the FBI." He got accepted and was in it for five years. In the late '40s, he got out. After that, he came back and joined the law firm with his brother in Brunswick. Richard Russell had just made one of the partners a federal judge, so the firm just had three people: Mr. Bennett, Mr. Reese, and John Gilbert. So they needed James, and he was delighted to come back home. John and James were fourteen years apart. They were good lawyers and honest. They didn't charge by the hour. If they had to take depositions, they just called a lawyer instead of riding first class. Growing up in poverty, they understood people.

Ben Gilbert graduated from the medical school in Augusta and served in the Pacific. He had to operate on injuries for two years, and he never got over it. It was a horrible thing for a young man. He was later a pediatrician in Gainesville, Georgia and much loved. He'd sit up all night with patients and go out in the country to them. My grandson, who is a doctor, says old people come up to him and say, "Dr. Gilbert, are you any kin to Ben?" It makes him proud to say, "He's my grandpa's brother."

We moved to Brunswick in 1946 and lived at Brunswick Villa near Arco. There was no telephone and no pavement. We didn't have iceboxes. I had to walk two or three blocks to get to a telephone. There was no drainage. They had septic tanks. One of my boys, Jim, got rheumatic fever. Dr. Galen was a Jewish doctor who came to see Jim every day and took a blood sample every Thursday. He charged $15 a month. He had been under occupation in Germany. His folks were Russian Jews. Once, when I was seven months pregnant with Ernest, I dropped a bottle of grapefruit juice in front of a house, and the lady ran out and said, "Oh, dear! I'm sorry." I told her, "Nothing's wrong. My sack broke [laughs]." I was so embarrassed I never walked on that path again.

My husband was born in Brunswick in 1918, two days before the [World War I] Armistice. He was the sixth child and the sixth son of Mrs. Gilbert, his mother. His father was O. P. [Osceola Pinckney] Gilbert from Mississippi. He married Zuleme Jordan from Wrens, Georgia, near Augusta. O. P. was pastor of the First Baptist Church in Brunswick. He gave a sermon titled "The End Is Not Yet" just before my husband was born. Some ladies in the church visited the parsonage after his birth and told his mother, "If we had a sixth son and our husband preached a sermon–The End Is Not Yet–we would divorce him." Of course, O. P. was preaching about a number of things, including the war.

Going to Church

There was a man whose name was Urbanus Dart [see Bill Brown narrative], who gave lots of churches the land they built on. The original Brunswick Baptist "church" met in the Glynn Academy schoolhouse, built in 1840 on Egmont Street. There were many more colored members [seventy slaves] than white members [nine]. They founded the First Baptist Church in 1858. I imagine the colored people sat in the balcony. Everybody moved out during the Civil War because they feared the Yankees would come, which they did. The church now is on the corner of Mansfield and Union Streets. The pastorium [parsonage] was right next to the church. The First African Baptist Church on Amherst Street was built after the Civil War. Their members built it themselves. They didn't even use any nails. They just cut wood beautifully. For our 130th First Baptist Church anniversary, the preacher from the First African Baptist Church made the best speech. He said, "Once a long time ago, there was a big continent across the sea shaped just like a pork chop." He went on to say that these people came under duress from Africa. "Where they landed, we don't know. No matter where they were, though they couldn't dance or do a lot of things, they all sang about what's going to happen when they get to Heaven." You can listen to the music from those days, everything from "Swing low sweet chariot/Coming for to carry me home" to "All of God's children got shoes/When we get to Heaven, going to put on the shoes/Going to strut all over God's Heaven." It was such a sweet sermon.

Yellow Fever

Brunswick had a yellow fever epidemic in 1893. The preacher at the church left, and it made everybody furious because he didn't stay to help. Most people would go away to relatives' houses in the country. A lot of people died. But there were people who came because you don't get yellow fever again once you've had it. So groups came to places like Brunswick to help. A lady named Sister Esther Wallace came from somewhere like Memphis. She stayed and opened a restaurant. When I came to Brunswick in 1946, she lived on Newcastle Street above one of the stores. The Zells were also here. They had a downtown store. They must have been Russian Jews, because their name was Zelmenovitz, which was set in tile in front of their store. Carley was the oldest boy. He wanted to live in three centuries, and he did. He was born in the 1800s and died a few years ago [2006] at the age of 106.

Sunday School

Mr. and Mrs. Gilbert were poor and walked everywhere when they first got to Brunswick. He was the First Baptist preacher from 1915 to 1930 during the Depression. He'd get chickens for payment. One of Mrs. Gilbert's boys, Courtland, had polio. They had two schoolteachers living in the pastor's house to have somebody there to teach Courtland and to help make money. She fixed the upstairs attic for the other five boys to live. It must have been hot as blazes up there. My husband, James, was the baby. I asked her why she never taught Sunday school. She said, "I had six boys to get dressed for Sunday school, including one lame boy. I had the only piano, so they [the choir] practiced before church. There wasn't a toilet at the church, so I had to fix the towels and clean up for the choir. And I had to have a nice lunch ready for the preacher when he came home. Do you understand why I couldn't teach Sunday school?" I said, "Yes, ma'am. I won't ever ask you again." She was a lovely lady. She went to Waycross when they opened that Baptist [retirement] village. I'd go to see her once a week. If I missed, I'd think, "Oh, gosh. She's going to fuss." But she'd say, "I woke up this morning and knew something good was going to happen, and here you are." I'd ask, "How do you feel?" She'd say, "With my fingertips. How do you feel?" She set for me a good example not to make my children feel guilty now that I'm old. She was so patient and dear.

Artistry

I'm really an artist at heart and did two hundred children's portraits in my lifetime. I did a few oils and a lot of pastels and watercolors. I chiefly like to do it like Mary Cassatt. She was a woman that was in that group with the first French Impressionists. Her brother was head of the Pennsylvania Railroad. I took art lessons for twenty years from Bill Hendrix on St. Simons. He'd gone to art school in New York and was at the High Museum. He got a Fulbright scholarship to come down. As soon as my children were old enough to stay by themselves or had a sitter in the afternoons, I went every Tuesday to his studio with several of my friends and stayed all day painting. He asked me to come to his daughter's wedding because I was so fond of him. Well, she had a horse, and the horse was her maid of honor. They put a hat on it. A judge, also one of his students, performed the service in their yard. Bill and Mittie are buried at Oglethorpe Cemetery. He has a death mask and a little poem on his headstone. It is the most intriguing thing you've ever seen. He must have done his own death mask. He was good at doing things like that. Scares you to death. He's lying there with his eyes closed. It looks exactly like him except that it's all black. Mittie died after he did. She has one, too, but it doesn't look much like her.

I left the Baptists because they were closing in on me. I was on the World Mission Board for eight years. That's when they tried to get into a hierarchy. They wanted you to believe the world was made in seven days. Women couldn't be deacons. All that kind of thing. It was very painful to me. Now, I'm in a really good Presbyterian Church on St. Simons, and I'm happy. They have women deacons, pastors and associate pastors. They try to give half of everything they get to charity, and they do, just about. They send missions to help HIV patients in Honduras and funds to places in Africa where they lack water. I went to Africa once when I was in the Baptist Church. It made me understand about the poor people there. It's unbelievable how we still don't love each other. We fight and hurt each other. It's sad to me.

NOTES

[1] "After Eli Whitney's invention of the cotton gin in 1793, cottonseed actually became a problem. Some was plowed back into the soil, and only a small fraction was needed for planting, so the rest rotted as the mounds of cottonseed grew. About the time of the Civil War, the cottonseed processing industry began to develop, and by 1897 it was time for action. Businessmen from Tennessee, Mississippi, Georgia and Texas met and formed The Interstate Cottonseed Crushers' Association.... the name of the organization was changed to the National Cottonseed Products Association (NCPA) in 1929." http://www.cottonseed.com/aboutncpa/default.asp, accessed February 26, 2011.

[2] Penfield, Georgia was established shortly after 1829 in Greene County and named in honor of Josiah Penfield (c.1785-1828), a Savannah merchant and silversmith, who bequeathed $2,500.00 and a financial challenge to the Georgia Baptist Convention to match his gift for education purposes. The Convention organized a manual labor school which opened in 1833 as Mercer Institute (renamed Mercer University in 1837), in honor of Rev. Jesse Mercer of Greene County, a major contributor to the matching gift request.
Wikipedia, http:// en.wikipedia.org/wiki/Penfield_Georgia, accessed February 26, 2011.

[3] The First Baptist Church of Savannah was one of a very few Southern coastal churches that did not close during the Civil War. The story is told that Pastor Sylvanus Landrum preached on one Sunday in late 1864 to a congregation made up largely of Confederate soldiers, and the next Sunday to one of Union soldiers, Savannah having surrendered during the week. http://www.visit-historic-savan nah.com/first-baptist-church.html, accessed February 26, 2011.

[4] "Vitaphone was a sound film process used on features and nearly 1,000 short subjects produced by Warner Bros. and its sister studio First National from 1926 to 1930. Vitaphone was the last, but most successful, of the sound-on-disc processes. The soundtrack was not printed on the actual film, but was issued separately on 12- to 16-inch phonograph records. The discs would be played while the film was being projected. Many early talkies, such as *The Jazz Singer* (1927), used the Vitaphone process." (The name "Vitaphone" derives from the

288

Latin and Greek words, respectively, for "living" and "sound."). Wikipedia, http://en.wikipedia.org/wiki/Vitaphone, accessed February 26, 2011.

[5] "Pio Nono College, named for Pope Pius the Ninth, was founded by the Catholic Church in 1874 but became St. Stanislaus in 1889 when Jesuits acquired the school to train initiates for the Jesuit priesthood; it burned in 1921 and was never rebuilt." New Georgia Encyclopedia, http://www.georgiaencyclopedia.org/nge/Article.jsp?id=h-782, accessed February 26, 2011.

Robert Eugene Woodward

Bob Woodward recalls a time before television and the Internet when one's worldview was shaped by books, Hollywood movies, and magazines like Life *and* Time; *when black and whites used different entrances for the same theatre; and when boyhood friends were known by their nicknames. He came along at a time in American history when technology and transportation infrastructure merged in ways that for the first time allowed teens to venture thousands of miles by themselves with little planning and no adult oversight. In the early 1950s, Bob and a friend took an impromptu road trip–Jack Kerouac style–to find Lizzie Miles, an aging blues singer in New Orleans' French Quarter.*

Bob Woodward

My name is Robert Eugene Woodward. I was born on November 21, 1934 in Augusta, Georgia. My memories go back beyond my first awareness of things such as social boundaries and prejudices. I grew up in a decidedly rough section of town known as Harrisburg. At one time, it was a small town outside of Augusta. As I understand it, Harrisburg and Augusta once competed for a stake in the tobacco industry, which had moved here from South Carolina and North Carolina because those states had depleted their soils by growing tobacco over and over again. A man named Ezekiel Harris came to Augusta around 1790 or 1795 from Edgefield, South Carolina to establish a town to compete with Augusta for the tobacco trade. The area he developed became known as Harrisburg, and over time, it became a haven for blue-collar workers.

From the date on one of the local cotton mill buildings, 1840, that's about the time the cotton industry really picked up around Augusta. I do recall when Augusta was a haven for cotton brokers. A lot of cotton came in, was brokered, and shipped out or processed into cloth in one or more of the local mills. There were railroad lines in close proximity to the warehouses. I saw horse-drawn wagons loaded with bales of cotton going up and down Reynolds Street, which runs parallel to the [Savannah] river. There were cotton warehouses and brokerage firms down there. The mill owners built a number of houses near the Harrisburg cotton mills and rented them to their employees. When I was little, horse-drawn wagons would deliver ice and coal to neighborhoods around town. All the streets in Harrisburg are paved now, but I can remember when many of them were dirt.

We swam in creeks and in the river; there were no swimming pools available. There is a network of canals that run through Augusta that supplied water for the textile mills, but I was told not to swim in the canals because at that time they were dumping raw sewage into them. When I was a kid, Harrisburg was a safe area and had numerous family-owned grocery stores and other small businesses. None of that is the case today.

I don't recall there being a great amount of animosity or hostility among my immediate family members towards blacks. I never heard my dad speak badly about them other than there was no question but that he thought he was superior to them. I'm just being candid. There was a time when a lot of black females in Augusta would do laundry for whites, including people who lived in Harrisburg whose socioeconomic condition was not much better than the blacks. Black ladies would walk through neighborhoods with large bundles of someone's laundry tied up in a sheet and balanced on their heads, with another bundle under each arm. They would come and pick up the laundry and take it home. They would wash it out in the yard in a big black pot, stir it with a boat paddle, hang it out to dry, and bring it back to the family. But I was amazed that these ladies could walk those distances with that large bundle on their heads and more bundles under their arms.

One day, I commented on it in front an adult. I said, "How does that black lady balance that bundle on her head?" The adult was a male, and he looked at me and said, "That's not a lady. That's a woman." I wanted to know what's the difference, and he said, "White females are ladies. A black female cannot be a lady. She's a woman." At the time, I didn't know much about race relations or what prejudice was based on, but that did not make sense to me, and things have always had to make sense at some level for me to accept it. I decided right on the spot that henceforth, any time I referred to any grown female, it would be as a lady. That was my way of saying, "To hell with you. I'll decide that sort of thing for myself." To this day, I refer to any adult female as "lady."

I am not and have never been a racist. I have no qualms with anybody based on their race or their ethnicity, but I am prejudiced in the broadest meaning of the word, in that we all prejudge things. An example would be that if I see a man walking towards me who is well dressed and obviously comfortable in his own skin, then the chances of me having a discussion with him on art, politics, literature, or what-have-you are much better than with the guy who is coming right behind him who is having trouble walking because his pants are down around his knees. I make that sort of prejudgment. I assume in that word picture I just drew that the guy in the suit was white and the guy with his pants down around his knees was black, but if you transpose them–if you had the guy in the suit being black and the one with his pants down around his knees being white–I would still make the same judgments about the two of them based on their appearance. I would not believe anyone one who told me they did not do pretty much the same thing.

Initially, grade school was a little traumatic for me. I was shy and always small and had to learn real quick how to defend myself. I had something of a black sheep uncle who was pretty rough-and-tumble. He knew what I had ahead of me, and he taught me some fundamentals. After that, things improved. Grade school was called John Milledge.[1] He figures prominently in Augusta and Georgia history.

I started grade school when I was five. My first grade teacher, Mrs. Moore, for whatever reason, took an interest in me. I lived one block away from school. She and I developed an understanding that I would go home from school and come back with my bulldog. They would lock the doors after school let out, but her classroom was on the first floor on the corner. She would help me lift my dog into the classroom through the window, then I would climb in and dust the erasers for her and re-sort the flash cards, which they used to teach students numbers and letters. I had a real fondness for her because she showed a genuine interest in me. She early on taught me how to sound words and to spell them. Looking back on it, she had a lot more influence on me than I knew at the time.

Grade school went from first grade through seventh. After that, I went to Richmond Academy. High school was four years [through 11th grade]. I loved high school and reluctantly graduated. The first three years I attended, it was all male and military. My senior year, they combined the boys and girls high school–Tubman. Teachers at Richmond Academy were somewhat characters in their own right. It was prevalent for people in and around Augusta to have nicknames. One of the teachers was named "Snake" Nixon. Another was "Big Six Lucky," who got his nickname from his days playing football. Just about everybody had nicknames, particularly around Harrisburg. It was just sort of a tradition, and I loved the nicknames. I knew guys named Cotton, Wimpy, Swifty. Coot Connors was a tough guy in grade school. A bunch of us were in the schoolyard one day, and somebody addressed him as Coot. We were getting to the age when we started noticing girls. Coot said, "I don't want to be called Coot anymore. I want to be called by my real name." Well, I didn't know what anybody's real names were. All we knew were the nicknames. So, one of us said, "What is your real name?" He said, "Lester," and all of us started laughing. Someone shouted out, "Hell, I'd rather be called Coot than Lester!" I remember running from Coot because he was bound and determined he was going to catch someone and beat the tar out of him. I've wondered since that time if having a nickname was economically predicated, because the people I knew who had nicknames were from areas like Harrisburg and Frog Holler, and places like that. They were not from up on the Hill–not people who had money. I only know of one person from the Hill who had a nickname. It was Q Ball. I don't know where that nickname came from.

Just before my teen years, most of the play activities we had involved sports and wrestling, which we called "wrasslin'," and I loved to wrestle. Even though I was small, if you learn a little about balance and leverage, you can take care of yourself. There was a man who lived next door to me who drove a taxicab. To supplement his income, he raised hogs. He knew a black family who lived on the edge of town. He paid them to let him keep his hogs there, and he would bring food for the hogs. Most of the food he took out there was comprised of throwaway items that neighborhood grocers would get rid of–produce that had spoiled. They would keep it for him. He would put the produce in these fifty-five gallon drums and once a week go out to the farm and slop his hogs, and I'd go with him. There were always five or six black kids around. It didn't take us long to break down whatever shyness there was between us, and we'd start wrestling. I remember vividly every time I'd go home, my stepmother would make me take my clothes off on the back porch before I came in so she could wash them, because I would be less than house-worthy at that point.

Church life was a fairly big part of my life until I hit sixteen. I went to church by myself. I didn't go as a family. I had lived with a cousin, who was five years older, and her mother from the age of two to five. After that, I lived with my dad and stepmother, and my cousin was living with her mother in another part of town. But she [the cousin] and I would meet at the same church, Central Christian on Crawford Avenue right in the heart of Harrisburg. I started going when I was five or six years old. I always got there early, and the janitor would let me ring the bell, which was a great thing.

Augusta had a professional baseball team called the Augusta Tigers. My uncle would occasionally take me to a game when I was nine or ten years old. The field was right across from where University Hospital is now along Walton Way.[2] I never was much for watching sports. I loved participating in them. But I went because I loved that uncle.

We had rationing during World War II. Meat was rationed–tea, sugar, tires, women's stockings–things like that. We didn't have an awful lot of anything, but we always had what we needed. My dad was a meat cutter at neighborhood grocery stores. He always knew enough people that he could barter to get what we needed. I would put ration stamps into ration books and then pull them out. I was maybe ten when I heard that the war had ended. Broad Street was where everyone liked to congregate back then, and you just instinctively knew that when you heard the announcement, that everyone who could was rushing down to Broad Street. I lived about four blocks from Walton Way, a main artery going to the downtown area, so I ran to Walton Way, and a car was coming down the hill without the first tire on it. He was riding on the metal rims, kicking up sparks as he went down the street. He was going to Broad Street with no tires to celebrate the end of the war.

I graduated from high school when I was sixteen. Then I went to Augusta College, which is now called Augusta State University. But I only went for six months. I was very impatient and wanted to get on with things. I didn't see that I was going anywhere with junior college. Just by observing what was going on in my environment–what people did for a living, the efforts they had to put forth–I determined very early on that I wanted to live on a higher scale than what I was accustomed to in Harrisburg.

Broad Street in Augusta is a wide street, I think second only [in the South] to Canal Street in New Orleans. I recall seeing trolley tracks on Broad. About two blocks on Broad Street, the main commercial street downtown, there were four movie theatres. One of the white theatres admitted blacks, but they had to sit in the balcony, and they came in and out of a different doorway than whites. I started going to movies at an early age–so early that I couldn't read the marquee well enough to know what movie was playing. At that time, they put still photographs in the foyer of the movie theatre, so you could get some idea of what the movie was about. I would walk into each one of the theatres and look at the stills and decide from that which one I might want to and see. My preference was westerns, war movies, and any sort of adventure movie. I also liked the kind of movies that portrayed a standard of living superior to what I was experiencing where people were mannerly, well dressed, courteous, educated. *Magnificent Obsession* was one. I couldn't read the poster, and I don't remember who was in it, I just remember being impressed by hearing the name of it during the movie. Occasionally, I would find myself in a theatre that was showing a musical, and that would just infuriate me. I would immediately get up and leave, because there was no way I could relate to people being in the middle of a conversation and burst into song. It interrupts the story, and the story is what I wanted. If I couldn't relate to it, I didn't want it.

Before I became aware of the appeal of books, I was reading weekly magazines. There was a newsstand called Home Folks right in the midst of where all the movie theatres were. It was a combination of magazines, paper stand, cigar store, bar, pool hall, and I was told you could place bets on sporting events there. The main bus stop was downtown right directly in front of Home Folks. While I was waiting for the bus to go back home after a movie, they would not object to my leafing through magazines, because I didn't have money to buy them. My favorites were *Life, Look, Collier's Weekly,* and *Saturday Evening Post* because they featured photographs. I always felt I got a lot out of seeing something. Once I became aware of magazines like *Time*–by then I would have a little job and could buy one– I'd always buy *Life* and *Time*. They'd pretty much cover the same stories, but *Time* would go into more depth in the text of the story, and with *Life* magazine you got to see what you were reading about. I thought that gave me a pretty good grasp of the subject. That was my window on the world. That and movies. This was before television.

When I was thirteen, one summer I got a job on a laundry truck that picked up and delivered laundry and dry cleaning. The route was in an area known as "The Hill," which was actually called Summerville, sort of the upper echelon of town. That summer of riding around in that truck was my first foray around Augusta outside of Harrisburg and another mill area called Frog Hollow, now where University Hospital and the Medical College of Georgia is located. Between those two neighborhoods there's a small area called Plum Nelly. The name is derived from it being "plum" out of Harrisburg and "nearly" in Frog Hollow. I began to traverse the Hill section where all the finer homes were and was blown away by the size of the houses, the grandeur of them, the expanse of lawn out front. The first one I went into, the lady asked me to bring the packages into the house. Up to that point, the only kind of flooring I'd ever seen in a house was either bare wood or linoleum. I stepped into that living room, and it was wall-to-wall plush carpet. I hadn't even seen that in movies, so it made a big impression on me. As I recall, it was a wheat color.

We had another customer who lived on Milledge Road whose name was Edison Marshall. He was a writer. As I understand it, movies were made from a couple of his novels. He was a big game hunter, which I didn't know until I made a delivery one day.[3] For some reason, rather than being greeted by the maid, he came to the door and invited me in and showed me his game room. It was a large room just filled with trophies of animals from all over the world on all the walls, bear and zebra rugs on the floor, and so forth. I'm sure he had good intentions, and his intent was to make a positive impression on this runny-nosed kid, but he actually made a negative impression because I left there thinking, *Why in the world would anyone want to kill all those beautiful animals?* I don't expect everything to be subject to my approval, so I just accept it as being different from my mindset.

From what I had learned from reading and movies, I got the notion that whatever kind of job I had, I didn't want to do anything but make marks on paper with a pencil. That seemed to me like the way to go. One day, I read the want ads and saw that one of the textile mills had a position open for an apprentice draughtsman. I just had a general notion of what drafting was, but I went in and interviewed for the job. I was seventeen at the time. Much to my amazement, the guy hired me. The only thing that saved me was that right next to my drawing table in the Engineering Department was a large bookcase filled with books on drafting, civil engineering, geometry, and that sort of thing. Every day at lunch, I would peruse those books.

After being there for nine months, I became aware of the Savannah River Site [a nuclear materials processing center], which was located about twenty miles away in South Carolina. I would hear people talking about the kind of money you could make working there. Then I saw that they were advertising for draughtsmen, but you had to be eighteen. When I turned eighteen, I applied for draughtsman. At that time, you either had to have a degree or five years of experience as a draughtsman. But the man who interviewed me said he would give me a job as an illustrator and perhaps I could work my way into becoming a draughtsman. An illustrator would generate graphs, charts, and diagrams, which computers can do now. After three years of that, they would consider you for apprentice draughtsman, so I became a mechanical draughtsman. We also did drawings for architectural designs because they were always building and renovating, and we did electrical drafting, heating, and ventilating.

The most satisfaction I got from drafting was from a side job I had. I went to work with a contractor who did design and construction of warehouses, stores on Broad Street, banks, churches, and renovations. In addition to working at the Savannah River Site, I worked for him in the evenings and on weekends for twenty-five years doing architectural drafting. I got more satisfaction from that than I did with mechanical drafting. His name as Harry Piehl Vankerkhoff, one of the most impressive people I've ever known. He and I developed a sort of father-son relationship. He had only a fourth grade formal education and became a brick mason, then job foreman, then contractor, and then became a structural engineer strictly by taking correspondence courses and hiring civil engineers and architects to tutor him in the evenings. For a while, he was going back and forth by plane to Atlanta to take a few courses at Georgia Tech. In the course of his career, he became a registered engineer in twenty-three states. He was highly respected. I knew of at least one occasion when he put some of his own money into a job to get it done right. He was originally from South Georgia and came from a childhood of privation. That sort of thing impacts some of us differently than others. He never got rid of the bitterness and resentment he had as the result of people expecting him to come to the back door when he was going to tile a bathroom at the house of what he referred to as the "landed gentry."

He was a true eccentric, and perhaps a genius. When I first starting working with him, I knew very little about architectural drafting. Without saying so, he conveyed to me that I would learn quickly, or I would be gone. His self-confidence was of a magnitude I had not encountered before, nor have I since. It seemed never to occur to him that there might be something he couldn't figure out, and he expected the same level of performance from others. Because of that attitude and his extreme impatience, when I would go to him for just a hint of direction, he would give me a look and go right back to his calculations without saying a word. I'm sure I would not have lasted long enough to figure any of it out if he had not asked me to proofread a bid he had dictated to his secretary one afternoon. There have been several times in my life when I have benefitted greatly by spotting errors others have made, and that was one of them. In addition to the bid being in error, the accompanying letter was poorly crafted. I marked it up and gave it back to him. I soon found myself writing all his professional correspondence, and over time, much that was personal. All with about the same level of direction he gave me with drafting. But fortunately, he had hit upon something I didn't need much help with, and performing that duty enabled me to hang in long enough to learn what I needed to know about architectural drafting.

Harry was meticulous with his structural calculations, and would go over them several times to ensure that they were correct. However, once I watched him calculate, on a renovation job site, the size of a needed column and its corresponding concrete footing, including size and positioning of reinforcing bars, with just a slide rule. I learned from one of the job foremen that he did that sort of thing frequently, especially doing renovations, where conditions often turn out to be other than what was expected.

Late in his career, he decided that he would do his structural calculations and analyses in German, despite the fact that he knew nothing about the language and not a hell of a lot more about English. A clue to his motivation to do so may perhaps be revealed by the fact that when I first met him his name was Harry Piehl. He later legally changed it to Harry Piehl Vankerkhoff, and later to Harry Piehl von den Kerkhoff. He was not the sort of man to explain his actions, but he informed me that the name changes resulted from things he had recently learned about his parents, whom he had no connections to, nor did he have any first-hand knowledge of them. I didn't quiz him. In typical fashion, he acquired books and tapes on the subject and hired a language professor from the local college to tutor him. After a surprisingly short period of time, he was turning out calculations in German, and not nearly as readily I became able to figure out enough of it, in context, to check his calculations behind him.

Harry was undoubtedly shaped by events during his formative years in South Georgia, and the effects stayed with him for life. He told me one time that he often wondered how much more successful he might have been if he had "been of the landed gentry" and had had someone to direct him. I replied that he probably would not have done as well, for he would not have had as much to prove to himself, nor the necessary inner demons to drive him. He liked that notion.

Harry is interred in a tomb/crypt in Magnolia Cemetery, which is a story unto itself. Harry was fixated on balance and proportioning in his designs, using the Golden Mean [or Golden Section] in his calculations, and he had a definite preference for odd numbers over even ones, as do I. He wanted a symbol to place on his stationery that might convey that, so I researched mandalas, found that one in a library book on the subject and drew it in ink to pass on to the printer. Years before he died, he bought a burial plot at Magnolia, and we executed drawings for the tomb/crypt's construction. He decided he wanted the mandala to be displayed there, so he had one cast in bronze. At the same time, I designed one depicting the unity of a mason's level, hammer, rolled up blueprint, and plumb line and bob.

Mandala at Harry Piehl Vankerkhoff grave, Magnolia Cemetery.
Source: http://flickr.com/photos/aconaway/251726097/in/photostream.

Sometimes I feel like I'm an archaeologist on a dig because I go through certain areas of town, and on a particular piece of land, I not only remember the building that was there before the building that is currently there, I can remember when there was no building there. It's a bit disconcerting in a sense, because you realize how long you've been here. We renovated a building on the corner of 7ᵗʰ and Broad that was five or six stories high. It had once been a hotel, and we renovated it into a bank. I don't think it's any longer a bank. We did some work on churches in town including one of the preeminent black churches near University Hospital. Among others, we renovated Ruben's Department Store down on Broad Street.

About 1953, I joined the Air Force. I went to San Antonio, Texas–Lackland Air Force Base–for basic training. I was twenty when I joined, much greener than my nine-year-old granddaughter is today. Being a reader of magazines and a movie buff, I had, at some level, bought into the prevalent notion that Southerners were intellectually inferior to people from other parts of the country. It took me about two days in basic training to realize that intellect, ignorance, stupidity, meanness, and all the other human characteristics are not geographically determined. Then I went to Biloxi, Mississippi–Keesler–for radar technician schooling. From there, I went to the base in Warner Robins, Georgia, attached to a mobile radar unit. It was educational–my version of going to college. I learned a lot by being in the military and being subjected to authority–people I didn't think were qualified to tell me what to do. But I learned to accept it, which has always been against my grain. I really enjoyed being in Biloxi, because it's in close proximity to New Orleans.

The year before I went into the Air Force, I had a friend, Bob Lamb, who shared a love of blues and jazz. We were eighteen years old, and neither of us had ever been anywhere of consequence, and we decided that needed to be corrected. We talked about going to New York or New Orleans. Our objective was to hear some real good jazz, other than on records. I didn't much like the idea of going to New York because I had read enough about it to be convinced it would be an experience in frustration since it was so large and intimidating. About that time, I read an article in *Time* magazine about a female blues singer named Lizzie Miles.[4] The gist of the article was that Lizzie had just recently returned to New Orleans and was performing at a club in the French Quarter. The writer gave the impression that if you wanted to hear Lizzie Miles live, then you needed to hurry up and come on, because she was getting up in years. So, we decided that would be our mission. We would go to New Orleans, and we would find and listen to Lizzie Miles. Bob's stepfather had an old Plymouth or Chrysler that he let us borrow. We drove in that heap to New Orleans. We left Augusta with $50 apiece. We filled up before we left, and the price of gas was twenty-five cents a gallon. I remember thinking we'd be better off when we got to New Orleans, because with all the oil refineries there, gas would have to be dirt-cheap. As it turns out, gas was twenty-seven cents a gallon there, which was sort of the beginning of my education on distribution and pricing.

When you look back on it, it's a study on being ignorant and uninitiated. We had absolutely no business striking out in that heap of a car, planning to be gone for a week, and with only $50 apiece. How we decided to stay at a YMCA, I have no idea. I don't think we had any idea where we were going to stay or what we were going to do once we got there, other than find Lizzie Miles. But we drove there in a day. We went through Columbus, Georgia and Mobile, Alabama and ended up at a YMCA on Lee Circle, where there is a statue of Robert E. Lee, and it was within walking distance of the French Quarter. We parked the car behind the Y and didn't start it again until we left to come back to Augusta. We either walked or rode the streetcars wherever we went. It was less than two dollars a night to stay at the Y for each of us. We ate one meal a day at an Italian restaurant called Tony's. For a dollar-seventy-five, you could get a platter of spaghetti with marinara sauce, a full loaf of French bread, and a pitcher of tea. Surprisingly enough, we did not get tired of that the whole week. Neither of us had eaten authentic Italian food before, and we absolutely loved it.

We found Lizzie Miles in some club in the French Quarter. Both of us just fell in love with the French Quarter. This was before it became quite the tourist haven it is now. It was replete with jazz joints, sidewalk artists all around Jackson Square, Café Du Monde with its little pile of sugar-powdered doughnuts, fresh air produce and fruit market, the Central Grocery store with the muffaletta sandwiches, which were invented there about 1906. At that time, we weren't really aware of these things because we were only having that one meal a day, but I came to know about them on subsequent trips to New Orleans. Lizzie appeared to me, at the time, to be an ancient black woman. She was probably only in her sixties. The first song we heard her sing was, "I ain't gonna give you none of my jelly-roll." Of course, we both loved that. I wasn't really blown away by the type of blues she sang. I really prefer my music edgier. I prefer Chicago style blues. She was wearing a long, sequin gown with brightly colored beads around her neck. A Dixieland band backed her up. Those guys could play anything.

We almost got arrested coming back. We came around the panhandle of Florida and cut up through south Georgia. I had read that Pensacola had the whitest beaches in that part of the country, and I decided I wanted to see that beach. When we got to Pensacola, it was nighttime, very dark. I realized I wasn't going to get to see the white sand, but I was not going to leave without walking on the beach. We parked the car along the road and walked across a dune onto the beach. I decided that we should also swim in the surf before we left. We started undressing and got down to our shorts. All of the sudden, we were encompassed with flashlights. It was the police. It turned out that we had walked through someone's property, and they had called the law. The guy knew we were just kids and told us we were going to have to leave. He walked us back to our car, and we left. We made it back from New Orleans in a day, too. I was so taken with New Orleans that I went multiple times while stationed in Biloxi. When I got married in 1958, my wife and I went there on our honeymoon. We took two days driving down there, but spent all our money while we were there and had to drive straight through coming back.

The relative innocence of the times should be better conveyed, and that brings hitchhiking to mind. To risk that today, from either side of the transaction, requires a death wish. Not so in the early fifties. My friend Bob Lamb and I hitchhiked all over Georgia, South Carolina, and once into North Carolina. The North Carolina jaunt remains the most memorable. Returning from a dance one Friday night, my date informed me that she would be leaving the next day to go on a week's vacation with a mutual friend and her family, further adding that they would be going to Lake Waccamaw in North Carolina. "Why don't you and Bob Lamb come up there to see us?" I didn't reply, but after taking her home I went by Bob's house, woke him up and asked if he was game for the trip. Since he was as adventurous as I, there was no doubt what his answer would be.

We left the next morning, overnight bags in hand, around five o'clock after briefly consulting and packing road maps. The first ride we got was with a black gentleman delivering a truckload of cantaloupes to the market in Columbia, South Carolina. At the end of that leg, as Bob was thanking the driver for the ride, I hoisted two melons from the back of the truck. Doing so has troubled me since, but I had no problem with it at the time. A succession of short, boring rides followed, and then we were picked up by two elderly ladies, probably much younger than I am today, and found ourselves sharing the backseat with an impressive array of hoes, rakes and shovels. After just a few miles, traveling at a speed not much faster than we could have walked, the driver asked which branch of the military we were in. Upon learning we were civilian high school students, she stopped the car and told us to get out, saying, "I never would have picked you up if I had known you wasn't soldier boys." We randomly repeated that line for years. Several rides later, we were picked up by two guys not much older than ourselves in a Coca-Cola delivery truck. The driver told us we would have to climb to the top of the truck and hold on tight, which we did. At the end of that ride we were wind-blown, somewhat shaken, but highly amused over what we had just done.

Eventually, we arrived at the lake, asked at the office which cabin the Pizzuttos had rented, and to everyone's surprise, we were sitting on the steps when they arrived. All, including us, were astounded that we had beat them there by hitchhiking. The girls were delighted, the mother seemingly bemused, and the father obviously annoyed. He was in the Army, stationed at Fort Gordon outside Augusta, and was in charge of all athletics at the Fort. He immediately, and wisely, put the two of us to work sweeping and mopping and everything else he could think of. We managed one dip in the lake with the girls and left before noon the following morning. The trip back to Augusta was not as memorable, but when the girls returned and spread the word regarding what Bob and I had done, he and I managed to draw a lot of interest from our investment.

Although I'm not at the point where I'm really comfortable saying I'm an artist, I paint landscapes, still lifes, and paintings from candid shots of people who, for whatever reason, catch my attention. I have two on the wall now, one of a woman I photographed on the beach in St. Augustine and another that I photographed on a beach in Virginia. I have a seascape that I did in Clearwater, one with the sun going down of the Chesapeake Bay, one with my three grandchildren looking out over a lake, things of that nature. These are oils paintings. I think I'm wired to be visually observant. I love words. I love music. But I really love looking at things. I subscribe to art magazines. I'll spend long periods of time trying to absorb just what the artist was doing.

I think all of us at various points in our lives, get very focused on a certain thing and wear it out before getting on to something else. There was a time when I wanted to more carefully and thoroughly organize my thoughts than I had prior to that, and I decided to write a series of essays on whatever subject came to mind. So I started to do that, but I could never finish one subject before I would find myself branching off on another, and I got really frustrated. Though I was not a poetry fan at that point, I decided to try it, since writing poetry is very disciplined, and there's probably more editing by way of trimming than with any other form of writing. It forces you to encapsulate your thoughts, to be more careful and selective with your choice of words. So, I started doing that, and I have a couple of loose-leaf binders filled with things that I wrote. They were written for my own enjoyment and enlightenment. I had the idea that if anyone else appreciated what I attempted to do, then that's just gravy.

Miscellaneous Information

What little education I have has essentially been self-education, and it never ends. Your world is as big or small as what you put into your mind—what you are aware of, what you understand, and how well you can piece together everything. There's really no such thing as miscellaneous information, because you never know when a little piece of data is going to tie together two very large areas of information that you're trying to better understand. Sort of like a jigsaw puzzle.

A friend and I once had a conversation about reality—trying to get a grip on just what we mean when we say, "This person is not really in touch with reality." There are as many realities as there are creatures that have the facility of awareness. But don't you need to separate reality from actuality? Reality is what you "realize," what you are consciously aware of, by virtue of your five senses, but there's a hell of a lot more that you're not aware of going on around you. The simplest example is that your "reality" of a tabletop is that it is solid. The "actuality" is that there is more space within that area between all the molecules

309

and atoms than there is matter. It's solid at your level of awareness, but when you get down to the atomic level, it's not solid at all. There is no fixed "reality." It depends on who or what perceives it, and from what point between wherever and infinity. I got to thinking how unfortunate it is that my awareness is fixed within my physical and intellectual confines. I can't see the world from anyone else's perspective. So a poem came from that:

> *what is the essence–the material quintessence*
> *the germ of this shifting sense of self?*
> *why am I only me,*
> *why does that have to be,*
> *why cannot awareness shift vantage points?*
> *why anchor me at all with the constraining chain and*
> *ball*
> > *of this Earth-bound, finite, floundering bit of flesh?*
> > *can death be birth at last–the opening of the hasp,*
> > *the freeing of awareness now fit for flight?*

That little poem is how I went about organizing that line of thought. Another one is more whimsical, but along the same lines when talking about the senses:

> *I am availed of senses, which number five;*
> *their unanimous contention is that I am alive.*
> *But a sixth suggests that may just be rumor;*
> *old sly…… dry……… sense of humor.*

In writing poetry, I was mindful of reducing my thoughts down to as few words as possible, but I was also mindful of the rhythm. I was a drummer and played in dance bands for a number of years. I think that's where the rhythm in my poems comes from. We played country clubs, wedding receptions, VFWs [Veterans of Foreign Wars], American Legions, and private parties within a 150-

mile radius of Augusta. One night, probably in the early 1960s, we were playing at what was then the Richmond Hotel, and I was on a break having a conversation with a black waiter. We got to talking about music, and I asked him what he thought of James Brown, because I love James Brown rhythms. The key to his music is that on every song he does, they accent the first and third beat rather than the second and fourth. The waiter said, "We," meaning black people, "really don't care that much about James Brown. It's his band that we love." But that was a lot of years ago, and I know that over time, most folks who like edgy music did come to love him.

At one point at the Savannah River Site, I was working on the design of fuel elements that went into the [nuclear] reactors. It was momentarily disconcerting. I had secret clearance. When I was working on fuel assemblies, I had to take my drawings off the board before I left every day and put them in a vault. This information was highly guarded. Years later, I took a couple of my grandchildren to the local museum here, and there on display was a cutaway of one of the fuel assemblies I had done. Right there for everybody to see it. What a difference time makes.

NOTES

[1] Colonial Governor of Georgia.

[2] Named for George Walton, Declaration of Independence signer.

[3] "1894-1967. Edison Marshall was a nationally known author and adventurer who once told *Grit* magazine: 'I went after the two big prizes, fame and fortune, and I got them both.' Born on August 29, 1894, in Rensselaer, Indiana, he moved to Medford in 1907, when his father George Marshall bought into the Rogue Valley orchard boom. Growing up in what is now the South Oakdale Historic District, Marshall nurtured his love of literature through his father's library of classics. Marshall graduated from Medford Senior High in 1913 and attended the University of Oregon from 1913 to 1916. While a freshman at the university, he sold his first story to *Argosy* magazine, giving him the confidence to pursue writing as a career. He joined the U.S. Army in 1918 and was stationed at Camp Hancock, Georgia [located near Augusta] where he met and married Agnes Sharp Flyth. Together, they moved to Medford within a few blocks of the Marshall family home. Their two children, Edison Jr. and Nancy Silence, were born in Medford. In 1921, Marshall won the prestigious O. Henry Award for 'The Heart of Little Shikara.' He also sold stories to pulp magazines and published several adventure books, including *The Strength of the Pines* (1921), which was set in Oregon, and sometimes wrote under the name of Hall Hunter. [Wife] Agnes Marshall, who had grown up in the South....never quite fit into Medford, and in 1926 her homesickness for Georgia prompted the family to move permanently to Augusta. Throughout the 1930s, Edison Marshall was a regular contributor of serial novels to *Good Housekeeping* magazine, with his name featured on the covers. He traveled around the world and earned a reputation as a big game hunter and adventurer in search of story material. He lived a quiet rural life in Georgia, claiming that he never read other contemporary authors. In 1941, he returned to novels with the publication of the historical romance *Benjamin Blake*, a Literary Guild selection and a huge success. Many popular novels followed during the next twenty-plus years—fictional narratives based on historical figures, including *The Upstart*, *Yankee Pasha*, *Infinite Woman*, and *Castle in the Swamp*. Readers who know local history and names can catch references to his Oregon roots in his writing. Marshall's first screen credit was *Snowshoe Trail* in 1922, followed by four more silent movies and five 'talkies' based on his books. Most

notable of the movies were the 1942 *Son of Fury*, based on *Benjamin Blake* and starring Tyrone Power, and *The Vikings* in 1958 with Kirk Douglas." http://www.oregonencyclopedia.org/entry/view/marshall_edison_1894_1967_, accessed June 16, 2010.

[4] "Lizzie Miles was the stage name taken by Elizabeth Mary Landreaux (31 March 1895–17 March 1963), an African American blues singer. Miles was born in the Faubourg Marigny neighborhood of New Orleans, Louisiana, in a dark skinned Francophone Creole ('Creole of Color') family. She traveled widely with minstrel and circus shows in the 1910s and made her first phonograph recordings in New York of blues songs in 1922–although Miles did not like to be referred to as a 'blues singer', since she sang a wide repertory of music. In the mid 1920s she spent time performing in Paris before returning to the United States. She suffered a serious illness and retired from the music industry in the 1930s. In the 1940s she returned to New Orleans, where Joe Mares encouraged her to sing again—which she did, but always from in front of, or beside the stage, since she said she had vowed in a prayer not to go on stage again if she recovered from her illness. Miles was based in San Francisco, California in the early 1950s, then again returned to New Orleans where she recorded with several Dixieland and traditional jazz bands and made regular radio broadcasts, often performing with Bob Scobey or George Lewis. In 1958 Miles appeared at the Monterey Jazz Festival. In 1959 she quit singing, except for gospel music. She died in New Orleans, from a heart attack, in March 1963." Wikipedia: http://en.wikipedia.org/wiki/Lizzie_Miles, accessed March 26, 2010.

313

Thomas Edwin Dennard, III

On his trek through Georgia in 1540, Hernando De Soto failed to find the source of Georgia's gold. Four-and-a-half centuries later, Ted Dennard discovered another source of Georgia gold–Tupelo bee honey. Ted's interest in bees has gone from a few hives in the woods to a stint as a Peace Corps beekeeper instructor in Jamaica and ultimately to founding the Savannah Bee Company®, an Inc. magazine 5000 Honoree and fastest growing private companies for 2009 and 2010. Savannah Bee honey is also a favorite of Oprah Winfrey's and has been featured in her magazine and on her web site. In 2007, the U.S Small Business Administration named Dennard's company Small Business of the Year in Georgia. His products have garnered numerous awards including the Flavor of Georgia "Winner" in 2007 and 2008, and Grand Prize winner in 2010.

Ted Dennard. Photograph courtesy of Taigan.com.

My name is Ted–Thomas Edwin Dennard, III. My grandfather was called Edwin, my father was Tom, and my parents wanted to call me something else. So my name,

314

Ted, comes from the initials, T-E-D. I was on December 9, 1965, 9:30 p.m. at the Brunswick hospital. Dad is from Pineview, Georgia. He was born in 1936. My mother, Marie Burton Dennard, was from Toccoa, Georgia. The Dennard side of my family could be French, and the Burton side is probably British. The family has stories about Sherman marching through Georgia. My great-great-grandfather died of a heart attack while working in the fields with his slaves. He's buried at Cedar Creek Cemetery.

I got interested in beekeeping early on. An old man, Roy Hightower, put his beehives on our family's land south of Brunswick somewhere around 1979–'80. Another man wanted to put his bees on our land, but the word going around was, "That guy wouldn't give you but a baby jar full of honey. Don't let him put his bees there." So my father, who knew Roy was a beekeeper, asked him to put his hives there. I was fourteen years old. Roy put his bees just off a little dirt road curve near my father's hostel in the woods. We put on all kinds of raincoats, rain pants, boots, bee gloves, and bee veils and marched to the beehives. In that 100-degree Georgia summer heat, we literally were soaking wet before too long. It was as if we had jumped into a swimming pool. Roy lifted the top of one beehive and puffed some smoke in there. From the few dozens of bees outside the hive, all of a sudden there are thousands of bees flying around and roaring with their wings. It was terrifying. They're everywhere around you. Fairly quickly, you learn that they're not trying to sting you, and you calm down a bit. We started pulling frames out of the hive and looking at the honey. I held up this one frame, which had different colors of honey in each section of the frame–a reddish honey, an amber or gold honey, a greenish honey. You could put your finger in each part of the frame and taste, and each one was distinctive. That was the first time I realized that honey taste could vary, and I was just blown away by that, and I still am. From then on I just loved it. I've had friends tell me since then, that I used to keep a cup of honeycomb next to my bed when I was growing up, which I had forgotten about. I took wax paper cups and filled them up with honeycombs we extracted so I could pull out a piece and chew on it.

There were about twelve hives. Roy taught me the ropes, and I thought I knew everything, but it wasn't until later that I realized I didn't know anything about beekeeping. I'm not saying Roy didn't know much. I just didn't fully understand. What I was good at was honey, not so much the beekeeping part. I just loved the honey. Roy died during that period, and I kept the hives going and kept getting honey out of them all the way through high school until I went to college.

Bees can fly many miles, but that's not a very efficient way to make honey because they'd have to burn so much of the nectar coming back. Their range is more like one or two miles. They'll fly as far as they have to without having to consume their honey source. The queen bees lay thousands of eggs a day, but that's not how they reproduce. They are a colony, a super-organism, and they reproduce by swarming. Once there's a lot of nectar coming in, meaning if they leave they'll have a good chance of surviving out there on their own, the old queen will lay eggs in queen cells. These cells are a little bigger. Right before one of those queen cells hatches, she can smell it. She will leave the hive with half the bees and half the honey, and they will go and make a new home. The new queen keeps the old hive going. It happens during the spring.

I have about a dozen hives on the Altamaha River on someone else's land. You just get permission to do it and give them some honey–the same way Roy did with us. The trees are going to be about a week to ten days late blooming this year because of the cold. All the tupelo honey production is an extremely tight window. Generally, it's a ten-day flow starting around the 22nd of April and finishing on the 5th of May. Last year, it was only three days. This year, we expect the honey to start flowing around May 1st. We'll take the boxes off of the hive around May 10th– whenever the nectar stops flowing. That's all you get until the next year. Other types of honey have longer production times. Sourwood honey has a four-to-six week production cycle.

I don't name the hives unless the bees are extremely aggressive, and then, it's not really a kind name. Sometimes a hive might be extremely bountiful, and I'll give it a friendlier name. I've never had a hive poached– knock on wood–and I haven't had any bears get at them. Up in the mountains, bears do get at hives. You learn where to put beehives through experience–trial and error. Over the years, you know where the good spots for honey are, and you recognize what would be good land.

Tupelo is my favorite honey and the favorite honey Savannah Bee sells. It's called tupelo honey because the nectar the bees collect is from the flowers of a tupelo tree.[1] Tupelo trees grow in riverbeds where cypress trees grow. In fact, it's called a tupelo-cypress ecosystem. They grow in the flowing water and on the banks. There are many species, but these are of the genus *Nyssa*, species *ogeche*.[2]

Ted on a Satilla River sandbar. Photograph courtesy of Jonathan Doster.

Honeybees have evolved with the plants over time. They were not too different from wasps at one point. It has been theorized that honeybees were essentially wasps eating insects, then they went after aphids, which make a sweet substance called honeydew, and from there, they bypassed insects and started living solely on flowers. For the last 150 million years, they've been developing with the flowering plant world. The plants harvest the sun's energy, making simple sugar. They put a little bit of these simple sugars in the flower which attracts pollinators that drink up the nectar, which is mostly water with a little sugar in it.

Because honeybees are so fuzzy and hairy and they wiggle a lot, they shake pollen grains from one plant off of their bodies down into the pistils of another plant. The shaking makes the pollen go down deeper into the pistil, ensuring that it's going to get pollinated, that it's getting cross-pollinated with multiple flowers which increases the genetic diversity of the seeds to come. The seeds have the encoding that will make them even more likely to be viable and grow. This causes the fruits to be more numerous and larger. The seeds encased in the fruit will be eaten by animals and spread even further.

This whole thing ends up with the bees benefiting the plants by ensuring their species will continue with strong genetic characteristics that make them less susceptible to maladies affecting that particular plant species. Honeybees have enabled those plants to out-compete other wind-pollinating plants. The way the world looks today is in large part because of these little pollinators and their relationship with flowering plants. Birds and other animals are benefited because they have access to more fruits. Even the oxygen in the air is ensured in part because bees help the plant world get a footing and stay strong, which also helps prevent erosion. So, there are a lot of immeasurable benefits that bees bring to the world around them. It's very poetic.

There are over a hundred crops Americans like to eat that are dependent on honeybees for pollination. For example, cucumbers need six to eight honeybees to visit that female flower which is open for only one day. Pumpkins, squash, watermelons, cucumbers need to have honeybees right there on them. Beekeepers now need to put hives on farms to ensure fruits are fully shaped. There are many plants that will bear some fruits, but they may be smaller, less numerous, or malformed if they don't get pollinated by honeybees. You may still get some fruits, but the production will drop off. Some crops, like almonds, need the bees in order to produce anything. People put bees on peppers, beans, blueberries. I have a beekeeper that takes his bees to the Vlasic® pickle farm. Some people put bees on tomatoes. Some beekeepers put them on oranges, though there's not enough evidence to prove they increase the yield. Apples are another crop that rely on bees, and strawberries… the list goes on and on.[3]

On average, one hive will produce 84 surplus pounds of honey, about seven gallons, meaning more honey than they will need to survive the year. Savannah Bee produces about 200,000–250,000 pounds of honey [16,000–21,000 gallons]. We get our honey from a loose-knit confederation of beekeepers. We have developed a relationship over the years where I know they can make the honey, and I guarantee a certain price per pound. When the honey season is over, they'll send samples. I'll review them, and we'll make a deal. The beekeepers range from here to as far away as Idaho where we get a honey we use for pairing with cheese. We get a fantastic acacia honey from an Italian beekeeping family at the foothills of the Alps. In the South, we would call the acacia a black locust tree. They were imported to Italy about two hundred years ago as an ornamental and took over. Now, in Italy, they can make a pure black locust honey, and we can't because we don't have enough black locust trees in concentration. Over there, the trees spread over larger areas.

Roy taught me about bees and beekeeping. My takeaway was the love of honey. Then I attended Sewanee, University of the South [Sewanee, Tennessee] studying philosophy and religion and ended up living in this really old cabin. The landlord, Archie Stapleton, was like a father to me. It's all in hindsight that I'm connecting the dots, but my time with him was an interesting one. He had a vineyard, a big garden, and bees. He was a super cerebral retired minister who taught me some amazing facts about honeybees–how the queen was born a worker, turned into a queen by eating royal jelly, lives forty times longer, lays 3,000 eggs a day, can determine if those eggs are male or female, fertilized or not, and nobody really knows how. Before, it was really about the honey. He taught me to be more interested in honeybees. Bees ventilate the hives. You can put your hand or face next to the hive entrance and feel them fanning air in and fanning air out. They're ripening the honey or drying out the honey. The nectar comes in at about 85% water, and they need to drop it down to about 17% water. It's not honey until they get to about 19%. It's considered unripened honey or nectar until it gets below that threshold, and below that threshold is that point at which it won't ferment and will never spoil and will be good forever. They also need to regulate the temperature to be 94 degrees Fahrenheit. That's the ideal temperature to incubate the eggs and have the larvae and pupae hatch and grow. In the summertime, they are fanning to keep the hive cool. When it gets too warm, they'll bring water into the beehive and fan their wings over it–evaporative cooling. In the winter, they're trying to raise the temperature, so they eat honey and gather into these dense balls of bees and start shivering and wiggling, which generates heat enough to maintain the ideal temperature even if it is zero degrees outside.

World Traveler

During college, I took my junior year off, in 1986, and went to Fiji, Australia, Tasmania, and New Zealand. Why? I don't know. I just wanted to go there. It was a bootstrapped trip down under. I was in Fiji for a month and spent most of my money there. Arrived in Australia with $200. Back then, you carried cash. We [young people] didn't have credit cards. I immediately went to work in a restaurant in Sydney for two months, saved some money, then went down to Tasmania and picked apples for a month. I went back to Australia and bought an old station wagon for 385 bucks, Australian, and drove it from Melbourne up the east coast [2,000+ miles] where I sold it to a German for 400 dollars. On the way, I picked up an Aborigine named Ramon who was hitchhiking. He ended up staying with me for about two weeks. He was a funny guy. He was really into his culture, but he was also into marijuana. Everybody we met, straight laced or not, be it in a restaurant or wherever, he would ask if they had some *ganja*–marijuana. It was bad enough that we, a black and a white, were traveling together. They were racist as all get out back then. Imagine driving through the South with a black guy wearing dreadlocks. I hope the racism was more so back then and not so much now. I hitchhiked back to Sydney, flew to New Zealand, hitchhiked around there for five weeks, and then came home after about eight or nine months of traveling.

You don't see many people hitchhiking anymore. I used to hitchhike home from college. One spring break, I hitchhiked from Tennessee down to Miami so I could catch a plane to Mexico. It just seems like it's a different era now. Maybe everybody's got a car these days.

Upon graduating from Sewanee, I joined the Peace Corps, and they wanted me to teach beekeeping. Again, bees crop up in my life, but I thought that was perfect. They sent me to Jamaica. I trained for three months, then served two years as a Peace Corps volunteer on the north coast in Saint Mary Parish. It is a remote area, bracketed between the resort areas. Ocho Rios is to the west of it, and Port Antonio is to the east. My job was to work with the Department of Agriculture that was based in St. Mary Parish, work with the beekeepers, and increase their ability to produce honey and make an income from it. I had a guy that served as my mentor there who lived about half a day's ride up a mountain valley. There was a beekeeping association just being formed, so it was perfect timing for me to get there and work with them. I served as a liaison between the dozens of beekeepers that were a part of this newly formed association. I worked individually with beekeepers every day and taught at five different elementary and high schools that had agricultural components, teaching the kids how to be beekeepers. That is where I learned to love beekeeping.

Decton Hilton (left), Jamaican beekeeper, Ted Dennard (right) as Peace Corps instructor.

It wasn't until then that I lost my fear of getting stung. They–the Peace Corps people–told me I had to. I wouldn't get any respect from the Jamaican beekeepers if I was afraid of being stung. I thought that was macho BS. But you had to just bite the bullet and go out there raw-paw. After a while, you realize the stings don't hurt that much. This past week, I was stung about thirty times. I realized in Jamaica that it really is better not to use gloves. Once you totally lose that fear of being stung, you get this amazing, Zen-like experience when you go near bees. That lack of fear opens you up to a great experience where you're just listening to the bees, watching, smelling, hearing the bees– a multi-sensory experience. You get lost in it. It's really a calming, meditative act at that point. You'll think you've been there an hour, and it will have been four hours. You have no idea how that much time has escaped.

Jamaica is a mixed bag of wealth and extreme poverty. People really do live in dirt floor huts up in the mountains. I had no running water, cooked on a little two-burner gas stove, but it wasn't primitive. I would have been considered well-off there. I was the only white person and was probably three miles from a telephone. They were suspicious in the beginning, but accepted me after a while. At first they called me "white blood-clot" [or claat] and some other names. Those are their expletives–blood-clot, bumble-clot. In the end, they called me "Honey Man."

What Life's About
My dad, a lawyer, told me not to get into law or rather, he showed me not to. He talked so poorly about the law profession for so long. His appreciation for it came later in life. One night, we were sitting around the table he said, "Do any of you want to go into law? We've got a pretty good little operation here." I said, "After all the terrible things you've said about it over the years, I can't believe

you're even saying that." There were many years where I owed the bank a tremendous amount of money and had no idea how I would ever pay it. I was working four or five jobs, literally scraping the scum off of housing projects bathtubs and resurfacing them, burning alive in the summer heat, sweating in stinky old clothes, wondering why I had not gone into law. I had no promise of making money or getting ahead at all at any time. I thought, "He should have given me some advice so I'd have a fallback position." But dad always counseled me, "Don't do anything just for money. Life's not about that." He's right now, but my mother wasn't wrong when she said, "Money won't make you happy, but not having it can make you unhappy."

The Savannah Bee Company came about from having a few jars of honey that I sold to one store. Richard Grayson, my college roommate, had a master's in mathematics. He was teaching school, and I was working different jobs. We were living in Savannah, broke as all get out, and thought, *We've got to get some money. This beekeeping hobby has got to pay for itself.* So, we bought an extractor for a few hundred dollars, which put us over the edge, and it was against my protestations that he did this. You take the wooden frames that hold the combs out of the beehive box, cut the wooden cappings off, and put the combs in the extractor, which is a centrifuge. The extractor is a stainless steel basket or cage inside of a stainless steel drum. The combs spin around inside the drum, which spins the honey out of the combs against the inner walls of the drum and runs down. When you're done, the combs are empty and open from the top just like they were when the bees started making them. You put the combs back into the beehive, and they start putting honey back in them. The bees don't have remake the combs.

We ended up buying these honey bear bottles, putting honey in them, and selling them in his girlfriend's (Jennifer, later his wife) store, called One Fish, Two Fish.

We quickly moved to glass jars. I started buying more bees and learned how to make tupelo honey. I decided to put the tupelo honey in pretty glass bottles, because it was so good, and I didn't want it to look like all of the other honey out there. I first put it in these French wine bottles around 1999, and it started selling all over. People called from all over the country wanting to buy the honey. After a couple of years of doing that, by 2001, there were about twenty-five stores. I decided I was going to do this more as a business. At the end of 2001, I took a leadership class, and I printed a brochure and a price sheet and went to the Atlanta Gift Mart in January '02. We won a bunch of awards including best food and best display. The name "Savannah Bee Company" came about by me not knowing where this was going to go. If I was ever going to have a retail store, I wanted it to be able to sell anything, not just honey. So, I thought the name needed to be broad and inclusive.

Savannah Bee Tupelo Honey

Oprah Winfrey or her people saw some Savannah Bee honey at one of the trade shows we attend. They were attracted by the packaging, tried it, liked the quality, and listed it as one of her favorite food items.[4] In hindsight, the French bottle packaging looks great, but I wasn't really thinking about it like that. Honey is our biggest seller. Honey-based body care products are about 20% of our business. More than half of the honey we sell is tupelo honey. Business is like a garden. You can plant anything you want, but it might not grow. If you knew it would, it wouldn't be fun. Bringing something to fruition and seeing it work is exciting. While we've gone from $50 a year to $3 to $4 million a year in sales, it's still the same. Our goals and growth are bigger and riskier, but it's still an adventure full of promise.

Since the mid-1980s, bee populations have been declining, and nobody knows for sure why. Some say it's mites, then we think it's the viruses, not the mites that is the problem. Mites are just the hosts for the viruses. In the late '90s, it was beetles that came over from South Africa that people thought caused the problem. It's always something. People spraying with pesticides and other chemicals. Loss of habitat is a factor. We don't know if it's genetically modified [GM] crops or the corn syrup that's made from GM corn, the inbreeding of the queen stock, the movement of bee hives to different crops. There are all kinds of theories. Most likely, it's a combination of everything. There are so many factors that it just caused them to start stressing out. The bees' honey production varies from year to year. The last couple of years have been bad due more to weather than colony collapse. It can vary geographically as well. There has been a general trend worldwide over the last year or two [2008-2010] where it was really bad. As a result, honey prices are the highest I've seen in my lifetime.

Bees have always followed me through life. When Richard, my brother, Jeff, and I were traveling through

Southeast Asia in about 1996, we were riding the Mekong River on a little riverboat. At one point, we started hiking off of a tributary and came across someone's beehives–little baby Asian bees. I talked to the owner and got to see inside the hives. That was very cool.

Changes

Georgia has changed a lot in my lifetime. It's a big, industrious state with tons of commerce, ports, agriculture, and forest. It's one of the top producers in the world. If it was a country, it would have the 22nd largest GDP.[5] Atlanta is a huge hub. It's tripled in size since I was born. I see a lot of progression in Savannah in terms of multi-cultural people in part because of SCAD [Savannah School of Art and Design] and the Army bases. Things are growing and progressive. Georgia's got a lot going for it.

I love where I live. Savannah is beautiful and filled with history, with a distinct culture but it also offers the finer things in life like great restaurants, music and film festivals, and just plain progressive thinking. The best part is the coast with its tidal saltwater marshes and creeks that lead to these fantastic remote islands with deserted beaches. The rhythm of the tides and the birds ties me into nature. From my house and dock, I regularly see bald eagles, manta rays, sea turtles, dolphins and the rising sun and moon. My beehives tie in to that connection with nature. The first blossoms of red maples in late January signal the beginning of spring, and each successive bloom excites me as the honeybees continue to exponentially grow in size and activity until the end of summer when the burning heat slows everything down to a sultry pace. Somehow, the timeless cycle of honeybees doing what they've been doing for over 100 million years grounds me to this place–to the present moment that hangs still against the chaotic change of life.

NOTES

[1] Tupelos are valued as honey plants in the southeastern United States, particularly in the Gulf Coast region. They produce a very light, mild-tasting honey. In northern Florida, beekeepers keep beehives along the river swamps on platforms or floats during tupelo bloom to produce certified tupelo honey, which commands a high price on the market because of its flavor. Monofloral honey made from the nectar of the Ogeechee Tupelo has such a high ratio of fructose to glucose that it does not crystallize. Wikipedia, http://en.wikipedia.org/wiki/Tupelo, accessed December 13, 2010.

[2] Genus *Nyssa* L.–tupelo; Species *Nyssa ogeche* Bartram ex Marsh–Ogeechee tupelo.
http://plants.usda.gov/java/profile?symbol=NYOG,Accessed December 13, 2010.

[3] Wikipedia lists over 120 crops that rely on bees for plant pollination.
Wikipedia,
http://en.wikipedia.org/wiki/List_of_crop_plants_pollinated_by_bees, accessed December 13, 2010.

[4] Savannah Bee Company honey is featured among *O Magazine's* food "Delights":
http://www.oprah.com/gift/The-Savannah-Bee-Company-Honey_1?cat_id-18, accessed December 13, 2010.

[5] Based on 2009 IMF (International Monetary Fund) and World Bank rankings.

Lewey Lawrence Cato

In colonial times, Georgia's produce was transported to distant markets by waterways–rivers, canals, and along the coastline. Then came the steam engine. Railroads began to crisscross the state in the early 1800s, linking small and large towns alike to a new network of commerce, and providing passengers with tickets to anywhere in the continental United States they wished to travel. Lewey Cato represents a by-gone era in Georgia, a time when young men aspired to work for "the railroad." Like his father before him, he possesses an innate understanding of anything mechanical. He began his career repairing steam engines and concluded it working on diesel engines.

Lewey Cato

My name is Lewey Lawrence Cato. I was born in Douglas, Georgia, on April 4, 1917. My father was Lawrence Cato. He was probably born in South Carolina. My mother was Mae Quinn. Momma was born in Graham,

Georgia right [southwest] out of Hazlehurst. They sold their farm and bought a place between Alma and Hazlehurst in the Satilla section of Georgia. They were raised Baptist but converted to Methodists later on. Two of Momma's sisters were nurses in the state institution at Milledgeville. Dad had a knack for anything mechanical. He was a lineman and worked in the plant for the Douglas Power Electric and Telephone Company.

He was also one of the best automobile mechanics of any type car. Dad, before he passed away, went to Atlanta. Momma fixed a money belt, which he wore, and he went and bought a 1917 Hupmobile.[1] During the 1918 flu epidemic, he was working on a car, lying on the floorboard, and contracted a bad cold, which went into flu and pneumonia. He died when I was twenty-two months old.[2]

I was raised Methodist. Our preacher, Tom Stanford stands out in my mind. He talked with me personally about my future life and what I should do. In fact, he was instrumental in me joining the Methodist church at twelve years old. One of his daughters, Mary, was my teacher in the intermediate grades in school. They didn't teach the Bible or have prayer in the classroom, but often I had at-ease conversations with her about happenings in the Bible.

All of my schooling was in Douglas. At that time, there were only eleven grades. We were strapped for money. I got any kind of job I could get. I handed out circular papers. I'd walk the streets and drop the papers in the parked cars. There was one theatre, The Rialto, in Douglas at that time. The Carrols owned it. Every Saturday they had a Western picture. Momma always let my sister, Lois, and I go to it. Tom Mix and Hoot Gibson made an impression on me. I listened to country-type music. Some of my friends were C. E. Thompson, Hugh Bussey, Wink Covington, Wink Rogers, and W. F. Coffee. Coffee County was named for his family. At that time, there was not too much mixing of blacks and whites. My school, Douglas High, was all white.

Momma's brothers, Kimpsey, Emmitt, and Pink Quinn, made an impression on me. I would emulate any fishing and hunting that they did. Her other brother, Walter, died in service during World War I. There were two lawyers in Douglas who were the most well-known. They were referred to as "Colonel." Colonel Heath and Colonel Mingledorff.

Coming up, I was the "fix-all" or the "fix-it" for the neighborhood with the encouragement of Momma. She always said she wished she could send me to Georgia Tech. The first thing I remember fixing was an automobile. I dropped the pan, loosened the rods, scraped the bearings, and put it back together. I just knew how to do that. It was in my blood, I suppose. I bought a motorcycle once for a few dollars. The engine was in a washtub, and the rest was in boxes. I bought it, put it together, and rode it off. More-or-less, it came natural.

When I graduated from school, I worked in a grocery store. I met my wife while I was working in Simm's Service Store one Saturday. It was in December around Christmas time. She came in with Roberta Peterson, a girl I knew, to buy Christmas supplies for needy families. And I thought she was one of the most beautiful things I had ever seen. I asked Roberta when I got the chance, "Who in the world is that?" She said, "Do you want to meet her?" I said, "Not right now. I've got to clean up." I was in my work apron. They came back later when Roberta told the girl I wanted to meet her, and Roberta introduced us. She was Hilda Johnson, from Hazlehurst, Georgia. She came to Douglas to attend South Georgia College, which was a two-year college then. We did not have a big, expensive wedding. Her family was very church-orientated, and one of the preachers really affected her and her family. We went to where the preacher resided and had two or three churches under his charge. It was down toward Brunswick.

While I was working at the grocery store, the news went around that you might could get on with the railroad. So, Mom went with me to the superintendent of Motor Power, George Crowder, of the Georgia & Florida (G&F) Railroad.[3] The Georgia & Florida ran through a more-or-less agricultural part of Florida, Georgia, and South Carolina. The general offices were in Augusta. It ran from Madison, Florida to Greenwood, South Carolina. He gave me an opening in the tool room, and I worked there a month-and-a-half and worried him every time he came out about putting me on my apprenticeship, which eventually he did on September 15, 1936. There, I learned anything about operating any of the machines–the lathes, shaper, planer–in the shop. There were many different types of lathes in the shop. Eighty-to-ninety craftsmen working in it. There was the coach shop, paint and lettering workers, a blacksmith, welders, boilermakers, machinists, electricians, and all the crafts had apprenticeships. They made me a mechanic on February 1, 1940. My job was to tear down and repair and rebuild any steam engine on the line. It included welding and running all type machines and assembling the steam engines. If one came in with something broken, I made the part and put it on. There weren't many wrecks to deal with. It wasn't a fast railroad. Just slow freight. There weren't too many improvements on early steam engines I worked on. We refined some of the design mistakes. It was an easy transition going from steam to diesel engines.

The G&F had a couple or three passenger trains. One of the best passenger trains was known as the Bon-Air Special, a special train that handled night traffic to Douglas. Ducoff's Hotel [Douglas-Coffee County] was the leading hotel rail passengers stayed at in Douglas. There were several other ones like Hunts, a big hotel, and the Hayes House–a room-and-board house. There were two railroads through Douglas, the G&F and the A, B, and C–Atlanta, Birmingham, and Coast, which later became the Coastal Line. I was allowed an annual pass and a trip pass. All other railroads honored the pass, and we honored their passes. Sometimes, an engine would break down on the line. We'd have to carry them another engine. One of the best trips I made, representing the railroad, was around 1940 on Seaboard going to Chicago and out to the General Motors diesel plant for training. Three of us went. I was general foreman, and I had an electrician and a machinist along with me. I won a set of leather-bound books on repairing locomotives embossed in gold with my name on them. It was for giving the best report on assembling and disassembling an engine and the effect of running a disabled engine.

By World War II, I had gone to the Seaboard Railroad. I worked out of Wildwood, Florida about twenty-five miles from Ocala. The train traffic in Wildwood was very heavy, going to ports of departure. There were quite a few German prisoners that worked in the shop yard, but not in the capacity of mechanics. They were more-or-less slave labor. Not having any knowledge of the German language, I didn't talk to any of them. You could motion–point, nod your head, things like that. If they looked big-eyed, that would be a question: "How do you do that?" We never had any problems with them. They may have liked it too much because some of the local girls began hanging around them. I was there six-and-a-half years. I went back to Douglas as general foreman of the shops I had served my time in. Ten years later, I went back to the Seaboard until retirement.

Vacation

We had three sons: Larry, Hobson, and Jerry. Most of our vacations were spent going back to the family farm one hundred miles away to gather produce and carry it home with us. We'd go to the seashore on occasion and stay with the Faircloths on St. Simons. They lived at Number 8 Oglethorpe Park. We'd go to the beach and do a lot of crabbing. Momma and Aunt Dee [Cordelia] knew how to dress a crab and gather the meat out of the shell and make stews, salads, and things like that. We'd crab at the pier and in the marsh.

Chief

I once had an Indian Chief 900 cc motorcycle. My wife wouldn't ride it. My three boys got on it with me one time, and she said she knew that with the three boys I'd be very careful, but if she got on there by herself with me, I would run it fast and clown with it. I never raced it professionally, just street running. On one occasion, a bunch of us boys came to Jacksonville, Florida. When we got into Jacksonville, it was night. We rode under one of the streetlights, and I glanced down at the register. It carried a white hand when it was doing top speed. It was 105 mph. That was around 1950.

Locomotion

All three of our sons got into the railroad business. That was a natural thing. I don't think I encouraged them other than, at that time, a railroad worker had a little better home life, financially. That may have encouraged them in selecting their life's work. Larry worked in the environmental department. Hobbie [Hobson] wound up as an engineer. Jerry followed in Larry's footsteps. By law, each rail facility that does maintenance on locomotives, has to have a treatment facility. They're regulated under the EPA [Environmental Protection Agency] as far as materials, waste products, used oil and things like that. We have treatment plants, discharge permits, and all environmental rules and regulations have to be obeyed. Most people don't think of railroads as having to do that, but they wash locomotives and handle petroleum–huge amounts. Hobson's son, Jimmy, is a conductor for Seaboard-CSX on a freight train. The conductor is in charge of the train. He gets the switch list when he starts his trip, and according to that list, they drop off so many cars at certain destinations.

I don't miss the heavy work that went on in the shop, but I do miss the association with the men working there. Nearly half of the employees were blacks. They did all of the menial jobs. Back then, they would hire blacks to do that rather than whites. In Georgia, over the years, there has been a marked improvement in the life of a black and the association of whites with them.

NOTES

[1] Hupmobiles were built from 1909 to 1940 by the Hupp Motor Company, Detroit, Michigan.

[2] "The most deadly epidemic to ever strike the United States occurred in 1918. As America prepared for war, a soldier at an Army fort in Kansas reported to the base hospital with flu-like symptoms. There, he was diagnosed as having a strain of flu that was called Spanish Influenza (since it was erroneously believed the strain had originated in Spain). Before the year was out, 675,000 Americans would die from the flu -- more than the total of all Americans to die in all wars in the 20th century. The 1918 strain of flu created not just an epidemic -- but a global pandemic causing 25,000,000 deaths. In the U.S., the epidemic's worst month [was] October, when almost 200,000 Americans died from the virus. October 1918 was also the month the flu epidemic hit Georgia." Digital Library of Georgia, http://georgiainfo.galileo.usg.edu/1918flu.htm, accessed February 6, 2011.

[3] "The Georgia and Florida Railway was organized in 1906 for the purpose of purchasing, building, and operating railroads in Georgia and Florida. Most of the G&F was assembled by John Skelton Williams, former president of the Seaboard Air Line Railway, between 1906 and 1911." http://railga.com/gafl.html, accessed February 8, 2011.

Mary Evelyn Gowen Wood & Charles Latimer Gowen

Hurricanes, World War II U-boat blackouts, a good ol' fashioned Georgia governor's race, a cold war missile defense system, school integration–these are some of the events witnessed and described in this narrative by Evelyn (Bootie) Wood who grew up in the age of hayrides and hydrogen bombs. Her accounts of life on the coast during the 1940s, '50s and '60s are followed up by her father's description of life there in the 1920s and a unique event in the annals of jurisprudence that occurred on the St. Simons pier.

Bootie Wood

I am Mary Evelyn Gowen Wood, better known by the nickname "Bootie." I was born in the old Brunswick Hospital in the south end of Brunswick on March 7, 1936. Dr. Robert Burford, our family doctor, delivered me. My parents were Charles Latimer Gowen and Evelyn Louise Williams Gowen.

The Gowens came to southeast Georgia from South Carolina about 1820. They lived near Beaufort in the community of Combahee Ferry, which must have been near Garden's Corner, just off present-day US Highway 17. No trace of the community remains today, but about two miles to the northwest on Old Church Road are the ruins of hauntingly beautiful Sheldon Church and churchyard. My great-great-great-great grandmother Mary (Polly) Keating Gowen is buried under massive live oak trees about one hundred feet behind and to the left of the church. She was married at age 15 to Lt. James Gowen, who was born in Virginia about 1743. Polly Gowen was, apparently, a very liberated woman for her time. Family histories document that she went into business for herself as a storekeeper. Also documented is a contract signed by Polly, her father, Richard Keating, and her husband, James, in which James agreed not to interfere with his wife's business and to ensure that neither he nor his heirs would be responsible for any debts she incurred. Polly died in 1813 at the age of 63. James and Polly' son, William, married Mary Harrison whose mother, Elizabeth, had moved to southeast Georgia with her husband, Lt. John Harrison, about 1788. When William and Mary died in an unexplained manner, both on the same day in 1820, their two youngest children, Barney and James, were sent to live with their grandmother Elizabeth in Camden County, Georgia. Barney Gowen lived in Camden County and never married. James Gowen, my great-great grandfather, stayed in what is now Glynn County and about 1839, married Anna Abbott, daughter of George Abbott and Mary Wright Abbott, daughter of Major Samuel Wright, Revolutionary War officer, of Orange Grove Plantation on St. Simons Island.

My father was born near Westgate, Iowa, where his mother, Edna Latimer Gowen, had gone for his birth. It was customary for her to return to her parents' home in Iowa, to give birth to her children. She made several trips back and forth to Iowa when her children were young, and my father told me about happy memories of his time there with his

Latimer grandparents. When his mother was able to travel, she returned with baby Charles to Brunswick, Georgia, where they lived with her husband, my grandfather, Clarence Blain Gowen. My father grew up in Brunswick with his brother, George, and his sister, Gladys. He attended the University of Georgia, graduated in the Class of 1925 with a law degree, and returned to Brunswick to practice law as a junior partner of Judge C. B. Conyers. My mother's parents were Rufus B. and Mary Wakefield Williams, and she grew up with them, her sister, Marjorie, and brother, Jack, in Franklin, Kentucky. She studied two years at Bethel College in Hopkinsville, Kentucky, and came to Darien, Georgia, with a teaching certificate around 1925 to teach Bookkeeping, French, and Latin. Darien was a busy little coastal town, and several of the schoolteachers lived together at a boarding house. Social activities were organized for the teachers with some of Brunswick's young men, and my mother and father met at one of these functions. Their friendship deepened, and my father proposed to her in his Hudson Speedster, parked overlooking the scenic McIntosh County marsh in Valona, near Darien.

They were married in Franklin on June 14, 1928, and returned to Brunswick to live. My mother worked during World War II in the office of Dr. Thomas, an eye, ear, nose and throat doctor in Brunswick. Later, she opened and operated a gift and antique shop, The Tabby House, located on St. Simons in a slave cabin that had been part of Retreat Plantation. When my mother started The Tabby House, there were remnants of newspapers still on some of the walls. Some residents believed ghosts would have to read everything on the walls before they could disturb you. Remnants of blue paint, which also kept out "haints," were still here and there on some of the walls.

Now a gift shop, the Tabby House was originally occupied by a family of slaves who adopted the name "White" after emancipation. Floyd White, the last occupant, was killed by a drunk driver near the Bloody Marsh monument.

My sister, Anne, gave me the nickname "Bootie." She was five years old when I was born, and she called me a "Bootie Bug" when she saw me kicking my feet, which were covered in little hand-knitted shoes, called booties. I was called Bootie Bug for a while, but by the time I started school, the nickname had been shortened to Bootie. My teachers in school occasionally called me Mary Evelyn or Evelyn, but the nickname won out and has stuck tight to me. As a young girl, I wanted to be called Meg, my initials, a very romantic name to my mind, but it never caught on. After my father came home to Brunswick to practice law and married my mother, we lived with my grandfather, a widower by the time I was born, at 1302 Dartmouth Street in Brunswick, a white Victorian house on the corner with Albany Street, which is still standing and, thankfully, presently being renovated by some new owner. During hot summers, we spent time at the cottage on East Beach that my grandfather built in 1936 and where my husband and I have lived for almost 50 years.[1] While on the island during those summer days, we often visited relatives who lived in several houses on the beach near the lighthouse. Whenever we traveled by way of the pier, I watched for the road to the Bottle House, and was thrilled when my father would turn in and take me to see it. It was an actual little house in the woods made by a gentleman, from hundreds of discarded colored bottles.

East Beach

My father told me about some of the things he and his brother, George, used to do for fun when they were boys. He said they used to walk from the pier to East Beach and swim the creek that ran from Bloody Marsh to the ocean and separated East Beach from the rest of St. Simons. You can still see a small marsh there today near the Coast Guard Station, where the creek ran out to the sea. The boys would walk up the beach to the high dunes at the end of East Beach, climb to the top, and marvel at the height of the dunes and their isolation from the rest of the island. I never heard my father mention wild horses being on East Beach, but I have heard from other native islanders that horses were on East Beach and also on other neighboring islands, including Sea Island and Jekyll.

In the Fall

When summer ended, the cottage was closed, and my family returned to Dartmouth Street in Brunswick. We lived there until Pearl Harbor Day, December 7, 1941, when we moved to 700 London Street, an apartment at the home of Eric and Lucy Tiller and family. Mr. Tiller was an accountant for Sea Island Company. My sister and I, respectively, were the same ages as the Tillers' son, Eric, and their younger daughter, Carol, and they became our good friends. We often played Monopoly on the porch of the Tiller's house which fronted on Union Street. In the fall, Eric and I gathered nuts from under several pecan trees

341

in the yard and sold them to Mr. Ike Aiken as he walked home from the bank in the afternoon: 10 cents a bag.

Education

I attended first grade at Sidney Lanier School in Brunswick. Wilma New was my teacher. By the next year, however, we had moved permanently to the cottage on East Beach, St. Simons Island. People who owned houses on St. Simons were expected to rent them to people who had come to the area to work at the shipyard in Brunswick [during World War II]. We did rent our cottage to some shipyard people, but they cooked in one of the upstairs bedrooms and burned a hole in the floor, and my parents decided to move to the island permanently. An elementary school was opened that year at a former Girl Scout camp called Camp Marion, at the end of 6th Street on East Beach [marsh side]. Morning and afternoon shifts were scheduled in order to have classes for all of the island children. I attended the afternoon shift, walking the short distance from my house to school. Miss Annie Baker was my teacher that year. She moved to Camden County sometime later. One of my memories of those walks to school is passing the artesian well that was located on the western side of Bruce Drive between 9th and 10th Streets, and which supplied water to East Beach. It cycled off and on during the day and was a familiar sound to us children as we walked and rode our bikes all over East Beach

We had a wonderful neighborhood at the end of East Beach. The Baumgardners, Gilberts, Gowens, Prentices, and Walkers lived within a stone's throw of each other. Between the five families, we had a dozen children, and there was always something fun going on in the neighborhood. We drew hopscotch squares on the hard-top road with oyster shells and hopped all afternoon. We played Kick the Can in the evenings until we were "whistled in" by our parents. We explored the tall dunes behind the Prentice, Walker, and Baumgardner houses. We swam in the surf in front of the Gilbert and Gowen houses for hours until our skin shriveled up, as various parents sat vigilant on the beach. We paddled around in the boat that was always tied up in the marshy, muddy, but enticing, slough by the Baumgardner's house. We crabbed in the mud flats that dropped off into Gould's Inlet near where the Blackbanks River met the ocean. Crabbing was one of our favorite activities, and the Baumgardner's cook, Belle, loved to catch supper by fishing and crabbing along with us. Crabs were extremely plentiful, and we always knew that, given enough time, we could come home with as many crabs as our parents wanted to cook and pick out. There were many adventures to be had in the dunes, along the mud flats, on the beach, and in the ocean. Occasionally, we children ganged up against each other and fussed and fought, but mostly we had a lot of good times together.

(L-R) Linda and Jimmy Prentice, Shirley Cooper, Sally Walker, Barbara Jean Prentice on boat in East Beach slough.

World War II

During World War II, everyone's car headlights were blackened halfway, and people who lived along the coast had to use blackout curtains. This was to provide protection against enemy submarines that were moving in the waters along the coast. One night, my parents were invited to a party at the Baumgardner's home down the street. During the party, guests were walking back and forth in front of a "picture window" which faced the ocean, laughing, and talking, and enjoying one another's company. No one noticed that it had gotten dark and that the blackout curtains hadn't been pulled. Soon, two air raid wardens appeared at the door to check out a report that the coast patrol had noticed that someone on the end of East Beach appeared to be sending signals out to sea. It was obvious what had happened, but the incident demonstrates the serious atmosphere that existed in wartime and the tensions that were felt in the community because of reported sightings of German submarines in the waters off of our coastline.[2] At the movie theaters, we watched newsreels and knew about President Franklin Roosevelt's battle against polio and the terrible crippling that resulted from contracting the disease. The feature film was often interrupted when the lights came up and ushers passed plates to collect contributions to The March of Dimes. We always made sure that we had at least one dime to put in the plate each time we attended. It was rare to travel any distance during World War II, because tires were rationed, but when we did travel, my friends and I would try to hold our breath all the way through towns where a lot of polio cases were reported. It seems that I can remember the number of cases in towns being reported on signs as you came to the city limits.

Sailors from the Blimp Base at Glynco [a U. S Naval Air Station] used to hitchhike rides to St. Simons. Our parents always stopped on their way to and from

Brunswick to pick up sailors. They came to meet and dance with local girls at the Casino near the St. Simons pier. A bowling alley and soda fountain were located where the library is now, and in the evenings a jukebox was rolled to the open-air patio for dancing. Wooden railings lined both sides of the patio, and people would sit on the railings and watch the dancers. A moonlit night, the scent of gardenias, girls in short shorts with summer tans, and sailors in their white uniforms made for a very romantic scene. The movie theater would let out about nine o'clock, and we younger children would sit on the railings and watch until our parents picked us up.

School Days

St. Simons School was opened in 1943, and my third grade teacher was Carolyn Butler. She told us about the local legend of Mary the Wanderer, and said she had actually seen Mary's ghost near her home on Butler Avenue. The only serious trouble I got into in elementary school happened in Mrs. Butler's class. A few of us girls ran around at recess untying other girls' sashes. Mrs. Butler called us up in front of the entire class to tell us why that was not a good thing to do!

The new school consisted of the cafeteria, stage, and the building facing Ocean Boulevard. There were rooms for six grades and additional rooms for offices. A large playground at the back of the school was bordered by woods, and the Murrah family lived in a house that was barely visible through the woods. Mary Murrah was the dietician at school, and her daughter, Anne, was one of my best friends. Ice cream, eaten in a cup with a wooden spoon, was a favorite treat.

Louise Connally was the sixth grade teacher and also our school principal. All of our teachers scheduled a morning Bible reading and the pledge to the flag. In Mrs. Connally's sixth grade class, we memorized Psalm 100 and several fairly lengthy poems. I was in a group of students from sixth grade who were taken into the principal's office and seated in small chairs in a semi-circle to listen to classical music while Mrs. Connally described what we were hearing. I suppose it was a kind of enrichment class. All students in her class learned folk dancing in boy-girl pairs, and dance performances were held from time to time. I once played the part of Santa Claus in a sixth grade play on the cafeteria stage. Wartime activities included bringing newspapers and scrap iron to school. These materials were weighed, and classes competed to see which one brought in the most. I bought stamps for stamp books that were turned into war bonds when they were filled. I think the school coordinated this effort, and it must have been a time-consuming extra job for our teachers.

Mr. Allen Burns was our bus driver. There was no road on the western side of East Beach then. There were only Bruce Drive and the side streets which were usually sand or shell roads leading to a few houses. There was nowhere for Mr. Burns to turn the bus around on Bruce Drive, so he turned east at 9th Street and traveled Bruce Circle to the corner of Bruce and 11th where he let out all the children who lived up at the end of East Beach. In my mind, I can still see Mr. Burns' watchful blue eyes in the bus's rear view mirror. Some of us girls were very much afraid of being reprimanded by him, and we were pleased to grow up and find that he was a very gentle, kind man, with a wonderful sense of humor. We kids walked home the remaining few blocks in all kinds of weather, and rarely did a parent meet us in a car. I recall sometimes leaning against the northeast wind as we walked home. Often, we girls had to suffer the sting of berries shot from peashooters pulled from the pockets of the boys on the way home.

In the 1940s on East Beach, Bruce Drive was the only paved road. Houses were built along both sides of Bruce Drive and were scattered along the side streets. At the ends of most of the side streets on the beach side, were houses facing the dunes and beach. Many of the houses were built with a large porch on the beach side to catch the sea breeze and, in those days, before air conditioning, with windows on all sides of the house to allow breezes from any direction to pass through.

Hurricane Season

Many people on the island stayed overnight in the school when a powerful hurricane was threatening. The school was one of the sturdiest and newest buildings, and it was thought to be a safe place to wait out the storm. This might have been the time that my father was in Atlanta attending a session of the legislature, and we girls and our mother were at home on East Beach. The wind began to howl, and the ocean was kicking up huge waves out in front of our house, when a Coast Guard sailor knocked on our door to say that things were getting dangerous, and we needed to leave our house. My mother was sewing at her treadle sewing machine when my sister and I went to her and said we needed to leave. She said, "I'm not leaving until Charlie comes home," and my sister and I replied, "You've lived your life, Momma, but we're still young!"

My mother was probably all of 40 years old at the time. We did spend a night at the school because of a hurricane once, and I was surprised that so many of the people we knew on the island were there also. I don't know whether my father got back from Atlanta to go to the school with us or not. I do know that in those days, we knew almost all of the permanent residents on the island by name and automobile.

Another hurricane scare occurred sometime in the 1940s. Our family had traveled to north Georgia by car to see the Georgia Bulldogs play football, and we were returning home late on Sunday evening. As we drove through heavy, driving rain across the causeway and crossed over the shaky wooden bridges, we could barely see out of the windshield of the car. My father had to lower his driver's side window and try to follow the white line in the middle of the road to keep from running off the causeway. In those days, we didn't get the early warnings on television, of course, and we depended solely on WMOG, the local radio station, to give us news of impending storms. I imagine we had the car radio on, but maybe the station had been shut down by the weather. I don't think we were worried about a direct hurricane hit, though, because we were headed home to East Beach.

We arrived home to find that the power was still on in the house, and everybody headed for bed upstairs, exhausted from the trip and the hazardous causeway crossing. I heard a noise downstairs, a sort of crash, but not very loud. My parents didn't seem worried enough to investigate, but I went downstairs to see what might have caused the crash. I couldn't see anything amiss until I looked through the French doors in the living room to see how wet the porch was with all the rain blowing through the screens. An amazing sight greeted me. There were all the boards and roofing shingles of our porch roof sloshing in water back and forth where our porch floor should have been! My father came down to investigate, got his flashlight, and tried to determine what had happened. Had the ocean come up to the house and washed our porch away? Was our house in imminent danger of collapsing? Because it was so dark and so windy, my father decided not to try to investigate outside. He told us to pack a small bag, and said that we were going to leave and see if we could find rooms at Queen's Court down at the pier. We were able to get two rooms there, and that's where we spent the night, not knowing what we would find at our house in the morning.

The next day, we found that it was not water from the ocean that had collapsed our porch. What had happened was related to the wooden bulkhead my father and John Gilbert, our next door neighbor, had constructed along the high water mark in front of our houses. The bulkhead rose up above the sand several feet, and the construction people had built a sort of "stile" where we could cross over to get to the beach. People from our part of East Beach had made a path from Bruce Drive through our yard in order to get to the beach. The path was well-used and had made an indentation in the landscape. It developed that we were draining all the rainwater that had backed up on East Beach during the storm out to the beach under our house! When the porch foundation on the south side washed out, the porch had come down.

We got a new porch after this unusual event, and a new path to the beach was made through the bushes along 14th Street, the first time that side road had ever been opened up to foot traffic. 14th Street remained only a path to the beach for many years until Charlie Buffington built a little house close to the beach between 13th and 14th Streets and needed automobile access to his house.

Toward the end of the decade, extensive development came to East Beach, and the neighborhood at the end of Bruce, as we kids had known it, changed drastically. One of our favorite pastimes was romping around in the massive, very tall sand dunes that stretched along the western side of East Beach from 13th Street to the northernmost tip. The tops of the dunes had these scrubby little sea myrtles on them. We could climb to the top of the "mountain" behind the Prentice's house and look out over Bloody Marsh and see the Bloody Marsh monument in its location on Demere Road.[3] At the very end of East Beach, we could climb the highest dune, probably 30 feet, and peer over the tip-top and see the Sea Island bridge and dock, but we could also look down and see a lady we knew only as "Cousin Laura," sunbathing in the nude on her sun porch.

Bill, Sally, and Gracia Walker pose for Christmas picture on
interior dunes of East Beach.

East Beach, located on the eastern shore of St. Simons Island, 1953
(left, courtesy of Royce Wood) and 2011 (right, Google Earth© image).
The footprint of the interior sand dunes are visible in white extending
to about 6th Street on the 1953 photograph. Note the extensive accretion
of land on the eastern (right) side of the 2011 photograph.

The decision to take down "our dunes" to make room
for more houses was very bad news to the children in the

neighborhood. When the bulldozers arrived, we got cardboard and crayons and made signs protesting the destruction of the dunes. We fastened the signs to sticks and carried them back and forth in the area of the bulldozing. We thought we were making a huge protest, but it's doubtful that many people other than the bulldozer operators, our parents, and a few neighbors were aware of our efforts.

It was a very sad time for us children, and it also was a topic of conversation when our parents gathered on one of the neighborhood porches in the evening to have drinks and cool off in the sea breeze. The adults said that Count Gibson,[4] a former Georgia Tech professor whose home was one of several along the sand road that continued along the beach beyond the paved portion of Bruce Drive, was of the opinion that taking down the dunes would cause the wind patterns along the beach to change, and in turn, cause the ocean to come in onto the land. Beach erosion did begin about that time, causing several homeowners, my father and John Gilbert included, to build wooden jetties along the remaining dunes in front of their properties, parallel to the beach. Our jetty, or bulkhead, was visible into the 1950s, but it has become covered by sand in the years since then.

One day, should it become uncovered, it may be a huge surprise to people who have no idea it is there. In later years, a wooden groin was built near Gould's Inlet at right angles to the ocean, extending out into the water to try to trap the shifting sands. It has washed away over the years and has been replaced by the wooden pier there now. From that time of significant erosion in the late 1940s and early 1950s until now, the sand has covered what remains of these and other wooden structures.

When Hurricane Dora came in 1964, we went to Willacoochee, Georgia, where my husband's aunt lived. Her name was Madge McCranie. For a few years, we had been nursing a little dune out in front of our house. We had thrown our yard trash out there, and the sand had caught on. Sea oats were beginning to grow, and we were so proud of it. When we got home to the island, we were sure it would be gone, but it wasn't. The water came up close, but it didn't take anything away. It's very strange because it really did a number down near the school [several cottages were washed away]. The rock wall that was put in place after Hurricane Dora in 1964 has been covered and uncovered from time to time in the intervening years. Today, the rocks are more covered with sand than at any other time since they were placed there.

In about 1965, the first rocks and riprap were placed at the end of Bruce Drive at Gould's Inlet, and development of a little park there began to take place. Erosion can happen, however, from time to time as the sands shift along the coastline, and, in the spring of 1989, we and two other homeowners on the beach between 14th and 15th Streets got permits to place broken concrete riprap along the high water line. Most of this material is covered by sand and even dunes now. As anyone who lives on the beach knows, an absolute truth is that the ocean gives and takes.

The Campaign

In 1954, the year I graduated from Glynn Academy, my father ran for governor of Georgia. He had been Glynn County's representative to the state legislature for almost 20 years, had made good friends locally and all over the state, and had been encouraged by many of them to enter the race. Nine candidates were in the running, and my father and his supporters felt that a run-off election was a possibility and that he stood a good chance of being in it. So our family embarked on a family-style summer campaign, during which we drove all over the state meeting people and giving speeches from the back of a truck. Anne was by then a reporter for *The Atlanta Constitution* and took a leave of absence from the paper to join us.

We kicked off the campaign in July with a rally in Jesup. Somewhere, there is a home movie of the rally. My first cousin, Jimmy Fendig, and our friend, Eric Tiller, both high school classmates who had graduated with me in May, joined our campaign team as "advance men" who, with Edwin Fendig, Sr., traveled ahead of our family to coordinate our visits to courthouse squares in county seats all over the state. We had a covered truck, similar in size to the ones in which we had hayrides, decorated with "Gowen for Governor" banners, and it was pulled up as near the town's courthouse as possible, sometimes on the lawn outside the courthouse.

Evelyn, Bootie, Anne, Charles Gowen (and Skipper) prior to campaign, July 1954.

Grady Reeves, a professional "entertainer", acted as master of ceremonies and drummed up the crowd. He worked for an advertising firm in Alabama, which was hired to handle some aspects of the campaign. He wore horn-rimmed glasses and a cowboy hat, made corny jokes over the microphone, and lip-synched to amplified country music. He was quite a sight, and people came out of the restaurants and stores along the main streets to see what the ruckus was all about. At the appointed time, our family would arrive by car, pull into a space reserved for us, climb up steps onto the truck platform, and take our seats. Grady would then introduce my mother, sister, and me, and we each said a few words to the crowd before he introduced Daddy, who launched into his campaign speech.

After the speech, my sister and I walked into the crowd with iron skillets in case there was anyone who wanted to contribute money to the campaign. The idea behind the skillets was psychological. We thought anyone who gave money would be more likely to remember "Gowen" on Election Day. I was always surprised at the people who responded to us. We actually raised enough money from our skillets to pay for the gasoline in the old black Plymouth car our family drove that summer. I had had my driver's license for two years and was trusted to be the driver of the car, a responsibility I took very seriously. My sister, Anne, sat in the back seat with her portable typewriter in her lap, pounding out stories about our campaign for Georgia newspapers as we drove along the highways.

We were on the road for weeks, staying overnight with friends or sleeping in motels and hotels around the state. We traveled all over the state, making scheduled speeches in the county seat towns and stopping occasionally along the way to hand out brochures in gas stations and general stores. Our first day of campaigning after the rally in Jesup found us making speeches near the railroad tracks in Portal, then on the courthouse lawn in Statesboro, and, finally, in the center of town in Brooklet. Thinking about that day later, we decided on the following words to describe the three diverse Bulloch County audiences, respectively: suspicious, curious, and generous. In Portal, a very small group of people gathered, but several men leaning back in their chairs against the wall of one store didn't appear to be paying us any attention. In Statesboro, on the courthouse lawn, a fairly large crowd gathered in pairs and small groups all along the streets near our truck. That evening, in Brooklet, we had a very responsive, sizable crowd who put the most money collected that summer into our skillets. Our first day was behind us, and we were on our way!

My father's platform, highlighted in his campaign speech, was "honesty, decency, and economy in government." He was in favor of paving farm-to-market roads, and he was for "separate, but equal schools," among other issues that summer. Schools were segregated in the South, but the Supreme Court had ruled just weeks before the campaign that segregation was unconstitutional in the landmark case *Brown vs. Board of Education of Topeka, Kansas*. None of that summer's seven candidates for governor advocated integration of schools.

1954 Georgia Governor's race cartoon.

As Election Day drew closer, the Alabama advertising people organized Talkathons in the cities that had television stations–Macon, Columbus, Augusta, and Atlanta. I believe my father also appeared on television in Albany. These sessions were call-in shows that went on for hours, during which, my father answered questions from people who made calls to a telephone bank at the television stations manned by volunteers. It was an effort to use the relatively new media of television to promote my father's platform and build up to a dramatic finish just before the election. The Atlanta Talkathon was the biggest "show," and my father was on the air continuously for 24 hours. Probably as a result of the Talkathons, our campaign showed strength in these cities. However, the county unit system was in effect in Georgia, allowing rural counties to control the election, and Marvin Griffin of Bainbridge, outgoing governor Herman Talmadge's choice, won the election.

Charles Gowen (center), Grady Reeves (right) campaign coordinator, Photo by Robert Symms for Morgan Fitz, Herald Building, Augusta, GA.

Our family took consolation in knowing that many people considered my father the "best man in the race," and "too good to be governor." Political cartoons often showed him above the fray while the other candidates battled it out down below. For me, the opportunity to visit all areas of the state at a young age and meet many interesting people was both educational and extremely enjoyable. One sidelight of the campaign is that Anne met and fell in love with Jack Spalding, a reporter for *The Atlanta Journal*, who was covering [former Georgia Agriculture Commissioner] Tom Linder, another candidate for governor. Jack began

357

showing up at our campaign stops. We would gaze out from our seats on the truck platform, and there he would be, leaning up against a building, watching and listening. He would hang around and talk to us after the speeches, and he and my sister began to spend time together. They were married in June the following year. Jack was a delightful, wise, and witty man and a great addition to our family. He was editor of *The Atlanta Journal* for many years.

Eisenhower

I heard my father say many times, when asked about the race, that the best thing that ever happened to him was "not being elected governor." He also joked that if all the people who told him they voted for him actually had voted for him, he would have been elected. But many people thought he would have made a great governor for Georgia. He was intelligent, honest, generous, and hard-working, a man with many friends and a great sense of humor. He had been involved in the political process in Georgia for many years. He also enjoyed life immensely, had a great memory, and was a superb storyteller. He loved to travel, participated in interesting events, and attracted interesting people.

I recently came across a thank-you letter to him from General Dwight Eisenhower, before he became President, thanking my father for letting him off the hook for making a speech on Sea Island, probably to the Georgia Bar Association, that my father had arranged. Apparently, the General was needed elsewhere, and my father delivered the speech on General Eisenhower's behalf. In 1962, at the age of 58, when many of his friends were thinking about retirement, he was invited to become a senior partner in the law firm of King & Spalding in Atlanta, where he practiced trial law for 20 more years. He and my mother enjoyed life in Atlanta where they lived the rest of their lives.

Fortunately, my father wrote about some of the events and people of importance to him. [See following narrative. Another story of his stories is posted at: http://freepages.genealogy.rootsweb.ancestry.com/~gowenr f/nl199201.htm]

Races

Relationships between black and white people on the island seemed friendly and respectful to me during my growing-up years. When we lived in Brunswick on London Street, we had a nurse and cook named Dicy Ford. Most evenings, I rode with my mother or father to take Dicy home to her husband, Richy, after she had worked all day for our family. Richy was blind and was by himself all day while Dicy was working. They lived in a small, unpainted house with a neatly swept dirt yard located near where the former Perry School Building is now on Stonewall Street. Later, Sam and Onie Lee Davis worked for us and lived on the west side of Albany Street, near Gloucester, in a house that was part of a row of "shotgun" houses. Onie was baptized at St. Perpetua Church in German Village[5] on St. Simons Island, and raised on Little St. Simons Island where her family worked. After Onie and Sam were divorced, Onie lived on St. Simons in the Harrington neighborhood and cooked for our family. When I was a young girl, I sat on the kitchen stool while she cooked and listened to her stories about hunting parties that were held on Little St. Simons and about visits of the Bishop of Georgia to St. Ignatius Episcopal Church [located in Jewtown, a black community on St. Simons] where she was a member and altar guild chairman. She often spent nights during the week in a room attached to our garage. Later, she married Mansfield "Speedy" Jackson, who had a nightclub in Harrington. Onie, Mansfield Jackson, and Onie's nephew, Alfred Williams, were some of the last members of St.

Ignatius Church before services for black members were discontinued.

My father, mother, and sister were charter members of St. Simons Presbyterian Church. I became a member when I was baptized at the age of 12. I was the youngest person in the church choir for a few years and was active in the youth program as a teenager. Two people at St. Simons Presbyterian who were important influences in my life were the minister, The Rev. Dr. James T. Gillespie, or "Dr. G," as we called him, and Mrs. Edwin Fendig, Sr., who had been known to me as "Aunt Emwynn" for many years, even though we were not actually related. These two people were instrumental in shaping my faith through their teachings and actions. I became an Episcopalian when I was confirmed at Christ Church, Frederica, my husband's church, in 1960. The priests and people of Christ Church have been positive influence on my life during the past 50 years.

The Teachers Paved the Way

I attended Glynn Academy in the Class of 1954. Some of my favorite teachers were Malcolm Magaw, an English teacher who encouraged me to think and write; Lula Howard, our unique and brilliant Latin teacher; Beulah Lott, Bernice Tracy, and Oren Lunsford, math teachers of high intellect with great expectations, Rod Scott, who made chemistry and physics so much fun; Clyde Stapleton, who brought American history to life, and Jane McLeod Faircloth, who coached our graduation speeches. Rose Moore, Ruth McDonald, Dick Wooten, May Joe Bunkley, Gena Sullivan, Earl Stapleton, Carolyn Willis, and Sara Upchurch were all teachers who inspired and encouraged me and made learning fun.

University of Georgia

Cheerleaders were chosen by the student body, and I was part of a group of several students who were elected after putting on what we thought was a clever and enthusiastic group presentation on Memorial Auditorium stage. We loved cheering for our Red Terrors and enjoyed working on routines together. My friends and I had great respect and admiration for Sidney Boswell, superintendent of schools, and Jim Warren, Glynn Academy principal. Indicative of the times in which we were living was the topic assigned to me as one of the speakers for graduation, "Civic Responsibility in the Hydrogen Age." I was awarded a Freshman Scholarship to the University of Georgia and was always proud of having attended one of the best high schools in the state.

Growing Up

Children growing up on St. Simons in the 1940s and 1950s had lots of opportunities for fun. There were the beach and the ocean, several swimming pools, horseback riding, picnics, movies at the Old Casino, fishing, crabbing, Scout and club activities, bowling at the New Casino, and skating at the Airport Playhouse, at the dance hall at the end of Mallory Street near the pier, and later, on the top floor of the New Casino. For some reason, not understood by me at the time, my mother did not want me to "hang out" at the New Casino. Young people, including my sister who was five years older, had enjoyed meeting and dancing to the jukebox in the open courtyard at the Old Casino for years, but my mother refused to drop me off to spend time with my friends at the New Casino, and she wouldn't allow me to walk or ride my bike there. I felt she didn't understand or trust me, and, regrettably, it caused a rift between my mother and me for a while.

Then, when I was fourteen, Betty and Jack Lester moved to St. Simons. Jack Lester was president of the island's first bank, St. Simons State Bank. Betty and Jack had no children of their own, but they were concerned that there was no organized group for teenagers, so they started the Teenage Club, which met at the American Legion building at Gascoigne Bluff.[6] My mother let me go there and even to be picked up by several boys who had driver's licenses, because Betty and Jack were chaperoning the club. I had the happy, free feeling of being able at last to meet and "hang out" with friends somewhere other than at school or on the school bus. At the club we played records, danced, drank Cokes, ate snacks, played games, and, best of all, spent time with friends until we were delivered safely back home. Because I never broke the rules–amazingly, it never occurred to me to do so–I was allowed to attend the Teenage Club for the next couple of years. When we were in high school, hayrides around the island, the Glynn County area, and even up to McIntosh County were a popular form of entertainment. "Buzz," Daniel Lee Lane Krauss, lived on 6th Street, East Beach, and his family had cabins at Crescent, northeast of Darien. The parents of someone having a birthday party would rent a big truck with slatted slides and a driver. A bale or two of hay would be distributed on the truck bed, and the group would climb up on the truck, and, cushioned somewhat by the hay, head for the party destination, singing and laughing along the way. The trips to Crescent were especially memorable. When we arrived at the Krauss' cabins, we'd have a cookout and then take turns getting on a Tarzan-like swing that swung us across a ravine and back. Usually we had dates for a hayride, but sometimes church youth groups went on hayrides together in the island area. During Christmas holidays, we would stop and sing carols at the homes of people who were sick or elderly. Everybody loved hayrides, and we always had chaperones.

Royce Wood

Royce Wood was also growing up on St. Simons two years ahead of me, but I didn't become aware of him until the summer of 1948 when I attended a Boy Scout party where there was a celebration for a group of twelve boys who had attained Eagle Scout status under Scoutmaster Slim Fortier. Royce was one of the twelve and the tallest in the group. The party was held in the Scout building, a wooden structure located where the little league field is now. The Eagle Scout project was the clearing of a large field of palmetto plants to allow the creation of Mallory Ball Park. One of the ball fields was named Lefty Butler Field, in honor of the husband of Mrs. Butler, my third grade teacher. Mr. Butler was a strong supporter of sports for young people, and I think he may have played baseball professionally.

Two years later, during the summer of 1950, when I was an upcoming freshman and Royce was an upcoming junior at Glynn Academy, we sat together on the school bus each day and became friends. A year or two later we had become a "couple," attending school, church, and community events together. In 1952, Royce graduated from Glynn Academy and attended South Georgia College in Douglas before joining the U.S. Army where he was assigned to a Nike missile battalion near Indian Head, Maryland during the Cold War. Missile sites ringed Washington, D.C. to protect the Capitol from enemy attack, and Royce worked as battery clerk and radar operator for the site in Indian Head. This particular Nike Ajax missile was one type, and there was another one called Hercules. It was the duty of all the people on the site to keep them ready in case of an attack. The missiles were kept underground and brought up on elevators during training exercises.[7]

Royce and I were in love, wrote many letters back and forth, and enjoyed an occasional long-distance phone call. After my graduation from high school in 1954, I attended the University of Georgia year-around for three years. After Royce and I married in 1957, I took my last college course by correspondence and graduated with my class in 1958.

My first job was working as Editorial Clerk in the Reports Preparation Section of the Naval Propellant Plant in Indian Head. My office edited and prepared for publication technical reports that were sent to us by scientists working in the propellant area of the facility.

Our first child, Evelyn, was born in 1959 in Washington, D.C. while we were living in Maryland, shortly before Royce was discharged from the Army and we moved back to St. Simons Island. Daughter Laura was born at the new Brunswick hospital in 1961, and son David was born there in 1963. Royce was employed as a forester in the Woods Division of Brunswick Pulp and Paper Company, later Georgia Pacific, and worked there 37 years before he retired in 1996.

When our son, David, began kindergarten, I began thinking about going to work. Meg Way, my friend from St. Simons Presbyterian Church, encouraged me to think about a career in teaching. I had majored in Journalism in college and had taken a course called Journalism in the Secondary School. It would count toward my teaching certificate, but I would need a lot more coursework to become certified to be a teacher. Meg told me I could start teaching on a provisional certificate and take courses during the summer. I had been president of the PTA at St. Simons Elementary School and served as president of the Glynn County PTA Council, so I was already a supporter of teachers and education, and I decided that it might be a career in which I could be successful.

Segregation of schools was ending, and black students would be coming to formerly all-white public schools. I knew there would challenges coming in education with integration, and I thought I might be able to make a difference. I began teaching in 1968, and I believe the schools were integrated in 1969. When I look back on the timing, I realize that it was a good time to be training to be a teacher. With culture changes coming in education,

364

innovative teaching ideas would be needed, and teachers, more than ever, would need to be energetic, motivated, and well-prepared with strategies and techniques to meet the needs of all children, including those of the black students who would be in formerly white classrooms for the first time.

When I began my teaching career at St. Simons School, my third grade teacher, Mrs. Butler, was still teaching there. In a conversation we had one day while we were both waiting to use the mimeograph machine, she welcomed me to the staff. I made a comment about her long experience, and she told me that each year was completely different from the last, that I would find that each year had its own unique challenges and opportunities, and that nothing stayed the same from one year to the next. How right she was! Flexibility is probably a teacher's most important quality.

I taught fifth grade at St. Simons Elementary School for three years before being recommended by my principal, Dene Barone, to be the teacher to start the gifted program for children in each of the county's elementary schools. The gifted program grew through the years with state funding, but in the beginning, I worked as an itinerant teacher, meeting with students at each elementary school for a few hours once a week. Eventually, I was based at St. Simons Elementary School where there were enough students identified as gifted to warrant a full-time teacher. I met with students for one full day each week in the Challenge Program, and, for quite a few years, the students and I were able to design curriculum based on their interests. We organized our classes around subject areas like Astronomy, Endangered Species, The Middle Ages, Ancient Cultures, and Microbiology.

I took my children to Athens with me over several summers while I worked on certifications and graduate degrees in elementary education. They were good sports about participating in the sports program at Stegeman Hall at the university while I attended classes. Looking back on it, I realize they missed being on St. Simons with their friends during summer vacation. One day, they told me they were the only children in Georgia who were running laps at Stegeman Hall at eight o'clock in the morning during their summer vacation. My parents and my husband's mother helped take care of the children many times during those summers. My husband was lonely without his family. Everybody gave up things they would have preferred to have because I needed a job and wanted to be at the top of the pay schedule as soon as I could. I'm thankful to the people who sacrificed so that I could pursue my career.

I retired in 1996 after working 28 years in the Glynn County School System, but I am still friends with quite a few of my former students because we are in touch through Facebook. Now, I volunteer on the board of CASA Glynn, Inc., supporting the mission and activities of my church, and serving as treasurer of my high school class. I feel the need to declare a second retirement so that I can be available to spend more time with our grandchildren and great-grandchildren and do more travel and reading while I have the energy and eyesight, respectively. A source of great happiness for my husband and me is the realization that we have been able to live almost all of our lives in one beautiful community with all of our children, grandchildren, great-grandchildren, and closest relatives nearby. For this blessing, we are grateful to God every day.

Charles Latimer Gowen

Charles Latimer Gowen, Bootie Wood's father, was a young lawyer at the time of the 1927 trial he relates below. He also describes the racial demographics on the island, which hadn't changed much since the end of the Civil War. The 80% black population he describes in the 1920s is now less than 4% of the island's residents according to the 2010 census.

Charles Latimer Gowen

In 1927, St. Simons was on the threshold of development but still much the place it had been when the only access was by boat. The permanent population was small, probably two hundred or less, divided about 80% black and 20% white. The white [Stevens and Taylor] families lived at Frederica, The Mills [Gascoigne Bluff], near Bloody Marsh, and in the Pier section. The blacks lived principally in the South End centered around the intersection of Arnold [now an extension of Mallory Street] and Demere Roads, in the Obligation Pond-Harrington area and Jewtown. Relations between the races were excellent and each respected the other. Crime was almost unknown, and no one had reason to fear for their safety. Most of the roads were either sand or paved with oyster shells. The causeway from Brunswick was only four years old. The summer cottages were strung along the beach from the Arnold House [near the present King & Prince hotel] to King's Retreat [present day Sea Island Golf Course] with some open areas. Most of these were without heat and not suitable for year-round use.

It was in this setting that a civil trial was held that had great public interest at the time. This was the controversy: Mr. B. F. Mann and some associates subdivided a tract of land lying to the west of Ocean Shore Boulevard and south of Arnold Road called "Ocean Breeze." Small tracts of land owned and occupied by colored people lay between the subdivision and Demere Road on the west and along most of Arnold Road to the north. Some lots were sold in the subdivision in 1927 and a few houses built. On the northeast corner of Demere Road and Arnold Road was the residence and store of Joe Follins, and just to the east was property owned by Sam Proctor. Sam worked for our family business in Brunswick until 1917, when he was drafted and served in the Army. The Proctors were a prominent St. Simons colored family, and well-liked and respected. Upon his discharge, Sam returned to St. Simons and built a pavilion on his property which he called "Proctor's Emporium." It was enclosed by latticework and had a dance floor and a soft drink facility. This was the only facility of its kind on the Island for colored people. During the summer on Saturday nights, Sam had a band and held dances there as a commercial venture. The houses that had just been built in Ocean Breeze brought white people for the first time near the South End black settlement, and Mr. Mann and a few of the Ocean Breeze residents employed a Mr. A. A. Nathan, a Brunswick lawyer [later a judge], in an effort to close Proctor's Emporium.

At that time, the Georgia Code provided for summary abatement of nuisances in a Justice Court proceeding before two justices of the peace and twelve freeholders of the county. Mr. Nathan filed such a suit, and it was served on Sam Proctor who came to Brunswick to discuss his defense. When we had agreed on a fee, Sam said, "Mr. Charlie, if I hires your company to defend me, I don't want you to lose my case." With this injunction, I began work and developed that Sam had a band of five or six pieces who played each Saturday night from about 8:00 p. m. to midnight. These dances were well patronized not only by the St. Simons colored people, but also by the summer cottager's servants whom they had brought to St. Simons with them, from Atlanta, Macon, Waycross and other points. The Emporium's customers seemed to have conducted themselves well, and the place was considered orderly by the law enforcement people.

The principal complaint of the plaintiffs was that the music was loud, and in these pre-air conditioning nights the windows were always open to catch the breeze, hopefully a sea one. The nearest house in Ocean Breeze was about three or four hundred yards away from Sam's place.

At that time, Clifford Postell was the only Justice of the Peace on St. Simons. Since the law required two justices to act, Judge Postell brought a justice of the peace from Brunswick. My memory is not clear, but probably it was Judge Symons. On the appointed day for the trial, Sam and I and his witnesses arrived at Judge Postell's courthouse, which was a one room building on the west side of Demere Road opposite its intersection with Arnold Road. When we arrived, there were some twenty or thirty spectators and witnesses besides the freeholders who were to act as a jury. The justices conferred and announced that it was impossible to accommodate that many in the courthouse and that the trial would be moved to the ocean pier, where it would be cooler and where the crowd could be accommodated.

This was the same pier used by the steamboats before the causeway was built. It had a cover over a portion of the dock and a few benches where patrons could wait for the boats and be somewhat protected from the sun and weather. It was under this cover that the justices assembled us. While the law in force then provided for twelve freeholders, I believe Mr. Nathan and I must have agreed on six, probably allowing each side to strike three from the panel. Moving the trial to a more central and cooler location increased the number of spectators, and we must have had close to fifty by the time the trial began in midsummer.

Mr. Nathan presented his case, taking about an hour, and the testimony centered on the music and particularly the crashing of cymbals and the beating of the drums. I had Sam testify about keeping an orderly place and that the music wasn't necessarily loud. His witnesses confirmed his testimony. Unfortunately, one of Sam's white witnesses, on whom he had counted, used the delay incident to the changing of the scene of the trial to imbibe too freely, and we couldn't use him.

At the conclusion of the evidence, arguments to the jury began. Mr. Nathan had the opening and conclusion. When my turn came and I began my argument, the [intoxicated] witness we hadn't used realized he had been overlooked, stood up and called to me and pointed to himself and tried to take the witness chair. I got him quiet and was just getting into my argument when all the jurors suddenly jumped up, ran to the other side of the pier, and some of them jumped into the ocean. It was to save a summer resident who had gotten beyond his depth and was crying for help. After he was rescued and the jurors returned to their seats, we finished the arguments, and the Justices has us all retire a short distance away while the jury deliberated. After fifteen or twenty minutes, the Justices called us back, and the verdict was in Sam's favor. When this was announced, the summer visitors broke into applause, and the [white] lady nearest me said, "Thank goodness, I won't have to go home. You see, our servants told us if Proctor's Emporium was closed, they were going to leave, since it was the only fun they had."

So, St. Simons' largest attended and perhaps, the only jury trial ever held on the Island, ended after interruptions not usual in the administration of justice. Proctor's Emporium continued to operate until Sam died of cancer some ten years or so later.

NOTES

[1] Like Sea Island, East Beach is a Holocene (10,000 BC) formation that came into existence some 35,000 years after the main land area of St. Simons Island was formed during the Pleistocene period. Taylor Schoettle, *A Naturalist's Guide To St. Simons Island*, (St. Simons: Watermarks Printing Company, 1993), 58.

[2] Five merchant ships were sunk off the Georgia coast by German U-boats during World War II.

[3] Bloody Marsh is the site of General Oglethorpe's ambush of Spanish soldiers on July 18, 1742. The Spanish, under the command of Governor Don Manuel de Montiano, invaded St. Simons with a force of 2,000. The skirmishes at Gully Hole Creek near Frederica and at Bloody Marsh represented the last clashes between Spanish and British forces north of the Florida border.

[4] Count D. Gibson is the author of *The Sea Islands of Georgia: Their Geologic History*, University of Georgia Press, 1948.

[5] A section of the island originally occupied by German Salzburgers (German Lutherans) under Oglethorpe and later owned by the Wylly family. "These families made their living by planting and fishing, selling their wares to the Frederica settlers and to the officers of the Regiment." Orrin Sage Wightman and Margaret Davis Cate, *Early Days of Coastal Georgia* (St. Simons Island, GA: Fort Frederica Association, 1955), 226.

[6] Gascoigne Bluff is the site of Georgia's first navy. The bluff is named for James Gascoigne, captain of the Sloop-of-War, *Hawk*.

[7] Project Nike was a U.S. Army project, proposed in May 1945 by Bell Laboratories, to develop a line-of-sight anti-aircraft missile system. The project delivered the United States' first operational anti-aircraft missile system, the Nike Ajax, in 1953. A great number of the technologies and rocket systems used for developing the Nike Ajax were re-used for a number of functions, many of which were given the "Nike" name (after Nike, the goddess of victory from Greek mythology). The missile's first-stage solid rocket booster became the

basis for many types of rocket including the Nike Hercules missile and NASA's Nike Smoke rocket, used for upper-atmosphere research. Wikipedia, http://en.wikipedia.org/wiki/Project_Nike, accessed May 3, 2011.

Hugh Hinton (Sonny) Gibson

Dr. Hugh Gibson was born during the Great Depression. He grew up in Albany, Georgia and moved to Jeffersonville at an early age. He attended a military school, and later, prompted by his mother's death, pursued a medical degree in obstetrics. He talks about growing up in a segregated society and is candid in his assessment of race and culture today.

Dr. Hugh Gibson

My name is Hugh Hinton Gibson. Hinton was my grandfather's name. I was born February 14, 1936 in Macon. Dr. Thompson delivered me. My parents were Marion and Walter Scott Gibson. My mother was a Hill from Macon, and my father was from Albany, Georgia. I grew up in Albany, a relatively small, typical slow-moving southern town. My mother was a house mom, and my father worked for the railroad as a switchman, which entails switching, unhooking, and unswitching cars and setting up

374

trains. It was pretty labor intensive. In the beginning, we lived in an apartment. After several years, it must have been when we were five or six, my grandfather, Hugh Hinton Hill, bought my mother and father a home that was a three bedroom brick home located in the central part of the city and located right across from the school.

We grew up there and went to grammar school in Albany. There were two grammar schools that were side-by-side. One was for the first three grades, and the other was the third through the sixth grade. My sixth grade teacher was a lady named Miss Calhoun, and I had some very fond memories of her. She taught all the subjects. This was just sixth grade class where she taught everything. We had about twenty-five to thirty students in that class and didn't leave it except for lunch and recess. The school hours were from about 8:30 to about 3:00 o'clock. I had a younger brother, Buddy (W. S. III). After school, we played together and no specific games. We played touch football, catch–those sorts of things. I have no idea where my nickname, Sonny, came from. Nicknames then were often more benign and acceptable than some of the ones you hear today.

Cars

From Albany to Atlanta then was probably a three-hour drive on Highway 41. To see chain-gangs on the road was not an uncommon sight. My grandfather had a number of different cars. He was sort of a car fancier. He had Packards, Studebakers, Buicks. My uncle was a big believer in Chryslers, and he always drove a Chrysler. I learned to drive his Chrysler. A lot of my experience driving was when I came back to live in Macon in a Pontiac sedan my uncle had.

The Parents

My mother and my father had a very stormy relationship in their marriage. My mother had had one year

375

at Wesleyan.[1] She was a very talented, smart person. She could play the piano and the violin. My father was a nice looking fellow who, to put it bluntly, was useless. He worked on the railroad, and he never really did anything constructive. He was one of those folks where the grass is always greener on the other side, and if something happened, it was always somebody else's fault and not his. He, apparently, in the early years of my life, did a lot of drinking and gambling. I didn't have any idea at that time what was going on. My mother separated from him several times, and we came back to live in the Macon area. One year, we were living in Jeffersonville, right outside of Macon. My grandfather had been raised up in the country and had bought a dairy farm in Jeffersonville. My brother, my mother, and I spent a year there. It was fun to live there because we had several dogs and horses. My role was not one of any labor.

Segregation

Black and white relations were pretty typical for the area when I was growing up. It was a purely segregated society at that time. There were schools for the whites, schools for the blacks, separate drinking fountains, separate restrooms. There were a number of restaurants and things like that the blacks could not go in. Some of the workers or tenants on the farm were blacks. Some of the black children became acquaintances.

Carrying On

I went to the Baptist church growing up. Services were typical of most Baptist churches–the music and the preaching. I was never heavily involved. I did some Sunday school, but I really didn't like it. For some reason, there was no continuity about it. It was a haphazard happening. The people who came varied from time-to-time. I just had no real interest in it. Church was something I did because I was supposed to do it.

When I was in the sixth grade, my mother died. She had been pregnant and was threatening to lose the pregnancy, was hospitalized. She was put to bed rest and apparently had a massive pulmonary embolism. When she died, there was no way my father could take care of us. At that point, my mother's family dropped in. They were really kind of my parents the rest of my life. Her sister, Dorothy, who was called Dot, lived in Albany, and she came to stay with us to keep us in school. It was so very evident that wasn't going to work. So my family, primarily my grandfather, arranged for me and my brother to go to a military prep school–Georgia Military Academy in College Park right outside of Atlanta. It's now Woodward Academy. It was certainly a shock for both of us. We were at the same school, but separated. I would say there were maybe five or six hundred students there. It was divided into the grammar school and the high school. At that point, I was in the high school part of it. It was all on the same campus. In many ways, it was very fortunate for me in that it gave me a sense of purpose and a certain amount of discipline that shaped the rest of my life. You got up at daybreak every morning, made your bed, put on your uniform, marched to breakfast, marched to class, then marched to lunch, marched to dinner–you had a certain time for lights out. It was a pretty strict, well-disciplined, good academic environment.

During my high school and college days, the social life in Macon revolved around fraternities and societies. Since the schools were segregated by sex, we didn't have the usual social life most communities had. So, a lot of social activities involved high school fraternities and sororities that sponsored social events. At the end of each year, right after high school was out, all the sororities and fraternities had house parties down on St. Simons. That carried through the years I was in Mercer. We would take chaperones and just hang out wherever we could find a place to rent.

377

Some of my grandmother's family lived in Atlanta, and we were pretty well taken care of. I had an uncle whose name was Sam Foster, a bachelor and an executive in the Coca-Cola Company. He took an active interest in my brother and me because our mother was one of his favorite people. Our time off campus was limited. We were not given the license to go all over the city. We could go into College Park, but that was the extent of it unless we were with family.

Coming Back

I listened to a lot of pop–Johnny Matthis, Jo Stafford, Ella Fitzgerald, Louis Armstrong–but I also listened to a lot of classical music. I was never really very fond of country-and-western and listened to that very little. Now, I listen more to country music, jazz, and some of the pop music. Some of the soft rock is okay.

After we finished our second year at military school, we came back to live with our aunt and uncle in Macon. We lived on Hines Terrace in the central part of town. Macon was bigger than Albany and was more urban but not as urban as Atlanta. It was a pleasant place. We lived in a nice neighborhood. There was a milk and ice cream factory there called Dixie Dairies. It was present in central and South Georgia from Macon to Augusta to Albany. My uncle was an executive in the business.

I entered what was then the Lanier Junior High School, which was an all boys' school at that time. Education was segregated not only by race; it was segregated by sex. It was an ROTC military high school. Having been at a military school, I accepted the military discipline a lot better than a lot of people did.

At the Carhop

I grew up at the time a lot of area musicians were beginning their careers. One of the first people who really made it was Little Richard.[2] When I was in high school,

Little Richard used to be a carhop at one of the drive-ins [movie theatres] frequented by the teenagers. He would do the hambone[3] and put on a show for people. Carhops would take your order and put the tray on your car window.

High School

My interest in medicine first occurred to me when my mother died. I did very well academically in high school, was on the honor roll, and was the number two man, a lieutenant colonel in the ROTC, my senior year. I was tall for my age, so I played basketball for three years at Lanier High School and made the all-star regional team. My sophomore year, our team played for the state championship. I played very little in that game which was in Atlanta at Georgia Tech. We played North Fulton High School. It was a pretty close game. As a senior, I was captain of the basketball team. I was the center at six feet, four-and-a-half inches. At that point in time, Lanier High School was a powerhouse in high school athletics. My senior year, our football team won the state championship. There was fellow named Theron Sapp[4] that was in my high school class who went to [the University of] Georgia. I was too near-sighted to play football, and you couldn't play with glasses. This was before contact lenses.

College Life

My maternal aunt and uncle were the ones we lived with initially, but then, my grandmother developed breast cancer and died. My grandfather had bought a bigger house, and we all moved in together. The last year or so of my high school years were spent living with my grandfather, aunt and uncle, and my brother. I always wanted to study medicine, but my grandfather was a very successful businessman. Around this time he had sold his dairy to Bordens. He accumulated a lot of Borden stock. To keep busy, he developed an air-conditioning and refrigeration business where he would sell commercial air-conditioners, and he also sold commercial soda fountains. Because he needed somebody to take over his business, I decided I would go to Georgia Tech with the idea of being a mechanical engineer. I stayed for two quarters, but it became very obvious to me that engineering was not my forté. I did well academically, but mechanical drawing was something I could never figure out. So, I decided that this was foolish. I loved Georgia Tech, but I decided I wanted to leave there so that I could go to medical school. At that time, Georgia Tech didn't have any biology or anything that would qualify you for a premedical course.

My grandfather was on the board of trustees at Mercer. I had thoughts about staying in Atlanta and going to Emory, but it was decided that I would come to Mercer, which I did. I was hell-bent to get through college and get into medical school. After leaving Tech after the winter quarter, I came back and went straight through, graduated a year early at Mercer and got into the Medical College of Georgia in Augusta. This was 1957.

I was still in the ROTC at Mercer. After graduation, I went to summer camp up in Virginia at Fort Lee. I was commissioned a second lieutenant. After finishing the summer program, I went to medical school. While I was there, I spent one year in the reserve in a medical unit. One of the important things that influenced my life is that I had always been very nearsighted and had to wear thick glasses. When I got back to Mercer and got into the ROTC, they didn't want to take me the last two years because of my eyesight, but there was a captain there who thought I had some unusual abilities, and he got a waiver so that I could finish, and I got my commission.

After a year at medical school, I had the option to get an honorable medical discharge, which I did. I finished medical school in 1961. My senior year, I had met and married my wife, who is from Augusta and was a graduate of the Medical College of Georgia School of Nursing. My wife is also an artist and has painted all her life. She graduated a year before I did. I came back to Macon and did a rotating internship at the Macon hospital. During my last year in medical college, I decided I wanted to go into OBGYN. I had applied for the program and got accepted with the recommendation that I come to Macon to do the internship. After I finished the internship, I went back to the Talmadge Memorial Hospital in Augusta and did my residency, which was four years. During my first year of residency, the professor of ophthalmology diagnosed that my optical problem was glaucoma, and they started me on a treatment.

Back in Macon

My grandfather was the dominating factor in my life in lots of ways. He had come to me after my first son was born to tell me that he wanted my wife to stay at home, so he gave us a stipend to support us financially through my internship and residency. So I finished my residency and decided to come back to Macon and open a practice by myself. When I came back to Macon, I shared an office with Dr. Thompson, the fellow who delivered me when I was born. He was, at that time, pretty much doing an office practice. Macon has been a very good medical town though it has suffered from a lot of hospital politics. We have had, for the most part, neonatologists here. I started out by myself and after a couple of years, developed a relationship with Ed Rogers who was already established. We became partners and had several people added through the years. We got up to as many as four partners, but that seemed to come and go like a lot of marriages. I have no idea how many children I've delivered over the years. It seems that patients begin to go into labor in the middle of the night. As a resident, I delivered babies outside the hospital because we couldn't get them to the delivery room. I've been called by friends who had dogs, but I told them I wasn't a veterinarian and couldn't help them out [laughs].

I practiced obstetrics until about 1996 or '97. All through this time, I had a lot of problems with my eyes. I had surgery and cataracts. The crowning blow was I developed a corneal degeneration in one eye. That gave me monocular vision, and I had to quit deliveries and surgery. For three or four years, I did primarily an office practice. Dr. Rogers had retired at that point. I had one other partner who needed someone who could take calls. He and I eventually parted ways when I got to the point my disability would pay me as much to be disabled as it was to work.

Growing Up

Having grown up in a segregated society always concerned me. I couldn't figure out why blacks had to use their own bathroom and drink out of their own fountain and why we all went to different schools. I'm sure that there were strong feelings in the South at that time about the differences between blacks and whites. In reality, I never had any opportunities to be with blacks other than the black friends I played with on the farm. They seemed like pretty good people, but the society was very segregated, and that's the way it was. Society seemed to have this idea that we were pretty well-developed as far as what was right and wrong and what you could do and what you couldn't do. There was a lot more respect for your friends and the individuals. I know that I had and have some friends that have a lot of anti-black feelings. I have to confess that as I get older and some of this stuff in today's society is stuffed down my throat, I find that I become more of a racist. The Southern culture was one of being a gentleman, being genteel, respect for your peers. I think that's all disappeared. In some respects, it's not politically correct in our society to have those feelings anymore. There was a segment of white society we generally referred to as rednecks, who were very racist. These tended to be people with a poorer family background, less educated, who had more menial jobs than some of the rest of us did. I say I've become a racist, and it's primarily because the government, society, and the black folks have kind of stuffed all this stuff down our throats, when in reality, the South was probably not that much more segregated than the North, although we have taken much of the blame for the black-white schism.

The thing that bothers me about this is that it has become so one-sided. The South had a proud heritage. It was primarily an agrarian society. Blacks and whites had a lot of camaraderie. To acknowledge that and to support it now, really is not politically correct, if you understand what I mean. Integration has dumbed-down society. Education is not what it used to be. I came to Macon with the idea that my children were going to go to a public school. I didn't want to put them in a private school, but it became very obvious to me that things had changed, so all of my kids were educated in private schools.

A Hobby

My hobbies since retirement have been computers and photography. Lately, I've been photographing a lot of wildlife, birds in particular. I extract the image on the computer and use it on some sort of artistic background.[5] With digital photography–being able to make a photograph, download it, and process it on the computer–you can do some interesting things.

It's amazing to me how many things have changed in my lifetime. I, and many of my friends, feel like we were very fortunate that we came along at the right time, considering the people born around the early-to-late 1930s to have had a good life. Most of those of my era were too young for the Second World War, too old for the others, so a lot of us who might not have survived [war], survived on that alone. It is sad to see things change as much as they have. If I thought they were changed for the better, I would applaud, but I can't find many things to applaud this day and time.

NOTES

[1] "Chartered as the Georgia Female College on December 23, 1836, Wesleyan is the world's oldest (and the first degree-granting) women's college.... In 1843, the Georgia Conference of the Methodist Church assumed responsibility for the College, and by an act of the state legislature changed its name to Wesleyan Female College (in honor of John Wesley, the founder of Methodism). In 1917 the 'Female' was eliminated from the title, and the school assumed its present name of Wesleyan College." Wesleyan College web site, http://www.wesleyancollege.edu/About/HistoryoftheCollege/tabid/134/Default.aspx, accessed February 26, 2011.

[2] "Little Richard, an American singer, songwriter, musician, recording artist, and actor, considered key in the transition from rhythm and blues to rock and roll in the 1950s.... Richard Wayne Penniman was born in Macon, Georgia, the third of 12 children born to Charlie 'Bud' Penniman, Sr. (10 April 1910–12 January 1952), and his wife Leva Mae (née Stewart). He grew up in a religious family in which singing was an integral part of their lives; they performed in local churches as The Penniman Singers, and entered contests with other singing families. His family called him 'War Hawk' because of his loud, screaming singing voice. His grandfather, Walter Penniman, was a preacher, and his father's family were members of the Foundation Templar African Methodist Episcopal (AME) Church in Macon... Penniman lived in a black neighborhood; he had some contact with whites but, due to racial segregation, he could not cross the line where the whites lived."
Wikipedia, http://en.wikipedia.org/wiki/Little_Richard, accessed February 26, 2011.

[3] A dance style that involves stomping and slapping/patting the arms, legs, chest, and cheeks.

[4] Theron Coleman Sapp, nicknamed Thundering Theron and the Drought-Breaker, (born June 15, 1935) is a former American football running back for the Philadelphia Eagles and Pittsburgh Steelers of the National Football League. He attended the University of Georgia (UGA). Wikipedia, http://en.wikipedia.org/wiki/Theron_Sapp , accessed February 26, 2011.

[5] Dr. Gibson won honorable mentions in several area photography competitions.

Dorothy Bragg Headden White

Dot White, from Hawkinsville, grew up in the horse-and-buggy days when dirt roads outnumbered paved ones. She was 16 when she first set eyes on the Atlantic Ocean. Her father sold mules to farmers before tractors were the norm and helped establish harness racing training facilities in middle Georgia. She recalls days when the local telephone operator knew everyone in town and where they were–or should be–at any given moment of the day. Dot was Governor Melvin E. Thompson's secretary when he became embroiled in the now legendary "three governors controversy." She also has the distinction of having impersonated Minnie Pearl longer than Sarah Cannon, Minnie's creator.

Dot White

386

My name is Dorothy Bragg Headden White. We're supposed to be in the line from General Braxton Bragg. My parents were Lowell and Emma Gussie. She was a McLeod from Pineview, Georgia. I was born on December 8, 1919, on a little farm about three miles west of Hawkinsville, Georgia. Doctor Burns delivered me. I had an appendectomy at five months. They had to drive me to Macon on wet clay roads to the hospital. There was an intestinal obstruction, and they just went ahead and took out the appendix. We moved to Hawkinsville when I was a little baby. I've actually seen a picture of me in a horse-and-buggy.

Left: Dot, age 4. Right photo: Dot White, center, age 5, sister Jane (l) and neighbor, Mickey Daniels (r).

My father and his father, Jim, were in a business called Bragg Livestock Company. In those days, before tractors on the farm, they had horses and mules. Bragg Livestock had stables in Hawkinsville. He would make trips by car to Fort Worth and St. Louis, buy a [train] carload of mules or horses, and sell them to the farmers. They had a blacksmith shop and some other things on the side. We went through the Depression years, and farmers had to keep on going. They had to have those mules to plow, but they couldn't always pay the bills. I remember those days. I never felt like I was poor, and yet you had your on- and off-seasons.

One of my friend's father had the Chevrolet dealership, and she knew she had a pretty good living. She could buy some right cute clothes that I couldn't buy [laughs]. Jamie McLeod–my best friend–her father was a rural letter carrier, and that was a guaranteed salary of about two hundred a month, which was really good. But my dad couldn't count on regular income. I never felt I was that lacking in what I needed, and nobody had much. We'd hear people talking about soup kitchens and food lines, but we had farms outside of town, and we always had some produce from them, so we had plenty to eat.

Daddy worked hard. He was an entrepreneur in those days of the Depression, trying to make a living in this and that. He started a coal business. He had coal shipped in and provided that for the town. He grew up on a farm and loved horseback riding. Once, he and a friend raced their horses down Broad Street. So he was interested in training horses, and he started harness racing in Hawkinsville and trained his own horses. In fact, it's become a big thing. It's central as a training place for harness racing. The federal government put money into building four hundred stalls and built two new tracks.[1] People come down from Michigan and other place(s) to train their horses, and then they move on when it's time to race. They go to Pompano Park, Florida, or go back to Michigan. We don't have pari-mutuel betting in Georgia, so they have to move on.

My daddy once took a pharmacy course, and he knew animals. Hawkinsville didn't have a veterinarian, so Governor Talmadge, Gene, sent a man down from Atlanta and said, "I'll let him go around with you for about a week and see what he can do about taking care of animals." Well, Daddy followed him for a week, and the man said, "You can be a veterinarian." Now days, you'd have to get an animal husbandry degree, but mainly it was inoculating and birthing animals–simple things. He kept doing different things to provide for his family. When the town finally voted to have a liquor store in Hawkinsville, he thought, *I can manage that. You don't drink when you run a store.* It just about killed my mother. She didn't want that. The Baptists were about to kick him out of the church. I don't think they ever did, but he ran that package store on the main street for a while and made more money than he ever made in his life.

Family Time

I had one sister, Jane, and a brother, Lowell, Jr. We called him Bubba. My mother was so very anxious that her children would grow up in the Baptist Church. When I was five and Jane was three, my mother would get us ready in our Sunday school dresses and say, "Now, hold hands, and walk to church together." We walked about two blocks. When we crossed the street, she'd say, "Stop and look both ways." We went to church every time the doors opened. My grandparents were very active in the church. I could hear my grandfather, Jim Bragg, singing about a block before I got to the church. He was a great, honest, good man. With just a handshake, he could get money from the bank and do business. He was a big hunter. Always brought a turkey for Thanksgiving.

As children, we would play under the streetlights at night. There was no air-conditioning, and people were out on their porches. We were barefoot a lot as kids. In the summers, I wanted to be in Pineview because I had my cousins, and we had so much fun. Pineview was about twelve miles away down a dirt road. We had a car, a Ford, even during the 1920s. My mother would say, "Lowell, I would like to go down to Pineview, and I promise I won't go over twenty-five miles-an-hour." There were no restrictions in Pineview. We'd walk out of the house at breakfast, and they [the cousin's parents] wouldn't see you to until dark, but you were being fed at some cousin's house somewhere. Nobody worried about your safety because everybody was kin to everyone else. We'd have bales of cotton out in the yard and jump from one to the other, sing songs and cut up, go down to Pappy Jacks [swimming hole] and Bluff Creek. That's where I learned to swim. Nobody taught you how to swim. You'd get in an old rubber inner tube and see if you could take it off and swim. My cousins were Jamie and Cleo McLeod, Jane Lou McLeod, Tom Dennard, Wilma Nell Clements. Her daddy had the Clements Drugstore where we hung out. They once had a railroad through there, and they still have a little red caboose from that train. They built a little park around it and made a little museum within the caboose.

There was a little independent telephone company in Pineview run by Mr. and Mrs. Wilson–Sarah Wilson–and they wouldn't sell out [to AT&T]. They liked what they were doing. You'd turn those handles on the wall, and you'd have to yell into the phone. You'd say, "Mrs. Wilson, would you ring Jane Lou?" She'd say, "Well, honey, I think she just left for Cordele. Looked to me like she had about three in the car. Wonder why they didn't take you?" That kind of thing. My Aunt Edith's daughter went to Alabama. She was a Phi Mu. My aunt said, "Mrs. Wilson, will you try to get the Phi Mu house in Tuscaloosa?"

After about a year of this, Mrs. Wilson said, "Miss Edith, I want to ask you something. What kind of a house is it that Anne lives in?" Just funny things like that. James McCallister, one of my friends in Atlanta, called and said, "Would you see if you can ring Uncle W.T.?" Mrs. Wilson said, "I think he's gone home for dinner...No, I called there, and they said he's already left, but he usually stops by cuddin [cousin] Annie Owen's house. You want me to ring there?... Well, lawd, they said he has gone, but I think he's already gone back to the gin." And the Atlanta operator is on the line, too, listening to all of that. From Hawkinsville, it was long distance to call Pineview twelve miles away, and you'd have to scream.

Southern Decoration Day

In April, all the school children in Hawkinsville would walk from the school to our downtown auditorium. Several old Confederate veterans would be on the stage for the program. It was Southern Decoration Day. We'd go out to Cedar Creek Church near Pineview, and clean up the cemetery and have dinner. My grandfather, John McLeod, is buried there. That was on April the 26th. Now, it's Memorial Day. I knew three or four men who fought in the Civil War. One, they called Uncle Bud. I think Lanier was his last name. He was old then–an old man walking up the street real slow with a cane. I can see him now, walking along, dressed in black with a black hat, white beard.

I learned to drive a Model-A in my driveway. I was driving by thirteen years old. I don't remember having a driver's license. Parents just let you start driving when you felt like you could. Around town, in high school, girls would get a group together. "Can you get your car for about an hour?" someone would say. We'd drive up and down the main street and look at the boys. The roads were dirt when I was a child–mud clay. We thought driving to Macon was a trip. Occasionally, you'd see chain gangs working on the side of the highway picking up trash. I don't remember paved highways until much later.

I went to Hawkinsville Elementary and High School. We'd walk to school, walk home for lunch, walk back to school, and walked home. We walked everywhere. The whole school was eleven years. It burned when I was a senior, but they rebuilt. Miss Mae Woodward was the first grade teacher. Very strict little lady. We had to be perfect–stand up straight and turn around on our feet–regimented.

We pledged allegiance and learned the Lord's Prayer in school in homeroom. We'd march to chapel, which was in the school auditorium. We sang songs like "Work, For The

Night Is Coming," "We've A Story To Tell To The Nations," "Santa Lucia." I tell my children that I made all A's in everything. I started to major in math in college. Ginger, my daughter, is teaching algebra now. I couldn't work an algebra problem now if my life depended on it. My children say, "Are you sure you were salutatorian?" They laugh about it.

The Ocean

I was probably sixteen years old before I saw the ocean. I thought, what a big pond of water [laughs]. Jamie McLeod would go to Jacksonville Beach every summer with her parents. And they included me on that trip. There were no swimming pools–you had to go in the ocean. We'd wear rubber bathing caps and get sunburned everywhere. We'd lie out and try to get a good tan–real brown. How ridiculous. I have spots all over me to show for it.

Dot White at age 21 in front of Hawkinsville home.

School Days

M. E. [Melvin Ernest] Thompson was our principal from grades one through about eight. He was born in Millen, Georgia. He took a liking to me and a few other girls. We didn't have much, but he thought we were smart, I guess. When it came time to go to college during the Roosevelt days, he helped me get an NYA–National Youth Administration–Scholarship. I had two years of college, secretarial courses–typing, shorthand, accounting–at GSCW, Georgia State College for Women, in Milledgeville. I got there on a Greyhound bus. It was about sixty-five miles through Macon and over to Milledgeville. It took a couple of hours at least. None of us students were allowed to have cars. We weren't even allowed to get in a car, they were so strict. Even on a date, we couldn't go beyond the flagpole on the campus. Be in by 10:30. Lights out by eleven o'clock. That's when most social life starts at universities now. We had very famous people come and entertain–James Melton, The Lyceum Attractions, Lonesome Eddy and Jeanette MacDonald, a singing duo. When I was in college, I told people I knew the name of everyone in Hawkinsville and the name of their dogs. Well, I did!

Gone with the Wind

I went up to Atlanta in 1937. I was standing on a little ol' soapbox down on Peachtree Street when they had the *Gone With The Wind* parade with Clark Gable, Carole Lombard, Vivian Leigh, Margaret Mitchell–all of them. Clark Gable and Carole Lombard [his wife] were seated on the back of a convertible where they could see the crowd and wave. They were going to the Georgian Terrace Hotel where they stayed, right across from the Fox Theatre. You could just about reach out and touch them. *Gone With The Wind* was premiering at the Fox. It was very special.

Dot White (right) at Georgia State College for Women with Margaret Smith. Margaret would later marry Joseph Hazelwood, a Marine Corps pilot. Their son, Joseph Hazelwood, Jr., was captain of the *Exxon Valdez*.

While in Atlanta

I learned to type on an old-fashioned pica. Later, I used an electric. That was modern. I can still do shorthand, but who wants that now with computers? Mr. Thompson would visit the campus to check on us. By then, he was the state school supervisor in Atlanta. By the time I finished my two years, he had become Assistant State Superintendent. So he gave me a job in his office at the capitol in Atlanta in 1937. I took a Greyhound bus to Atlanta on Highway 41, the Dixie Highway. It was paved by then. My roommate, Margaret Smith, and I would come home for the weekend. We'd get back into Atlanta about nine o'clock at night and walk from the bus station right through downtown Atlanta over to catch a streetcar out to Decatur. We weren't afraid at all in those days. You don't get out in Atlanta anymore like that.

I lived on Sycamore Street in Decatur with eight girls in one big boarding house run by an elderly couple, Mr. and Mrs. Greene. He was a retired attorney. In order to make money, they opened up this big home they had. There were four bedrooms for girls, two to a room. They had all graduated from Agnes Scott, except my roommate and I were from GSCW. All the girls worked for the telephone company mostly, and she and I worked for the state Department of Education. It was great–three meals a day for $27 a month, room and board. We worked in the state office building right across from the capitol. We got to work on a 5-cent streetcar ride. You had to change on Edgewood and walk about three blocks up a hill in high heels to get to the office. We wouldn't dare be caught without our high heels, rain or shine.

Dot White (l) with cousin Jamie McLeod (Hickman), 1942.

After I left Mr. and Mrs. Greene's house, I lived in an apartment on Ponce de Leon with four girls. We called it Grammar Manor. We did our own cooking, but you couldn't even buy meat, beef or chicken. We'd make spaghetti and cut up a hotdog. Everything was going to the

[WWII] soldiers. We didn't have gasoline to run the cars. If anyone had a car, it didn't go far. You traveled by bus or train. We had sugar rationing. People were limited on what they could have–leather, rubber–everything. When I married, I bought a little girdle that had no elastic in it. Atlanta then was like a great big country town. I mean, I knew Atlanta. I knew everything about Atlanta. We didn't have any real skyscrapers back then. We thought the Regency Hyatt was something when they built that. My goodness alive, you can't even find it now. And now, of course, Atlanta has turned into a New York. What would be considered out in the country was out past Northside Drive or Peachtree Road. My roommate in college was from Dallas, Georgia, which was thirty miles from Atlanta. That's part of Atlanta now. Alpharetta and those towns are now part of the city. It's just something else now.

Cleo McLeod (Wagner) left with Dot, age 19, and Lowell, Jr.'s tame fox.

During World War II, there was a shortage of good teachers. The government issued a wartime teaching certificate to people with just one year of college. My mother wanted to start teaching, and she barely had a year at Shorter College before she married. I figured up her transcript to get her that one-year and counted a music course or something that hadn't been counted to get her up to thirty semester hours. She was a wonderful teacher and librarian and taught for the rest of her life in Pineview. During summers, she went to GSCW and Peabody College in Nashville to improve on her certificate and increase her pay scale. She built it up to about three years.

I went to some southern state teachers' workshops, which is how I met my husband. We were in Daytona Beach for two weeks at the Southern States Conference. I was sent down as secretary along with two girls from Tallahassee. We were secretaries for the convention. I met my future husband one year, and the next year, we became engaged. He was from the State Department of Tennessee. His name was Herman Headden. Back in Atlanta, I was dating Georgia Tech and Emory boys and just having a good time. The Emory boys might drive over and get two or three girls and go on to Ma Beatty's, a little hangout where you could have a coke and dance to the jukebox.

You couldn't do much that cost much money. Then, I married this man [Headden] who had two little girls, Ruth and Nancy. Their mother had died, and so I had them. Then we had three more children, Henry, Cherry, and Ginger. I was not in the Baptist Church forever, because I married a Presbyterian from Nashville, Tennessee and raised my family in the Presbyterian Church until finally, I converted him to be a Baptist [laughs].

By then, M. E. Thompson was Lieutenant Governor. Gene Talmadge, who had been elected governor in 1946, died before taking office. Mr. Thompson had been elected by the people to be Lieutenant Governor, and he thought he should move into to the governorship, and most people thought that. But Herman Talmadge, being Gene's son, thought that he needed to go in. It went back and forth for a while.[2] Mr. Thompson moved into the governor's mansion for about a year. Then, they had another election. He was elected by the people [won the popular vote] but didn't win the county unit vote, and Herman won out. But that's okay. Mr. Thompson served for a while. I was his secretary while he was governor, which entailed typing, shorthand, keeping his schedule, and typing some of his speeches. He got invited to some parties that were pretty highfalutin, but many times, he didn't care to be a part of some of those parties and declined the invitations. My family thought I was very fortunate to be employed by him. As governor, he bought Jekyll Island for $675,000.

They named the bridge that goes over to the island M. E. Thompson Bridge. All those old homes–Rockefeller, J. P. Morgan–were very run down because they hadn't been used since the 1890s. There was no way to get to Jekyll except by boat until they built the causeway and bridge, which was maybe fifteen years later after the state bought Jekyll. He thought the island could be used for teacher meetings and statewide conferences. After he lost out to Herman Talmadge, he went to Valdosta and went into business for himself. He eventually got Parkinson's. Mr. Thompson was like a second-father to me, a real guiding light in my life.

Going Home

When I moved to Tennessee with my husband, it took me about two years to be happy in Nashville because it was very hillbilly–country, dirty. If we went home to Hawkinsville at Christmas time, it was an all-day drive, maybe twelve or thirteen hours. This was before the interstate highways were built. Once we went to the Isle of Skye in Scotland. When I got to the front step of Dunvegan Castle, the McLeod [MacLeod] ancestral home, I said, "Grandpa, we're home! [laughs]."

Being Minnie Pearl

I started impersonating Minnie Pearl in the 1940s. We were at a party one night, and people were doing little impersonations, and I thought, *What can I do? I'll see if I can do Minnie Pearl.* Some man there said, "Come to my school, and do Minnie Pearl for my students." Then, one thing led to another, and I've been doing it since about 1947 and still doing it. It's just fun, because people laugh. You go to nursing homes, and people think you *are* Minnie Pearl. "Oh, here she comes. We always used to see you on *Hee-Haw.* You were so good!" I just say, "Thank you." They believe I'm the real one.

[In character] A man put a gun right in my ribs and said, "I want your money or your life." Then he frisked me all up and down. I said, "I don't have any money, but if you do that again, I'll write you a check!"

Dot White as Minnie Pearl in 2001.

That's one of her jokes. I told Minnie once, "I try to do a good job impersonating you." She said, "I'm glad you're doing it, because I won't live forever, but I'd like for Minnie Pearl to live right on." She had a real sweet spirit. She [Sarah Cannon] was teaching school, and she just decided make up this Minnie Pearl character. Through the years, it's worked. Her sister was one of her writers. They'd grown up around Centerville, Tennessee and knew a lot of country kids. Minnie Pearl was just a girl who loved everybody, and everybody loved Minnie. Just a country girl. This doctor in my church, Dr. Horace Watson, was going on a trip to lecture at the Hadassah Hospital in the Holy Land and said, "Dot, why don't you come and bring your Minnie Pearl hat." So I went with him and his wife, and the hostess at the hospital came to escort us to the right place. I was dressed like Minnie, and she tapped Mrs. Watson on the shoulder and said, "I don't know if your friend knows it or not, but the tag is still on her hat."[3] It was fun. I'm 90, but mentally and emotionally, I'm probably about thirty-five years old.

Dot White on her 90th birthday.

Hawkinsville

Hawkinsville is twice or three times as big as it was when I was growing up, but it's still not on an Interstate like Perry. Perry has more hotels and everything now. We're still more of a residential community. When I go back home, I go around Atlanta. People say, "Well, you're from here. Don't you know how to get through Atlanta?" I say, "No, I don't."

I'm proud of Georgia and perk up every time somebody mentions Georgia. I love the state.

NOTES

[1] "Hawkinsville is home to one of the largest harness racing training facilities in the country. The town has had a long history of horse racing, and celebrates the Hawkinsville Harness Horse Festival every spring." Georgia.gov,
http://hawkinsville.georgia.gov/05/home/0,2230,8969499,00.html;jsessionid=5C202B3B89-13713DC054A3D4D6BB4E4D, accessed March 7, 2011.

[2] The "three governors controversy" involved outgoing governor, Ellis Arnall, lieutenant governor Melvin Thompson, and Gene Talmadge's son, Herman, who had received write-in votes. In January 1947, the state legislature elected Herman Talmadge governor. He served two months in that capacity before the Georgia Supreme Court ruled the legislative election invalid. Thompson served as governor until the 1948 general election.

[3] Comedienne "Minnie Pearl always dressed in styleless 'down home' dresses and wore a hat with a price tag hanging from it, displaying the price of $1.98." Wikipedia,
http://en.wikipedia.org/wiki/Minnie_Pearl, accessed March 9, 2011.

William Waddell Winn

Columbus-born Billy Winn is a journalist and historian whose great-great-grandfather drew up the original plans for the city and served as a physician to both whites and Creek Indians. Winn grew up when the main industry in town was cotton mills that ran day-and-night. Like many Southerners, he recalls listening to Civil War stories as a boy: "Grandmother lived with us, and meals were a series of battles. We fought the Battle of Manassas at breakfast, maybe Chancellorsville at lunch, and Gettysburg at supper. To this day, I can't eat a piece of fried chicken without thinking about Pickett's charge." As a news reporter, Winn covered much of the Civil Rights Movement, including press conferences with Dr. Martin Luther King, Jr. and other leaders, as well as Dr. King's funeral. While working in Atlanta, he met Pulitzer Prize-winning journalist Ralph McGill, whose influence lives on in Winn's work.

Billy Winn. Photograph by Fred Fussell.

My name is William Waddell Winn–"WWW." My mother did that to me. Because I had trouble spelling my middle name (it's "Waddell," but I spelled it "Waddle" until I was in college), a lot of my elementary school classmates called me "Waddle." Waddell was my grandmother's maiden name. I was born in the old City Hospital of Columbus, Georgia, September the 9th, 1938. My father was Dr. John H. Winn, and my mother was Dorothy Clason Winn. She was from an Old South family with roots in Georgia and Alabama. My father was born in Hamilton, Ontario, but he had lived in North Carolina as a young man. His ancestors were part of the Irish Famine immigrants who came over to America in 1846 or '47. After a number of years, they moved to New York, where they could make a better living, and ultimately, to North Carolina. They were very poor, but hard working. They were textile mill people and settled in Concord, North Carolina, where my father's father worked in the mill. He somehow managed to get Daddy and his two brothers through medical school. I suspect my father moved to Columbus because he got his father a job in a mill here.

Columbus was a big textile mill town with miles of mills on the Chattahoochee River. When I grew up, the mills were going 'round the clock. Lots of lint in the air, too, and cotton bales stacked all over the riverfront. You can read about them in Carson McCullers' *The Heart Is A Lonely Hunter.* Carson's real name was Lula Carson Smith. She was born in Columbus.

My father went to the University of North Carolina at Chapel Hill and got his medical degree from Vanderbilt. I think his brothers did the same. My mother's family was different from Daddy's. They go back to 1827 when my great-great-grandfather came here. He was one of the trustees of Columbus in 1827-'28 when the city was founded. He was a doctor, too. Part of Momma's family settled in Columbus, and another part settled in Russell

County, Alabama, right across the Chattahoochee in a little town called Seale, Alabama. My father came here in 1920 to be a practicing physician not long after World War I, during which, he had been in the Medical Corps stationed in the Midwest and the West Coast. He went through the 1918 pneumonia epidemic in the army. That's what the Medical Corps people stationed in the United States remember about World War I. He was a very quiet guy and would not talk much about himself. His first wife died in childbirth, and so did the child. Daddy died when I was thirteen years old.

College Life

I went to Columbus High School and then to Vanderbilt for one year, transferred to Emory, and dropped out my senior year, and went into hiding, trying to educate myself the way I wanted to. I went through an intense period of just reading because I felt I wasn't getting what I really wanted in school. Plus, I was a wild and crazy kid. My mother and uncles wanted me to become a doctor, but I knew I wasn't doctor material. There are a lot of people alive today who would otherwise be dead if I had been a doctor. It was a forced education, and I rebelled against it. What I did do, is I found a little nook on North Highlands Avenue in Atlanta at St. Charles Public Library, a small, but wonderful place. I sat down there for I forget how long reading anything I could get my hands on. Even in my teens, I haunted the public library in Columbus. Early on, I started reading black literature–John Henrick Clark, W. E. B. Du Bois, Langston Hughes, Richard Wright, James Baldwin, Ralph Ellison. Zora Neale Hurston was a favorite, and Ernest Gaines, the short-story writer. When I got to reading American literature seriously in the St. Charles Library, I read through the whole shooting match starting with the 1920s and '30s to the present. Ostensibly, I was going to Emory, so I was living on campus in dorms and

405

the KA [Kappa Alpha] house, and part of the time in little apartments in the area.

Billy Winn, student council president, Columbus High School.

The Journalist

When I went to work for the *Atlanta Journal* for $65 a week, my wife and I had a very inexpensive place on Briarcliff Road. I got into journalism by accident. In my teen years, I was much under the influence of Ernest Hemingway and F. Scott Fitzgerald, [John] Dos Passos, and that crowd, and decided I wanted to be a writer. One day, I went into the *Journal* on Forsyth Street, never dreaming I'd get a job. Harold Davis was the city editor of the *Atlanta Journal*. We hit it off. I was interested in the classics, and that was also a passion of his. He eventually got a Ph.D. in history. When I started at the paper, I couldn't even type. He sat me down in front of a typewriter, gave me an assignment, and away we went. At that time, they had a marvelous copy desk with several published novelists on it, including Rudy Burke, George Wallace's old sparring partner. It was a challenging group of people. My first assignment was to do a story on an African-American woman who was some sort of phrenologist. She lived in Decatur, east of Atlanta, in a spooky house up on a hill. She had skulls all around her room, dozens of them. So I interviewed her. She may have been a conjure woman–I don't know. When I turned my story in and it made it to the copy desk, one of the copyreaders came over to my desk and said she liked it. Made my day.

I was with the *Journal* for four or five years in the 1960s during the Civil Rights Movement. The *Atlanta Constitution* was the paper with the reputation in the business. Ralph McGill was editor of the *Constitution,* and I think Gene Patterson was still there. That was the morning paper. The *Journal* was considered the more conservative of the two papers and came out in the afternoon. I turned in copy beginning about noon during the day. I had to come in about 7:30 in the morning. The *Constitution* got out before dawn with Ralph McGill's column on the front page. In those days, the papers were trucked all over Georgia. The *Journal* came out in the late afternoon, but I'm no longer certain what time. It was the evening paper, the one Atlanta people read when they got home from work.

College annual photograph of Billy Winn.

Ralph McGill and I got to be friends, or at least good acquaintances. I had lunch with him at Gold's Café shortly before he died. Reese Cleghorn[1] was there. Reese was the backbone of our editorial page and went on to edit the *American Journalism Review* in Washington. McGill was the guiding spirit of the *Constitution* and of southern journalism.[2] Of course, he was roundly hated by large portions of the white population. I knew him mainly through his work. I was just a kid at the time, still in my early twenties, so we were not intimate, but he gave me advice. He told me–begged me, really–not to go back to Columbus under any circumstances. He was such a powerful influence in my life and still is. He was a very courageous guy, and God knows what he put up with in his struggle to change white attitudes toward blacks. He literally gave his life for it. People tend to forget the real threat of violence that lay behind white attitudes towards blacks in those days. Once, I wrote a piece for the *Journal* on the decline of family farming in which I mentioned the children of a white family in rural Stewart County. When I went back to visit the little town where the family lived, I was greeted by the irate father of those children. He put a .357 in my face and said he would kill me if I ever mentioned his children again in "those Ralph McGill newspapers." The way it was in those days. If something like that could happen to me, imagine the threats McGill got every day. It wasn't easy for McGill to break through the curtain of blind hate that was ingrained in white racism at that time. You could extend your voice too far and lose all credibility with the people you needed to influence the most, and many people thought Ralph did. But he got the ball rolling. He stood up when the heat was hottest, when the battle was just getting engaged in many ways. Certainly in the popular culture, his influence was important in changing some of the white attitudes. Of course, he had to be educated by black people himself. In one instance, he was making a speech, and black college students hooted him down. He got a real lesson in what was actually the reality on the street for black people. It did work a sea change on him. He did learn, and he did grow. He was a man caught in a storm trying to do the right thing.

Columbus in the 1950s and '60s was terribly racist. Ralph had a lot of friends in Columbus when he was a sports writer. He'd come down here to bird dog trials, go hunting and fishing with judges, lawyers–the powerful people, and he'd go to the Georgia-Auburn game, which was played in Columbus in those days at [A. J. McClung] Memorial Stadium. When he began to speak out on race– become a turncoat on the race issue–they treated him as a traitor. Later, he was to come down here and speak on one occasion and was met by a group of whites at the city limits and told to turn around and not come back. He had to go back to Atlanta. Columbus was, for years, one of the roughest places to be if you were black or a white liberal.

I didn't take McGill's advice not to return to my hometown. As much as anything, I moved back to Columbus because of something Dr. Martin Luther King, Jr. said not long before he was killed. Dr. King had a tremendous influence over my life. We weren't friends or anything. I just knew him from covering him. I'm sure if he were alive today, he wouldn't know me from Adam. I don't mean he took me aside and said go to Columbus. He sometimes would say to all of us reporters who covered him in Atlanta that we should go and work for the movement among our own people because they were the ones that really needed it. This stuck in my mind. I never thought I'd actually get a chance to do it though. I liked him very much although he was always late for meetings and press conferences, a real pain to reporters on deadlines. He'd always come into meetings smiling, tell a joke or something on himself. You couldn't stay mad at him. He had such courage, and of course, he was carrying a tremendous weight on his shoulders. He also had a good personality, something that doesn't always come through on TV. He was likable as a person.

I have many memories of Dr. King and the scene in Atlanta during the Sixties. I also covered Julian Bond, John Lewis, Rev. Ralph Abernathy, Hosea Williams, Andrew Young, James Bevel, William Holmes Borders, Jesse Jackson, Vernon Jordan, C.B. King, Joseph Lowery, Dr. Benjamin Mays and many other figures in the civil rights movement. We all covered them because the Southern Christian Leadership Conference office was in Atlanta and Ebenezer Baptist Church, Daddy King's church, was right down the street on Auburn Avenue. I kept a photograph of McGill, King and W.E.B. DuBois on my office wall at the *Columbus Ledger-Enquirer* for many years, but I packed all that stuff away long ago. Sometimes it seems like a dream and sometimes, like a nightmare.

The first time I really took note of Dr. King's moral power was when I saw and heard him speaking from the back of a pick-up truck beside the Georgia capitol. It was a moonlit night in the Sixties. The power and rhythm of King's voice captivated me, as it did the other people in the small crowd that had gathered there on the sidewalk. I no longer remember what his subject was–maybe it had to do with the effort to keep Julian Bond out of the Georgia Legislature, a disgraceful and sadly ludicrous moment in the state's history. The *Journal-Constitution* had a schizophrenic attitude toward the civil right movement in those days. Not everybody at either paper agreed with McGill. Some of the editors were flatly racist, and sometimes, the composing room would misspell King's name on purpose. I recall the news that Dr. King had won the Nobel Prize was played far back in the paper. And when some reporter asked our managing editor, Bill Fields, when we were going to cover Selma he said, "When it gets to be news." Those are the kind of things you can't forget.

Once, I got an interview with John Lewis, then one of the leaders of the Student Non-Violent Coordinating Committee or SNCC. Lewis was supposed to be hard-edged, but I found him to be sensitive and humane. He talked of his concern for the young people of both races who were dropping out of school to join the movement. He wondered aloud what was going to become of them when they got older, how they were going to make a living. There was genuine concern in his voice, and I thought the interview was revealing of another side of this young man who was a leading figure in the civil rights movement. I hustled back to the *Journal* and typed up the story and turned it in to our city editor. The city editor read it quickly and handed it back to me, saying, "I've laid in one too many foxholes to print that."

I was in the newsroom of the *Atlanta Journal* when we learned that Dr. King had been assassinated in Memphis.

We had a different city editor by then, John Crown, an ex-Marine. He told me to get to Memphis as fast as I could. I had to borrow $54 from Crown to pay for my airfare. Memphis shocked me. There were National Guard troops everywhere, machine guns on street corners around the old Peabody Hotel, which is where most of the media gathered. The whole scene was depressing and ineffably sad. The streets of the city seemed gray and dingy. Of course, most of us were depressed. By luck, I stumbled into a meeting of civil rights leaders–I guess they were mostly members of the Southern Christian Leadership Conference–in a room at the Peabody Hotel. I had no right to be there, but nobody said anything to me, so I just leaned back against a wall and listened. What I heard was a debate over the very future of America, whether to burn it down or try to save it. After considerable debate, much of it emotional, the group voted overwhelmingly to save the nation, to urge calm and patience in the face of the terrible tragedy that had just happened. I remember being very proud of that.

As to Dr. King's funeral, I recall the enormous number of people of all races who attended, the celebrities standing on almost every corner by which the cortège passed, the wagon and mule team leading the way, Mahalia Jackson singing "Precious Lord"–off key. After that, everything is just a blur. I think now that I was in shock. Many people were. Ralph McGill died shortly after that, I think in 1969. Then Bobby Kennedy was assassinated. In less than a decade we had lost John F. Kennedy, Martin Luther King, Ralph McGill and Bobby Kennedy. The world in which I had imagined a role for myself just seemed to crumble. It was a surreal time, at least for me.

After that, I sort of drifted. Worked for *Atlanta Magazine,* did some freelancing, lived in New Orleans for several years. Eventually, I landed a job as editor and publisher of an experimental non-subscription magazine, *Good Life,* which was aimed at wealthy readers. It was my one attempt to make some real money out of journalism. It failed, and as the man in charge, it was my fault. That failure, however, also led to my coming to Columbus and taking a job with the *Columbus Ledger-Enquirer*, first as a senior writer and then, for the last 13 years, as editor of the editorial page. Funny the way life works out. Dr. King still is much in my thoughts although all that I witnessed in Atlanta now sometimes seems like it took place in another life.

Columbus is a complicated place with a hidden history that is equal to the history of any place I know about. It's got everything. Columbus was founded as a result of the 1827 land lottery engineered by Governor George M. Troup, who was known as the "Oracle of State Rights." I think he did more than any other man, including John C. Calhoun, to fix states' rights views on the South. He was the best-known voice primarily because he led the effort to forcibly eject the Indians from Georgia. His voice was heard in Alabama, Mississippi, and Louisiana where movements began to remove the Indians west of the Mississippi River to Indian lands in Oklahoma. He used his influence in a verbal war with President John Quincy Adams to win a place for the states' rights view on a local level and the national level. He was one of the South's first real demagogues. While the national debates were taking place in Congress and later, over the Removal bill of 1830, he was digging his heels in on the local level. Most people think that states' rights grew out of the Civil War, but it grew out of the struggle to get rid of the Indians from our western lands, our southern states that used to be called the Old Southwest, but which we now call the Southeast. States' rights grew out of Georgia's efforts to get rid of the Indians, who at that time, occupied half of the state. These were the Creek or Muskogee Indians.[3]

Several members of Troup's inner circle came to Columbus from Milledgeville. His personal secretary,

Mirabeau Lamar,[4] his chief aide-de-camp, Seaborn Jones, and very influential judges and lawyers moved here; men like Eli S. Shorter, Alfred Iverson, John Banks, James S. Calhoun, to name a few. They had a heads up, no doubt, that if they moved to Columbus, they could a get a lead in acquiring Indian lands in Alabama. These men became speculators in Creek Indian lands. In the course of the next twenty years, they defrauded, cheated, and used every imaginable method to acquire Creek lands. By 1836, they were able to run the Creeks west of the Mississippi with the help of Andrew Jackson and others. But basically, it was done by that cadre of men who were around with Troup at the state capitol in Milledgeville.

My great-great-grandfather on my mother's side, Edwin Louis DeGraffenried, came in 1827 and was part of the five trustees who laid out the city.[5] He was a physician and was a surgeon for the Creeks during a smallpox epidemic. I know I'm influenced by his defense of the Indians and his work with them. They were grateful to him for what he did.

"Embryo Town of Columbus On The Chattahoochee...Drawn with the Camera Lucida by Capt.ⁿ B. Hall RN, Engraved by W. H. Lizzars [sic]." Likely engraved by William Home Lizars, who, like Basil Hall, was from Edinburgh, Scotland. Image courtesy of *Columbus Ledger-Enquirer*.

I have his portrait on the wall. As children we always thought he was shaking his finger at us, telling us to behave. The frightening thing about the portrait, which used hang in our living room over the fireplace, was that his eyes seemed to follow you wherever you went. That, and the fact there was a hole in the canvas that somebody told us, probably grandmother, was put there by a Yankee sword.

Portrait of Edwin Louis DeGraffenried, courtesy of the Historic Columbus Foundation.

Recently, a group from the Creek Nation in Oklahoma was visiting Columbus, young and middle aged people. They were looking for sites that were important to the Creek Removal period to raise the consciousness of their people and to reclaim that history. I took them down the Chattahoochee River to Fort Mitchell, one of the places from which the Creeks were gathered by the U.S. Army and sent to the west in chains. Many people died, and many committed suicide rather than leave their home. They walked them to Montgomery where they put them on riverboats to Mobile and New Orleans and up the Mississippi to the Oklahoma Territory. After that, many other removal parties left. We had natives going west as late as 1848, a long removal period and an agonizing time for the Indians. The land was their larder, and they had an attachment to specific geographical areas and the plants and animals there. So I showed them the old fort. One of the Native American's family had originally lived in what is now Eufaula, Alabama, and he wanted to go the site of old Eufaula Town. He was the first in his family to return there.

We went to the site of the old Indian village, and it seemed to be a very important moment for him and the others. It was moving to see them have such a reaction. Of course, there's nothing there, just an empty field located on a beautiful peninsula in the Chattahoochee River. Most people would just look on it as barren ground, but for them it was home. When the Indian Nations moved west, they took local place names with them. You'll find a Coweta, Eufaula, Ocmulgee [Okmulgee], Muscogee [Muskogee] and other town names out there. Later, the lands stolen from the Indians became the basis of the cotton kingdom throughout the South. We wanted the land for planting cotton, and we got it.

Almost nobody in Columbus remembers the Creeks anymore. Columbus was one of the places that made the Civil War, and it sits like a stone on our memory. I was a diver for years and started scuba diving when I was thirteen or fourteen years old. I read Jacques Cousteau's *The Silent World* and got a rubber suit and aqualung very young. I'd go out into the country by myself to lakes and ponds and swim with the turtles and bass and other fish. I dove on a sunken Civil War gunboat and saw the cannons. The gunboat was called the *Chattahoochee*. We also had an ironclad here being built during the war. Both of them were burnt and sunk in the Chattahoochee River. The Yankees came here a week after Appomattox. General Wilson, the Union commander, sunk the ironclad. The gunboat boilers had exploded down river, so it had sunk previous to their coming here. Both vessels have been reclaimed and are now on display in the local Confederate Naval museum.

My great-grandfather, James Fleming Waddell, was in command of the Confederate artillery at that last battle, the date of which was practically carved into my grandmother's forehead. Grandmother lived with us, and meals were a series of battles. We fought the Battle of Manassas at breakfast, maybe Chancellorsville at lunch, and Gettysburg at supper. To this day I can't eat a piece of fried chicken without thinking about Pickett's charge.[6]

Columbus history is full of interesting characters. Thomas Brewer, a local African American physician, was some guy and should be a subject for a novel. Dr. Brewer and my father came to Columbus at the same time in 1920. Daddy and his partner worked with Dr. Brewer informally. He helped them, and they helped him, particularly with some of his more complicated diagnoses, because he was primarily delivering babies. Dr. Brewer was shot and killed in a downtown clothing store in 1956 during the time of the Montgomery bus boycott. He was head of the NAACP here and also head of a successful movement to eliminate the all-white primary in Georgia at the time, a very important effort for African Americans then and now. He was instrumental in integrating the police force, he got public parks integrated, and he was trying to get integration in the schools. Totally fearless. African-Americans here in Columbus called him "Chief." He was hated by the white community and threatened many times. After he was shot and killed, the professional blacks in Columbus–the lawyers and doctors–left, including Dr. McCoo whose daughter, Marilyn, went on to be a famous singer. Those families went to Oakland, Los Angeles, San Francisco, and Cleveland. They just dispersed–a Diaspora. Terribly damaging to the city. It was years and years after that before the African-American community recovered leadership.

When I was growing up, I knew something was wrong as far as race goes. I don't want to claim too much, because I was in every way a regular white, macho, typical teenage boy, but I knew the race thing was off base. I was raised by a black cook in our family, Betty Crowell Jackson, who was in many ways more like a mother to me than my own mother. She gave not just nurture, but love. I know that many young white boys who grew up with black maids have this romantic notion of that relationship. After all, she was working for us, and I was the son of the guy she was working for. Anyway, I worshiped her, but I saw how she was treated and mistreated. One time, Betty had made some boiled custard ice cream for grandmother. Grandmother and I were sitting at the table eating dinner alone in the house, and grandmother found a grain of sugar in the ice cream. She called Betty out of the kitchen and chewed her out.

I remember looking up at Betty's face as she was standing in the kitchen door and these tears were flowing down her face. I've never forgotten that moment. It just tore at my heart, mainly because of the affection I felt for her. There were a number of experiences like that. I recall having family dinner at grandmother's house one day when the subject of James Reeb, the white minister clubbed to death in Selma in 1965 came up. "He got just what he deserved," grandmother said. "Pass the chicken, please." I can't forget stuff like that.

The Written Word

I began to read at a fairly early age, maybe as a means of escape. We had a wonderful librarian in Columbus, Loretta Lamar Chappell. I started coming across books in the library that were so different from the culture I had grown up in. I don't know whether Miss Chappell or some other librarian was putting the books where I would come across them or not. They may have. I read a short story by John Henrik Clarke called "The Boy Who Painted Christ Black," which had a profound effect on me. I read it at just the right time. I began to ask some questions. For some reason, when I was just a kid, I read Jomo Keenyatta's *Facing Mount Kenya*, and I came across Albert Schweitzer's *Out Of My Life And Thought*. That got me to thinking differently. The culture at the time was so anti-black that I can make no claims for myself, because almost anybody who spent their daily life surrounded with the attitudes toward people of color, as we used to say, would have been affected by the experiences I had. It really isolated me and still does.

White people always want to talk about how much better things are. You don't hear many black people, even today, saying how much better things are. We have had progress in the election of public officials. We even have a black U. S. congressional representative from this area, Sanford Bishop. In terms of government, everything is desegregated but really not integrated. We have many public schools that are virtually all black and white. The neighborhoods are mildly desegregated at the edges of them. Some of the wealthier blacks have managed to integrate some of the better suburban real estate developments. Whether there has been much progress in changing the human heart, I question that.

Another reason I came back to Columbus was because in the 1970s we had a serial murderer here, the "Stocking Strangler," who raped and killed seven elderly women,

419

several of whom were upper-class and well-known in the city and friends of my mother. I was in Washington and had a contract with Time-Life Books to write a book on infectious diseases at fifty-cents a word, a fortune to me at the time, so I could afford to move. My aunt was living alone, and I came back to stay with her during the stranglings. It was a dream to come back to Columbus and write about my hometown. Fingerprints ultimately did the killer in. His name is Carlton Gary. He stole a gun from a house, and they traced the serial numbers on that gun back to the house and found out where the man living there got it. The gun came from a distant Gary family member in Alabama who told the police he sold it to Carlton. Once they had his name they ran it through NCIS, identified him, and found his prison records in Syracuse, New York. They found him in Albany, Georgia, arrested him, and brought him back to Columbus. He's now on death row at the facility in Jackson, Georgia. He's had many appeals.

Columbus has always been active in sports. We all went to ballgames and played sports. I played baseball as a pitcher and was a guard in basketball. A number of major league teams have been in and out of here. The Cincinnati Reds did their spring training here [1912]. In my childhood, this was a St. Louis Cardinal's farm team. The Georgia-Auburn football game was played here [1916-1958].

Hunting and fishing were really important here. There was a subculture where anyone who could scrape two nickels together would buy bird dogs and get a little plot of land out in the country, maybe the old farm that their grandparents owned before they moved to town. Everybody rode horses. They had bird dog trials. The bird dog handlers would train them and take them to somebody's land and put them through trials in which the dogs would locate and point to birds. All of this was done according to very rigid rules and high standards. The dogs were put through the paces. They tried to make the dog break the point and run after the bird. While this was going on, there was a lot of bourbon being drunk. It was the old Southern scene.

Columbus is also a military town. Without Fort Benning, Columbus wouldn't exist. Since we lost the textile industry, Fort Benning is the economic engine. It's the major player of the economy in the area. This is very much a pro-war town from that point of view. The real positive effect of the fort is that it has brought more educated people into the community and has had a leavening effect on racial and social attitudes. Many of the people from Fort Benning choose to retire here, go into second careers, open businesses, and they have assumed leadership positions in the city. They make a real difference. A lot of the black troopers, staff sergeants, and civilian employees have become effective leaders in the community. They had a little more money than many of the local blacks, many of whom are still very poor. Their own educational status was usually higher than most of the local blacks. So they've had a positive effect on the black community as well.

The History

AFLAC [insurance company] has made a lot of millionaires and has a very positive financial effect. The development of the Columbus Regional Healthcare System, has had a tremendous effect on the city. In the absence of the mills, these companies along with Synovus [banking], Total System Services, the credit card processing company, have been the lifeblood of modern Columbus.

The Georgia countryside, compared to when I was growing up, is haunted, almost empty. It's called the "Second Georgia" by the state politicians. It's poor. It's lonely. The family farms started disappearing right after World War II. Black people left the farms in the 1940s for the city when mechanization took over. Most of them moved to any major city in the state. The small towns are fighting to survive. They have to have a major industry in order to survive. If they don't have one, they are slowly dwindling away. The family farms are now colossal super-mechanized farms. At the same time, I love driving out in the countryside. We have "studio farms" now, where well-educated couples are running fifty-acre specialty farms, growing grass-fed beef or raising some exotic fruit. The towns are trying to develop a tourism attraction. Lumpkin, for example, has a historic village called Westville. Each town tries to have something like that. Dawsonville has long been known as the peanut capitol of the world. Americus is the watermelon capitol. They've all got something going. My neighbor, Fred Fussell, has a wonderful show-and-tell he does about the rollaway four feet high neon signs parked out in front of businesses that move from town-to-town and change the little exhibit info on them–whatever the local attraction might be.

I did a history of St. Luke Methodist Church, *Line of Splendor*. People around here keep asking me why I did it. They know I'm a lapsed Episcopalian. For one reason, we have two or three social histories and a good short history, but no really detailed history of the city. Most people don't read up on their local history. So I thought maybe I could do histories of institutions that people have some relationship to, and they might be more inclined to read them. Then I could work in bits and pieces of the history of Columbus. That's why I did a 600-page history of St. Luke. It's almost as much a history of Columbus as it is of the church. An added incentive was that most of the financial leaders and power brokers of Columbus are or were members of St. Luke, including those land speculators who founded the city. Their descendants still go to St. Luke church, and they have run Columbus either *sub rosa* or openly as political leaders, financial leaders, social doyennes, the whole business. I worked out a deal with the minister, a great guy named Hal Brady, so that I could talk about race relations openly. I got a chance to write more honestly about racial matters–who had tried to keep blacks out of churches, and so forth–than I have ever been able to anywhere else. Now, I'm doing a book on the city hospital for the same reason. I'm trying to put together a network of these books. I don't know if it's going to work, but it pays some of the bills and allows me to write about things that matter, at least to me.

NOTES

[1] Later, dean of the University of Maryland Philip Merrill College of Journalism from 1981 to 2000.

[2] Ralph McGill, as editor and publisher of the *Atlanta Constitution*, was a leading voice for racial and ethnic tolerance in the South from the 1940s through the 1960s. As an influential daily columnist, he broke the code of silence on the subject of segregation, chastising a generation of demagogues, timid journalists, and ministers who feared change. When the U.S. Supreme Court outlawed segregated schools in 1954 and southern demagogues led defiance of the court, segregationists vilified McGill as a traitor to his region for urging white southerners to accept the end of segregation. In 1959, at the age of sixty-one, he was awarded the Pulitzer Prize for editorial writing. Source: The New Georgia Encyclopedia, http://www.georgiaencyclopedia.org/nge/ArticlePrintable.jsp?id=h-2769 , accessed January 23, 2012.

[3] Troup negotiated the Treaty of Indian Springs with his cousin, William McIntosh, the son of a Creek Indian and a Scottish trader. In signing the treaty, McIntosh authorized the sale of all of the remaining Creek lands (primarily in southwest Georgia) to the United States. Although he acted as principal chief of Coweta, McIntosh represented only a small faction of the Lower Creek tribe, and his authority to sell the land was questionable. He and several other chiefs who signed the controversial treaty were murdered by angry members of the tribe who felt that the chiefs had betrayed the interests of their people. U.S. president John Quincy Adams withdrew the Indian Springs Treaty and negotiated a federal treaty that would have given the Creek Indians slightly more land. Troup refused to recognize the new treaty and began removing the tribe with state militia forces. When Adams threatened to send in federal troops to enforce the federal treaty, Troup began organizing the state militia force, preparing to fight the U.S. Army in the name of state's rights. Adams, however, was not willing to go to war over the fate of the Creek Indians and allowed Troup to have his way. Source: The New Georgia Encyclopedia, http://www.georgiaencyclopedia.org/nge/Article.jsp?id=h-2822, accessed January 23, 2012.]

[4] Lamar established a newspaper in Columbus, Georgia, the *Columbus Enquirer*....In 1836, he was elected vice-president of the Republic of Texas under Houston.... Lamar was the unanimous choice

to replace Houston as president in 1838, and was inaugurated on December 1, 1838. Source:
http://en.wikipedia.org/wiki/Mirabeau_B._Lamar, accessed January 23, 2012.

[5] Founded in 1828 by an act of the Georgia Legislature, Columbus was situated at the beginning of the navigable portion of the Chattahoochee River and on the last stretch of the Federal Road before entering Alabama. The city was named for Christopher Columbus, its founders likely influenced by the writings of Washington Irving. The dimensions for the city streets were drawn up by Dr. Edwin L. DeGraffenried with an eye toward wide boulevards in the European manner. Across the river, where Phenix City, Alabama is now located, Creek Indians lived until their removal in 1836. Source: http://en.wikipedia.org/wiki/Columbus,_Georgia, accessed January 23, 2012.

[6] When the outbreak of war came in 1861, the industries of Columbus expanded their production and Columbus became one of the most important centers of industry in the Confederacy. During the war, Columbus ranked second to Richmond in the manufacture of supplies for the Confederate army. In addition to textiles, the city had an ironworks and a sword factory as well as a shipyard for the Confederate Navy. Unaware of Lee's surrender to Grant and the assassination of Abraham Lincoln, Union and Confederates clashed in the Battle of Columbus, Georgia on Easter Sunday, April 16, 1865, when a Union detachment under General James H. Wilson attacked the city and burned many of the industrial buildings. The inventor of Coca-Cola, Dr. John Stith Pemberton, was wounded in this battle. The owner of America's last slave ship, Col. Charles Augustus Lafayette Lamar, was also killed here. A historic marker has been erected in Columbus marking the battle by Wilson's troops as the "Last Land Battle in the War Between the States." Source:
http://en.wikipedia.org/wiki/Columbus,_Georgia, accessed January 23, 2012.

Oscar Cruz

Oscar Cruz is a second-generation migrant worker who has worked Georgia's onion and cotton crops for more than 27 years. Cruz's narrative portrays yet another aspect of Georgia in transition, and is a classic tale of immigrants moving to America and improving their lot with each succeeding generation. His parents came to the state as migrant workers, speaking little, if any, English. Oscar is more assimilated into the culture than his parents. He's fluent in English, and he has risen in the ranks from field laborer to foreman and mechanic. His children–the third generation of his family to live in Georgia–are even more acculturated and have no plans to labor in the fields.

My name is Oscar Cruz. I don't have a middle name. "Cruz" in Spanish means "cross." I was born in Del Rio, Texas, February 27, 1964. Del Rio is about 150 miles from San Antonio going west. Mom was born in Monterey, Mexico. My Dad was born in [Cuidad] Acuña, Mexico.[1]

I went to school in Florida, Illinois, and Ohio. My parents were following the migrant work. In Ohio, we lived at a migrant camp in cabins the farmer had. There were three or four people in each cabin. We used to do pickles, cucumbers, tomatoes. In Florida, we picked grapefruits, oranges, and strawberries, and we lived in apartments provided by the company we worked for.

A cousin of my dad invited him to Illinois to work at asparagus. From there, we went to Wisconsin to work in cherries and strawberries. Then, my Dad met a guy in Wisconsin who invited him to Florida. We went to Florida in 1970. There were a lot of kids working in the fields in those days. They don't let children in the fields now. I was working the fields in 1969, so I was about five years old. I

426

met my wife in Florida. I did crop work in Dade City, Vero Beach, and Ruskin, Florida. I used to go to North Carolina, too, from 1981 to '93. I picked cucumber, bell pepper, and sweet potatoes.

In 1980, my Dad's brother-in-law invited him to work in Georgia doing onions. So we started coming to Georgia every year and just decided to stay permanently. We stayed in Lyons where there were trailers we could rent. I came here in 1980 and stayed permanently in 1994 and never had any problems with anyone. I'm a Georgia citizen!

I like picking onions. The soil in Toombs County makes Vidalia onions special. I like onions on hamburgers, steaks–anything. We work almost seven days when we can. On Sundays, we just work half a day. My family goes to church in the morning. We got to go wash clothes, get groceries–all that. The other days we go until the body tells us it's time to quit the work. We start at seven o'clock in the morning and knock off at six o'clock or 6:30.

This year, onion harvesting started the first week of April. It ends about the first week of June. Right now, we are around the corner to finishing the crop. I've been doing it for so many years. Some people work faster than others. It all depends on the person. We get paid by the bucket–$.38 a bucket. Some people can do about 350 buckets a day. If the onions are big, it takes about 40 or 45 onions to fill a bucket. If they are medium-size or small, it takes more onions.

When I'm finished with the onion crop, I rest until the middle of August or the beginning of September. Then I go and do cotton in Statesboro. There, I'm the service man–the mechanic. I fix module builders and get paid by the hour. The module builder is a machine that presses the cotton in the field.[2] The farmer puts the cotton inside the builder. It presses the cotton, which they call modules. It makes a big, long block of cotton about thirty-to-forty feet long and way higher than your head. It's a big machine. The machines are automatic. They have sensors, pressers, hydraulic hoses, motors and shafts. Sometimes they break, and I'm the one who fixes them.

First, I was a module truck driver. I learned how to fix the modules myself. I've been doing it for eight years. The company I work at has sixty module builders. They furnish them to the farmers, and there are a lot of farmers. Sometimes, all the machines are working, sometimes one breaks. I'm in one town, and suddenly one breaks, so I go to another town. The farthest I go is about 50 miles from the company I work at. Sometimes it takes no time to fix a machine. It all depends on what they tell me is wrong. When I'm going down the road, I'm thinking about what to check. When I get there and see it, it might only take me five minutes to fix it. I fix them pretty good, so it takes a while to break one.

Cotton harvesting starts in September and ends the last week of January or the first week of February. When I'm in the cotton season, the onion planting starts in November and finishes about the middle of January. So I'm doing both jobs at the same time. They pay by the foot–$2.60 every hundred feet [of planting]. In the mornings, I go over here to onions. After a couple of hours, I go back to the cotton.

A tractor makes holes in the ground, and we plant the onions. The people kneel down or bend over. That's the way we plant them. To harvest them, a tractor digs out the onions, and we cut the root and cut the top. You might say it is hard work, especially right now–the sun–so hot. I guess somebody's got to do it.

We live in a house now. I rent it. Lyons is a small town, but we love it. A lot of people know who I am. What I do to relax or have fun, I go see my daughter play softball. Sometimes we go to dances. In summer, we go to Six Flags in Atlanta or Water Adventure–things like that. We also go to Texas for vacation. It's been a while since we went there. I've got family–aunts and uncles–in San Antonio. I've got cousins at the border of Mexico. I don't know anything about inside of Mexico. I just go right at the border where my cousins live. I've never really been *in* Mexico.

My mom and dad are still alive, thank God. My dad is 80 years old, and my mom is 71. They live about five minutes from my house. They never had any problems with racism that I recall. We never did. My dad knows a little bit of English. He speaks it when he wants to. My mom understands English a little bit, but she just doesn't want to speak it. I can't spell in Spanish. I can't even read Spanish. My oldest can read and write Spanish a little bit, but my youngest don't know much of it at all. If I tell them something in Spanish, they don't know what I'm saying. They don't read or write Spanish.

I've been working twenty-seven years with Stanley Farms. It is a good company to work for. Just imagine twenty-seven years working someplace with no problems at all. I love it, and it's great. I'm a foreman. I recruit people to cut onions. Almost every year you have different workers. Last year, I had some guys who had been coming with me for ten-to-twelve years straight. Last year was the last time they came. They said they decided to go another route. This year I still have three or four from the previous year. Right now, there are about twenty-eight on the crew. We're about to finish the onion crop, so some have left already. New workers keep going until they get the hang of it. Some people prefer working in the fields. Some people don't like to work in the fields. They prefer to go to the grader, where they grade the onions and put them in boxes. The bad onions are cut into little pieces. They throw them in the field, and turn the dirt over with tractors.

I don't want my kids to be working in the fields. That's the reason I wanted them to finish school, because I know what kind of work it is in the fields. I know. I've been doing it since I can remember. So that's why my kids don't go to the fields to work. My oldest [son] is a welder. My oldest daughter works for a law firm. My third one graduated last week. I still got a girl who is fourteen. The one who graduated already said he doesn't want to go to college. I don't know about the one who is still in school.

When we were moving state-to-state helping my Dad, I just got to eighth grade, if I'm not mistaken. Sometimes I think to myself, *I should have been in school.* There's no telling what I should have done. Thank God my three oldest have finished school. I was raised in the agriculture field. That's how it is.

NOTES

[1] Cuidad Acuña is located on the US-Mexican border across from Del Rio, Texas.

[2] The cotton module builder is a machine used in the harvesting and processing of cotton. The module builder has helped to solve a logistical bottleneck by allowing cotton to be harvested quickly and compressed into large modules which are then tarped and temporarily stored at the edge of the field. The modules are later loaded onto trucks and transported to a cotton gin for processing.... In the US today more than 90 % of the cotton harvested is compacted with module builders.... A module builder is about 9 meters (30 ft.) long, 4 meters (12 ft.) high and 3 meters (10 ft.) wide.... After loading the cotton into the module builder, a hydraulic compactor moves up and down along the length of the machine. This process is repeated every time that...cotton...is unloaded into the module builder until a module is built up and discharged through the tailgate of the machine. The module is stored on the field and the module builder is moved into a new position to build up another module. Wikipedia, http://en.wikipedia.org/wiki-Cotton_module_builder, accessed June 1, 2011.

Mack Francis Mattingly

Indiana born Mack Mattingly came to know this state, its people, and its rich opportunities as an IBM salesman traveling Georgia's back highways for twenty years. A term in the United States Senate and ongoing service to the state and nation since then, give Mattingly a unique perspective into Georgia and the changes he has seen over the last 60 years.

Senator Mack Mattingly

I first came to Georgia in 1951 during my service in the Air Force. I was stationed at Hunter Air Force Base in Savannah and knew almost immediately I would live the rest of my life here. I was born in Anderson, Indiana at the height of the Depression on January 7th, 1931. Like men

432

across America at that time, my dad worked incredibly hard to make his way and support his family. He had only an 8th grade education, but he taught himself much through those years. At first, he struggled just to find work, then found a job as an assistant salesman at a small town furniture store which years later, he wound up owning and operating. Even now, people still remember my dad and mother and the furniture store he owned. I have always been proud that I began my career in sales–like my dad, an entrepreneur.

Now, everywhere in the U. S. it is important to remember that until World War II, most people didn't move large distances during their lifetime. When radio and television brought the world to our homes, it changed how we thought of the world. But it was the Second World War that carried hundreds of thousands of servicemen and women all across the globe, and that, combined with the availability of air passage, profoundly changed how people–especially young people–viewed life.

I graduated from high school in 1949, went to Indiana University and then entered the Air Force with the outbreak of the Korean Conflict. I was stationed in New York, Louisiana, Georgia, Illinois, and Saudi Arabia. But it was my time at Hunter that something connected. Certainly, I liked the people of South Georgia, the ocean, the beaches, the temperature. I was a kid, and this was definitely not the North, and there was no snow. So, initially that was it, but then I began to feel a part of this place. And for a young man raised in an entrepreneurial world, the opportunities in Georgia were obvious and exciting. I returned to Indiana after the service, completed my degree, and within a few years, moved my family here.

I found a job with IBM Corporation in Savannah as a sales representative, and that was a true defining moment in my life. I was a northern born guy in a southern state with a large sales district, and in order to survive, I had to develop and use every bit of those sales and character instincts I'd

433

learned from my dad and my own brief experience. IBM was a wonderful company to work for, and through that job, I not only learned customer skills and how to turn sheer determination into success, I also learned Georgia. I was on the road driving from town to town four and five days a week. I learned every road and every town, every good restaurant and where the best coffee could be found– and I met people. Wonderful, wonderful people. I learned what mattered to them and what they were worried about in their towns, in their state, and in their country. I learned from them. And they made me a Georgian.

There are some things about Georgia that will never change. The topography, for example, is extraordinarily diverse. This certainly impacts how the culture of the people has developed and indeed, from the mountains and hills, to the plains and farmland to the seashore, one finds not only different geography and climate, but different sociology. Likewise, there is also a lot of cultural diversity historically and with the influx of people from everywhere over the past several decades. One of the main things that made me settle in Georgia was the great attitude of welcoming of people from the outside, and while that can make it hard to maintain our cultural identity and history, still, it helps us grow beyond ourselves into a far more richly complex and diverse society as a state.

Likewise, there is a great deal of diversity in the job market across the state. Recently, I spoke with a man from Australia about the move overseas of the textile industry. I pointed out that there are still some textile companies here along with the carpet industry, but what is remarkable to me is that this state is so vibrant and progressive that the textile industry we lost was replaced by other industries. Agriculture in cotton, peanuts, tobacco, soybeans, onions, corn, and tree farming continues to grow. Kaolin, granite, pulp and paper are major industries. Military bases in Augusta, Columbus, Albany, Savannah, Hinesville, St.

Marys, Atlanta, Marietta, Valdosta, Warner Robins and the Federal Law Enforcement Training Center in Brunswick create opportunities not only on the military bases for civilians, but also for associated industries that surround them, and the same holds true for every other industry.

Atlanta has evolved into a mega hub for an incredibly rich and diverse array of national and international corporations–Coca Cola, Delta, UPS, Home Depot, Chick-fil-A, Arby's/Wendy's, Intercontinental Hotels, CNN, Mindspring, Earthlink, Holiday Inns, Waffle House, Rayovac, Equifax, Haverty's, and Scientific Atlanta to name a few. Tourism is a major industry, and we have two major ports competing head-to-head with every other port in the United States–and winning.

Camden and Glynn Counties, for example, are typical of a lot of places in Georgia outside the metro Atlanta area. Years back, there wasn't much in Camden County other than the pulp and paper manufacturing company and a shipping company that stored munitions in St. Marys. Then the submarine naval base was built there, and Camden County became one of the most prosperous counties in the state of Georgia, drawing servicemen and women and their families from all across the United States.

When Glynco [Naval Air Station] left Brunswick, the efforts of a small group brought Gulfstream and the Law Enforcement Center to Brunswick. That's what I'm talking about. Somewhere instilled in the psyche of our people is the understanding that crises always breed opportunities for new ways of thinking and new ways of doing things.

That's the greatest resource of the state of Georgia. It's the opportunity I saw when I came here and joined IBM. It has never changed, and it is a passion that can serve us for generations to come if we recognize it. Clearly, despite challenges that come and go, Georgia is healthy and thriving. We know we're on the right track because so many people continue to come to Georgia to vacation and live. People find what we have found–acceptance in business and in the heart. They come with new ideas, start new businesses, and create opportunities for others, making Georgia surely one of the most traditional and progressive states in the Union. Georgia keeps moving forward because of the opportunities and because of people who see those opportunities and put them to work.

Writer and oral historian Stephen Doster is the author of fiction and non-fiction, including two oral histories. He was born in Kingston-On-Thames, England and raised on St. Simons Island, Georgia. His literary works are focused on Georgia and the Georgia Coast. He holds degrees from the University of Georgia and Vanderbilt University and currently resides in Nashville, Tennessee with his wife, Anne.